The Cradle of Knowledge

Learning, Development, and Conceptual Change
ใ$CC Lila Gleitman, Susan Carey, Elissa Newport, and Elizabeth Spelke, editors

The Cradle of Knowledge
Development of Perception in Infancy

Philip J. Kellman and Martha E. Arterberry

A Bradford Book
The MIT Press
Cambridge, Massachusetts
London, England

This book was set in Palatino on the Monotype "Prism Plus" PostScript Imagesetter by Asco Trade Typesetting Ltd., Hong Kong, and was printed and bound in the United States of America.

Library of Congress Cataloging-in-Publication Data

Kellman, Philip J.
  The cradle of knowledge: development of perception in infancy /
  Philip J. Kellman and Martha E. Arterberry.
    p.   cm.
  "A Bradford book."
  Includes bibliographical references and index.
  ISBN 0-262-11232-9 (alk. paper)
    1. Perception in infants. I. Arterberry, Martha E. II. Title.
  BF720.P47K45   1998
  155.42′2—dc21   97-34269
                                                      CIP

For our parents

Contents

Series Foreword

This series in learning, development, and conceptual change includes state-of-the-art reference works, seminal book-length monographs, and texts on the development of concepts and mental structures. It spans learning in all domains of knowledge, from syntax to geometry to the social world, and is concerned with all phases of development, from infancy through adulthood.

The series intends to engage such fundamental questions as:

The nature and limits of learning and maturation: the influence of the environment, of initial structures, and of maturational changes in the nervous system on human development; learnability theory; the problem of induction; domain-specific constraints on development.

The nature of conceptual change: conceptual organization and conceptual change in child development, in the acquisition of expertise, and in the history of science.

Lila Gleitman
Susan Carey
Elissa Newport
Elizabeth Spelke

Preface

More than three centuries ago, the philosopher John Locke recounted the query he received from his friend William Molyneux:

> Suppose a man born blind, and now adult, and taught by his touch to distinguish between a cube and a sphere.... Suppose the cube and sphere placed on a table and the blind man to be made to see: ... [could he] by his sight, before he touched them ... distinguish and tell which is the globe, which the cube? (Locke, 1690/1971, pp. 121–122)

Locke and Molyneux answered in the negative. In their view, only by learning to interpret the sensations of vision and associating them with touch could visual sensations become connected to a notion such as *form*.

How we obtain knowledge through the senses has long intrigued philosophers and scientists. Many have sought to understand the nature of perception by asking how it begins, and their answers have anchored conceptions of human nature and formed the foundations of theories of knowledge.

It is striking that Molyneux posed his question about what untutored perception might be capable of in reference to an *adult*. Given that the experiment was imaginary, why not ask about perceptual responses uninfluenced by a lifetime of thinking and learning; why not ask about a human infant? Apparently, the idea of assessing perception in the helpless human infant was considered too far-fetched even for thought experiments! In this regard, not much had changed in 1947 when Austin Riesen wrote, "The study of innate visual organization in man is not open to direct observation during early infancy, since a young baby is too helpless to respond differentially to visual excitation." (Riesen, 1947, p. 107)

We wrote this book because more recently, the study of human perceptual development turned out to be possible after all. Over the past several decades, researchers have discovered windows into the human infant's perceptual world. Although unable to speak, point, or locomote, even newborn infants respond in subtle ways that reveal aspects of their sensory and perceptual experiences. Through diverse and often ingenious efforts, researchers have exploited these responses to reveal perceptual competence, test hypotheses about processes, and infer neural mechanisms. Some of the answers they have uncovered would have surprised Locke and Molyneux, as they have surprised modern researchers.

Why do we care about how perception develops? The reasons are those that have kept these questions in the forefront of intellectual debate for centuries. The beginnings and workings of perceptual knowledge bear on fundamental questions of both epistemology and psychology: What links ideas in our minds to external reality? Are perceptual processes that connect the mind to the world inherent in the mind or are they constructions from experience? Today we know these questions unfold at several interacting levels. How does energy carry information and how can it be extracted by perceptual systems? To what extent has sensitivity to structured information, and the neural circuitry that carries out perception, developed through the evolution of perceptual systems, and how much does perception become organized through experiences of the individual? Do the basic processes of perception differ across individuals depending on their personal histories?

It is sometimes argued that questions of nativism versus empiricism are misguided—that all development is an interaction between organism and environment. Perceiving organisms must of course eat and breathe, and their perceptual systems will deteriorate if not stimulated. These interactions with the environment, however, do not answer questions of whether organisms come equipped innately or maturationally to pick up information and represent their environments in meaningful ways. The study of perceptual development can and, as we will see, often has answered such questions.

We also care about perception as a prerequisite to understanding other aspects of human cognitive and social development. The developing infant's interactions with the physical and social worlds are both enabled and constrained by what can be perceived. What has recently been learned about perception, we suggest, requires a new account of development. The discovery that human beings begin the path of development at quite a different place than previously suspected has many consequences.

Finally, the study of perceptual development sheds light on the character of perception itself and its place in the mind. Early in this century, the Gestalt psychologists contended that relationships are most important in perceiving and that intrinsic mechanisms in the nervous system respond to these. As the century draws to a close, this lesson is still not fully appreciated. Students of cognitive science, neuroscience, and psychology often think in terms of sensation (or basic filtering of stimulus energy attributes) and cognition—general inferential processes that "recognize" or "make sense of" sensory inputs. Yet a wealth of evidence points toward autonomous perceptual mechanisms that stand between sensation and cognition. More than half of the cerebral cortex appears to be dedicated to perceptual information processing. This massive allocation of brain-power may serve primarily to extract stimulus relationships and produce abstract, meaningful descriptions of reality. There may be no better way to acquire an appreciation of the character and function of perception than by studying its development.

In writing this book, we have stayed close to the methods and data of scientific research on infant perception. A simpler and neater story could have been told with fewer details; no doubt such a story would have better suited some purposes. On the other hand, the story of infant percep-tion research is one in which experimental findings are replacing centuries of conjecture about the origins of the mind. Like conjecture, interpretation of data has pitfalls, and these are not easy to prevent or remedy with-out keeping in view the methods and results on which conclusions and generalizations depend.

We are grateful to many people who devoted their valuable time to comment on this book as it evolved. Richard Aslin, Kathy Cain, Claes, von Hofsten, Nava Rubin, Bill Wilson, and several anonymous readers provided very helpful comments on one or more chapters, and we bene-fited from helpful discussions with Martin Banks, Randy Gallistel, and Rochel Gelman. We thank Christine Massey for an especially thorough reading of the book and many insightful suggestions. We owe a special debt to Elizabeth Spelke who heroically made detailed comments on *two* versions of the manuscript. Her wisdom has improved our presentation of many ideas and helped us sharpen our arguments on some contro-versial matters. Daniel N. Robinson originally convinced PJK some time ago to begin a book on infant perception and also suggested the title. We appreciate his inspiration and hope the final product was worth the wait. None of our colleagues who graciously assisted bear any responsibility for any errors that might remain in the book.

We gratefully acknowledge grants BNS 89-13707, BNS 91-20969, and SBR-9496112 to PJK from the National Science Foundation and awards to MEA from Gettysburg College that supported in part our writing efforts as well as much of our own research reported here. We also thank the editorial staff at MIT Press, especially Amy Brand and Deborah Cantor-Adams, for expertise, insight and patience, and Leah Miners for capably compiling the index. PJK thanks his wife Pam for her patience and sup-port, and Julie, Laura, and Kim for demonstrating firsthand the miracles of perceptual development during the writing of this book. MEA thanks her husband Bill for his encouragement. Finally, the data about which we have written have come from thousands of infants and their parents who selflessly gave their time to participate in research in laboratories all over the world. They have our enduring gratitude.

Although a more personal dedication appears on another page, in an important sense this book must be dedicated to the many researchers who have labored earnestly and creatively to unlock the secrets of perception in infancy. Their discoveries fill these pages, and our efforts would not have been possible without theirs. We hope this book does their work justice, for they have written an important chapter in the study of the mind.

Chapter 1
Views of Perception and Perceptual Development

Perception forms the portal between reality and knowledge. It is the gateway through which matter and energy in the physical world lead to ideas in the mind. An enigmatic bridge, it appears as biological activity from one end and conscious awareness from the other. In the theater of the mind, it is the opening scene.

In giving us contact with the world, human perception is proficient and unobtrusive. The world simply appears to be there, in all its dimensions and detail, from even a brief glance. To walk, we place our feet on some surface whose location and solidity are obvious. To grasp, we reach to where an object is. We turn toward a speaker, knowing before turning where and often who they are. The accuracy and transparency of perception mislead the casual observer, and sometimes the expert, into thinking that knowing through the senses is uncomplicated.

In the development of the individual, perception is pivotal. Learning about the physical and social worlds, and acquiring language, all rely on the products of perception. To the extent perceptual ability is lacking at the beginning of life, these tasks must be postponed. Developing perception becomes the central task of early development, as many theorists have suggested (e.g., Piaget, 1954).

In seeking to understand perceptual development we encounter several key questions. How does perception get started? It is easy to demonstrate that the senses function from birth. But do they reveal a world of objects, situations, and events? Or do they serve up at first only the "blooming, buzzing confusion" suggested by William James (1890)? When perceptual knowledge is attained, how does the process work? To explain how a quantum of light absorbed by a photoreceptor in the eye initiates an electrical signal in the nervous system involves many complexities. Equally mysterious, however, are processes that determine from many rays of light—each carrying no information about how far it has traveled—the position, size, and shape of an object several hundred feet away. Moreover, perceptual abilities are not static; they change with development and experience. Which of these changes depend on simple growth or the maturation of new mechanism, which depend on learning to interpret the inputs to the senses, or acquiring skill in selecting information? How do perceptual changes cause and result from changes in other cognitive and motor abilities? To begin to pose such questions, we need first to consider the character and function of perception.

ASPECTS OF PERCEPTION

One reason the study of perception is so fascinating and complex is that it involves questions of fundamentally different kinds. We can discover these different aspects by looking at almost any perceptual phenomenon and asking what needs to be explained.

Issues of Representation and Process

Consider the display in figure 1.1a. We see five objects varying in shape and color. The same five areas are rearranged in figure 1.1b. Now things look different. We notice three objects, not five, and the objects have acquired some interesting qualities and relationships. The circle on the left has become translucent; we can see part of another object through it. The circle on the right is pierced by the middle object. The middle object is seen as a whole despite having two visible parts separated by a gap on the right and a differently colored part on the left.

This example illustrates that perceptual experience is not a simple inventory of stimulus inputs. Both figures 1.1a and 1.1b may be straightforwardly described as containing five regions of certain colors at certain positions on a flat surface. Indeed, this is exactly the type of description used by the computer on which the displays were created to send instructions to the printer. There is no depth, nothing transparent, and no interpenetrating objects. Your perceptual system handles these inputs very differently, mapping the five simple regions into three objects, one of which is translucent and one pierced by another.

As a second example, consider the three cylinders in figure 1.2. Which is largest? Most observers report the cylinder nearest the top of the page as largest and the one nearest the bottom as smallest. In reality the cylinders do differ slightly in size, but the order is opposite to the way they appear: the cylinder lowest in the figure is largest. Your visual system has transformed the input into an ordering of perceived size opposite to that actually present in the input.

In these examples, the transformations between the stimulus inputs and what is perceived depend on relationships in the stimulus. As the Gestalt psychologists argued long ago, perception is not merely a response to local stimuli; it depends on *patterns* in space and time. A crucial part of the

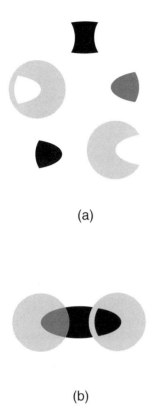

(a)

(b)

Figure 1.1
Organization in perception. The 5 visible areas in (a) appear as 3 perceived objects in (b).
(See text.)

task of understanding perception is finding out what dimensions, features, and relationships we extract from the inputs. We seek to determine how these are represented and what further processing is required to produce the objects, scenes, and events of our experience. These questions address the level of *representation and process* in the study of perception.

We might set out to study perception in the infant or the adult with this goal alone. By manipulating stimulus inputs and measuring what is perceived, we can obtain data allowing us to build theories about perceptual processes. This task is central but not sufficient. One limitation is that in pursuing this task alone, we would end up with a catalog of curiosities. On receiving stimulus pattern *a*, the visual system engages processes *b* and *c* leading to our perceiving *d*. We would lack a deeper understanding of our catalog of transformations. We could say nothing of why a visual system should take pattern *a* and end up with percept *d*.

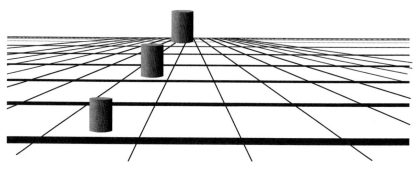

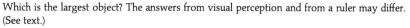

Figure 1.2
Which is the largest object? The answers from visual perception and from a ruler may differ. (See text.)

Issues of Ecology

Let us look again at figure 1.1. It is remarkable that this arrangement of color patches on a piece of paper should evoke the perception of one object passing through another, or five patches making three objects. But consider, if three objects were positioned in space in the proper way, and if one were translucent, then the projection to the eyes could be the same as what we get from the picture. Where one object passed behind the translucent one, that part of the display would appear different in surface lightness, while its boundaries maintained their continuity with those not covered by the translucent object. In other words, the percepts rendered by the visual system are physically plausible—that is, they could be caused by a suitable physical arrangement in the world, given the laws of optics.

A stronger claim can be made. The technology for placing precise arrangements of ink on paper is a relatively recent human invention. In the natural world, the one in which animals evolved over millions of years, if your eyes received the patterns in figure 1.1, you would almost certainly be confronting an arrangement of a translucent object and two others—the scene your visual system says is there. To make such a claim, we need to know a great deal about the ecology—about what goes on in the physical world and how it produces patterns of light sent to our eyes. Put informally, it would be very improbable for five separate physical objects to come together in such a way that their boundaries displayed the continuity we see in figure 1.1. Moreover, certain lightness relations in the scene are exactly right for a translucent surface, and certain positional relations are exactly right for one object penetrating another, but these relations would be quite coincidental otherwise.

Similarly, you may have already silently protested during our discussion of figure 1.2. There is something reasonable about the perceived size order of the cylinders in the figure. The objects appear to rest at different locations on a surface, and due to the appearance of the surface as receding in depth, the objects appear to be at different distances. A superficial approach to perceiving object size might use only the projective sizes of objects; a deeper analysis would address the geometry relating physical size, depth information, and projective size that holds in our physical world.

We now see that our understanding of perception must involve—in fact, must begin with—the study of the world to be perceived. We call this the *level of ecology* in the study of perception. Although sensation and perception have been studied systematically for several hundred years, a clear understanding of the importance of this level has emerged only in the latter part of the twentieth century. The first stop on the road to understanding perception is a rigorous analysis of the *task* of perception—what is to be perceived—and the ways in which environments make *information* available to accomplish the task.

Issues of Biological Mechanism

To capture, represent, and transform information requires mechanisms of considerable complexity. How does perceptual processing take place in the nervous system? This is the question of the level of *biological mechanism*. When we consider non-biological information-processing systems (machines) along with biological ones, we might prefer Marr's (1982) label—the *level of hardware implementation*. In some ways, this level requires the least introduction. Everyone knows that to understand vision, for example, we need to know about the retina, about rods and cones, and about where optic nerve fibers project in the brain. If one develops a vision problem, the facts of biological mechanism are most relevant to its causes and treatment.

Although we may speak of this level as a single category, it encompasses various levels of its own. Each sense involves specialized receptors and associated mechanisms designed to bring to the receptors a particular form of energy from the outside world. In vision, for example, the lens and cornea refract incoming light rays onto the retina, and several different muscle groups allow the eyes to be pointed, focused, and converged, to optimize the pickup of information. Beyond the receptors, neural mechanisms are wired to register key features in energy patterns; these in turn feed into various neural streams specialized for extraction of higher-order information. Still other neural mechanisms must integrate

Table 1.1
Three levels of analysis in the study of perception.

Level of Ecology	Level of Representation and Process	Level of Biological Mechanism
What is the perceptual task? What information is available for perceiving? What constraints simplify the task?	How is information extracted? How is information represented? What computations are performed?	What biological mechanisms accomplish the extraction, representation and processing of perceptual information?

information from different processing streams and different senses to produce our coherent experience of objects and events.

MULTIPLE LEVELS IN THE STUDY OF PERCEPTION

We have now introduced three levels important in understanding perception—the *level of ecology*, the level of *representation and process*, and the level of *biological mechanism*. Table 1.1 indicates the kinds of questions asked at each level. In this section, we take a closer look at each level to sharpen the issues within and between levels that guide our study of infant perception.

The Level of Ecology

What are the tasks of perception, and what information is available to do these tasks? J. Gibson (1966, 1979) pointed out the central importance of these questions and argued that answering them requires study of the way environments interact with energy to provide information. In vision, he called this enterprise *ecological optics*. The term *ecological* designates facts at a level relevant to perceiving organisms. Not every fact about the physical environment is relevant. We are concerned with the physical world within certain spatial and temporal ranges. In spatial terms, our concerns lie primarily between about a tenth of a millimeter and ten thousand meters. In this range, the texture and topography of surfaces and the shapes and sizes of objects are relevant to our activities. At one end of this range, we may be concerned with minute variations that make a surface rough or smooth or with tiny markings on visible surfaces. At the other end, we can set and maintain a course with reference to distant mountains. The physical distances between stars and the distances between molecules, in contrast, may be preconditions for our existence but are not ecologically relevant for guiding behavior. Our perceptual concerns are likewise confined in time. Organisms may apprehend and react to changes or events in the environment unfolding in milliseconds or hours but not to those occurring in nanoseconds or centuries.

Within these ranges, what sorts of information about the physical world are important? Complex perceptual systems belong exclusively to mobile organisms, and we can understand much about perceptual function from that simple fact. In the first place, the task of moving through the environment requires selectivity and guidance. We need to know about surfaces of support in the world, about footholds and dropoffs, about obstacles and passageways. To maintain posture and balance as we locomote, we need ongoing information about our own position relative to surfaces of support and to gravity. Next, there are the aspects of the physical world—including objects, events, and the spatial layout—that we need to apprehend if we are to do anything useful by moving. Objects, which are coherent, bounded, material units, often are inanimate, such as rocks, plates, and pillows. Many of their properties are important to our interactions with them including their forms, sizes, rigidity, and composition. Other entities we perceive, such as people, cats, and spiders, are animate and may pose danger, provide protection, comfort, and companionship. With those of our own species, it is important that we perceive emotion, demeanor, action, and intention, as well as spoken language. Analogous to the boundaries in space that specify surfaces and objects, we perceive *events*—sequences of motion or change that are in some sense coherent and separate from other goings on.

This brief description of the subset of the physical world relevant to perception is illustrative, not exhaustive. Certain ways of thinking about perception lead to the possibility that its full scope is surprisingly wide. Besides surfaces, objects, people, and events, connections among physical events—causality—and among social ones—social intention—might be detected by perceptual mechanisms rather than constructed from learning about the world. After understanding more about perception and its development, we will be in a better position to consider these possibilities.

Ecology and Information

What about the *optics* in *ecological optics*? Information, like objects and events, must be appropriate to spatial and temporal scale. Thus, Gibson argued that ecological optics is not fundamentally concerned with tracings of single rays of light or the absorption of quanta by molecules emphasized in traditional geometric and physical optics. Instead, we attempt to identify information produced by interactions of volumes of light with objects and surfaces at a scale relevant to perceiving organisms.

Marr (1982) emphasized the need for formal *computational* accounts at this level. How can the objects and events of the physical world be

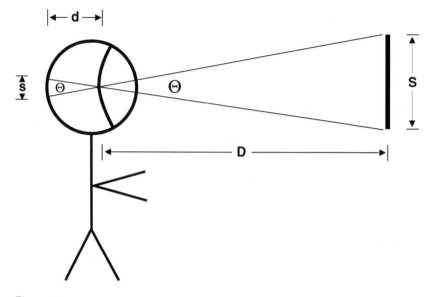

Figure 1.3
Size and distance relations. *S* is the real object size; *D* is its distance from the observer; *s* is the projected size at the retina; *d* is the distance from the nodal point of the eye to the retinal surface; Θ is the visual angle projected by the object.

determined mathematically from informational variables available to the perceiver? Often, obtaining a unique and accurate answer requires the use of *constraints*. A constraint is an assumption about the way the world works that may be incorporated into perceptual computations to restrict their possible outcomes. The most powerful constraints derive from general and enduring features of our physical world. For example, objects in our world have spatiotemporal continuity. In order to move from one place to another, they must pass through positions in between. Objects do not appear at one place, vanish, and materialize some distance away. A perceptual system that incorporates this premise will exclude percepts of discontinuous objects that would otherwise be compatible with available information.

As another example, consider again perception of object size. What information is there for perceiving size? The projection of a viewed object takes up a certain portion of our field of view; we call this *projective size* or *visual angle*. Projective size is a poor guide to physical size because it varies with viewing distance. There is, however, an invariant relation between physical size, projective size, and distance: the ratio formed by the object's real size and its distance is the tangent of the visual angle. Figure 1.3 illustrates. The projection of the object onto the eye can be gotten by drawing straight lines from points on the object through the nodal point[1] of the eye to the retina. If distance can be registered, a perceptual processor that incorporates this relationship can compute real size from visual angle, available at the eye of the observer, and registered distance. This mathematical relationship concerning size and distance is in the first place a fact about the world we live in—that is, a fact about optics and projective geometry. An important part of the study of perception is to determine when such relationships are incorporated as constraints in perceptual processing. Such constraints may be inborn or maturational, presumably resulting from evolution under consistent conditions (Gibson, 1966; Johansson, 1970; Shepard, 1984). On the other hand, some theorists have suggested that constraints may be discovered through learning by the individual (Helmholtz, 1885/1910; Wallach & O'Leary, 1982).

This example of size perception can be extended to illustrate the importance of thorough ecological analysis. Although it was long believed that physical size could be recovered perceptually *only* by using distance information, J. Gibson (1950) noted a relational variable that offers size information without using distance. On a textured surface whose texture elements are relatively uniform in size, the visual array projected to the eye contains a *texture gradient*. The projective sizes of texture elements decrease as the surface extends farther away from the observer. In figure 1.2, the spaces between the grid lines form a texture gradient and provide an appearance of depth. Gibson noted that an object resting on a textured surface will occlude the same number of texture elements no matter what its distance. Object size, then, might be gotten in relation to texture element size. Seeing two objects at different distances as being the same size might not require using equations about size and distance; rather, they can be directly compared to the texture elements at their location.

The relation between projective size and distance applies equally to viewed surface texture and viewed objects, allowing us to obtain size by their relation without using distance information. The usefulness of this relation also depends on the fact that, due to gravity, most objects in our environment rest on ground surfaces.

The example underscores the primacy of the level of ecology in understanding perception. Many advances in understanding perception have come from the discovery of stimulus relationships that provide more direct information about some physical property than do simple variables. If we have limited or misleading notions about information, we may not understand what is detected and computed by perceptual systems. Even where many details are known about the neurophysiology of perceptual systems, an understanding of which details are relevant and what brain mechanisms need to extract and compute depends on a clear ecological or computational account of perception.

The Energy World

We have so far said little about the role of *energy* in sensation and perception. In terms of functions or tasks, we have emphasized not perception of energy (e.g., seeing light) but perception of physical structure, such as objects and surfaces. In terms of means, we have emphasized the pick-up of information. But how does information become available? We are able to perceive only because the material environment around us is awash with energy. We are constantly immersed in seas of acoustic vibrations, electromagnetic waves, chemical and temperature gradients, and much more. Only some of this energy is available to our senses. It is sobering to realize that while standing in your living room, thousands of cellular telephone calls, paging signals, air traffic control transmissions, and commercial radio and television broadcasts are passing undetected through your body.

Energy links the physical world of material structures and events to the perceptual world in which objects and events are represented. We see a table not by direct contact but by means of the light it reflects. Due to the evolution of specialized systems for receiving them, we are sensitive to certain forms and ranges of energy.

Perception begins with energy interactions at sensory receptors. At the same time, this first step has given rise to many misconceptions about perception. One is that we can understand perception by understanding local responses to energy. Another is that what we *perceive* is energy. Perceiving properties of energy is in fact a means, not an end. Perception informs us more about matter than energy, by means of patterns in ambient energy. In the final outputs of perception—what we experience or represent—our knowledge about energy per se is generally poor. For example, in a lighted room, we perceive the layout of surfaces of varied reflectance, but we have little or no sense of how much light, in absolute terms, comes to the eye from each surface (Gilchrist, Delman & Jacobsen, 1983).

It may seem so intuitive that what we hear is sound and what we see is light that the disavowal of these notions is shocking. But these notions are arbitrary, as we can readily grasp by thinking about the causal chains involved in perception. Consider: Causal interactions of objects with light send patterns of light to the eyes. A pattern of light as it hits the retina *is* the last step in the causal sequence of sight that lies in the physical world, *outside* of our biology. Perhaps this fact underlies the idea that what we see is light. But the causal chain continues. Light goes no further into the nervous system than the retina, where it gives rise to electrical signals. Significantly, no one would claim that seeing occurs in the retina; it occurs in the brain. The light is left behind as subsequent electrical events take place en route to later destinations in the nervous system, where perceptual representations and conscious experiences are produced. In this causal chain from objects to light patterns to electrical signals to perception, what should lead us to single out light as the thing that is perceived? It makes no more sense to say we see light than that we see electrical signals in the retina!

The fact is, the causal chain of perception carries information about all of the steps. Patterns of cortical activity contain information about light patterns *and* about retinal electrical patterns *and* about objects in the world. Singling out one of these as what we perceive is arbitrary, except on functional grounds. In the use and evolution of these causal sequences in biological systems, the important properties extracted are usually those far back in the causal chain: objects, spatial layout and events. Sometimes a property of energy *is* a salient output of perception—as when a sound is loud enough to cause pain. What we most often find in the descriptions we obtain from perception, however, are behaviorally important aspects of the physical world's material structure, not its energy characteristics.

Explaining perception, then, must include accounts of the catching of energy by receptors. But it requires much more. As our description makes clear, perception is determined by events that occur both earlier and later. Perceiving what is in the world is possible because interactions of energy with objects produce patterning across space and time. These patterns in spatial temporal relationships are often not even definable in terms of local receptor activity. Discovering and specifying precisely patterns in energy that provide information to perceptual systems is our task at the level of ecology.

The Level of Representation and Process

The function of perception is to provide accurate representations of the world to organisms and to guide their action. These representations and the processes that derive them comprise what we labeled the *level of representation and process*. Much of what needs to be explained in perception is what these representations contain and how well they correspond to the physical world. In the study of infant perception we compare the scope, accuracy, and detail of the infant's perceptual world to the physical world as well as to the perceptual world of adults.

In calling the outputs of perceptual processes *representations* we use the term broadly. We certainly mean to include characterizations of the outputs of perception as *descriptions* of the environment (Pylyshyn, 1973; Marr, 1982). We do not mean to imply, however, that the outputs of perception are always accessible to consciousness. Some theorists (Gibson, 1966; Turvey, Shaw, Reed & Mace, 1981) view the outputs of perception as leading to the adjustment of ongoing action in perception-action loops, rather than as comprising explicit descriptions to be thought about, remembered, and so on. A standing person, for example, makes periodic postural adjustments to compensate for detected sway. The visual or vestibular registration of sway is seldom conscious. For our purposes, registration of knowledge about the environment (or self) will count as part of the perceptual world, whether or not it is conscious or accessible to other cognitive processes. Although the differences among these cases are interesting, they are not particularly well illuminated by studies of infant perception. It is often tractable to test an infant's registration of some aspect of the environment, but it is much harder to distinguish whether it has been registered implicitly or made explicit in the subject's awareness. Our methods do give clues about such distinctions, however.

The first step in understanding representation and process is some account of infant perceptual competencies. Much of our focus is on research revealing these. What aspects of the environment are perceptible by infants? Which of the multiple sources of information used by adults are usable by infants? Prior to the last few decades, these questions were sources of speculation and controversy but not of experimental research. In this book we show that these questions have been answered to an impressive extent in many perceptual domains.

Direct versus Algorithmic Perceptual Processing

How to characterize representation and process in perception has been controversial. Marr (1982) argued that perceptual processes are "algorithmic," in the sense that the outputs of perceptual processes depend on a sequence of representations and operations on them. Our label is more neutral about the character of perceptual processes. Some seem aptly described as algorithmic. In other instances, perception may involve not a sequence of representations but a more direct mapping from stimulus relations onto perceptual outcomes, as emphasized by Gibson (1966, 1979). The issue of whether perception involves direct mappings or intermediate representations has been hotly disputed (Gibson, 1966, 1979; Johansson, 1970; Hochberg, 1974; Epstein, 1982; Runeson, 1977; Ullman, 1980; Fodor & Pylyshyn, 1981; Turvey et al., 1981; Cornman, 1975). A related issue is whether perception must be described as inferential in the sense of requiring assumptions about the world to constrain the possibilities consistent with the input (Fodor & Pylyshyn, 1981). An example may help illustrate these issues in understanding the character of perception.

Consider an object approaching an observer at a constant velocity. The size of the object's optical projection increases in size as it comes closer. Knowing when the object will contact the observer, however, might seem to require calculation. At a certain instant, the object projects a certain size on the retina of each eye. If the object is familiar, its distance may be calculated using the same geometry we considered earlier. The real size of the familiar object is retrieved from memory. Distance to the object may be computed from the projected size (visual angle) and the real size. Another distance calculation taken after a known time interval could be used to calculate velocity. Then, if velocity is constant, the *time to contact* could be derived from the object's last position and its velocity. This algorithmic approach would require acquiring, storing, and comparing projective sizes and distance estimates along with accurate timekeeping. The sensed visual angles, as well as the distance estimates, are intermediate representations used to obtain the final result. The inferential character of the process is obvious.

Lee (1974) provided an alternative analysis of this problem. Omitting mathematical details, the main result is that time to contact is specified directly by a higher-order optical variable. This variable is a ratio of the optical position of the approaching object's boundary and its first temporal derivative (*optical velocity*). The latter refers to the rate at which a contour or feature changes position on the retina. The upshot is that a ratio of two variables available at the observer's eyes mathematically specifies time to contact, without any need for computations involving distance and object size.

Now suppose a sensory system is wired so as to function as a detector for this higher-order variable. The only mental representation involved with such a detector might be its output—that is, time to contact. Indeed, empirical evidence suggests that perceptual systems in a variety of species do extract this information, and it is used to guide important behaviors (Lee & Reddish, 1981). It is in this sense that perception may be direct: properties of the world may be detected by perceptual mechanisms sensitive to relational variables in the stimulus; computations on intermediate representations may not be required.[2]

Studies of infant perception have not settled the question of whether perceptual processes are algorithmic or direct. Such studies suggest that the answer may vary across perceptual domains. We need to ask the question of representation and process separately for different perceptual abilities.

The Level of Biological Mechanism

The study of the machinery in the nervous system that allows us to extract, represent, and transform information is a rich and multifaceted enterprise. Studies of sensory psychophysics seek to define the range and limits of sensitivity of sensory systems to particular dimensions of energy. Taking a developmental stance, we seek to characterize changes in these sensitivities and theorize about their causes in neural maturation, learning, attention, motor development, and so on. Correlated with these efforts is direct investigation of physiological mechanisms underlying sensation and perception in animal subjects. Some of these studies address truly perceptual issues—such as how we detect and represent the positions of objects in space—whereas others are concerned with limits of sensory receptivity that constrain the pickup of information. Some research is undertaken in the hope of understanding and treating defects of perception. This concern involves almost solely the level of biological mechanism. If you wish to build a computer vision system, you will want to understand ecology, and the representations and algorithms used in human visual perception. If your vision becomes cloudy, however, you should consult an ophthalmologist.

One of the fundamental insights of the study of information processing is that the levels we have discussed are not reducible to each other. The specialist who understands algorithms for computing depth from differences in images given to the two eyes probably does not also perform cataract surgery, and vice versa. Neither is using concepts and relationships that will ultimately be replaced by the other's. One important reason is that hardware implementation (biological mechanism) is not unique. Given a task, and a process for doing that task, there are many possible implementations. Thus, an account of perception can be scientific and precise at the ecological and process levels yet reveal little about the details of the actual hardware. The accounts of the information, representations, and processes could be transferred to another physical system—for example, a computer-based vision system. The latter system could exploit the same constraints, pick up the same information, perform the same mappings or computations, and achieve the same representations as a human perceiver. The computer vision system would not have retinal ganglions cells, cortical neurons, or neurotransmitter substances; instead, it would use integrated circuit chips made from silicon or germanium.

The converse insight is sometimes less well understood. But it is one key to understanding perception and perceptual development, as well as information processing in general. That is, a detailed account of biological hardware alone does not explain perception. Accounts of ecology and process are not facts about neurons or integrated circuit chips or of any particular physical instantiation. They cannot be gleaned from ever more precise maps of neural firing and transmitter uptake. In fact, the reverse is true; choosing which observations of hardware are likely to be important rather than incidental requires knowledge of the task and the processes of perception (Marr, 1982; Putnam, 1975; Chomsky, 1980).

In this book our primary focus is on ecology and process. This emphasis is in part due to the impossibility of treating all of the levels adequately in one book. A truly massive amount of information is available on biological mechanisms alone, and the research has varied goals. Our focus is *perceptual knowledge*—how perceivers come to know the world around them, what processes achieve this knowledge, and how they change over time. But this is a statement of emphasis and not exclusion. Most scientists who work in cognitive science and neuroscience at any level would agree that work at each level informs the others. Indeed, we appear to be on the threshold of a remarkable era in which the facts at various levels connect and constrain each other far more than has previously been the case. Among the reasons are more precise quantitative theories about information and process, along with powerful new techniques for probing brain mechanisms. Accordingly, we have quite a bit to say about physiological mechanisms, but we stress those facts that clearly connect to the acquisition of perceptual knowledge, such as ways in which what we know at the biological level constrains information processing. Chapter 2 is devoted exclusively to this topic, and physiological aspects arise in our treatment of many other topics as well. Where our discussion of topics in the anatomy and physiology of developing sensory systems is less than comprehensive, the reader may consult several excellent sources (Bronson, 1982; Banks & Salapatek, 1983; Noback & Demarest, 1986; Simons, 1993).

STARTING POINTS OF PERCEPTION: TWO GENERAL VIEWS

We have seen that understanding perception involves three levels of inquiry—ecology, representation and process, and biological mechanism—and connections across levels. But we have not yet mentioned perhaps the most remarkable fact of all: the landscape—of perceptual processes, mechanisms, and even ecology—is dynamic, not static. From the beginning of each human life (earlier, in fact), it is constantly forming and changing. These are the phenomena of development and learning. In this book we examine early perception in various domains, such as object, space, motion, intermodal, and speech perception. In each case, we attempt to discover the starting points and paths of development of important perceptual abilities. In most cases, two general views compete to describe how perception begins and develops. One family of views—which we label *constructivism*—is empiricist in spirit, emphasizing the construction of perceptual reality through extended learning.[3] The other family of views —which we label *ecological*—encompasses a more nativist approach, emphasizing the role of evolution in preparing human beings to perceive. We introduce and examine each view in turn.

Constructivist Views of Perceptual Development

How might we know the world through our senses? The general answer given by constructivists has dominated theorizing about perception in philosophy and experimental psychology for more than two centuries. Constructivist views begin with the fact that sensory receptors, such as rods and cones in the eye, do not apprehend objects directly; each responds to a tiny region of impinging energy. As a result of their activation, receptors give rise to characteristic sensations, such as brightness at a particular location on the eye. Perception—knowing something about the objects and events in the outside world—consists, in constructivist views, of somehow making sense of these sensations. The process is like an inference: we must guess, hypothesize, or imagine what external objects might produce our sensations. Since many possible objects could give rise to particular sensations, the process can succeed only through learning. We learn which sensations co-occur and succeed one another, what visual sensations predict about tactile sensations, and so on. Drawing on memories and associations of past sensations, we construct a coherent interpretation of the causes of our sensations. This construction is the world we perceive. From this perspective, *perceptual development must consist of an extended period of learning to interpret sensations before meaningful perception of coherent objects and events is possible.*

Constructivist views about the building of perception out of sensation originated with British empiricist philosophers (Berkeley, 1709/1910; Hobbes, 1651/1974; Locke, 1690/1956; Reid, 1785/1969). These views were further elaborated by key figures in early experimental psychology (Helmholtz, 1885/1925; Wundt, 1862; Titchener, 1902), by modern perceptionists (Hochberg, 1981; Wallach, 1985), and by developmental theorists (Piaget, 1954, 1976; Harris, 1983). The specific ideas of these theorists differ somewhat but share the main features of our schematic account.

The arguments for constructivism were originally logical ones. Two are particularly instructive for understanding both the constructivist stance and departures from it. We label these arguments the *ambiguity* and *capability* arguments.

The Ambiguity Argument
In his 1709 *Essay toward a New Theory of Vision*, Berkeley (1709/1910) asked how we might possibly obtain reliable information through the visual sense. Berkeley pointed out that the projection of an object onto the retina of a single eye is inherently ambiguous; an infinite number of variously sized and shaped objects in the world could give rise to the same retinal image. If visual patterns are ambiguous, some nonvisual information is needed to disambiguate them. Berkeley suggested that the nonvisual information was provided by the oculomotor cues of accommodation and convergence. *Accommodation* refers to changing of the thickness of the lens to bring images at different distances into focus. *Convergence* is the turning inward of the eyes so that the two eyes image

the same point in space. In each case, the muscular contractions required to accomplish the task would correlate with physical distance to the target, and these muscle sensations could provide cues to depth. Berkeley argued that these muscle sensations might also start out as meaningless but could come to signify depth by association with experiences of reaching for and contacting objects.

The ongoing influence of Berkeley's ambiguity argument derives in part from its logical validity, assuming his characterization of the stimulus to be accurate. Only in the past several decades have challenges to his analysis of visual information been fully articulated and their consequences considered. These developments form the foundations of an ecological perspective, as we will see.

The Capability Argument
The growth of experimental physiology in the nineteenth century gave rise to perceptual theorizing rooted in knowledge of basic sensory capacities. Progress in sensory physiology centered on basic elements, such as individual sensory receptors and electrical conduction in individual nerves. An almost inevitable consequence was a strong emphasis on local activity in sensory nerves in attempting to explain perceptual knowledge. Particularly influential was the formulation advanced by Johannes Müller (1838). Müller, often considered the father of experimental physiology, was concerned with the physiological basis for differences in sensory qualities across the senses. When the eye is stimulated, normally by light but also by pressure or other means, we have sensations of brightness and color. As the example illustrates, characteristic sensations are a function less of the external stimulus than of the particular sensory apparatus affected. Müller called this idea the *specific energies of nerves*. The qualities possible in each sense derive from specific properties of the particular sensory nerves. (As Müller also considered, we now know that the nerves themselves do not differ in the various sensory systems; Müller's insight accordingly is transferred from the nerves themselves to the separate brain areas to which different sensory nerves project.) Müller's notion of specific nerve energies is profound in making clear that sensations inhere in the observer and not the world. It suggests a way of thinking about perception, however, that is less fortunate. Consider a few of Müller's doctrines (Müller, 1838):

I. In the first place, it must be kept in mind that external agencies can give rise to no kind of sensation which cannot also be produced by internal causes, exciting changes in the condition of our nerves....

III. The same external cause also gives rise to different sensations in each sense, according to the special endowments of its nerve....

V. Sensation consists in the sensorium's receiving through the medium of the nerves, and as the result of the action of an external cause, a knowledge of certain qualities or conditions, not of external bodies, but of the nerves of sense themselves; and these qualities of the nerves of sense are in all different, the nerve of each sense having its own peculiar quality or energy....

VIII. ... The information thus obtained by the senses concerning external nature, varies in each sense, having a relation to the qualities or energies of the nerve. (pp. 27–33)

We recount Müller's doctrines in detail to give a sense of the logic of a sensation-centered view. Any sensory effect could have multiple causes and moreover reflects more the properties of the nerve affected than anything else. Taken together, we can call these doctrines the *capability* argument. By their nature, the senses have only the capability of producing one kind of product—sensations. These characteristic sensations of each sense reside in the observer, not in the world.

Taking the capability argument at face value, it becomes baffling how we might move from having sensations to having knowledge about the external world. To the philosophically unsophisticated, it seems that perception puts us in contact with objects and events in the outside world. Given the capability argument, this cannot really be so. At best we construct, guess at, or imagine the world. We do so by cataloguing, associating, and reasoning about sensations. Achieving perceptual knowledge must consist of inferring the causes of our sensations. We might even be predisposed to do this. In Müller's words, "The imagination and reason are ready to interpret the modifications in the state of the nerves produced by external influences as properties of the external bodies themselves" (p. 27).

The ambiguity and capability arguments are not entirely distinct. Berkeley's claim that a ray of light striking the retina carries no information about how far it has traveled can be seen as a capability argument. However, the arguments are somewhat different. Berkeley's argument concerns the patterns (images) coming to the eye, irrespective of the sensory apparatus from the retina on. The capability argument is an argument about sensory mechanisms. It is in the nature of the sensing process that all the observer can really acquire are sensations, and these are results of specific neural activity within the observer.

In subtle or overt form, this inference from the capabilities of individual receptors or neurons to explanations of perceptual capacity still characterizes much work in sensory physiology and perception. It also characterizes some descriptions of perception by cognitive scientists. Specifically, it is often assumed that the senses deliver some raw or uninterpreted data that is then worked into meaningful form by cognitive processing, incorporating expectations and prior knowledge ("top-down" processing) to obtain the result.

Constructivism: Dissent and Modernization

Problems with the classical constructivist view have often been pointed out. Kant (1781/1902) questioned how our representations of the world could ever originate from sensory input alone. The fact that we have coherent experience presupposes modes of mental organization, such as the dimensions of space and time, into which our sensory experiences are arranged. A different sort of dissent came from the physiologist Hering (1861–1864), who emphasized the functioning of the two eyes as an integrated system that apprehends depth directly. Binocular disparity—differences in retinal positions in the two eyes stimulated by a target—might allow direct detection of depth without learning. Hering's claims attack both the capability argument, since the perceptual system can be seen as responding to relationships rather than local stimulation, and the ambiguity argument, because the characterization of the visual stimulus in terms of single retinal images is considered to be mistaken.

Despite these dissents, extreme constructivist views dominated experimental psychology until the early twentieth century. At that time, the Gestalt psychologists mounted a comprehensive attack on the notion that percepts are built up from local sensations. Their demonstrations and arguments suggested that *patterns* are fundamental to perception, whereas sensations are incidental. Form or pattern, they asserted, is not a sensory concept at all. The Gestaltists made this point using a variety of demonstrations of *transposition* phenomena. Consider a square made of red lines. From the constructivist perspective, the total experience of viewing the square is the collection of various sensations of discriminable locations and the redness and brightness at each. Thus, "the whole is the sum of the parts." The Gestaltists pointed out that one can easily change all of the sensations, however, while preserving the form of the square. A square constructed from black dots, changed in size and positioned elsewhere on the retina, is nevertheless a square. Thus "the whole is different from the sum of the parts." A melody illustrates the concept for temporal patterns. One can change the constituent notes while preserving the melody, so long as certain relationships among the notes are preserved. Conversely, presenting the original sensations in jumbled order destroys the original form.

Despite its telling arguments and demonstrations, the Gestalt critique was unsuccessful at dismissing constructivist views of perception's origins. Part of the problem was the lack of a successful alternative view. Perceptual organization, the Gestaltists suggested, resulted from the activity of field forces in the brain, a notion that received little support and has since been abandoned. In addition, constructivist views evolved to meet some objections, while retaining their emphasis on learning in perception. The modified views elaborated Helmholtz's (1885/1925) notion that experience might lead not only to stored sensations but to the abstraction of perceptual rules that could be used in the interpretation of future sensory impressions (Brunswick, 1956; Hochberg, 1978). Brunswick (1956), in particular, argued that the Gestalt laws of perceptual organization could be learned by experiences with objects. Such neo-Helmholtzian views have remained influential to the present time (Hochberg, 1981; Nakayama & Shimojo, 1992; Harris, 1983; Rock, 1983).

Ecological Views of Perceptual Development

A different perspective on perceptual development—an ecological[4] view —starts from radically different premises about perception. Its basic ideas[5] were elaborated by J. and E. Gibson (J. Gibson, 1966, 1979; E. Gibson, 1969, 1984; see also Johansson, 1970; Shepard, 1984).

A basic premise of ecological views is that the perceiving organism is awash not only in energy but in information. Ambient energy is structured by its interactions with objects, surfaces, and events. These interactions are lawful, resulting in a detailed correspondence between patterns in ambient energy and the structure of the environment. The specificity of the patterning of energy by the physical layout makes the environment knowable via detection of structure in the array of energy (Gibson, 1966). A second major premise is that perceptual systems evolved not to allow the organism to have meaningless sensations but to pick up information in energy patterns. The focus is on the perceiving apparatus as an integrated system for information extraction rather than on activity at single receptors or even simple summing of such activity in multiple locations. Receptive elements and individual nerve fibers are parts of larger devices whose circuitry is set up to extract useful information.

The organism is considered to be *actively* involved in the pursuit of information. Take the visual system as a case in point. More than a passive array of retinal receptors, it is an active, highly coordinated, information-seeking system. Ciliary muscles change the shape of the lens, focusing light on the retina. The two eyes turn inward or outward to place the same point in space at the center of each. The eyes may turn as a unit to follow a moving stimulus or focus on a particular feature of an object. The head may also turn or the observer may move her body to improve her view of a scene. These attunements are closely linked to events in the environment and the perceiver's behavior. The organism's behavior allows it to actively extract information, and this information in turn guides ongoing behavior (Gibson, 1966).

On this view, *perceptual development begins with meaningful contact with the world,* although some perceptual systems may mature after birth, and skill in picking up particular information may improve with practice. This developmental starting point differs conspicuously from that in the constructivist account. If perceptual systems have evolved to pick up meaningful information, perceiving objects and events may not require a long learning period. Perceptual systems may no more have to "learn to interpret" sensations than they have to learn which portions of the electromagnetic spectrum interact informatively with objects. Perceptual systems may be richly structured devices specialized to take patterns as inputs and produce meaningful, functionally useful, descriptions of objects and events as outputs.

To be plausible, ecological views must incorporate some answers to the ambiguity and capability arguments of constructivism. Let us consider these answers. As before, we use visual perception as our example, as it has been most central in debates about these issues.

Answering the Ambiguity Argument
Berkeley's analysis of ambiguity is technically correct if one considers only the information available in a momentary image projected on a single retina. Human perception, however, does not work that way. In the first place, as Hering (1861–1864) described, the two eyes can work together as a system to detect depth from differences in the optical projections to the two eyes. Even more important, perhaps the best information available to perceivers is extended in time, and perceptual systems are equipped to utilize such information (Gibson, 1966). Looking with a single eye through a peephole, a three-dimensional scene may be indistinguishable from a photograph or photorealist painting. When the observer views a scene or photograph while walking, however, the optical transformations across time differ drastically. Assuming the environment to be at rest, the pattern of optical changes furnishes unequivocal information about the three-dimensional spatial relationships in the scene, with the relations between optical transformations and the real scene specified by the laws of projective geometry. It has been claimed that this *kinematic* information given by observer or object motion is fundamental to ordinary perception. The momentary retinal image considered by Berkeley may be a degenerate input to perceptual systems (Gibson, 1966, 1979; Johansson, 1970).

Answering the Capability Argument
The reply to the capability argument is complementary to the reply to the ambiguity argument. Gibson (1966) argued that perceptual systems are geared to detect structure in ambient energy rather than properties of

the energy itself (such as intensity or wavelength of light). Although the separate senses have their characteristic sensations, "sensation is not a prerequisite of perception, and sense impressions are not the 'raw data' of perception—that is, they are not all that is given for perception" (Gibson, 1966, p. 48). Perceptual systems actively extract higher-order information from incoming stimulation. The specialization of perceptual systems to detect information about the environment (and about the self) are the results of evolution (Gibson, 1966; Johansson, 1970; Shepard, 1984). Over evolutionary time, perception has come to exploit enduring regularities or constraints of the physical world.

The ecological rejoinders to constructivism undermine the *logical* case for learning in perceptual development. Empirical investigations become central. Does perception give a meaningful representation of the world from the beginning? Can available information that is abstract and extended in space and time be used by naive perceivers? Despite available information and the possibility of evolved mechanisms of information pickup, the meanings of sensory patterns might nevertheless be learned, and the most optimal information might not be utilized. Moreover, the facts might differ for different perceptual abilities: development might conform to the ecological view for some capacities and fit a constructivist account in other cases. We cannot decide by logic alone; we must pursue these questions by observation and experiment.

PERCEPTUAL CHANGE

Perception changes. Details of surface texture obvious to an adult are invisible to a 2-month-old infant. The same infant makes no use of differences in the projections to the two eyes, although these specify vivid depth to a five-month-old. Through the lifespan, perceptual change continues. A student pilot peers out the window, unable to locate the airport in the midst of roads, buildings, and streams, while her instructor spots it effortlessly. Perceptual skills attained through experience underlie expert performance in many domains.

Less apparent is what exactly changes. How does the infant perceiver differ from an older child or adult? What is the role of learning? Of maturation? Is there only one kind of perceptual learning or several? Are processes of change in early perceptual development similar to or different from the perceptual changes that occur later in life as adults develop expertise in particular domains?

One class of change—perceptual change due to *maturation* of the nervous system—may be unique to the first year of life. We will encounter many examples, including visual acuity and stereoscopic vision, in chapters 2, 3, and 4.

Against this backdrop of maturing sensory capacities, we attempt to assess the role and characteristics of learning in perception. Investigators of every theoretical persuasion agree that learning changes perception. What is hotly disputed are the nature and implications of the changes. In particular, from the two general views of perception come two different answers—answers that imply radically different understandings both of the learning process and of the experienced perceiver. J. Gibson and E. Gibson (1957) called these opposing views of perceptual learning *differentiation* or *enrichment* theories. These two notions of perceptual change will be useful as landmarks as we consider early perceptual development. We explore them in turn.

Enrichment: Perceptual Learning in the Constructivist View

Enrichment describes the notion that meaning must be added to the raw data brought in through the senses. What we mean by *meaning* is reference to the outside environment. Thus perception can furnish knowledge about the environment (or misunderstandings of the environment from misperception). Sensation does not implicate an external world. The notion of enrichment is a necessary companion to classical ideas about the starting point of perception. If the senses deliver to the observer only meaningless sensations, some process must add meaning for knowledge of the outside world to be attained.

Different possible enrichment processes have been proposed. Constructivist views have often emphasized associations based on contiguity in space or time and also similarity. Such associations apply both to current stimuli and to stored memories of earlier sensations. For example, when the observer is presented with an apple, the various locations at which red is sensed are linked by contiguity in time and space and by similarity. These sensations can call up earlier ones, based on similarity and perhaps recency in time. Association with sensations of touch has often been accorded special status, as in Berkeley's famous (1709/1910) dictum "Touch educates vision."

Knowledge of an external object is comprised of a combination of current sensations and those called up from memory. In structuralist psychology, the former was called the *core* and the latter the *context*; meaningful perception was held to be possible only adding the context to the core (Titchener, 1902). One of the most famous accounts of perceptual knowledge as enrichment was given by Helmholtz (1885/1925, p. 152) and has become known as Helmholtz's rule: "Such objects are always imagined as being present in the field of vision as would have to be there in order to produce the same impression on the nervous mechanism."

The world we perceive comes about as an act of imagination using current sensations and associated ones from memory. Helmholtz also emphasized another aspect of enrichment—namely, the abstraction of general rules from experience. He contended that perceptual experience leads inductively to the formation of abstract perceptual rules. These rules, in turn, function as premises in inferencelike perceptual processing; thus, perception has the character of *unconscious inference*.

The most detailed view of enrichment, and the one most influential in theories of infant development, is Piaget's (1952, 1954, 1976). Reality is constructed out of sensorimotor experience. At first (Piaget; 1952),

> There is not involved, it goes without saying, any interest of the child in the objects themselves that he tries to watch. These sensorial images have no meaning, being coordinated neither with sucking, grasping or anything which could constitute a need for the subject. Moreover, such images have neither depth nor prominence.... They therefore only constitute spots which appear, move, and disappear without solidity or volume. They are, in short, neither objects, independent images, nor even images charged with extrinsic meaning.... Still later ... the visual images acquire meanings connected with hearing, grasping, touching, with all the sensorimotor and intellectual combinations. (pp. 64–65)

Unique in Piaget's analysis is the idea that interpretation of sensations comes about not merely from association with other sensations but with *action*. Connecting self-initiated movements and their sensory consequences forms the basis of the growth of knowledge about oneself and the world.

Differentiation: Perceptual Change in the Ecological View

Ecological views suggest that meaningful contact with the environment is possible without the necessity of enrichment. There is no stage in development in which the senses yield an uninterpreted product; perception is always directed to the external environment. Ecological views do not, however, assert that perception is unchanging through the lifespan. In fact, perceptual changes with experience are dramatic, both in early development and in later life. The type of change is what Gibson and Gibson termed *differentiation*. The environment provides a wealth of information, far too much to be extracted all at once. Moreover, the new perceiver lacks skill in information extraction. With experience, perceivers develop selective skills. Perceptual learning considered as differentiation learning is the development of precision and speed in the pickup of information.

In her classic work *Principles of Perceptual Learning and Development*, E. Gibson (1969) described these changes: with experience in a particular domain comes increasing specificity of discrimination, more optimal deployment of attention, and discovery of higher-order perceptual structure.

An interesting feature of perceptual learning is that it sometimes seems to occur without explicit reinforcement or even feedback. Mere exposure may be sufficient. Gibson also advanced an interesting conjecture about the content of perceptual learning. Learning primarily consists of learning *distinctive features*. These are attributes within a stimulus set that are relevant to distinguishing members of a set. What is interesting about this claim is that not all aspects of objects are said to be learned from exposure to the objects. Rather, the contrasts among members of a stimulus set come to the fore in perceptual learning. This idea makes interesting predictions about exposure to particular stimulus sets and transfer of what is learned.

PROSPECTUS

In what follows, we examine experimental research on the development of perception to determine the ecological and constructivist foundations of perceptual competence, the character of perceptual processes, and the sources of change. Research in infant perception has already shed considerable light on these issues. We will see that some claims of constructivist and ecological views must be abandoned or modifed, while others have received strong support. There may even be some hope of reconciling key ideas from conflicting general views of perception into a single coherent whole. We return to these issues in chapter 12, after we have more thoroughly explored the infant's perceptual world.

Notes

1. The *nodal point* is the point of intersection of all rays that pass through the optical system of the eye undeflected. Other rays of light leaving in slightly different directions from a given object point will arrive at the same image point, but they will get there by being deflected due to refraction by the eye's optics.
2. The process may nevertheless be inferential in the formal sense that it depends on certain assumptions or constraints incorporated into perceptual machinery (Fodor & Pylyshyn, 1981; Marr, 1982; Shepard, 1984). For example, the optical changes characteristic of object approach could be mimicked by nonapproaching objects whose sizes expanded (and visible texture and so on changed) in particular ways. It can be argued that the perceptual process mapping quantitative aspects of optical expansion onto perceived time to contact is constrained such that it cannot deliver the perceptual outcome of the nonapproaching, mutating object. Such a constraint reflects the improbability of such objects in the world. Gibson argued that even this formal notion of inference can be avoided: perception can be explained by information, without resort to internalized constraints or implicit assumptions. The interested reader is referred to Gibson (1979) and Turvey et al. (1981). Criticism of this view may be found in Fodor and Pylyshyn (1981) and Ullman (1980).

3. In other domains of cognitive development, constructivism may have other connotations and contrast strongly with, rather than subsume, associationist accounts.

4. Although the terms are similar, it is important to distinguish the *level of ecology* in the study of perception from *ecological views of development*. The level of ecology refers to facts and concepts about how physical environments make information available for perception. It is theory-neutral in the sense that any theory of perception must include analyses at this level. Ecological views of perceptual development embrace the idea that perceptual mechanisms have evolved to pick up information about functionally important properties of the environment. The closeness in terminology reflects a shared emphasis on lawful relations in the physical world as crucial to understanding both how perception works and how it evolved. An alternative term for the level of ecology is Marr's (1982) *level of computational theory*. This label has the virtue of avoiding the dual use of *ecological* but can be confused with *level of representation and process*. Analyses of potential information (computational theory) are not the same as specific procedures—computations—for processing information, but the distinction is often blurred.

5. The ecological view developed here is a hybrid. It is generally consistent with the viewpoint elaborated by J. and E. Gibson; some particulars are closer to the positions elaborated by Johannson (1970), Braunstein (1976), and Shepard (1984).

Chapter 2

Physiological and Sensory Foundations of Perceptual Development

More of the human brain is devoted to perceptual information processing than to any other function. Vision alone, it is estimated, involves over thirty different areas and 40 to 50% of the entire cerebral cortex. Adding other senses, it appears that the bulk of cortical processing serves functions of perception.

Even so, the whole brain weighs only several pounds and could be held in our two hands. Thinking of the brain this way, as a small object, we might suspect that a focused scientific effort would readily reveal how it works. Unfortunately, inspection at a finer grain gives us a different view of the difficulty of the task. Neurons—the units of information transmission in the brain—number about one hundred *billion*. Their functions are realized in their connections with other neurons, and these *synapses* number approximately 10^{14}, or about a thousand for every neuron. Connectivity on such a scale makes possible awesome computational power but also makes the task of describing in detail how computations are carried out in the brain a daunting challenge. Most visual areas, for example, are known to be connected to each other, and the hypothesis that each is connected to every other cannot be ruled out by existing data. It is no wonder that the human brain has been claimed to be the most complex device in the known universe.

When we seek to understand the brain early in life, we add to this complexity the dimensions of growth and change. Whereas some plasticity can be found at later ages, never are the changes so extreme and rapid as in the infancy period. Before birth and beyond, the vast neural machinery of perception is under construction. Its status at any given age inevitably decides the potentials and limits of perception in the infant.

Animal species are classified as *altricial*, meaning helpless and immature at birth, or *precocial*, comparatively mature, mobile, and functional. In such a classification, *homo sapiens* is designated as altricial. While not born with its eyes closed, as are kittens and many other altricial species, the human newborn is nonetheless relatively immobile and long dependent on its parents for care. These are just the outward manifestations. On the inside, the newborn has an incompletely developed brain, and other parts of its nervous system continue to mature for some time after birth.

Yet the extent of postnatal development should not obscure the fact that much perceptual machinery is already in place at birth. Compared to other altricial species, humans are perhaps unique in that all sensory systems become functional before birth (Gottlieb, 1971). The newborn opossum, by comparison, is born without eyes or ears. Gottlieb (1971) considers humans and other primates as "unique in having combined the precocial pattern of sensory development with the altricial pattern of motor development" (p. 118).

In this chapter, we consider aspects of physiological development and sensory limitations that make possible and constrain the acquisition of perceptual knowledge. The division of labor between this chapter and our later topics comes from distinguishing two types of questions and research on infant sensory and perceptual development. In later chapters, our primary focus is on perceptual knowledge—knowledge of objects, spatial layout, and events. Our present concern is with sensory limits and changes in them caused by physiological development. These outer boundaries of receptivity, such as visual acuity, do not directly reveal what is perceived and represented, but they place constraints on it. Sensory maturation in human infants has implications for early perception, for development in general, and as a practical matter, for attempts to study infants' capabilities.

THE HUMAN INFANT'S NERVOUS SYSTEM

Linking the infant's physiology to sensory and perceptual functioning is a difficult undertaking. We are limited by what is known about physiology and perhaps even more by our modest knowledge of how structures and events in the nervous system carry out perceptual processing. On the behavioral side, measures of sensory and perceptual function in infants are somewhat blunt instruments. The result of these compounded uncertainties is that our conclusions about specific physiological limitations on perception must be tentative. More encouraging is the fact that progress is occurring rapidly in all of the domains relevant to understanding brain and behavior. As a result, hypotheses about neural links to perception, and their developmental patterns, are becoming more plausible, precise, and testable than they were even in the recent past.

Neural Development

Soon after conception, development of the nervous system begins. Cortical neurons begin to form at 10 weeks gestation and are completed around eighteen weeks (Casaer, 1993). Once neurons form, they migrate, under the guidance of chemical gradients and of glial cells (see below), to genetically programmed sites in the nervous system. Formation of the cortical layers occurs from the deepest layer out toward the surface of the cortex (Jacobson, 1991). On reaching their destinations, neurons begin a branching process that allows each to form a thousand or more connections with other neurons (figure 2.1). Dendrites, the parts of a neuron that receive signals from other neurons across synaptic junctions, grow in treelike fashion, earning the process the colorful name *dendritic arborization*. Different brain areas follow different timetables. Differentiation of the visual cortex occurs between 25 and 32 weeks of gestation (Purpura, 1975), whereas differentiation of the cerebellum, a structure that controls movement, begins much later and continues to almost 3 years of age (Casaer, 1993).

Synaptic Development
Neuronal interactions occur primarily by chemical activity across synapses (figure 2.1). Across these gaps, branches from a neuron's axon may trigger the electrical discharge of another neuron. Synapse formation in the human cerebral cortex increases greatly after neuronal migration is nearly complete in the second trimester of pregnancy (Huttenlocher, 1994). Most occurs after birth, however, especially in a burst of activity between 2 and 6 months of age. During this time, the number of synaptic contacts increases by a factor of 10, reaching a total number that is approximately double that typically found in young adults (see figure 2.2). The overproduction of synapses is corrected by a synapse elimination process that begins around 1 year of age and is completed by 10 years (Huttenlocher, 1994). At least in the visual cortex, this elimination process results from a pruning of unstimulated dendritic connections rather than by programmed neuronal cell death (Huttenlocher, 1990).

Animal studies suggest that both synaptic growth and pruning are related to experience. Increases in synapses have been reported for young rats reared in complex environments and adults under some circumstances (Greenough, Black & Wallace, 1987). Synapse increase is correlated with an increase in skills such as maze learning (Greenough, Volkmar & Juraska, 1973; Holloway, 1966; Greenough et al., 1987). Conversely, particular kinds of stimulation and the acquisition of specific behavioral patterns may be accomplished by selective pruning of synaptic connections and probably selective neuronal death as well. One example is the formation of ocular dominance columns in the visual cortex. For binocular vision, the brain must keep track of which information comes in through which eye. In the monkey, there are originally overlapping inputs from the two eyes in binocular areas. Eventually, a sorting occurs into alternating bands

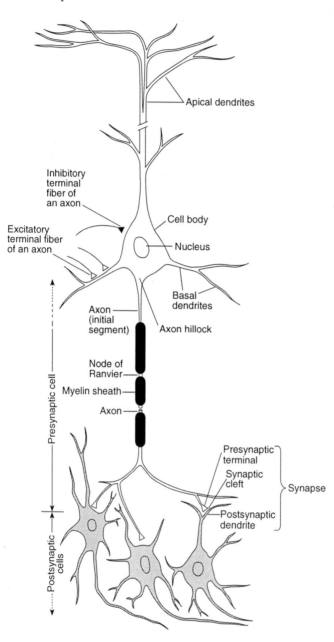

Figure 2.1
Schematic representation of a neuron and synaptic junction. Reprinted with permission from
Kandel, E. R., Jessell, T. M., & Schwartz, J. H., *Principles of neuroscience* (3rd ed.), Appleton &
Lange, 1991.

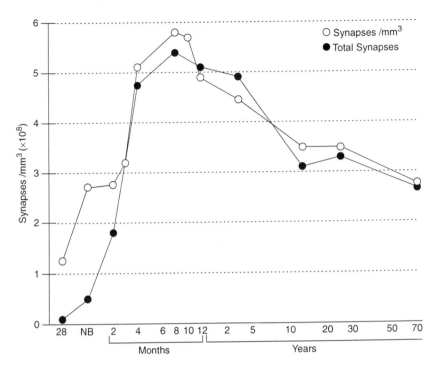

Figure 2.2
Changes in synaptic density across the lifespan. "28" indicates density estimates at 28 weeks gestation and "NB" indicates density in newborn infants. Reprinted from *Neuropsychologia*, *28*, Huttenlocher, P. R., Morphometric study of human cerebral cortex development, pp. 517–527, copyright 1990, with kind permission from Elsevier Science Ltd., The Boulevard, Langford Lane, Kidlington OX5 1GB, UK.

("columns") of cells, each responsive to only the left eye or the right eye. It is likely that this formation of ocular dominance columns results from the pruning of synaptic connections, and it is known to be affected by visual experience (LeVay, Wiesel & Hubel, 1980; Guillery, 1972). If both eyes receive normal visual input, a competition process leads to the normal alternating bands. If one eye is denied visual experience, it ends up represented by narrow bands, whereas the experienced eye's projections terminate in wider bands (LeVay et al., 1980).

Myelination
In the central nervous system, neurons are interspersed with ten to fifty times as many *glial cells*, which do not carry information but act as a support system. Among their many functions, they add structure, separation, and insulation and remove debris. Certain kinds of glial cells are responsible

for the process of *myelination,* the covering of an axon by a glial cell membrane, which greatly increases the conduction speed of the neuron and lowers its action potential threshold. With its new *myelin sheath,* the neuron's conduction speed increases from about 2 m/sec to 50 m/sec.

Increased myelination over the first months of life facilitates sensory responses and complex motor patterns. Myelination may be especially important in tracts connecting separate brain areas. Casaer (1993) mentions a number of developmental milestones that occur around the same time myelination occurs between separate brain sites.

Functional Regions of the Brain

At birth, the nervous system is more mature toward the periphery and less mature centrally. This may in part account for why infants are equipped with a large number of reflexes but few intentional movements within the first few weeks of life (Brandt, 1979).

Gottlieb (1971) reviews evidence of an invariant sequence of the development of sensory systems in a number of mammalian species. The evidence suggests that earliest sensitivity emerges in the tactile sense, usually somewhere in the head region, followed by vestibular sensitivity (indicated by righting responses), auditory sensitivity, and visual sensitivity (the latter two indicated electrophysiologically or behaviorally). Various species of birds show this same sequence. Its invariance is remarkable given that the various mammals that show it have evolved independently for at least 70 million years, and the avian species split off much earlier.

The significance of this pattern is not clear. Is it adaptive somehow? Is it optimal from an engineering standpoint because certain requirements for developing the individual systems make this ordering optimal? Or does it reflect phylogeny? In the evolution of sensory systems, tactile and vestibular systems probably preceded auditory and visual ones. We have no way to decide this issue. It is, however, intriguing that the ordering appears to go from proximal to distal: sensitivity is first to direct contact and body orientation and is followed by the senses of audition and vision that are used to detect more remote stimuli. The order suits the priorities of the developing organism, which will be able to withdraw from a noxious stimulus or reorient itself long before it can locomote toward or away from a remote object or event. Perhaps this functional interpretation of the order of appearance of sensory systems is most likely. As Gottlieb (1971, p. 106) put it: "On logical grounds, evolution is a consequence of nature's more successful experiments in ontogeny." We normally think of developmental patterns as being consequences of evolution, but in fact the success of certain patterns in the individual's development determines which developmental patterns persist.

In humans, all four of these systems—visual, auditory, tactile, and vestibular—appear to be functional before birth but with varying levels of maturity. We consider these, as well as the gustatory and olfactory systems, and motor development, below.[1]

VISUAL SYSTEM ANATOMY AND PHYSIOLOGY

Exquisite specialization for detecting spatial variation is the hallmark of the mammalian visual system. From a point on an object, reflected light sets out in many directions, yet the optics of the eye capture this light and ensure that rays reaching the eye from a single point end up focused on a unique point on the retina, while light from other directions is placed elsewhere. The close packing in the retina of about 7 million cones and about 120 million rods serves not only to catch most entering light but to preserve information about its direction of origin. This information makes possible the detection of changes in the input across the plane of the retina and ensures that they correspond to spatial changes in the optic array outside. The changes in the optic array often derive from important differences in objects, surfaces, orientations, and arrangements in the world. Systematic linkages from patterns in objects, space, and events, to patterns in the optic array, to patterns in the observer's nervous system make it possible to obtain knowledge of the world through the senses. Optimizing the extraction of this knowledge is the incredible engineering of the eye: adults resolve spatial details (for example, in Vernier acuity—discriminating the misalignment of two lines) twenty to thirty times smaller than the diameters of individual retinal receptors! These feats of spatial precision are only in progress in the newborn.

The Eye

From birth to early adulthood the human eye grows about 50 percent in axial length (distance from the front of the eye to the retina at the back). Because the size of the image on the retina increases with eye depth, we would expect newborns' visual acuity to be worse than adults by one-third, given this factor alone. The fastest growth in eye size occurs during the first year, with axial length changing from about 16 mm to about 20 to 21 mm, making up about half of the difference between the newborn and adult size of about 24 mm. Some other basic optical factors that might affect visual sensitivity, such as pupil size, transparency of the ocular media, and transmittance of the lens, probably do not significantly limit early vision relative to adult characteristics.

At the retina, however, we find a number of factors that make newborns' vision dramatically worse than adults'. For adults, fine detail and color are detected primarily in the fovea, a 1- to 2-degree central region of the visual field. Visual acuity in the fovea is 2.5 times better than at 10 deg out in the periphery and eight to ten times better than at 40 deg out. In the newborn, however, the fovea is strikingly immature. Newborns' cones, the photoreceptors in the fovea that provide color and high spatial resolution, are spaced about four times further apart than those of adults (Yuodelis & Hendrickson, 1986).

More limitations are evident when we examine individual photoreceptors. In adults, the cone is a long, thin structure that has an *inner segment* that catches quanta of light and funnels it (using the same principles as fiber optics) to the *outer segment*, where it can be absorbed by molecules of photopigment to trigger an electrical signal. An example of an individual cone from an adult is shown in the light micrograph in figure 2.3b. For an infant, the entire cone is much shorter (figure 2.3a), and the inner segment has a much more bloated shape. The outer segment is so short that it is barely visible between the outlined inner segment and the pigment epithelium (PE) layer. Analysis of the shape of the infant's inner segment (Banks & Bennett, 1988) suggests that it would not function as an effective waveguide; therefore, light reaches the outer segment to initiate a photochemical response only if it is aimed directly at the aperture of the outer segment.

The probable effects on visual efficiency of the spacing and shape of newborns' cones were calculated by Banks and Bennett (1988). Whereas adult cones catch about 65% of the light hitting the foveal area, the neonate's arrangement catches only 2%! Figure 2.4 shows schematics of the adult and infant eyes, illustrating the coverage problem. Obviously, most light hitting a newborn's fovea never contacts a photoreceptor.

The Visual Cortex

Visual processing of spatial detail, crucial for pattern, object, and event perception, is carried out in cortical visual areas. Projections extend from the optic nerve leaving the eyes to the lateral geniculate nucleus in the thalamus (a subcortical relay station) to the visual cortex. Another important visual pathway is entirely subcortical, extending primarily from the peripheral visual fields to the superior colliculus in the midbrain. This pathway appears to subserve rapid orienting to stimuli appearing in peripheral vision but does not process much pattern detail.

Anatomical observations indicating that the visual cortex is not fully mature at birth (Conel, 1939–1963) and several aspects of infant visual performance have led to the hypothesis that the newborn's visual processing is entirely subcortical (Bronson, 1974, 1982a, 1982b). Newborns show saccadic eye movements to track slow-moving stimuli and orient

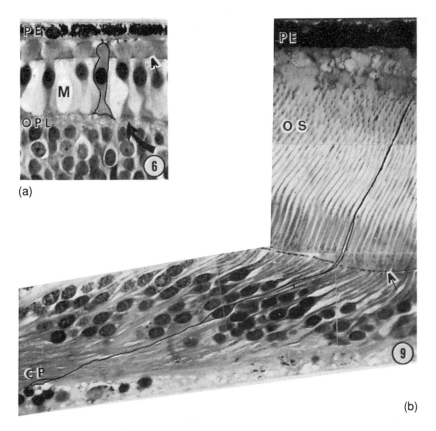

(a)

(b)

Figure 2.3
Development of cones. Single photoreceptors are outlined for a 5-day-old infant (a) and a
72-year-old adult (b). Reprinted from *Vision Research*, 26, Youdelis, C., & Hendrickson, A. A,
Qualitative and quantitative analysis of the human fovea during development, pp. 847–855,
copyright 1986, with kind permission from Elsevier Science Ltd., The Boulevard, Langford
Lane, Kidlington OX5 1GB, UK.

more readily toward stimuli in the temporal (near the ear) than the nasal
(near the nose) visual fields, characteristics that could be controlled by
subcortical orienting mechanisms. Moreover, brain electrical responses
(see below) to properties that are known to be processed in the visual
cortex, such as edge orientation, are weak or absent in the first 6 weeks of
life.

The notion of the "decorticate" newborn fits the bulk of behavioral and
electrophysiological evidence. In extreme form, however, it is contra-
dicted by several lines of behavioral evidence showing perceptual competence and implying some cortical function. Several aspects of visual

(a)

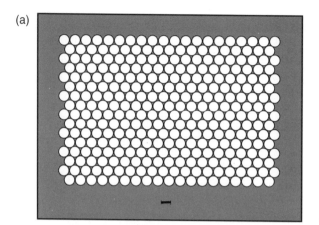

(b)

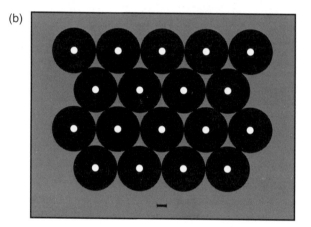

Figure 2.4
Schematic foveal receptor lattices for an adult (a) and a human newborn (b). The reference bars at the bottom of each panel represent .5 min of arc. White areas represent the effective light collecting areas. Redrawn from Banks & Crowell (1993).

performance that would require cortical involvement have been clearly documented. Habituation effects, when a stimulus is shown repeatedly over time, transfer from one eye to the other (Slater, Morison & Rose, 1983). Some sensitivity to edge orientation, which requires responses from cortical units, can be found in newborns (Slater, Morison & Somers, 1988; Atkinson et al., 1988). Moreover, evidence suggesting shape constancy in the newborn (Slater & Morison, 1985) would be difficult to explain in the total absence of cortical function (see below). As we see below, a number of basic sensory functions, such as sensitivity to orientation, direction of motion, and spatial phase, all appear weak at birth and much more robust six to eight weeks afterward. None of these, however, appears entirely absent even in tests at the earliest ages. Some interesting suggestions about the relation of early visual attention to neurological maturation are given by Johnson (1990). The infant's visual behavior is primarily controlled subcortically in the earliest weeks of life, but some cortical interactions with subcortical pathways are also evident. The cortical activity may involve at first only certain layers of cortex and processing functions that mature earliest. In particular, it is possible that for the neonate, more detailed pattern information may be taken in than can be used to influence attentional behavior. This hypothesis may help to reconcile the absence of certain electrophysiological responses and the weakness of certain sensory sensitivities in the newborn with some rather remarkable indications of perceptual competence that we explore shortly.

BASIC VISUAL CAPABILITIES

Our immediate concern, however, is to consider the sensory consequences of the infant's immature fovea and visual cortex. The incomplete maturation of the infant's nervous system constrains early visual sensitivity in numerous ways, limiting resolution of spatial and temporal detail as well as sensitivity to contrast, orientation, motion, depth and color.

Spatial Resolution

A common way to assess spatial resolution is in terms of *minimum separable acuity*, the smallest spacing between pattern elements that can be resolved. When the whole pattern consists of parallel dark and light stripes of constant widths, we can characterize spatial resolution in terms of *spatial frequency*—the number of black and white stripe pairs per degree of visual angle. Such patterns, often referred to as *gratings*, may contain gradual variation from black to white following a sinusoidal pattern (sine wave gratings) or abrupt changes from homogeneous dark stripes to light ones (square wave gratings). Grating acuity is characterized by the highest frequency distinguishable from a solid gray pattern having the same luminance as the average of the black and white. It is often convenient to assess an adult's vision by having the subject identify letters of different sizes. Tested this way, acuity is usually described in terms of the Snellen scale, a ratio comparing what the subject sees at 20 feet (or 6 m) to the distance required for similar spatial resolution by a standard observer with good vision. Thus, 20/40 means the observer's resolution at 20 feet is the same resolution as the standard observer would have at 40 feet. In spatial frequency terms, 20/20 vision corresponds to a resolution of stripes of about 1 min of arc (about 30 cycles/deg). (Holding your thumb about 10 inches away from your face, you could resolve about 75 black and white bands within the width of your thumbnail at this resolution.)

Newborns have far worse visual acuity than adults, perhaps about 1 to 2 c/deg, or 20/400. Acuity improves in almost linear fashion to near adult levels over the first eight months of life (Norcia & Tyler, 1985). Several different methods have been used to estimate infant visual acuity, and results have varied somewhat with method. By taking a closer look, we can get some sense of this variation and also some acquaintance with the methods used to measure infants' sensory and perceptual capacities.

Assessing Visual Acuity: A Methodological Digression

The topic of visual acuity and its measurement presents a convenient opportunity to introduce methods for measuring infant perception. These basic methods and variants of them have produced the findings we discuss in later chapters. The methods differ in the kinds of infant responses measured by the experimenter. We can distinguish four categories of methods:

- *Stimulus-specific behavior* A few classes of stimuli produce characteristic behaviors. Some of these are reflexes, whereas others appear to be functionally appropriate, voluntary actions. A characteristic response to a stimulus can allow us to infer, at minimum, that the observer detects the stimulus. If the stimulus evokes an adaptive response, we may be able to infer that the stimulus conveys meaningful information about the environment. When a person walking alters her path to avoid a pothole, we infer that she detected the existence and location of the hole. A similar close coupling between certain stimuli and characteristic behaviors allows us to infer what the infant perceives. Unfortunately, this method is limited in scope because of the modest behavioral repertoire of young infants.

- *Visual attention responses* Some of the most successful behavioral methods exploit general exploratory behavior and characteristics of infant visual attention. They include infants' tendency to look at any pattern in preference to a blank field, and the tendency to look more at novel stimuli after repeated exposure to a particular stimulus or class of stimuli (*habituation and recovery*).

• *Conditioned operant behavior* Operant methods rely on conditioning and discrimination-learning paradigms. After a response is trained (reinforced) in the presence of a particular stimulus, the experimenter can test for generalization of that response to variations in the stimulus.

• *Physiological measurements* In these methods, sensory or perceptual response is inferred from measured physiological variables, such as electrical activity in the brain or heart rate.

In considering research on visual acuity, we present examples of all but the operant method. In later chapters, we see many other examples from these categories; operant methods, although used less often, have played an important role in studies of speech perception, as described in chapter 8.

Stimulus-Specific Behavior   Some of the earliest measurements of newborn visual acuity (Gorman, Cogan & Gellis, 1957, 1959) used the reflexive following pattern called *optokinetic nystagmus* (OKN). OKN is elicited when a subject looks at a large, repetitive moving pattern: it consists of a rhythmic sequence of slow tracking eye movements followed by saccadic jumps of fixation back toward the straight-ahead direction. Gorman et al. used OKN to study acuity by presenting infants with a moving square-wave grating covering most of the visual field and moving either left or right. A reliable OKN response was taken to indicate that the infant could resolve the grating, and acuity was estimated as the smallest stripe width to which 75 percent or more of the infants showed OKN. Newborns' acuity was estimated by Gorman et al. to be about 1.3 c/deg (20/450 in Snellen notation).

OKN methods have also been used to chart the course of improvement in acuity with age. Fantz, Ordy, and Udelf (1962) found that visual acuity improves from approximately 1.5 c/deg (20/400) at 2 weeks of age to greater than 6 c/deg (20/100) at $5\frac{1}{2}$ months. These acuity estimates agree reasonably well with others obtained since (see Banks & Salapatek, 1983, for a review).

The use of OKN illustrates how sensory function can be inferred by measuring a behavior elicited naturally by a particular kind of stimulus. In later chapters, we see cases in which this method is used to infer perceptual knowledge. Examples are infant eye blinking and head retraction, which have been interpreted as indicating the infant's perception of an approaching object (see chapter 3), and infant reaching to the nearer of two objects, interpreted as showing perception of relative depth. There are three characteristic limitations that apply to inferences about perception from such stimulus-specific responses. First, young infants have a

very limited repertoire of responses, much less stimulus-specific responses, so little of perception can be studied using these. Second, where
perceptual knowledge rather than sensory function is at stake, it may be
difficult to ascertain the perceptual basis of a response. In the case of a defensive maneuver in the face of an oncoming projectile, the infant may
truly be aware of the object (and apprehensive), or the response could be
a kind of a reflex, executed without real awareness.

The third limitation is that the peculiarities of the response must be
well understood. In the case of OKN, there are several difficulties (Dobson,
1980). The stimulus must be a uniform grating, large enough to attract the
infant's attention; the procedure works best when the display fills the entire visual field. OKN may be weak or absent in a sleepy or slightly fussy
infant, a drawback common to most response measures used with infants.
Then there is the curious asymmetry in the infant's OKN response when
one eye alone is tested. Under 3 months, OKN occurs monocularly if the
motion of the stimulus is in a temporal to nasal (ear to nose) direction but
not if the motion of the stimulus is reversed (Atkinson & Braddick, 1981).

Visual Attention Responses   Studying infant perception requires methods that are quick, reasonably simple, and reliable. More than any other
single development, the pioneering studies of Robert Fantz opened up the
study of infant perception by meeting these requirements (Fantz, 1956,
1958, 1963). The *visual preference method* invented by Fantz rests on the
insight that the ability to explore the environment visually, unlike most
other motor skills, is present very early in life. Moreover, visual exploration tendencies can be used to make inferences about what infants perceive. In Fantz's studies, a subject was positioned in front of two adjacent
viewing screens with differing displays, If subjects spent reliably more
time attending to one display, with display position changing randomly
over trials, then they must have been able to discriminate the two displays. Variations on this simple idea have been responsible for many important findings about infant perception.[2]

Use of the visual preference method to assess early visual acuity is
straightforward (Fantz, Fagan & Miranda, 1975). Presented with two side-
by-side display screens, infants will tend to look more at a display containing visible contours than at a blank field. To assess acuity, subjects are
presented with a display of alternating black and white stripes on one side
and a homogeneous gray display on the other. A reliable preference for
the striped side indicates some ability to resolve the stripes. By varying
the width (spatial frequency) of the stripes, one can estimate visual acuity
(grating acuity) as the smallest visual angle of stripes that are discriminable from the blank display.

Some refinements of the test have produced an efficient and accurate
clinical technique known as the *forced-choice preferential looking (FPL) method*

(Teller, 1979). Infants are presented simultaneously with two displays. For tests of grating acuity, one display is a stationary, high-contrast, square-wave grating, and the other is a homogeneous gray field having the same space-averaged luminance as the grating pattern. Left-right position of the grating is varied randomly across trials. On each trial, an adult observer makes a forced-choice judgment about the grating's location (left or right). The observer makes this judgment solely from looking at the infant, based on any aspect of the infant's behavior. The idea is that better-than-chance responding by the observer, based on any aspect of the baby's fixation or behavior, must indicate that the baby is responding differently to the two displays. Generally, the most informative behaviors are direction of gaze and duration of looking, but there is no requirement that the adult observers utilize, or even be aware of, any specific indicator. Following each trial, the observer receives feedback regarding accuracy. This feedback helps the observer to identify the most informative behaviors of the infant. FPL methods yield acuity estimates similar to OKN methods (Banks & Salapatek, 1983). Acuity estimates for 2-week-olds are 1.3 c/deg; these estimates increase to 5 c/deg by 6 months of age.

Physiological Measurements   A different approach is to use not overt behavior but some physiological response to indicate sensory or perceptual activity. In estimating infant visual acuity, *visual evoked potentials* (VEPs) have proven useful (Marg, Freeman, Peltzman & Goldstein, 1976; Sokol, 1978; Pirchio, Spinelli, Fiorentini & Maffei, 1978; Norcia & Tyler, 1985). The VEP is an electrical response to a discrete stimulus or stimulus change recorded from the visual cortex by means of electrodes placed on the surface of the scalp. In order to isolate responses specific to the stimulus from ongoing brain electrical activity, responses to many discrete stimulus presentations are averaged (*transient VEP*) or a periodic stimulus (such as a contrast-reversing grating, where stripes change from dark to light over time) is used, and signals are analyzed for modulation at the stimulus frequency (*sustained VEP*). A reliable response component at the modulation frequency indicates some sensitivity to the stimulus. Ideally, visual acuity could be estimated as the spatial frequency for which the VEP amplitude falls to zero. In practice, this proves impossible because of background noise, so the estimated zero point is usually extrapolated from the data using the assumption that near threshold, acuity declines as a linear function (Norcia & Tyler, 1985; Sokol, 1978).

VEP studies in the 1970s and early 1980s produced acuity estimates similar to behavioral and OKN measures in the first month of life but indicated considerably higher levels from about 2 months on (see figure 2.5). The discrepancy may be related to differences in what is being measured by VEP and behavioral techniques; the specifics of how these cortical electrical signals relate to perceptual experience are unknown. Dobson

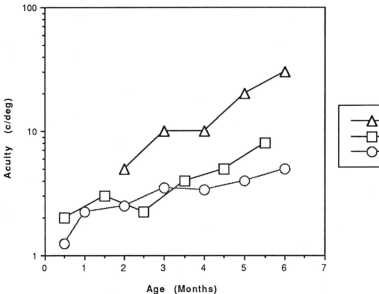

Figure 2.5
Estimates of infant visual acuity by age and experimental procedure. From Banks, M. S., &
Salapatek, P. (1983), Infant visual perception, in M. Haith and J. Campos (Eds.), *Handbook of
child psychology* (Vol. 2). Copyright © 1983, John Wiley & Sons. Reprinted by permission of
John Wiley & Sons, Inc.

and Teller (1978) point out that the typical averaging techniques in VEP
studies may pick up subthreshold signals that are unavailable to the infant
on a trial-by-trial basis. Differences in scoring methods may account for
some of the disparity as well. The extrapolation of threshold functions
to the point where the VEP is undetectable represents a more liberal
criterion than the 75 percent detection used in FPL studies. If acuity is
assigned based on a lower percentage (55 or 60 percent), there is better
agreement across methods (Dobson & Teller, 1978).

An innovation that increases the precision of VEP measurement is the
sweep VEP technique (Norcia & Tyler, 1985; Norcia, Tyler & Hamer,
1990). In this technique, a contrast-reversing grating stimulus changes
spatial frequency in linear steps every .5 sec. Perhaps the primary advantage of this method is that a 10-sec sweep can yield useful data across the
spatial frequency range more quickly than with separate trials at different
frequencies. This efficiency makes the method less susceptible to changes
in the infant's attention and general state (Norcia & Tyler, 1985).

Sweep VEP results show a linear increase in grating acuity to nearly
adult levels over the first 8 months (see figure 2.6). The most interest-

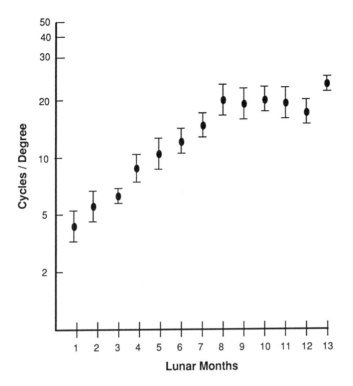

Figure 2.6
Increase in grating acuity in infants over the first year of life as measured by sweep VEP. Reprinted from *Vision Research*, 25, Norcia, A., & Tyler, C., Spatial frequency sweep VEP: Visual acuity during the first year of life, pp. 1399–1408, copyright 1985, with kind permission from Elsevier Science Ltd., The Boulevard, Langford Lane, Kidlington OX5 1GB, UK.

ing contrast with earlier data is that newborn acuity, estimated at about 5 c/deg, is three to five times higher than earlier VEP and behavioral estimates (Marg et al., 1976; Harter, Deaton & Odorn, 1977).

This major discrepancy in acuity estimates is difficult to interpret. It highlights the major issue regarding physiological indices of sensory and perceptual function: what does the measurement mean? For VEPs, there is evidence that the electrical signals come from an early stage of cortical processing. If so, then reliable evoked responses to a display indicate that the signal has made it through the optics of the eye, through the geniculostriate pathway at least to the visual cortex. Regardless of what other questions there may be, reliable VEP results indicate which signals are passed to a certain point in the nervous system.

But what do measured VEPs mean about what the infant sees? If we knew that the VEP is a physiological marker of sensory experience, then

we could accept VEP estimates of acuity. Lower sensitivity indicated by
behavioral measures would be due to infants' inconsistent attention or
their weaker preferences for barely visible stimuli. Suppose instead that
we knew that the VEP comes from a neural process before sensory experience emerges; then it would vouch for an intact optical-neural pathway
to some point, but it would not estimate visual acuity. Behavioral estimates of acuity would then be preferable for deciding what infants see.
Unfortunately, we do not know enough about the VEP to decide.

We have the same problem with behavioral measures, but the direc-
tionality is different. With physiological measures, we cannot be sure that
a *positive* response indicates that something has been *perceived*. With
behavioral measures, we can be comfortable that a positive response
indicates perception at some level. On the other hand, a *negative* result in
behavior is almost always uninformative. Perception is not the same as
action, nor does it always lead to action. An infant may detect a stimulus
but fail to show an overt response. In this regard, a good physiological
measure may have advantages, in showing that some internal response to
a signal did or did not occur at some level of the nervous system.

We may view these methodological uncertainties as obstacles to our
immediate goals or as useful windows into the deeper issues in understanding perception and the mind. The root problem here is the *mind-body
problem*: how does activity in the nervous system produce knowledge,
guide behavior, and give rise to perceptual experience? We understand
the connections only in a vague, correlational way. With continued
research and new technology, we can expect the correlations between
neural activity and behavior to become more precise. It is not clear, however, when or whether such developments will provide an account of how
physiological activity connects to conscious experience. Without such an
account, we must accept uncertainty in any attempt to use a physiological
measurement as an indicator of perceptual experience.

Peripheral Acuity

Our combined discussion of methods and visual acuity have featured research about acuity presumably involving foveal vision. What about visual
acuity in the rest of the visual field? For adults, acuity drops off steeply
going from fovea to periphery. For the infant, however, the fovea at birth
is less mature than the peripheral areas of the retina. Sireteanu, Kellerer,
and Boergen (1984) investigated the development of infants' acuity in the
peripheral visual field. Infants' acuity at about 10 deg from the fovea was
tested in infants between the ages of 24 days and 13 months. Sireteanu et
al. found an increase from 1.6 c/deg to 3.2 c/deg between 2 and 4 months
of age. They found no significant improvement in peripheral acuity be-

tween 4 and 11 months of age. The difference between foveal and peripheral acuity thus appears to be considerably less than for adults. From birth to adulthood, acuity will become six to twelve times better in the fovea but only two to three times better in the periphery.

Implications of Spatial Resolution for Perception
Methods based on behavior, FPL, and OKN agree rather well, as do original VEP methods, especially in the first few months of life. Better acuity estimated by the sweep VEP technique may be a true improvement in measurement and may indicate that early visual resolution is much better than previously thought. All of the methods indicate a monotonic (roughly linear) improvement in grating acuity through about 8 months of age.

Despite variations in methods and their attendant theoretical uncertainties, available acuity estimates provide strong clues about the level of visual detail in the infant's visual world. Newborn acuity is between 1.5 and 5 c/deg or between 20/400 and 20/120 Snellen. With grating acuity at the low end of this range, the newborn could resolve a stripe width of 20 min. Missing would be much textural detail of distant surfaces; small text would pose a problem if the infant could read. Acuity would not, however, pose much of a problem for detecting the layout of surfaces in ordinary environments, the shapes of common objects, or fine texture of near objects. At a viewing distance of 20 inches, for example, a texture element 1/8 inch in diameter would be resolvable. The hole in a small letter *o* in ordinary book print should be resolvable from 10 inches away. Interestingly, there is evidence that deletion of high-frequency (fine-detail) information has little effect on adult pattern recognition (Ginsburg, 1978). Similarly, von Hofsten (1983a) notes that an infant's acuity, although far inferior to an adult human's, is about the same as that of an adult cat. If cats could read, their acuity might prove something of an impediment, but their perceptual-motor behavior is quite good. There are additional considerations raised by the young infant's contrast sensitivity (see below), but grating acuity in and of itself does not pose a major obstacle to early perception, perceptual development, or attempts to study them.

Contrast Sensitivity

Acuity measurements provide information about the visual system's ability to resolve detail under conditions of high contrast. Another basic determinant of visual sensitivity is *contrast*—the range of luminance in a pattern. One standard measure is Michelson contrast, defined as

$$(L_{max} - L_{min})/(L_{max} + L_{min}),$$

where L_{max} and L_{min} designate the maximum and minimum pattern luminances, respectively. This measure ranges from 0 to 1, increasing with the difference between the darkest and lightest areas in a display.

Contrast threshold, the minimum contrast needed to detect a pattern, varies with spatial frequency. An adult contrast sensitivity function (sensitivity equals 1/threshold value) is shown in figure 2.7a. We can recognize several well-known features of this function. Sensitivity is highest in a middle range of spatial frequency, with the optimal frequency (detectable with least contrast) at about 3 to 4 c/deg. Above 10 c/deg, sensitivity decreases steeply and cuts off around 30 c/deg for adults, corresponding to the limit of visual acuity.

Compared to adults, newborns' contrast sensitivity is not impressive. Figure 2.7b shows data from several laboratories (Atkinson, Braddick & Moar, 1977a, 1977b; Banks & Salapatek, 1978, 1981; Pirchio et al., 1978). Sensitivity increases over the first 6 months, especially for high spatial frequencies. The low-frequency fall-off is not consistent at 1 month but steepens between 2 and 6 months. With age, the range of detectable spatial frequencies (acuity) increases, and peak contrast sensitivity shifts rightward, matching the adult peak at 3 to 4 c/deg by about 3 months. These results have been found with both moving and static gratings, although infants appear to be more sensitive to moving as opposed to static gratings of low spatial frequencies (Atkinson et al., 1977a).

Implications of Contrast Sensitivity for Perception
Banks and Dannemiller (1987) point out that, although infant contrast sensitivity is poor relative to adults, it is quite sufficient to detect many of the intensity variations in common objects and spatial layouts. To use their example, under normal illumination, a human face often gives contrasts of .7 to .8 between skin and hair. Sensitivity at threshold for a contrast of .7 would be 1.428; it can be seen in figure 2.7b that 1-month-olds exceed this sensitivity throughout most of the range of spatial frequencies they can detect. As we concluded regarding acuity, these limitations of early vision would be expected to affect pickup of fine spatial details. Minute textural variation and subtle gradations of intensity may not be visible to the young infant. Perception of ordinary objects and events in well-lit environments is not greatly limited by contrast sensitivity.

Another point to keep in mind is that poor contrast sensitivity does not imply that above threshold, contrasts are less noticeable for infants than adults. Due to the possible operation of a compensation process, *contrast constancy*, it is possible that apparent contrasts remain in correspondence with actual (physical) contrasts more than would be expected from the infant's CSF (Banks & Dannemiller, 1987). The infant's threshold may be higher, but above this threshold, the appearance of different contrasts may be similar for adults and infants.

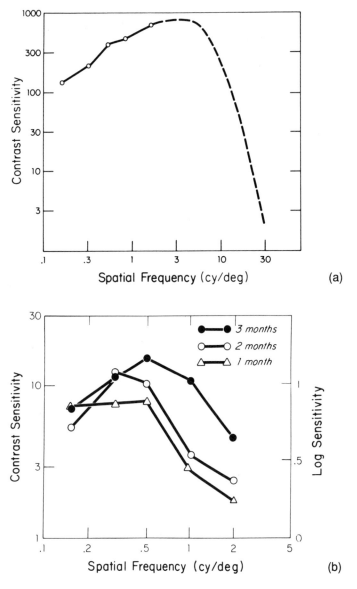

Figure 2.7
Contrast sensitivity functions for (a) adults and (b) 1-, 2-, and 3-month-old infants. Reprinted with permission from Banks, M. S., & Salapatek, P. (1978), Acuity and conrast senstivity in 1-, 2-, and 3-month-old human infants, *Investigative Ophthalmology and Visual Science, 17,* 361–365.

Mechanisms of Development in Constrast Sensitivity and Acuity

An elegant means of quantifying early visual capacities, tracking changes, and inferring the mechanisms of developmental change is the *ideal observer* analysis (Geisler, 1984, 1989), pioneered in the study of infant vision by Banks and his colleagues (Banks & Dannemiller, 1987; Banks & Bennett, 1988; Banks & Shannon; 1993; Banks, Geisler & Bennett, 1987). In this method, known sources of optical error (spherical aberration, chromatic aberration, diffraction due to the pupil, clarity of the optic media, and errors in image focusing) are quantified. Added to these effects are estimated effects due to immaturities in neonates' photoreceptors and their cumulative effects on vision estimated theoretically. The resulting estimates are compared to estimates of infant visual performance obtained from experiments. In general, these analyses suggest that infants' acuity and contrast sensitivity in the first 6 months of life fall well below the levels that should be possible given limitations that are known. Ideal observer estimates predict, based on preneural mechanisms, a 1.3 log unit (twentyfold) decrease in contrast sensitivity and a .6 log unit (fourfold) decrease in grating acuity. Observed data show larger decrements. Because infants' contrast sensitivity is worse than predicted by the ideal observer model, infants' limited vision is not due solely to optical and photoreceptor immaturities. Banks and Shannon (1993) suggest that other postreceptor mechanisms account for infants' poor performance. Possible mechanisms are intrinsic neural noise, such as random addition of action potentials in the visual cortex, inefficient neural sampling, poor motivation to respond, and so forth.

Orientation Sensitivity

It is now well established that initial cortical processing of visual input involves neural units selective for orientation, retinal position, and spatial frequency. Each of these dimensions of selectivity is crucial for the extraction of information for perception. Orientation in particular would seem to be required for all later processing concerned with recovering object boundaries, form, and texture. Yet some evidence indicates that orientation sensitivity is rather weak in the earliest weeks of life (Braddick, 1993; Braddick, Wattam-Bell & Atkinson, 1986).

Using visual evoked potentials, one might expect to pick up a cortical electrical response to periodic alternations of orientation of a grating stimulus. Braddick, Wattam-Bell & Atkinson (1986) presented orientation reversals at about 8 per second and observed little VEP response until 5 to 6 weeks of age. Newborns' lack of orientation responses did not seem to reflect more general deficits; even the 1-week-olds showed reliable responses to phase reversals (switching of dark and light areas) in the same stimuli. Slower modulation (3 reversals/sec) produced evidence of an orientation-specific response between 2 and 3 weeks (Braddick, 1993). These characteristics of orientation responses seem to be paced maturationally; preterm infants of the same gestational age showed responses similar to full-term infants, suggesting that duration of visual experience is not relevant (Atkinson et al., 1990).

Orientation sensitivity has also been studied behaviorally, using a method that has been widely applied to problems in infant perception—habituation and recovery of visual attention. The topic of orientation sensitivity provides an opportune juncture to elaborate this method.

The Habituation Method

In habituation studies, duration of visual fixation to a particular display is measured over several trials. *Habituation* refers to the fact that infants' fixation times to a particular stimulus decline over time. For example, if the oriented grating shown in figure 2.8A was presented to an infant observer over repeated trials, looking times would decline. After this decline, looking times to the same display and to a display of changed orientation could be measured. Here we encounter a second useful characteristic of infant attentional behavior. Habituation will generally be

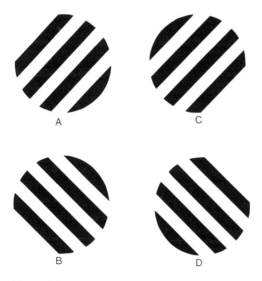

Figure 2.8
Stimuli used to test infants' orientation sensitivity. Infants were habituated to one of the four grating patterns shown. After habituation, infants habituated to (a) or (b) were tested with patterns (c) and (d), while infants habituated to (c) or (d) were tested with (a) and (b). Reprinted with permission from Slater, A., Morison, V., & Somers, M. (1988). Orientation discrimination and cortical function in the human newborn. *Perception, 17,* 597–602.

specific to properties of the stimulus presented. If a noticeably different stimulus is presented, recovery of looking time—dishabituation—will occur. Thus, dishabituation can be used as an index of perceived stimulus novelty. The ingenuity of investigators in manipulating what is repeated and what changes from trial to trial has allowed many important questions about perception to be posed using this method. A discussion of the key concepts and historical roots of the habituation method may be found in the appendix.

Habituation studies of newborn orientation discrimination were conducted by Slater et al. (1988). Their subjects were 16 newborns (mean age = 3 days, 18 hours). After habituation to a high-contrast square-wave grating (striped pattern) oriented 45 deg from the vertical, they were presented with a pair of displays containing two patterns, one matching the orientation seen during habituation and one shifted 90 deg (45 deg from the vertical in the opposite direction). To control for possible responding to local stimulus features (such as the black area at upper left), the phase (position of black and white stripes) was reversed in the test displays from what it had been during habituation. Referring to figure 2.8, subjects habituated to patterns A or B were tested with the pair shown in C and D, and vice versa. On the first test trial, infants looked on average 77 percent at the stimulus in the novel orientation; 15 of the 16 infants looked more at the novel stimulus. This result was confirmed by Atkinson et al. (1988).

Implications of Orientation Sensitivity for Perception

Clearly, some maturational process operates to improve orientation sensitivity from rudimentary beginnings to full function around 2 months of age. Infants do demonstrate orientation sensitivity from birth, however. The studies directly demonstrating their sensitivity have important implications. For one, they clear up a great mystery. VEP studies had suggested that infants might be "orientation blind" until 5 to 6 weeks. But as we see later on, behavioral studies of form perception indicate impressive innate abilities (Slater et al., 1988; Fantz et al., 1975; Slater & Sykes, 1977) that are difficult to explain without assuming sensitivity to contour orientation. A second implication is a lesson that arises often in infant perception research: negative results are largely uninformative. Failure to observe a certain ability might indicate that infants lack it, but it might instead indicate their inattention, their lack of preference among discriminable stimuli, domination of their fixation by some other stimulus attribute, and so on. In the case of negative VEP results on newborn orientation sensitivity, it seems likely that some maturational process produces more robust orientation processing, and related VEPs, by 2 months of age. The failure to register infants' orientation sensitivity via VEP methods could be explained by such changes; speculation is complicated by the fact that we do not really know much about the relation of VEPs to neural processing. Braddick (1993) considers some possible mechanisms of development as well as some limitations in interpreting VEP data about the development of orientation sensitivity. It is, in any case, sobering to find infants acting with so little regard for the electrophysiological data!

Finally, several theoretical studies have suggested that basic dimensions of visual sensitivity, such as orientation and spatial frequency, can be produced by interactions of modifiable neural networks with the statistical properties of the visual environment (von der Malsburg, 1973; Olshausen & Field, 1996). Although the idea of the "self-wiring" of the nervous system from environmental input seems to be gaining steadily in popularity, the evidence largely contradicts this idea as an account of human visual development. As we have seen, sensitivity to basic visual dimensions, such as orientation, can be demonstrated in human newborns. These results are consistent with studies of cortical cell receptive field properties in neonates of other species (for a review see Banks & Salapatek, 1983). Evidence for inborn orientation selectivity, for example, can be found in kittens and even more clearly in monkeys (e.g., Wiesel & Hubel, 1974). In chapters 3 and 4, we will consider evidence that the inborn perceptual abilities of humans extend even further, encompassing important aspects of three-dimensional spatial perception and sensitivity to some relationships that define visual configurations, such as faces.

If the general notion of the "self-wiring" visual system is incorrect, what can elegant simulations of self-organizing systems tell us? They may in the first place help us understand how visual cortical organization emerged over evolutionary time. The statistics of the natural environment may have exerted their influence on our genetics rather than on the individual's neural development. Second, although many basic visual functions appear at birth in humans, we have noted some do so quite weakly. The rapid improvement in many visual functions in the first six to eight weeks of life has been argued to involve maturational influences such as myelination, but it may also involve attunement of neural circuitry under environmental input. Earlier we mentioned one example—the influence of visual input on the formation of ocular dominance columns in visual cortex, a development important for the computation of binocular depth information.

Temporal Aspects of Vision

Information carried by motion or change is crucial to visual perception of the environment's stable properties, such as the three-dimensional layout, as well as changes or events occurring within it. Early sensitivity to motion and change would be a prerequisite for the infant to tap this reservoir of dynamic information. Conversely, early immaturities or limitations in temporal processing would constrain early perception in important ways.

The basic sensitivities that allow access to the world of changes and events are several. These include detection of motion, its direction, and its speed. They also include the ability to resolve the onsets and offsets of stimulus changes (temporal resolution).

Temporal Resolution

Analogous to the ability to resolve changes in luminance that unfold across a spatial dimension, temporal resolution is an important aspect of a visual system. For a light blinking on and off there will be some rate of flicker too fast to resolve visually, and a constant light (more or less the average of the light and dark episodes) will be seen. The highest frequency at which the flicker is detectable is called the *critical flicker frequency* (CFF); for adults the CFF varies with factors such as stimulus contrast but is around 60 Hz (cycles per sec) under the best conditions.

Studies of infant CFF have employed either visual preference measures or a particular electrophysiological indicator, the electroretinogram (ERG). In FPL studies, a spatially homogeneous display with a given frequency of flicker is paired with another display that presumably appears as unchanging. Choosing the brightness of the unchanging display poses a challenge. Suppose that the flickering display is not detectable as such by the infant's visual system but that the averaging characteristics of the infant's system are unknown. It would be hard to be confident that the brightness chosen for the unchanging display matched the brightness of the flickering display. In the absence of such a match, a visual preference might be observed based on the difference in perceived brightness. A clever way of avoiding this problem has been employed in CFF studies with infants (Nystrom, Hansson & Marklund, 1975; Regal, 1981). The "unchanging" comparison stimulus is in reality a flickering display whose frequency is well above the adult's CFF, presumably undetectable as flickering by infant subjects. Whatever the temporal averaging characteristics of the infant's system, the two displays should match in the event that no flicker is detected in either one.

Nystrom et al. (1975) obtained CFF estimates using a visual preference procedure with 6- and 10-week-olds. Unpatterned, flickering stimuli of 1, 5, 10, and 20 Hz were all preferred to the 100 Hz comparison stimulus. Nystrom et al. also tested all possible frequency pairs among their stimuli. In all cases not involving the 100 Hz stimulus, they found preferential fixation of the higher frequency. Regal (1981) studied infants longitudinally as well as cross-sectionally at 1, 2, and 3 months of age using an FPL procedure. One of the displays on every trial flickered at 75 Hz, above the

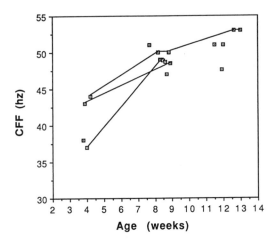

Figure 2.9
Critical flicker frequency (CFF) as a function of age. Reprinted from *Vision Research, 21*, Regal, D. Development of critical flicker frequency in human infants, pp. 549–555, copyright 1981, with kind permission from Elsevier Science Ltd., The Boulevard, Langford Lane, Kidlington OX5 1GB, UK.

adult CFF and assumed to be unvarying for infants. On each trial, the observer judged the location of the lower-frequency stimulus; CFF's were defined as the frequency at which observers were 75 percent correct. Figure 2.9 shows the results of this study. Connected points indicate data from the same subjects tested at different ages. On average, CFFs were estimated at 41 Hz at 1 month of age, 50 Hz at 2 months, and 51 Hz at 3 months. Under similar conditions, adult CFFs averaged 53 Hz. These results indicate that temporal resolution of these high-contrast stimuli is adultlike by 2 months and not drastically different at the earliest age tested (1 month). Regal also tested a few 2-month-olds on reduced luminance displays. He found that the falloff of CFF with reduced luminance closely matched that shown in adults.

ERG studies use an electrical potential at the retina that undergoes detectable changes with changing light intensity. ERG correlates well with detectable flicker when high stimulus intensities are used. Findings using this measure indicate that by 2 months of age responses appeared adultlike (Heck & Zetterstrom, 1958; Horsten & Winkelman, 1964). One study (Heck & Zetterstrom, 1958) found reduced CFF in infants 1 month or younger, with a 15 Hz CFF at the best (highest) illuminance on the first day of life (compared to CFFs around 70 for 2-month-olds and adults). In the study by Horsten and Winkelman (1964), in contrast, essentially adultlike performance was obtained from the earliest ages.

The observed ERG does not necessarily indicate that flicker is perceived or even necessarily what frequencies are able to be processed beyond the retina. Nevertheless, the convergence between ERG and behavioral data is impressive. Specifically, both indicate essentially mature patterns by 2 months. Also, the CFF at 1 month estimated by Regal (1981) using an FPL procedure closely matches the ERG-based result at one month reported by Heck and Zetterstrom at similar illumination levels.

Before 1 month, the available data do not fully mesh. No behavioral data exist, but according to ERGs, newborn CFF is either considerably worse than for adults or similar to adult levels. Stimulus conditions and ages tested were similar for the two studies; the reason for the discrepant data is not clear.

A more comprehensive description of temporal properties of early vision could be given by measurement of infant temporal contrast sensitivity functions (Banks & Dannemiller, 1987). Analogous to spatial CSFs, these would depict, for a given illumination level, the amplitude of intensity modulation required for detection of flicker. Thus, a temporal CSF would plot amount of intensity modulation (actually one over the modulation) against frequency. Adult temporal CSFs show a bandpass characteristic: for high illumination levels, sensitivity is greatest between about 5 and 40 Hz, dropping off steeply on both sides. We do not know of systematic studies testing whether infant flicker sensitivity requires greater contrast for low frequencies.

Implications of Temporal Aspects of Vision for Perception
Temporal resolution in the human visual system reaches adult levels earlier in life than spatial resolution and appears to be reasonably good from the beginning of life. Since processing of temporal change underlies perception of motion and events, one possible consequence is that visual perception of motion and events might be comparatively advanced and proficient relative to detection of fine spatial detail.

Motion Detection
Infants detect and attend to motion from birth. Their range of perceptible velocities is smaller than in adults but adequate to process most ordinary events. We defer much of our discussion of visual sensitivity to motion and its underlying mechanisms until we examine motion and event perception in chapter 6.

One major sensory limitation deserves mention here, however. A requirement for extracting useful information about objects and events is *directional sensitivity*. Motion direction is probably encoded by mechanisms in the visual cortex. Research suggests that this sensitivity is weak or absent in the first several weeks of life.

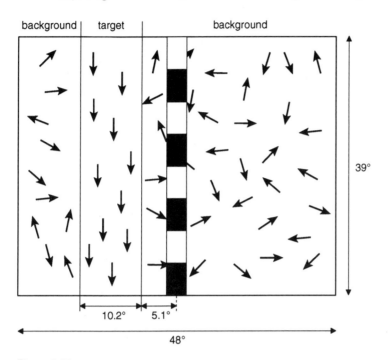

Figure 2.10
Display used to study infants' directional sensitivity. The two display panels differed by the presence of a vertical strip of coherently moving dots in the center of the left-hand panel. All other motions were random in direction. The center column of rectangles was used to attract infants' attention to the center of the display and disappeared during each trial. Reprinted from *Vision Research, 32*, Wattam-Bell, J. (1992), The development of maximum displacement limits for discrimination of motion direction in infancy, pp. 621–630, copyright 1992, with kind permission from Elsevier Science Ltd., The Boulevard, Langford Lane, Kidlington OX5 1GB, UK.

Two methods have been used. In *visual evoked potential* (VEP) studies, directional reversals at a certain frequency were given in arrays of moving random dots (Wattam-Bell, 1991). VEP responses at that frequency were not found until 6 to 8 weeks of age, depending on the whether slower (5 deg/sec) or faster (20 deg/sec) velocities were used. (Responses to the slower velocity emerged earlier.) Similar findings were obtained using behavioral measures, specifically the visual preference procedure. One condition paired a display with a region of dots moving in a consistent direction with another display having random dot motion (see figure 2.10). Whereas 15-week-olds showed robust preferences 8- to 11-week-olds showed only weak evidence of sensitivity, although they did look more at the coherent motion at the slowest velocities tested (Wattam-Bell, 1992).

More recent studies using visual preference and habituation methods with 1-month-old subjects found no evidence that infants discriminate a field containing regions of coherent dots moving in opposite directions from a field containing dots moving in a uniform direction (Wattam-Bell, 1996a, 1996b). One-month-olds do discriminate moving from stationary dot fields at velocities of 10 deg/sec and above, and they showed some ability to distinguish coherent from incoherent motion patterns. Wattam-Bell (1996b) argued that the latter two tasks could in principle be done without directionally sensitive mechanisms, and that the results involving the opposite-direction versus uniform-direction fields is a better test for directional sensitivity. This ability appears to be present by six to eight weeks (Wattam-Bell, 1996b).

These results are consistent with the possibility that directional sensitivity first emerges at six to eight weeks of life (Wattam-Bell, 1992, 1996a, 1996b). Before this time, infants may be sensitive to motion, or temporal change at least, but may not extract information about direction.

The possibility that directional sensitivity is absent at birth seems paradoxical given that even newborns will track, using saccadic eye movements, a moving stimulus. Also, as we described earlier, a moving, repetitive spatial pattern produces OKN (Aslin, 1981; Barten, Birns & Ronch, 1971; Dayton, Jones, Steele & Rose, 1964). Both OKN and early visual tracking may, however, depend on subcortical mechanisms (Atkinson & Braddick, 1981). It is plausible to believe, then, that the young infant possesses directional sensitivity implicitly in largely reflexive tracking mechanisms but that directionally sensitive mechanisms that contribute to perceptual representations (that is, those in the cortex) mature sometime after birth.

Many of infants' most sophisticated early perceptual achievements that we explore later in this book depend on information carried by motion. It is surprising that directional sensitivity seems so poor at the beginning. We consider further its implications for particular perceptual abilities when we explore object and motion perception in chapters 5 and 6.

Oculomotor Function

Aslin (1993) aptly summarized the importance of oculomotor adjustments (accommodation and convergence) in human vision:

> The mature human visual system has evolved the capacity to (1) select a small portion of the retinal image for close attention; (2) optimize the quality of the retinal image by adjusting its posterior focal distance to match the plane of the retinal receptors; and (3) direct

and maintain the two foveas on the object of attention despite changes in object distance. The ability to adjust the optics and binocular alignment of the eyes to match an object's viewing distance affords great efficiency in gathering detailed information about a real-world scene. (p. 30)

Clearly, human vision is a specialized information acquisition system, not a passive receiver of information. It aims, follows, focuses, triangulates, and readjusts continually in response to information received and in support of ongoing action (Gibson, 1966). Perhaps clues to the robustness of early visual function can be found in the status of these oculomotor adjustments.

Accommodation

The earliest study of infant accommodation suggested that newborns' eyes had a fixed focus around 19 cm but that accommodation improved through the first 3 to 4 months to nearly adult levels (Haynes, White & Held, 1965). A limitation of this study was the use of a fixed-size target. Given newborns' relatively poor visual acuity, the decreasing image size at farther distances may have been inadequate to drive an accommodative response (Banks, 1980). Further research equating target visual angle at different distances and using a variety of ingenious methods (for a review, see Aslin, 1993) has revealed that, despite larger errors than adults, even newborns are capable of reasonably accurate accommodation and adjustments in the appropriate direction for targets at within a range of about 75 cm or less (Aslin, Shea & Metz, 1990; Banks, 1980; Braddick, Atkinson, French & Howland, 1979; Brookman, 1980; Hainline, Riddell, Grose-Fifer & Abramov, 1992; Howland, Dobson & Sayles, 1987). Some more recent estimates indicate reasonably accurate responding up to 150 cm (Howland et al., 1987). Investigation of the dynamics of accommodative responses in infants 2 to 10 months old suggest a response rate of at least 4.6 diopters/ sec, similar to adult values.

Convergence

Early studies of convergence found that even in newborns, convergent eye movements in target-appropriate directions were present. The accuracy of convergence was reported to be quite variable but improving within the first few months of life. Newborns studied by Slater and Findlay (1975) showed convergence in the appropriate direction with target distances between 12.5 and 50 cm. Accuracy was good between 25 and 50 cm but not at 12.5 cm. Aslin (1977) investigated 1-, 2-, and 3-month-olds' ability to converge and diverge to a target moving in depth. He found that infants at all ages generally exhibited divergence when the target moved away and convergence when the target approached, but with age, the frequency of making a convergent or divergent movement in the appropriate direction increased. The youngest infants showed least accurate convergence for targets at the nearest viewing distance (12 cm). In a study with targets between 25 and 200 cm (Hainline et al., 1992), infants even at the youngest age tested (26 to 45 days) showed appropriate slopes relating convergence to target position. The authors characterized convergence as essentially adultlike, even in the youngest group.

Implications of Oculomotor Function for Perception
Within the first few months, infants can accurately accommodate and converge their eyes with varying target distances. These functions are somewhat more error-prone than for adults, and variations occur with drowsiness and attentional fluctuations (Banks, 1980; Atkinson, 1984). For convergence, accuracy is initially poor at very near distances (less than 15 cm) but surprisingly adultlike beyond. Basic oculomotor adjustments begin early in infancy to guide and enhance the pickup of visual information. Their role may extend even further. The muscular adjustments that accomplish accommodation and convergence provide distance information for adults and may possibly do so for infants. We consider this possibility when we examine space perception in chapter 3.

Binocular Depth Perception

Sensitivity to binocular disparity seems to be absent in the first several months of life. It emerges at about sixteen weeks on average, with stereoscopic acuity rapidly reaching adultlike levels (Fox, Aslin, Shea & Dumais, 1980; Held, Birch & Gwiazda, 1980; Petrig, Julesz, Kropfl, Baumgartener & Anliker, 1981). We consider the details of the development of binocular depth perception in chapter 3.

Color Vision

Color is one of the most captivating aspects of visual experience. More than any other basic visual attribute, color seems to be involved with emotional and aesthetic responses. Surprisingly, the functional importance of color vision remains unclear. Consider watching a movie in black and white. The perception of people, objects, spatial layouts, and events works well despite the absence of chromatic information. So what does color add? It is likely that adding chromatic variation to a scene (or evolving color vision mechanisms, to take the species' rather than the filmmaker's perspective) improves detection of differences, aiding perception of object boundaries and surface texture. Adjacent surfaces that may not differ in their effects on a single visual mechanism may present differences to a system based on three visual mechanisms of differing sensitivities across the wavelength dimension.

Whereas they may enhance detection of differences, biological color vision systems are not good detectors of specific wavelengths. (Any color experience may be the result of various combinations of wavelengths of light.) Moreover, the light from a surface that reaches the eye depends both on the surface absorptive and reflective characteristics as well as the wavelength composition of the light source. Thus, the spectral composition of light reflected from a particular patch of a surface does not by itself specify any property of the surface or the illuminant. Comparisons across regions in natural scenes may allow detecting a surface's characteristics apart from illumination changes, due to *color constancy* mechanisms. Whether color is most important for enhancing differences in the visual input or for revealing particular surface properties through constancy mechanisms remains an interesting topic of discussion.

Inquiries into infant color sensitivity began over a hundred years ago (see Bornstein, 1978, for a review), yet research before 1975 did not provide much in the way of a definitive statement regarding color vision's origins. The study of infants' color vision is difficult because researchers must distinguish infants' responses to colored stimuli from responses to other aspects of such stimuli, such as lightness.

To understand how researchers have solved such problems requires a little background. Perceived qualities of color are responses to the physical dimension of *wavelength* or frequency of light. Wavelength refers to the distance between successive crests in waves of light. Because light waves move at a constant velocity, this distance between successive wavecrests is inversely related to the frequency of waves passing a given point in a unit of time. Electromagnetic radiation spans a vast spectrum of frequencies, most of which do not give rise to any visual sensations. Specifically, the visual part ranges from wavelengths of about 400 to 700 nanometers. (A nanometer equals one one-billionth of a meter.)

Wavelength and Color Sensations

The relation between wavelengths and color sensations is a bit complex. Single wavelengths of light cause particular color experiences; for example, a wavelength of 485 nm will appear as blue and one of 680 will appear to be a slightly yellowish red. The converse relation is much more complicated and often misunderstood. When we experience a particular color, it does not imply anything about the presence of particular wavelengths of light. Many different combinations of wavelengths can give rise to *metamers*—indistinguishable color sensations. Another way to put this is that as visual perceivers, we are not very good wavelength detectors.

These facts about color vision derive from the underlying mechanisms. *Cones*, the photoreceptors responsible for color vision, come in three types. They differ in terms of their *photopigments*, light-sensitive substances that absorb light. Each photopigment absorbs light across a range of wavelengths, described by its *absorption spectrum*, the probability of absorbing quanta of light at different wavelengths. Neural impulses produced when cones absorb light provide the signals on which color sensations are based. Now comes the subtle idea: a photopigment's selectivity involves the probability of absorbing light quanta of different wavelengths, but the *effect* of absorbing a quantum of light is the same for all wavelengths. Put more simply, when a photoreceptor produces a neural signal, that signal carries no information about what wavelength caused it. Thus, a cone receptor and its neural consequences do not encode wavelength. The color sensations experienced by an observer depend solely on the patterns of activity across the three cone types. The three types of cone receptors—S, M, and L cones—can be distinguished in terms of whether their peak absorption probability falls in the short, middle, or long wavelength part of the visible spectrum. Whereas it can be said that the best stimulus (most probable absorption) for a cone type lies at a particular wavelength, any combinations of light that produce equivalent effects on the three mechanisms will be indistinguishable.

Isolating Color Sensitivity

The study of color vision is complicated by the fact that stimuli vary along several dimensions. Besides chromatic *color or hue*, there is *brightness* (related to light intensity) and *saturation* (roughly, how much the purity of a color is reduced by mixing with broadband light; pink is a desaturated red). Isolating responses based on these separate sensory qualities with infants is difficult. Infants might discriminate two stimuli differing in hue, for example, on the basis of some attribute other than hue, such as a brightness difference. Teller and Bornstein (1987) provide an analogy that illustrates the brightness problem:

> In a black and white photograph of an everyday scene, objects are still clearly visible; a red ball and a white ball are still distinguishable from each other because the white ball looks white and the red ball looks grey. There would exist some exact shade of grey ball which, in the photograph, would be indistinguishable from the red ball, but we could only find the right shade for the grey ball by trial and error, or by knowing the spectral characteristics of the two balls and the photographic film. Similarly, even a totally color blind infant

would see a red and white checkerboard as checkered unless the squares happened to be perfectly matched in brightness *for that infant.* (p. 206)

Matching displays in brightness for a particular adult does not guarantee that the displays will be matched in brightness for infants. Several procedures have been devised to separate infants' responses to hue from responses to brightness. One is to estimate the infant's *spectral sensitivity function*, the relative sensitivity across the wavelength continuum. Then, differently colored lights can be matched for brightness, theoretically leaving only a hue difference as a basis for discriminating between them. Unfortunately, it is hard to be precise about the infant's spectral sensitivity function, and it may vary across individuals as well. Nevertheless, matching chromatic stimuli for approximate brightness is usually a starting point for infant color vision research. From this starting point, brightness of the stimuli can be varied while holding only a hue contrast constant, so that discrimination across the array of stimuli can be based only on hue—that is, there is no consistent brightness difference that could govern responses (Peeples & Teller, 1975; Oster, 1975; Schaller, 1975). In the study by Peeples and Teller (1975), stimulus luminance was varied above and below the matching brightness level. Eight-week-olds discriminated a red from a white stimulus at all luminances. Because small steps of luminance variation were used, we can infer that the red and white stimuli had matching luminance for at least one stimulus pair.

Early Color Sensitivity
What do these kinds of studies indicate about when infants first perceive color? By 2 to 3 months of age, infants' color vision is similar to that of adults' (Maurer & Adams, 1987; Varner, Cook, Schneck, McDonald & Teller, 1985; see Kellman & Banks, 1998, for a review). Results with 8-week-olds suggest that most color vision mechanisms function by this age (Allen, Banks & Norcia, 1993; Clavadetscher, Brown, Ankrum & Teller, 1988; Hamer, Alexander & Teller, 1982; Packer, Hartmann & Teller, 1984), although some deficiency in the short-wavelength cone receptors (S cones) has been suggested (Teller, Peeples & Sekel, 1978). Before 8 weeks, however, infants do not pass many tests of color vision at which 8-week-olds succeed. A great deal of recent work has addressed the nature of the younger infant's limitations in sensing color. Varner et al. found evidence suggesting an S cone deficiency at 4 weeks, whereas Hamer et al. (1982) and Packer et al. (1984) reported deficiencies in tests that would imply M or L cone deficits in adults.

Two explanations for these limitations are currently debated. One is that the problem is a true *chromatic deficiency* (Banks & Bennett, 1988), meaning that immaturity of one or more cone receptor types or post-retinal chromatic mechanisms is responsible. The other possibility, called the *visual efficiency hypothesis* by Allen et al. (1993; see also Banks & Bennett, 1988; Brown, 1990), is that neonates' color-sensing abilities are limited by their overall visual sensitivity. On this hypothesis, color vision machinery is in place in the neonate visual system, but the optics and photoreceptor characteristics do not allow it to be fully activated. Testing these competing hypotheses is difficult. It involves comparing luminance sensitivity with chromatic sensitivity, a task that is hard to complete in the earliest weeks when infants show little or no chromatic sensitivity on certain tasks. If overall visual efficiency limits color perception, the relative sensitivity to luminance and color should remain constant over develop-ment. If a specifically chromatic limitation decreases with development, chromatic sensitivity should improve relative to luminance sensitivity with age. Some recent experiments suggest that the deficiencies found before 8 weeks involving sensitivity to medium and long wavelengths are due to overall visual efficiency rather than a chromatic deficit (Brown, Lindsey, McSweeney & Walters, 1995; Teller & Lindsey, 1993; Teller & Palmer, 1996). On the other hand, deficiencies involving short wave-lengths in infants 4 weeks old and younger may well involve some immaturity in the S cones or postretinal neural mechanisms (Banks & Shannon, 1993).

"My Baby Likes Red"

Researchers of infant perception often hear parents assert that their child prefers red over other colors. If such early color preferences exist, they may provide insight into basic issues about human color sensitivity. Although the physical dimension of wavelength has no abrupt categorical boundaries, our perceived color qualities do. Moving up the wavelength scale from 400 nm, monochromatic (single wavelength) lights all have a bluish, and initially a reddish, component. The reddish aspect disappears by about 478 nm. As wavelength increases further, a greenish component enters making the lights blue-green and then green-blue until 505 nm. At that point the blue is gone, and the hue is uniquely green.

These observations relate to qualitative experiences of color. The studies we have considered so far tested discriminability of colors. Other research has attempted to address the categorical nature of color experience in infancy. Do infants share the color categories of adults, or are these cate-gories fashioned in part by learning or perhaps culture? Bornstein, Kessen, and Weiskopf (1976) tested infant categorization of color using a habitu-ation praradigm. Four-month-old infants were habituated to displays of one wavelength. Following habituation, infants were presented with three test displays. One display had the same wavelength as the habituation display (for example, a blue of 480 nm). The two other test displays varied from the habituation display by the same wavelength difference (for example, 450 nm and 510 nm). In this example, 450 nm is also perceived as bluish by adults, but 510 is perceived as green. Bornstein et al. found that looking time increased to the displays that crossed a categorical boundary more than to displays of a different wavelength that were within the same color category. This result provides some evidence that 4-month-old infants perceive color categorically as adults do.

Do babies prefer some colors over others? An attempt to compare infant and adult color preferences was conducted by Bornstein (1975). He asked adults to rate the pleasantness of wavelength patterns that are typically described as one hue (such as unique blue) or a combination of hues (such as blue-green). Bornstein's subjects generally rated unique hues more pleasant than combination hues. He then presented 4- to 5-month-olds with paired stimuli, where one member of the pair was a unique hue and the other a combined hue. With some exceptions, infants fixated unique hue stimuli longer than combination stimuli (figure 2.11a, b). These results are more suggestive than conclusive, but they are consistent with categorical perception of color stimuli and with some special status of unique hues. Parents may be correct when asserting their baby likes red, but their baby may also like blue as opposed to violet, yellow as opposed to orange, and green as opposed to blue-green.

Color Constancy

Our discussion of color has so far focused on infant responses to chromatic variation. An issue of higher order is that of color constancy, the tendency for an object's perceived color to remain the same across variations in illumination. As we noted earlier, the spectral composition of light at the retina is determined jointly by the wavelength composition of the illuminant and by reflective characteristics of a surface. The experience of an object appearing the same color when viewed outdoors in sunlight and then viewed indoors under incandescent light may seem mundane. From the perspective of perceptual science, it represents quite a puzzle (Brainard, Wandell & Chichilnisky, 1993). The problem is that the wavelength composition of sunlight and incandescent light are very different; as a result, the wavelengths entering the eye from a given surface change greatly depending on the illuminant.

Dannemiller and his colleagues (Dannemiller & Hanko, 1987; Dannemiller, 1989) have carried out the only studies of infant color constancy that we know of. Using CRT displays, they simulated changes in both the reflectance properties of surfaces and the spectral composition of the illuminant. Twenty-week-old infants who were habituated to objects viewed under one illuminant generalized habituation to the same objects with a

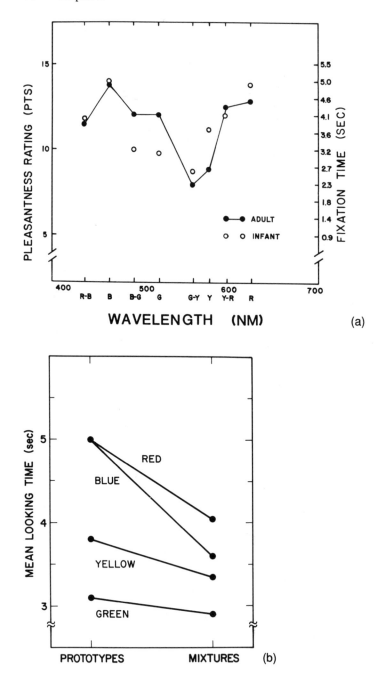

WAVELENGTH (NM)   (a)

(b)

changed illuminant. In contrast, 9-week-olds did not show this behavior; they dishabituated to the change in illuminant, suggesting a failure of color constancy at this earlier age. The reasons for these developmental changes in color constancy remain to be investigated.

Implications of Color Vision for Perception

The visual world of the infant by 2 months of age appears in color. From that age on, infants resemble adults in making chromatic discriminations. Moreover, young infants and adults appear to share color preferences for central colors and perceive the visual spectrum categorically. Using color to identify an object despite variations in illumination is an ability that appears somewhat later, around 5 months. Presumably, the encoding of color serves early perceivers in the ways that have been hypothesized for adults—aiding in segmenting the world into objects and highlighting textural features of surfaces, allowing them to be recognized or discriminated. Perhaps infants' early sensitivity to color also allows them the rich aesthetic and emotional responses to color that, although somewhat mysterious, contribute uniquely to human visual experience.

THE AUDITORY SYSTEM

Newborns can hear. Even before birth, by about the seventh prenatal month, development of peripheral mechanisms for hearing is nearly complete (Bredberg, 1968). As we consider in chapter 7, researchers have known for several decades that newborns often look in the direction of a sound (Wertheimer, 1961). But how well do infants hear? How do the limits of the infant's auditory world compare to the adults? In this section, we take up these questions.

Absolute Thresholds

The human infant's sensitivity to sound falls far short of adult levels. Absolute thresholds—the minimum physical energy detectable—are as much as 50 to 60 decibels (dB) higher than adult norms (Eisele, Berry & Shriner, 1975). Because the decibel scale is logarithmic (that is, its units are equal ratio steps), this represents a huge difference in the sound pressure

◄ **Figure 2.11**
(a) Relation between infants' fixation times and adults' pleasantness ratings for different hues. Wavelength is given on the x axis in nanometers, with letters indicating the appearance of single wavelength stimuli (R = red; B = blue; G = green; Y = yellow.) Open circles plot infant fixation times; closed circles plot adult pleasantness ratings. (b) Infants' fixation to prototype (unique) versus mixture (combined) hues. Reprinted with permission from Bornstein, M. (1975), Qualities of color vision in infancy, *Journal of Experimental Child Psychology, 19*, 401–419.

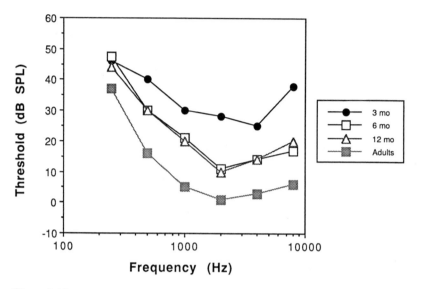

Figure 2.12
Average absolute thresholds for pure-tone stimuli for adults and 3-, 6-, and 12-month-old infants. Redrawn with permission from Werner, L. A., & Bargones, J. Y. (1992), Psychoacoustic development of human infants, in C. Rovee-Collier & L. Lipsitt (Eds.), *Advances in Infancy Research* (Vol. 7) (Norwood, NJ: Ablex).

level needed to trigger a sensory response. A 60 dB difference corresponds to a thousandfold change in sound pressure. This difference means that an adult can detect a whisper, but a newborn can just detect an average speaking voice.

Sensitivity varies by frequency. Figure 2.12 shows audibility curves across frequency for infants of 3, 6, and 12 months and adults from Werner and Bargones (1992). The curves, indicating relative sensitivity across frequency to pure tones (single frequencies), are similar in shape. These results were obtained using the *observer-based psychoacoustic procedure* (OPP), a variant of the forced-choice preferential looking procedure used in vision research (Olsho, Koch, Halpin & Carter, 1987). In the OPP, an observer may use any aspect of the infant's behavior to determine whether an infant is being presented with a sound. Following a judgment, the observer receives feedback regarding his or her accuracy.

About half of the difference between infant and adult auditory sensitivity is made up in the first 6 months, with improvement continuing into middle childhood (Elliott & Katz, 1980). Some insight into the mechanisms underlying these behavioral findings comes from studies measuring absolute thresholds using the *auditory brainstem response* (ABR). The ABR consists of low-amplitude electrical potentials generated by the activation of the auditory nerve and structures in the auditory brainstem, a subcortical part of the auditory pathway. These potentials occur within 10 msec following the onset of an auditory stimulus (Moore, 1982). The measure requires no overt behavioral response. Using ABR, Kaga and Tanaka (1980) found click-evoked thresholds in newborns within 15 to 20 dB of adult thresholds. The pattern of responses and the rate at which the growing child reached adult threshold levels was different from those found with behavioral measures. At low frequencies (500 Hz), adult response levels were reached by 1 month of age. This finding suggests that the rather slow progression of low-frequency sensitivity toward adult levels found in behavioral studies reflects changes occurring beyond the brainstem in the auditory system, probably cortical processing. Medium-to high-frequency sensitivity (4,000 Hz) reached adult levels between 3 to 7 months in the ABR studies. Most interesting, very high-frequency stimuli (8,000 to 12,000 Hz) produced thresholds at adult levels before 3 months, and thresholds at 16,000 Hz were on average 10 dB *better* than adults at both 1 and 3 months of age (Klein, 1984; see Werner and Bargones, 1992, for a review).

Superior infant ABR responses to very high frequencies may be related to hearing loss for high frequencies that occurs from childhood to adulthood. Whereas the child may hear sounds up to 20,000 Hz, adult limits are lower, cutting off at about 15,000 Hz (Moore, 1982). It is nevertheless unclear what to make of the discrepancies between behavioral and electrophysiological measures. In particular, analogous to electrophysiological measurements of the visual system, it is not clear that ABR responses indicate that the infant hears a stimulus.

Werner and Bargones (1992) sought to directly compare thresholds using ABR and OPP measurements. Subjects were presented with 1,000, 4,000, and 8,000 Hz tone pips lasting 5 msec. Infant and adult ABR thresholds were about the same at each frequency (see figure 2.13). Behaviorally, adult thresholds were on average 15 to 20 dB *lower* than their ABR thresholds, but infant behavioral thresholds were 15 to 30 dB *higher* than their ABR thresholds. Werner et al. suggest that this discrepancy may be due to the maturation of neural structures in the primary auditory pathway beyond the brainstem (auditory cortex) or to nonsensory factors (such as attention or motivation). Further work by Bargones and Werner (1994) provided some evidence in favor of the attentional hypothesis: adults may be much better than infants at selectively attending to a single frequency. This finding dictates caution in making the claim that infants hear less well than adults, but the magnitude of the sensitivity difference and its persistence in part until later in childhood suggest that development leads to improvements in both attention and auditory sensitivity.

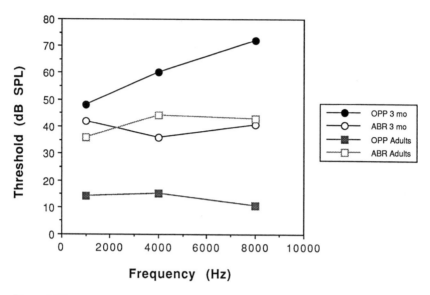

Figure 2.13
A comparison of auditory intensity (absolute) thresholds for adults and 3-month-old infants obtained by using a physiological measure, the auditory brainstem response (ABR), and a behavioral measure, the observer-based psychoacoustic procedure (OPP). Redrawn with permission from Werner, L. A., & Bargones, J. Y. (1992), Psychoacoustic development of human infants, in C. Rovee-Collier & L. Lipsitt (Eds.), *Advances in infancy Research* (Vol. 7) (Norwood, NJ: Ablex).

Differential Sensitivity and Frequency Resolution

Sounds of a single frequency are rarely presented in contexts outside of auditory threshold experiments. Instead, sounds follow one another, consist of multiple frequencies, and differ in intensity or loudness. Adults discriminate intensity changes between sounds as small as 1 to 2 dB (Sinnott & Aslin, 1985), whereas infant sensitivity is weaker, ranging between 3 to 12 dB at 7 to 9 months. Adults also detect smaller frequency differences than infants but not by much. With frequency signals between 1,000 and 3,000 Hz, Olsho and her colleagues (Olsho, Schoon, Sakai, Turpin & Sperduto, 1982a, 1982b) found that 5- to 8-month-olds discriminated approximately a 2% change; adults discriminated a 1% change. Infants discriminated higher-frequency tones (4,000 to 8,000 Hz) as well as adults.

Most environmental sounds contain combinations of frequencies. Frequency resolution is the observer's ability to perceive the individual components in a complex sound. An excellent paradigm for studying frequency resolution is *masking*; a threshold for one stimulus is obtained in the presence of a competing stimulus or masker. Studies using masking suggest that infants' frequency resolution thresholds are 10 to 15 dB higher than adults, but they are qualitatively similar. When the background noise level increases by 10 dB, both infant and adult thresholds increase about 10 dB (Bull, Schneider & Trehub, 1981).

Early audition researchers noticed that we perceive the parts of a complex sound more easily if the components have dissimilar frequencies (see Moore, 1982). This phenomenon has been conceptualized in terms of the *critical band* notion. A certain range of frequencies close to a target frequency will exert a masking effect, making detection of the target frequency more difficult. Frequencies outside of this critical band will exert a much reduced or negligible masking effect. Schneider, Morrongiello, and Trehub (1990) determined the critical band for 6-month-olds, 2-year-olds, 5-year-olds, and adults. They found that masked thresholds for all ages increased with bandwidth up to a critical width. Further increases in bandwidth did not result in increases in threshold. They also found that the size of the critical band did not change substantially with age. Thus, infants as young as 6 months have a critical band that is similar to adults, and changes in auditory filter width cannot explain differences found between adult and infant auditory thresholds.

Temporal Resolution

As we listen to music or speech, we process exquisitely subtle and complex information about duration and rhythm in auditory signals. Prerequisite to extracting such information is the capacity to assign boundaries in time to particular sounds and intervals between them. Such temporal resolution abilities are heavily involved in speech perception, auditory localization, rhythm perception, and the detection of signals in noise.

Not many studies have addressed the development of temporal resolution. One study was carried out by Morrongiello and Trehub (1987), who compared 6-month-old infants' temporal resolution to that of $5\frac{1}{2}$-year-old children and adults. Subjects were tested using an operant head-turn procedure. In this procedure infants are trained to turn their heads to one side when they hear a particular stimulus configuration (in this case a change in temporal sequencing). If infants make the correct turn, they are visually reinforced with an exciting toy, like a battery-operated, stuffed monkey banging on a drum. Morongiello and Trehub presented subjects with a sequence of 18 white-noise bursts and trained them to detect a change in duration of the middle 6 bursts or silence intervals between bursts. They found that adults discriminated changes as small as 10 msec, $5\frac{1}{2}$-year-olds discriminated changes of 15 msec, and infants discriminated changes of 20 msec. Performance was not affected by whether duration of the noise (burst) or the silence was varied. Thus, infants' temporal resolution is not as precise as adults, but it is not too bad either. When perceiving speech, many consonants are differentiated based on *voice-onset time* (VOT), the timing of laryngeal voicing and air release. The perception of /ba/ and /pa/ differ by a VOT of 25 msec. Infants' temporal resolution abilities are precise enough to distinguish these two phonemes. It is possible that early temporal resolution limits information processing of speech to some degree. Perhaps this limitation is one reason adults speaking to children use a different type of speech than when speaking to other adults. This speech, discussed in chapter 8, is slower, more exaggerated, and has longer pauses between linguistic elements. Modification of speech directed to infants may be one way adults, unknowingly, compensate for infants' less precise temporal resolution abilities.

Implications of the Auditory System for Perception

The infant's auditory capabilities begin before birth but do not reach adult levels for some months afterward. Absolute sensitivity, analogous to visual acuity, is quite a bit worse than the adult's, but the ability to discriminate among frequencies is good. Temporal resolution abilities also lag those of older children and adults. It is not clear whether these immaturities limit the young infant's ability to acquire information or guide behavior. Adults' absolute sensitivity may be greater than needed for the learning tasks faced by the infant. For an adult, detecting the sounds of events out of sight, far away, or of very low intensity may have adaptive value, but these may be irrelevant or worse for a young baby. Remote sounds that cannot be matched to visible events may actually be a distraction or impediment to some early learning. Evaluating such a conjecture would require a more detailed analysis of the developmental tasks of early infancy as well as an ecological survey of sound sources in the infant's environment. What we can say with greater confidence is that the infant comes into the world already an able auditory perceiver but becomes an even better one later.

THE SOMATOSENSORY SYSTEM

A variety of senses whose receptors lie in the skin comprise the somatosensory system. This system makes possible sensitivity to touch, pain, temperature, and more. Judging from infants' responses to hot liquids, a pin prick, or a soft stroke on the cheek, one might suspect that newborns' somatosensory system is well developed, and indeed it is.

The somatosensory system begins to develop during the sixth prenatal week with the appearance of synapses between sensory fibers and receptive neurons in the spinal cord (Okado, 1981). Development of the system approaches completion between the twentieth and twenty-fourth weeks of gestation (Kostovic & Goldman-Rakic, 1983), although full myelination is not completed until much later in childhood (Lauffer & Wenzel, 1986).

Touch

The relative maturity at birth of this system is easily seen in behavior. Infants typically respond to noninvasive touch with increased movement and increased heart rate. Touch contributes to the regulation of infant state and can play a role in eliciting and maintaining attention (Kisilevsky, Stack & Muir, 1991). Infants are also sensitive to the location of touch. Alert neonates will turn their heads reliably toward a tactile stimulus applied to the mouth on 93% of trials, toward an air puff on the cheek on 75% of trials, and toward a stroke on the forearm on 65% of trials (Kisilevsky et al., 1991). Moreover, infants show an integrated constellation of behaviors to a tactile stimulus. When stroked on the forearm, infants first move the stroked limb, then the head, and then the eyes to the side of stimulation (Dodwell, 1983). Perhaps even more striking is one of the oldest reports about infant responses to tactile stimulation. Watson (1919) demonstrated that when a noxious chemical stimulus was applied to the leg of a newborn infant, the infant was able to move the other leg to rub off the chemical (Watson, 1919). This finding is impressive not only in showing responsivity, but in suggesting some intermodal tactual-motor coordination of spatial information.

Besides indicating the locus of tactile stimulation on the body, the somatosensory system provides information about objects in the world. As we show in chapters 7 and 9, infants can determine properties of objects, such as surface characteristics and substance, from oral contact within the first month of life and from active manual manipulation later in the first year when more sophisticated motor skills emerge (for example, Streri, 1993).

Pain

Another important aspect of somatosensory sensitivity is pain. Do infants, as do adults, experience radically different sensory and emotional qualities from a stroke on the arm and a pin prick? The question of whether young babies experience pain has been of considerable interest from both theoretical and practical perspectives. Some medical procedures have been performed on infants without anesthesia based on the belief that infants are incapable of feeling pain. Given that infants' somatosensory system is well developed neurologically and that infants display clear emotional behavior to pain stimuli, it might be more reasonable to use anesthesia; indeed, this has become common practice.

Making a scientific case that an infant feels pain is nevertheless difficult. The difficulty points to one of the deepest issues in studying sensation and perception. The qualities of our sensations or the contents of our knowledge are known to each individual internally. In scientific research we never measure these directly. We can measure only behavior of some kind. We interpret the subject's behavior as indicating the presence of a particular sensation or percept when it gives us a simpler explanation of the observed behavior than we would have otherwise (Hochberg, 1968). The problem is worse in studying infants because they have a limited range of behaviors and in particular cannot give verbal reports. (Interestingly, the Latin root of the word infant—*infans*—means "one unable to speak.") Thus, we have less to go on in making the inference of sensory awareness or perceptual knowledge. As we have already begun to see, for many perceptual and sensory variables, experimenters can arrange circumstances that reveal perceptual knowledge. If an infant reliably looks more at one of two stimuli differing only on one dimension, the experimenter can infer that the infant is sensitive to the difference along that dimension. Pain presents one of the hardest cases for this kind of inference because a pain stimulus is normally accompanied by some other sensory event (that is, touch). A response indicating detection of the stimulus may not necessarily reveal that pain as opposed to mere touch was registered. Some of these complications exist in pain research with adults as well (Stevens & Johnston, 1993).

Regardless of the difficulty in interpreting pain research, investigators have attempted to identify behavioral and physiological responses to invasive stimuli (Anand & McGrath, 1993). Most newborns experience a number of procedures shortly after birth, some of which are invasive (for example, an injection of vitamin K into the abdomen, heel stick for blood sampling, circumcision), and these provide opportunities to study pain perception in very young infants. As compared to noninvasive procedures, such as the application of a disinfectant to the umbilical stem, full-term infants react to invasive stimuli with a common facial expression similiar to a pain expression seen in adults. This expression occurs within three seconds after the invasive action and consists of lowered brows, tightly shut eyes, nasolabial furrow, open lips, and a cupped, taut tongue (Grunau, Johnston & Craig, 1990). Accompanying this grimace is a rapid-onset, high-pitched cry. Preterm infants also show similiar responses to invasive procedures, depending on gestational age. Intensity of the characteristic facial "pain expression" increases with gestational age; infants between 25 and 27 weeks gestation do not show different facial expressions between invasive and noninvasive procedures (Craig, Whitfield, Grunau, Linton & Hadjistavropoulos, 1993). All of these observations are consistent with the idea that young infants, sometime after 27 weeks gestation, experience pain.

Implications of the Somatosensory System for Perception

The somatosensory system is functional at birth even though the system may not reach maturity until 3 to 8 years of age. Young infants can locate the source of touch and obtain information about objects from oral and manual exploration. Sensitivity to pain is found in newborns and even preterm infants.

GUSTATION AND OLFACTION

Gustation (taste) and olfaction (smell) function almost inseparably. As a case in point, the distinctive flavors of an apple or an onion come from a combination of taste and smell information. Most people know, however, that strictly speaking taste is defined as the activity of certain chemoreceptors ("taste buds") located on the tongue, sensitive to only four basic sensations: sweet, sour, salty, and bitter. Even so, it comes as a surprise to most that, tested with eyes shut and nose pinched closed, a person given a piece of raw onion will judge it to be a piece of an apple!

Four Taste Sensations

Research on the development of taste has centered around the four taste sensations. The adult form of the taste bud is present in the fetus at 13 weeks gestation. To study taste perception, researchers typically monitor infants' facial expressions following the placement of a substance in the infant's mouth or monitor the amount of intake of substances with different tastes. Obviously, inferring particular sensations from facial reactions or other responses is subject to the same difficulties we discussed in relation to pain. Some understanding of infant taste can be gleaned, however, from differences in response to different stimuli. Studies with newborns suggest that at birth infants can discriminate at least three of the four basic taste sensations—sweet, sour, and bitter (see Crook, 1987, for a review). Infants' sensing of saltiness develops within the first few months of life. When a large amount of salt is placed in the mouth, newborns show no particular facial expression (Rosenstein & Oster, 1988), and they show no difference in ingesting a salty solution and plain water (Beauchamp, Cowart & Moran, 1986; Beauchamp, Cowart, Mennella & Marsh, 1994). By 4 months, infants prefer salty concentrations over water. A similar change is found for bitter tastes. Newborn infants do not reject solutions laced with urea (although they do show a negative facial expression), whereas infants between 14 and 180 days do (Kajiura, Cowart & Beauchamp, 1992).

Olfactory Sensations

In contrast to taste, there are no "primary" olfactory sensations. Typically, to study smell, a cotton swab saturated with an olfactory stimulus is placed under an infant's nose, and a response, such as respiration changes, heart rate, leg withdrawal, or general activity, is measured. Studies of this sort indicate that newborns have a functional sense of smell. They show changes in respiration to anise acid (liquorice), asafoetida (garlic), acetic acid (vinegar), and phenylethyl alcohol (Engen & Lipsitt, 1965). Also, olfaction thresholds decline across the first few days of life, most pronouncedly so between the first and second day (Lipsitt, Engen & Kaye, 1963).

The discrimination and location of odors has been tested in the context of infants' ability to recognize their mother's breast pads. Macfarlane (1975) found that infants at 5 days of age will turn their head toward a used breast pad from their mother when it is paired with a clean one. By 6 days of age, infants show evidence of discriminating their mother's smell from that of another woman by preferentially turning toward their mother's used pad. Formula-fed infants also show the ability to discriminate their mother's odor from that of a neutral odor (Porter, Makin, Davis & Christensen, 1991).

Implications of Gustation and Olfaction for Perception

Infants' sense of taste and smell are fairly functional at birth. These senses work together to provide the infants with information about what substances they may or may not want to ingest. Moreover, smell may help infants recognize familiar objects and people in their environment.

MOTOR DEVELOPMENT

A main theme of this book is that much perceptual knowledge precedes action in early infant development. Compared to the development of perceptual systems, development of motor skills is slow. This observation reverses the traditional formula that perceptual knowledge originates from sensorimotor activity. Of course, perception and action do have important interactions as we show in chapter 9, but initial perceptual competence appears well before the infant can crawl or walk, reach or grasp in a coordinated fashion. For example, many of the young infants' visual capabilities are close to adult levels by 6 months of age, whereas self-locomotion may be just beginning at this time.

Because we discuss perception-action relationships in detail later, we restrict ourselves to a few topics here—a discussion of eye movements and a some general observations on the development of body movements.

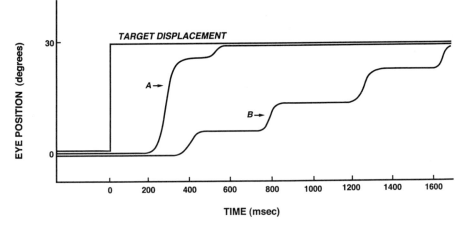

Figure 2.14
The time course of a saccadic eye movement to a target by (a) an adult and (b) a 2-month-old infant. Reprinted with permission from Aslin, R. N. (1987), Motor aspects of visual development in infancy, in P. Salapatek & L. Cohen (Eds.), *Handbook of infant perception: From sensation to perception* (Vol. 1) (Orlando, FL: Academic Press).

Eye Movements

Among the earliest coordinated motor movements are eye movements. We can distinguish in adults two types—saccadic and smooth-pursuit eye movements. *Saccadic eye movements* occur when a target is detected in the periphery and a large eye movement is executed to place the target on the fovea. Aslin and Salapatek (1975) describe adult saccades to a peripheral target as having high velocity and brief latencies and as being ballistic in nature (see figure 2.14a). *Smooth-pursuit eye movements*, in adults, are continuous or "smooth" tracking movements whose rate varies with the velocity of the target. Smooth pursuit allows the viewer to maintain the projection of a moving target on the fovea.

Although saccadic eye movements are present at birth, they do not take the form of adult saccades (Aslin & Salapatek, 1975). Whereas adults' initial saccades are matched to target distance, infants' initial saccades may cover only a fraction of the distance to the target, and subsequent saccades tend to be matched to the initial saccade in amplitude (see figure 2.14b). Bronson (1990) found that the average accuracy of infants' saccades remains unchanged between $3\frac{1}{2}$ and 8 weeks of age but improves by 11 to 14 weeks.

In contrast to saccadic eye movements, smooth-pursuit movements are hard to detect until about 2 months of age (Aslin, 1981). Infants younger than 2 months can track a moving object, especially if it is moving slowly, but they ordinarily make a series of saccades to follow the target. Some evidence (Roucoux, Culee & Roucoux, 1983; Shea & Aslin, 1990) suggests that smooth-pursuit movements can occur in infants younger than 2 months, but these have low gain (that is, they lag behind the target).

Body Movements

The earliest human motor development seems to reflect two general principles. First, development proceeds in a cephalocaudal direction—that is, it progresses from head to foot. Motor skills involving the head, neck, and arms appear before those involving the lower torso and legs. Motor development also progresses in a proximodistal direction—that is, development advances from the center of the body outward. Coordinated movement of the trunk and shoulders appears before coordination of the arms and hands.

Initially, many infant movements are actions guided by reflexes rather than under voluntary control. At birth, head control is limited to moving from side to side while infants are lying on their back. By 4 months, almost all infants can keep their head erect while being held or supported in a sitting position. Coordinated arm movements begin to emerge around 4 months of age, and manipulation skills become increasingly specified to object properties up to 12 months of age. (See chapter 9.)

The first form of self-produced locomotion is rolling. By 5 months, 90% of infants are able to roll over, and many are already on their way to some type of crawling (such as sliding around on the belly, scooting in a sitting position, or bear-walking in which only their hands and feet touch the ground). The average age for standing and the beginning of walking is $11\frac{1}{2}$ months of age, and 90% of babies are walking well by $14\frac{1}{2}$ months of age (Bayley, 1969).

Implications of Motor Development for Perception

In comparison with sensory development, motor development is delayed. This delay is extremely important for understanding the relations of perception and action, as we will see. It casts doubt on theoretical views asserting that perception first arises through action (such as Piaget's 1952, 1954, ideas of the sensorimotor construction of reality or Berkeley's "touch educates vision"). It suggests instead that the development of activity is preceded and guided by perceptual knowledge. But the effects inevitably flow in both directions. As motor skill develops, infants can more readily obtain information through their own actions. When one can reach, crawl, and walk, the world becomes more accessible and increasingly rich in opportunities for exploration.

The later development of infants' motor abilities has also profoundly influenced views of early perception. Because infants do not *do* much, they have been thought not to *know* much. Advances in the study of infant perception have depended crucially on investigators devising methods to exploit the few response capabilities of young infants. In turn, these methods have allowed us to discover that hidden within the relatively immobile infant is a surprising repertoire of perceptual competence.

Notes

1. This chapter is a bit encyclopedic and includes a number of topics not strictly necessary for understanding the material in later chapters. The reader interested in particular topics in infant perception might read this chapter selectively. The sections on basic visual capacities (pages 11–34) contain important general background and also serve to introduce research methods. The section on auditory sensitivity might be useful background for chapters 7 and 8. Other sections may be skipped without loss of continuity.

2. Another method based on visual attention—the habituation and recovery method—is perhaps the most widely used in infant perception research today. We introduce this method in the section on orientation sensitivity beginning on page 48.)

Chapter 3
Space Perception

No ability is more fundamental to human perceptual and cognitive development than spatial perception. If objects and events did not come coherently organized in a three-dimensional framework, the world would appear chaotic and mysterious. If two dimensions, up-down and left-right, were given but there were no depth, the idea that physical objects routinely come into and leave existence would be inescapable. Lack of a coherent spatial order was surely on the mind of William James when he characterized the world of the newborn as a "blooming, buzzing confusion" (James, 1890).

As we saw in chapter 1, the question of how space perception originates occupies a central place in perceptual theory. Logical arguments about the need for learning in perception were developed around issues involving space, particularly the "third" or depth dimension (Berkeley, 1709/1910; Helmholtz, 1885/1925; Piaget, 1954). Likewise, the ecological view's revised analyses of the information for perception centered on kinematic (and stereoscopic) information about space (Gibson, 1966; Johansson, 1970). The possibility that perceptual systems might have evolved to utilize such information is illustrated by visually guided, spatially oriented behavior in the newborns of some nonhuman species (Walk & Gibson, 1961; Hess, 1956). Yet neither the theoretical claims about the information available for perception nor studies of other species can tell us how human spatial competence emerges. The issues require experimental research with human infants.

Over the last two decades, researchers have taken up this challenge, and in this chapter we consider what they have discovered about the origins of human spatial perception. We focus on perception of the three-dimensional locations and relationships of objects and surfaces. A number of other spatial topics involving object properties, such as configuration and orientation, are treated in later chapters on pattern and object perception. Vision is primary, but other senses also contribute to spatial perception. We treat vision here; some aspects of auditory and haptic space perception are treated in chapter 8 on intermodal perception.

ECOLOGY OF SPATIAL PERCEPTION

The Task of Spatial Perception

What spatial aspects of the environment are important to human functioning? For upright, mobile organisms, maintaining posture and guiding locomotion are high priorities. Effective locomotion requires detecting the arrangement of obstacles and spaces between them and becomes even more critical at higher speeds, as when running. Besides locomotion, other actions require spatial information, from the simplest reaching and grasping, to the expert activities of a surgeon or a pilot landing a jet airplane on a heaving aircraft carrier at night. Both ordinary and extraordinary activities depend on accurate perception of distance and size, and many involve coordinating space, time, and motion. Beyond immediate action, spatial perception serves to establish representations of the environment that guide action in the future and form the bases of thought.

Important for understanding early spatial perception in *homo sapiens* is that human infants do few of these things. On average, a human infant does not crawl until 6 to 7 months, does not walk until about one year, and does not even reach effectively until 4 to 5 months. On attaining these milestones, the infant still remains relatively incompetent in finding its own nutrition or escaping danger. As we will see, however, spatial perception begins much earlier. What is its function before complex action systems emerge? Spatial perception, and early perceptual ability in general, may serve to advance cognitive and motor development. Despite the lack of motor skill, the infant can learn a great deal about the physical and social environments and can guide the attunement of emerging action skills through accurate perception.

Another function of early spatial perception might be to guide perceptual learning. As we described in chapter 1, two varieties of perceptual learning might occur—*differentiation learning*, more precise extraction of information with experience, and *enrichment*, the learning of new stimulus variables that come to specify spatial properties by correlation with already usable information. Some evidence in adult perception is consistent with the idea that new depth cues can be acquired by the latter kind of learning (Wallach & O'Leary, 1982). As we consider early spatial abilities, we discuss some sources of spatial information that may involve this kind of learning as well as those that depend on inborn mechanisms or neural maturation.

Information and Constraints in Spatial Perception

Space has three dimensions. To the physicist, space is normally isotropic, meaning its properties are the same in all directions. Visually, however, the three dimensions of space are not created equal. The optics of the eye map inputs from different radial directions onto different retinal locations. The ordering of targets in the environment from above to below the observer is preserved (although reversed) in the retinal projection, as is the ordering from left to right. Not given is the third dimension—the distance to an object reflecting light to the eye. Much of what needs to be explained in space perception involves distance. Not only is perception of distance important in its own right, but it is connected to many other perceptual properties, such as size.

Sources of information about depth and distance are remarkably numerous. Albert Yonas, a leading investigator of the development of depth perception, has remarked that "God must have loved depth cues because she made so many of them." Some order can be imposed by noticing that most depth cues in biological vision systems involve one of three different solutions to the problem of distance. We call them *parallax information, information based on assumed physical equality,* and *oculomotor information.* We also mention two other depth information sources that do not fit neatly into this categorization—*interposition* and *familiar size.*

Parallax Information
Parallax refers to differences in the optical projections of an object imaged from different positions. This information is the basis of triangulation: by measuring the direction of the moon from two widely separated locations a known distance apart, its distance from earth may be estimated. The same type of information is exploited in more than one way in human vision. *Binocular disparity* refers to differences in the projections to the two eyes from features in the environment (see figure 3.1). When we look at a point, that point is imaged in the center (the fovea) of each eye. Other points at about the same distance from the observer will project to corresponding retinal locations. Points at different distances will project to disparate locations in the two eyes, and the magnitude of disparity increases with distance from the fixated point. Disparity from points nearer than the fixation point can be distinguished from that due to points farther than it by the direction of disparity. *Crossed disparity* characterizes nearer points. The projection from a point closer than the fixation point will be more to the left in the visual field of the right eye and more to the right in the visual field of the left eye. You can easily demonstrate crossed disparity (figure 3.1b) to yourself. Hold up the index fingers of the two hands in a line extending in front of your nose, one at a distance from your nose of about 8 inches and the other at arm's length. Focus on the farther finger. You will notice that the nearer finger (keep fixating the farther finger!) appears as a double image. Now, close your left eye. You will notice that the right image in the double image of the near finger has

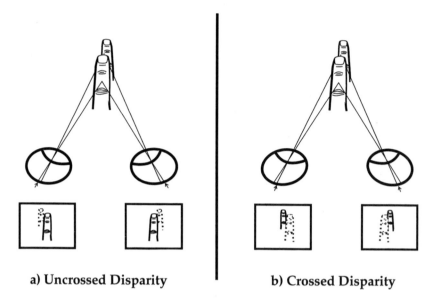

a) Uncrossed Disparity   b) Crossed Disparity

Figure 3.1
Illustration of binocular disparity. Uncrossed (a) and crossed (b) binocular disparity. The upper illustration depicts the physical viewing situation; arrows indicate the foveas of each eye. The rectangles in the lower diagram show the image given to each eye. The solid figure is seen as fused; dotted figures are visible as double images. (See text.)

vanished, meaning the right eye sees the left image (and the left eye saw the right image, before you closed it). This is what is meant by crossed disparity. *Uncrossed disparity* (figure 3.1a) refers to cases where the more leftward visual position is in the left eye, and the more rightward is in the right; such disparity comes from points farther away than the point of fixation. Again, hold up your two fingers, but this time focus on the nearer finger. You will notice the farther finger appears as a double image. This time, when you close your left eye, the left image vanishes. Because the left eye sees the left image and the right eye sees the right image, we have uncrossed disparity. The visible double images in this exercise help to make the point but are not necessary for the registration of disparity. For disparities below a certain amount, the visual world appears fused— that is, objects appear single. (Interestingly, both fused and visibly double images provide depth information.)

The relation between angular disparity and depth intervals in the world is not fixed. A given depth difference in the environment gives decreasing binocular disparity as a viewer moves farther away (disparity is inversely proportional to the square of distance). However, in combination with absolute distance information to some reference point in the environment, binocular disparity can provide highly accurate absolute depth intervals (Wallach & Zuckerman, 1963).

The same geometry underlies *kinematic information* about depth, except that parallax comes not from simultaneous use of two eyes in separate positions but from the changing position of the observer over *time*. A moving observer sees a constantly changing sample of the optic array. These transforming optical projections carry structural information about the spatial layout of the environment (Gibson, 1966, 1979; Johansson, 1970, 1975).

Kinematic information is multifaceted. Gibson (1966) proposed the term *optic flow* to describe the transforming optic array given to a moving observer. Certain properties of the global flow field indicate the observer's motion through space, guide locomotion, and control posture (Johansson, von Hofsten & Jansson, 1980; Warren & Wertheim, 1990; Crowell & Banks, 1993). For the most part these topics are discussed in chapter 9, dedicated to perception and action. Several more local sources of spatial layout information from motion are taken up in this chapter. Figure 3.2 illustrates four of these. *Optical expansion and contraction* can indicate relative motion between a target and the observer. For example, the projection of a moving object headed directly for the observer symmetrically expands over time, and, as we mentioned in chapter 1, such a situation provides optical information about the time to contact between the target and the observer. There is evidence that adult humans are sensitive to this information and that it, or related information, guides locomotive behavior in a variety of species (Lee, 1974). *Motion parallax* or *motion perspective* refers to differential optical change for points at different distances during observer motion. It can indicate relative and possibly absolute distance from the observer under some conditions. *Accretion and deletion of texture* refers to the gradual revealing or concealing of background texture when an object moves in front of a farther surface (or when an observer moves and views stationary surfaces at different depths). This form of information gives information about depth order (what is closer and what is farther away). Finally, the continuously changing optical projection of an object, given by object or observer motion, carries information about its three-dimensional form, allowing perception of *structure from motion*. This topic is treated when we consider object perception in chapter 5.

Parallax information, underlying both binocular and kinematic space perception, is preeminent in human spatial perception. A primary reason is its high *ecological validity*. The mapping between parallax information and three-dimensional arrangements is ordinarily unambiguous, at least in terms of depth order. Depth cues that can be presented in a flat picture (*pictorial cues*) are much more ambiguous (witness the fact that they can depict three-dimensional objects when only a two-dimensional surface—

(a)   (b)

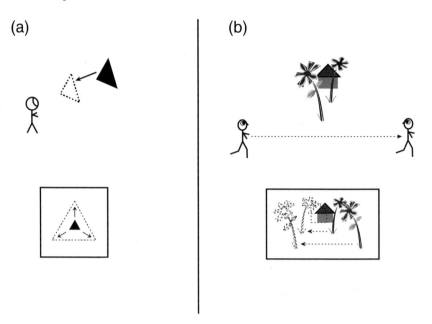

Figure 3.2
Depictions of four types of kinematic information about spatial relations. Top illustrations show the physical situation being viewed; bottom illustrations show the optical information available at the eye. a. *Optical expansion:* As an object approaches the observer, its projection at the eye expandes symmetrically. b. *Motion perspective:* As the observer moves, the relative positions of viewed objects change in the projection to the eye, with nearer objects displacing more than farther ones.

the picture—is present). To present parallax relationships without their normal causes in the three-dimensional layout, one must go to great lengths. A stereoscope may be used to present different images to the two eyes, or a virtual reality setup can give observer-contingent changes to simulate kinematic information. As a rough index of the relative ecological validity of these information sources, we may note the time sequence of human successes in simulating them. Realistic depiction of depth in paintings is hundreds—and some would argue thousands—of years old. The stereoscope, allowing simulation of binocular parallax, was invented by Charles Wheatstone in the nineteenth century. And effective simulation of observer-contingent motions to present a three-dimensional layout is only a decade or so old, with truly realistic virtual-reality technology maturing only in the last few years.

Information Based on Assumed Physical Equality
The pictorial cues to depth give information in a static, monocular view. A number of these cues rest on similar foundations (see figure 3.3). Pro-

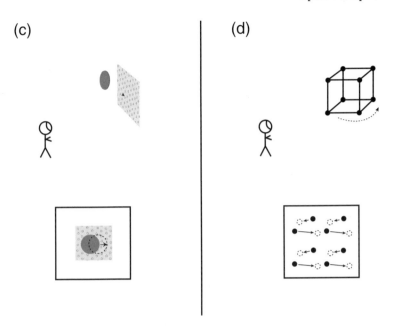

Figure 3.2 (continued)
c. *Accretion and deletion of texture:* Relative motion of an object and a farther surface leads to progressive occluding of background texture elements at the object's leading edge and revealing of texture elements at its trailing edge. d. *Structure from motion:* The rotation cube produces relative motions of its visible points in the projection to the eye; relations among these motion vectors specify the object's three-dimensional structure.

jective geometry dictates certain distance-dependent changes in images; for example, the visual angle projected by a given physical extent decreases with distance. Working this geometry backward, if two physical tokens (objects, spaces) can be assumed to have the same real size, them differences in their projective size can be used to order them in depth. This describes the depth cue of *relative size*. Due to *linear perspective*, the image of converging lines may indicate lines in the world, such as railroad tracks, that have constant separation but extend away in depth. *Relative height*, an often neglected and quite powerful cue, rests on the fact that more distant objects generally appear higher in the visual field. Here it is assumed that both objects rest on the ground and that the ground surface is generally flat. When these assumptions are met, relative height is a consequence of the fact that we ordinarily view our environment from some height above the ground surface. Gibson (1950) described the rich information in *texture gradients*. If it can be assumed that the physical tokens along a ground surface (pebbles, cornstalks, cobblestones, and so on) are stochastically uniform, then the decreasing projective size of texture

Figure 3.3
Examples of pictorial depth cues. a. *Linear perspective:* The escalators converge in the image.
b. *Relative size and relative height:* The more distant Gettysburg Battlefield monument projects
a smaller image, and its base is higher on the visible ground surface. c. *Texture gradient:* Image
size of visible texture elements decreases with their distance. Photographs © E. Christine
Merritt.

elements can indicate depth. Moreover, uniform surface texture may offer a direct means of size perception: two objects may be perceived to be the same sizes despite differing distances from the observer because they will occlude the same number of texture elements. Finally, *shading* rests on the fact that surfaces identical in their light-reflecting properties will appear brighter or darker, depending on their orientation to the light source. Variations in luminance can thus be used to perceive surface topography.

Information based on assumed physical equality is not as fundamentally rooted in the physics and geometry of our world as is parallax information. It is easy to display these pictorial cues to depth in situations where no depth exists, such as in paintings and photographs. In addition, it is not too difficult to find in ordinary environments violations of the assumed physical regularities on which these cues rely. Some converging lines are not parallels extending away from the observer, for example. Regular gradients of texture are common, but at the seashore, the average size of sand, shells, and pebbles decreases with distance from the water's edge. Many variations in surface luminance come from variations in surface reflectance rather than from differences in surface orientation. In all of these cases, pictorial depth cues may be inaccurate indicators of the spatial layout.

Oculomotor Information
Berkeley (1709/1910) proposed that visual information could be interpreted by association with muscular adjustments required for focusing the image (accommodation) and that converging the two eyes could provide information about the third dimension. Both of these adjustments should produce muscular sensations correlated with distance.

The physical facts that make these adjustments necessary are simply that (1) light moves in straight lines and (2) most surfaces (all matte surfaces) scatter incident light in all directions. Convergence depends only on the former: to view the same point in space, each eye must turn so that the fovea, the nodal point of the eye, and the target point are collinear. Accommodation is necessary because the closer a target, the more the eye admits a sheaf of light rays traveling in slightly different directions. Should these light rays from the same target point contact different retinal receptors, directional information would be lost. To get these divergent rays to focus on the same retinal location, more refractive power is needed for nearer targets. Changes in the thickness of the lens provide the variable refractive power.

Experimental appraisals of accommodation and convergence as distance information for adults have varied. Some early experimental work suggested a weak or negative relationship between accommodative strength and perceived nearness (Heinemann, Tulving & Nachmias, 1959). A comprehensive review of spatial perception in the early 1970s suggested that accommodation and convergence were at best weak cues (Hochberg, 1971). Later studies led to a revival of these cues, however (von Hofsten, 1976; Wallach & Floor, 1971). These studies found that oculomotor cues, especially convergence, can provide accurate information when measured indirectly. Perceived size, for example, can be accurately given by convergence information and retinal (projected) size information. Some of the earlier studies failed to find useful effects of these cues because of unexpected interactions of size perception on distance judgments, especially in tasks using targets of constant retinal size over a number of trials (Wallach & Floor, 1971).

Both accommodation and convergence are effective only at short ranges, up to 2 to 3 meters in adults. The similar geometry underlying both cues dictates that as distance increases, the adjustments required decrease drastically. Taking convergence as our example, consider two points 20 and 21.5 cm distant from the observer (directly in front of a point midway between the two eyes). Assuming the observer's eyes are 6.5 cm apart, the difference in convergence angles for fixating these two points is about .63 deg (about 38 min). In other words, changing convergence angle by .63 deg when viewing a target at 20 cm points the eyes at a location 21.5 cm away. For comparison suppose the eyes start out fixating a target 3 meters away. Changing the convergence angle by .63 deg in this case changes the fixated location by more than 1.5 cm. How much more? Now the eyes aim at a location 3000 meters away!

Other Depth Information Sources
Not all known depth cues fit into the taxonomy we have given. One important exception is the pictorial cue of *interposition*. Figure 3.4a illustrates. In the figure, it appears that the lighter object continues behind the darker object. Interposition, or overlap, thus gives us depth ordering. It does not give metric information about depth intervals or distance from the observer.

Interposition is a bit more intricate than it may first appear. *Why* do we see one object as going behind another? One idea is that the area whose boundaries change direction at the intersection is seen as behind. Thus, so-called T junctions might be the informational basis of interposition. This notion is serviceable for most cases, but counterexamples exist (Ratoosh, 1949; see figure 3.4b). The ecological regularity underlying interposition is that occlusion of one object's bounding contours by another object ordinarily produces T junctions. These junctions are less likely to occur from other causes. (Some complexities of interposition are discussed by Hochberg, 1971; for a discussion of the connection of interposition to

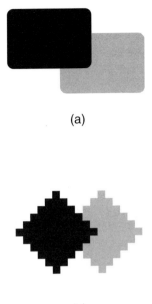

(a)

(b)

Figure 3.4
Two examples of interposition. a. Typical case, in which the surface whose contours end at contour junctions are seen as going behind the other surface. b. Problem case, in which the contour-direction change rule may not predict which surface appears in front (after Chapanis & McCleary, 1953). (See text.)

processes by which the visual system recovers the unity and shapes of objects under partial occlusion, see Kellman and Shipley, 1991).

A second cue that does not fit into our taxonomy is the depth cue of *familiar size*. If the physical size of an object is known, then the size of its retinal projection in a given instance may be used along with remembered real size to determine its distance. There is some evidence for the effectiveness of this cue for adults, especially when conflicting information is eliminated (Ittelson, 1953; but see Hochberg & Hochberg, 1953 and Predebon & Wooley, 1994 for conflicting views on the effectiveness of this cue in adult distance perception).

SPACE PERCEPTION ABILITIES AND PROCESSES

How does space perception get started? Which parts, if any, of the adult's arsenal of information sources can infants use? For convenience, we organize our discussion around four classes of information, based both on their ecological roots and on similarities in the mechanisms by which they are processed. For example, parallax information underlies both kinematic and stereoscopic information, but here we separate these because they appear to be processed separately. The four classes are kinematic information, stereoscopic information, oculomotor information, and pictorial depth information. This organization differs slightly from some other groupings (e.g., Yonas & Owsley, 1987).

An interesting conjecture regarding the development of space perception is that it may reflect the differing ecological validity of different information sources. Kinematic and stereoscopic information, we noted above, are less subject to ambiguity than are the pictorial depth cues. Early learning about the environment might be best served by reliance on only the most accurate sources of information, even if this means that some perceptual situations will be indeterminate (Kellman, 1993). We consider this conjecture in space perception and later in other domains where perception can depend on multiple sources of information.

Kinematic Information about Space

Kinematic information is arguably the most important source of spatial information for adults, given its precision and informativeness for spatial layout, guidance of locomotion, and skilled action. Kinematic information is also noteworthy in being unambiguous under reasonable constraints (e.g., Lee, 1974). For example, the depth ordering of viewed objects given by motion perspective when an observer moves her head back and forth is unequivocal, assuming only that the objects do not move contingent on the observer's movement. From the standpoint of ecological validity, infant perceivers might be expected to be equipped with mechanisms sensitive to kinematic information early in development. One might make the opposite prediction from other considerations. Much kinematic information is provided by observer motion rather than object motion. Because human infants do not self-locomote until about the second half year of life, one might expect mechanisms sensitive to kinematic information to arise at that time or later.

Kinematic Information for Approach

The optical projection of an approaching object expands symmetrically as the object comes closer to colliding with the observer. This kind of optical change carries information about the object's time to contact, and there is some evidence that adults use this information (e.g., Lee, Lishman & Thomson, 1982; Schiff & Oldak, 1990). Studies with other species indicate that optical expansion patterns elicit unlearned defensive responses (Schiff, 1965). Early studies of human infants 1 to 2 months old suggested that optical expansion displays trigger head retraction, raising of the arms and blinking (e.g., Ball & Tronick, 1971). Later work questioned the interpretation of head and arm movements (Yonas, Bechtold, Frankel, Gordon, McRoberts, Norcia & Sternfels, 1977). Infants may move their heads because they track visually the top contour of the pattern, and their relatively undifferentiated motor behavior may lead to the arms following along. To test this hypothesis, Yonas et al. presented a display in which only the top contour moved. Such a display does not specify approach of an object. From 1 to 4 months of age, infants showed as much or more head and arm movement to the single contour movement display as to the expansion display. It appears that tracking behavior may explain much or all of the apparent "defensive" movements by infants.

Paradoxically, however, it appears that both the tracking hypothesis and the original defense hypothesis are correct. Yonas et al. also measured eye blinking to their displays. In contrast to the head and arm movement results, infants blinked reliably more to a display specifying approach than the single contour. Reliable effects of blinking to approach displays, more than to control displays, have been found in several studies with infants from about one month on (Nanez, 1988; Nanez & Yonas, 1994; Yonas, Pettersen & Lockman, 1979; Yonas, 1981).

Motion Perspective

Little research has directly addressed motion perspective in perceptual development. Some investigators have conjectured that it may be an innate foundation of spatial perception (Walk & Gibson, 1961; Yonas & Owsley, 1987). But the evidence is thin. In classic studies, Walk and Gibson (1961) tested depth perception using a *visual cliff*, a glass surface through which animals could see a surface below. Newborns of several species refused to crawl onto the "deep" side of the cliff, and Walk and Gibson noted that these animals made lateral head movements that probably indicated use of motion perspective. Human infants cannot even be tested in the standard visual cliff situation until they begin to crawl (around 6 months of age), and they do not conspicuously show lateral head movements even then.

Von Hofsten, Kellman, and Putaansuu (1992) reported experimental results related to the development of motion perspective. They presented 14-week-old infants with an array of three vertical rods in a horizontal row, perpendicular to the line of sight. The infant was placed in a chair that moved laterally back and forth, and the middle rod moved a small amount parallel and in tandem with the chair. In one experiment, infants habituated to such an array in which the middle rod moved .32 deg/sec in phase with the moving infant chair. Afterward they were tested with two displays: one was spatially similar in that it consisted of three aligned, stationary rods; the other had three stationary rods with the middle rod displaced backward 15 cm, which gave the moving infant the same optical change patterns as in habituation. Infants generalized habituation more to the spatially different display having the same optical change as in habituation. The effect disappeared if the contingent motion was reduced to .16 deg/sec. Another experiment showed that infants were sensitive to the contingency between the optical changes and their own movement, as would be predicted if the optical changes functioned as motion perspective information.

The results are consistent with the idea that young infants utilize small contingent optical changes as information about object depth. All the dishabituation patterns fit predictions based on the use of motion perspective as an indicator of depth. But the results do not uniquely imply this interpretation. These dishabituation patterns might also be expected if infants responded to particular optical changes as well as the contingency of these optical changes on the observer's movement. In other words, the results do not unequivocally show that the optical changes were taken to indicate depth. These contingent optical changes do appear special in that infants' sensitivity to them exceeded that found in typical studies of motion detection by almost an order of magnitude (see chapter 6). Although this differential sensitivity would fit neatly with the idea that small, contingent motions are encoded as depth information, not motion, verifying this separation of systems will require further research.

Accretion and Deletion of Texture

Accretion and deletion of texture is a source of kinematic information for edges and depth discovered relatively recently (Gibson, Kaplan, Reynolds & Wheeler, 1969; Kaplan, 1969). During relative motion of two opaque surfaces at different depths, texture elements on the further surface become visible (accretion) or hidden (deletion) at the edges of the nearer surface. In random dot surfaces in which no other information is available, accretion and deletion of texture effectively specifies edges, form, and depth ordering of surfaces to adult observers (Kaplan, 1969; Andersen & Cortese, 1989; Shipley & Kellman, 1994).

Kaufmann-Hayoz, Kaufman, and Stucki (1986) studied shape perception from this kind of information. Three-month-olds who habituated to one shape specified by accretion and deletion of texture dishabituated to a different shape and vice versa. The result suggests that accretion and deletion of texture effectively specified edges and shape at this early age, although no inferences can be made about depth ordering from the data. Granrud, Yonas, Smith, Arterberry, Glickman, and Sorknes (1984) studied perception of depth ordering using a reaching procedure. Assuming that infants would reach preferentially to the nearer of two surfaces, they presented moving displays of computer-generated, random dot surfaces with vertical accretion and deletion boundaries specifying nearer and farther surfaces. Infants at both 5 and 7 months of age reached about 50% of the time to areas specified as nearer and 35% to areas specified as farther. (The remaining reaches were to edges or to two or more display regions.)

These results suggest that sensitivity to accretion and deletion information arises early. Later, Yonas and his colleagues raised questions about the basis of infants' responding. They pointed out that ordinary accretion and deletion displays might contain two kinds of information. Besides the actual appearance and disappearance of texture elements, there are different relations between moving texture elements and the boundary between two regions. On one side elements remain in a fixed position relative to the boundary; this side is nearer than the other. In the other region, elements move closer or farther from the boundary over time; this surface is farther. Tests with adult subjects show that the latter information (termed *boundary flow*) is usable as depth information when no accretion and deletion of elements at the boundary is present (Craton & Yonas, 1990). Craton and Yonas (1988) reported that 5-month-olds also responded to boundary flow information when no accretion and deletion was present. Further work may be needed to indicate whether accretion and deletion alone can specify depth order. The data do suggest that at minimum accretion and deletion enables infant perceivers to locate the boundaries between regions, since the boundaries (required to compute boundary flow) were not given in any other way in the Granrud, Yonas, et al. (1984) and Kaufmann-Hayoz et al. (1986) studies.

Stereoscopic Information

Stereoscopic depth perception is among the most precise forms of spatial information. For adults, it allows perception of absolute depth intervals, given some information about the distance of at least one visible point (Wallach & Zuckerman, 1963). Evidence suggests innate foundations for stereoscopic depth perception. Cortical cells sensitive to particular disparities at birth or after minimal visual experience have been found in several species (Hubel & Wiesel, 1970; Pettigrew, 1974; Ramachandran, Clarke & Whitteridge, 1977).

For humans, perception of depth from disparity arises by maturation in some infants as young as 2 to 3 months, with most infants first showing sensitivity around the 4th month. Research has employed preferential looking methods with stationary displays (Atkinson & Braddick, 1976; Held, Birch & Gwiazda, 1980) or with random dot kinematograms (Fox, Aslin, Shea & Dumais, 1980), along with the hypothesis that detection of depth specified by disparity leads to greater attention than a comparable flat display. Using visual evoked potentials, Petrig et al. (1981) estimated a similar age of onset of sensitivity.

Programmatic research on disparity thresholds was been carried out by Held and his colleagues (Held, Birch & Gwiazda, 1980; Birch, Gwiazda & Held, 1982). Visual preferences for a striped display containing stereo-scopic depth differences over a comparable flat display were studied longitudinally. They found reliable preferences at 12 weeks for crossed disparities and at 17 weeks for uncrossed. Improvement in stereoscopic sensitivity once it appears is strikingly rapid (see figure 3.5). Thresholds changed from greater than 60 min to less than 1 min of disparity in a few weeks. The lower estimate was limited by the apparatus (Held, Birch & Gwiazda, 1980) and is comparable to adult sensitivity under some conditions.

Disparity Sensitivity versus Depth Perception

Do studies of early binocular function indicate that infants see stereo-scopic depth or merely that infants can detect disparity differences? The issue is difficult to settle definitively. Control conditions employed in several studies, and studies examining spatial behavior tend to support the depth perception hypothesis. Held, Birch, and Gwiazda (1980), for example, found that subjects who showed clear preferences for vertical line displays containing horizontal disparity showed no such preferences when the display orientation was rotated 90 deg to give 34 min of vertical disparity (a condition that induces binocular rivalry for adults). Fox et al. (1980) reported that infants who preferentially fixated disparities looked away from displays with very large disparities that do not signal depth to adults. The result is most naturally interpreted as suggesting that ordinary preferential attention to disparity displays depends on perception of depth. On the other hand, it tends to suggest that disparities apart from stereopsis might affect infants' fixation. A different approach to the problem is to look for differences in spatial behavior based on disparity sensitivity. Granrud (1986) asked whether 4- to 5-month-old infants who were sensitive to binocular disparity showed different reaching behavior than infants at these ages who showed no evidence of disparity sensitivity. Two objects at different distances moved back and forth, perpendicular to the infants' line of sight. Under binocular viewing conditions, disparity-sensitive infants reached more frequently to the closer object than did disparity-insensitive infants. In a different context, Yonas, Arterberry, and Granrud (1987a) found that only disparity-sensitive 4-month-olds showed evidence that the three-dimensional form of an object perceived from kinematic information was matched to the same form specified by binocular dis-parity. On the basis of these diverse results, it seems safe to conclude that the onset of disparity sensitivity in human infants closely corresponds to their ability to perceive stereoscopic depth.

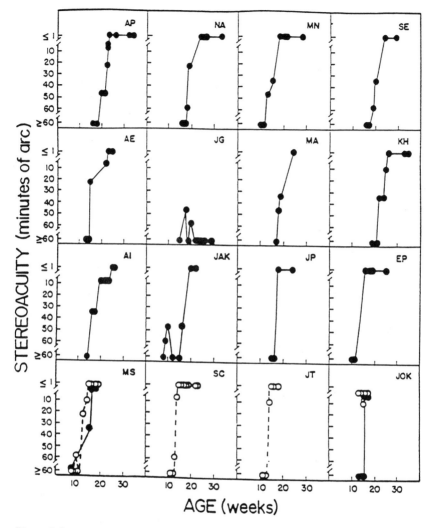

Figure 3.5
Stereoacuity estimates (in minutes of arc) as a function of age for individual infants. Reprinted with permission from Held, R., Birch, E., & Gwiazda, J. (1980), Stereoacuity of human infants, *Proceedings of the National Academy of Science, USA, 77,* 5572–5574.

Mechanisms Underlying the Onset of Stereopsis

The rapid emergence of stereoscopic acuity seems consistent with a maturational explanation. What matures? Possibilities include maturing of cortical cells sensitive to disparity, fine-tuning of convergence, or improving visual acuity that might facilitate disparity sensitivity. Evidence casts doubt on the latter idea. When both are measured in the same subjects, little or no change in grating acuity appears during the period in which stereopsis suddenly emerges (Held, 1993). Moreover, Westheimer and McKee (1980) tested adult stereoacuity under conditions that reduced their acuity and contrast sensitivity to approximate those of a 2-month-old infant. These manipulations reduced stereoacuity, but not enough to explain the absence of early sensitivity to large disparities. Development of convergence probably does not explain stereoscopic development because it would not explain differences in the timing of crossed and uncrossed disparity (Held et al., 1980). Interestingly, development of precise convergence may depend on improvements in disparity sensitivity, rather than vice versa (Aslin, 1987; Held et al., 1980). The most likely mechanism determining the emergence of stereoscopic vision is some maturational change in cortical disparity-sensitive units. In kittens, improvements in stereoscopic discrimination depend on changes in binocularly sensitive cortical cells (Timney, 1981; Pettigrew, 1974). Held (1985, 1988) suggested that human stereoscopic development depends on segregation of ocular dominance columns in layer 4 of the visual cortex. Initially, cells in layer 4 receive projections from both eyes. Between birth and 6 months, inputs from the two eyes separate into alternating columns receiving input from the right and left eyes (Hickey & Peduzzi, 1987). Since eye-of-origin information is needed to extract disparity information, this neurological development may be crucial in determining when stereoscopic depth perception begins.

Oculomotor Information

Accommodation

No research has assessed accommodation as a source of depth information in infancy. We saw in chapter 2 that when other limitations are avoided, infant accommodation appears to be reasonably accurate even in the early weeks of life. The early presence of accommodative function opens the possibility that accommodation could act as a depth cue, but this possibility remains to be investigated.

Convergence

In chapter 2 we saw evidence that convergence operates accurately by 1 month of age for distances beyond 20 cm (Hainline et al., 1992). If convergence is reasonably accurate, an important question is what could be the stimulus for eye movements leading to accurate convergence? Given the data on the development of stereopsis, binocular disparity does not seem to be a reasonable candidate before 3 to 4 months of age. Nor does accommodation-triggered vergence seem plausible, since accommodation is less accurate in the early weeks of life than is convergence. Hainline et al. (1992) suggested two possibilities. When targets are sparse or unique, convergence may derive from foveating the target in each eye. Alternatively, correlations in firing of cortical units sensitive to similar retinal positions, but driven by different eyes, could drive convergence. Currently little evidence is available to evaluate these hypotheses.

The studies we have so far considered concern the accuracy of infants' convergence rather than its relevance to depth perception. One study has addressed this issue. Von Hofsten (1974) tested 5-month-olds' reaching behavior while they wore convergence-altering glasses. The results showed that reaches were shifted appropriately toward positions consistent with convergence information. By 5 months, it appears that convergence can provide absolute distance information.

Convergence may provide distance information much earlier—perhaps from birth, although the evidence is indirect. Kellman, Hofsten, Vandewalle, and Condry (1990; Kellman & von Hofsten, 1992) studied 8- and 16-week-olds in a situation in which moving observers were tested for motion detection. The displays contained several stationary objects and a single moving object, with the moving object linked to the observer's moving chair (moving along a path parallel to it). Detecting motion in this situation requires distance information (Gogel, 1982). Infants showed evidence of accurate motion detection when they viewed the displays binocularly but not monocularly. Motion detection in the 16-week-old group may have been based on convergence, disparity, or a combination of the two, but it is unlikely that disparity is present at 8 weeks. The best explanation for 8-week-olds' motion detection in this situation is that it is based on distance information furnished by convergence.

Other results also point toward an early ability to extract distance information from convergence (Granrud, 1987; Slater, Mattock & Brown, 1990). These studies, discussed below, involve use of distance information in the perception of object size and shape.

Pictorial Depth Information

Much of what we know about the development of pictorial depth perception comes from a series of studies by Yonas and his colleagues (see Yonas, Arterberry & Granrud, 1987b, for review). Most of these studies used reaching as a dependent measure. Displays in which pictorial information specified that one object was nearer to the subject than another were presented to infants with one eye covered (eliminating binocular cues to depth). Preferential reaching to the nearer display was taken to indicate the effectiveness of a given pictorial cue.

Linear Perspective

The "Ames window"—a trapezoidal window developed by Adelbert Ames (Ames, 1951)—was used to study linear perspective by Yonas, Cleaves, and Petersen (1978). When an adult views the Ames window with one eye and from a sufficient distance, the window will appear tilted in depth, even though it is really perpendicular to the line of sight. (Binocular viewing reduces or eliminates the effect.) In the study by Yonas et al., 5 and 7-month-old infants viewed the trapezoidal window monocularly or binocularly on different trials, and reaching to the two sides was measured. Infants reached about equally to the two sides in the binocular condition, suggesting that any linear perspective information was overridden by binocular depth perception (as would be true for adults in near viewing of such a display). Under monocular viewing, 7-month-olds reached significantly more to the larger side of the window, but 5-month-olds did not. A consistent finding was reported by Oross, Francis, Mauk, and Fox (1987): infants 7.5 and 9.5 months of age, but not 5.5 months, perceived the illusory oscillation of a rotating Ames window display.

In a study using a combination of cues, Yonas, Granrud, Arterberry, and Hanson (1986) showed an upright, frontoparallel trapezoidal surface on which two objects were positioned at different heights. Linear perspective and texture gradient information created the impression of a receding ground surface on which two objects rested at different distances. (The display also contained the depth cue of relative height.) Under binocular viewing, infants at both 5 and 7 months of age reached equally to the two objects. Under monocular viewing, the 7-month-olds but not the 5-month-olds reached more to the lower object (which was specified to be closer by the pictorial depth cues).

Results from these several studies converge nicely in indicating that linear perspective indicates relative depth by 7 months of age.

Familiar Size

The depth cue of *familiar size* is unique in its importance for evaluating learning effects in space perception. Familiar size works this way: From the geometry of size and distance relations, the combination of a known object size and a given projective size can be used to compute the distance from the observer to the object. What is special about this cue is that it requires specific learned information—the object's true size. Strikingly, evidence suggests that infants do use this cue and that they come to do so with surprisingly little exposure to a unique object (Granrud, Haake & Yonas, 1985; Yonas, Pettersen & Granrud, 1982).

The first study of familiar size in infants (Yonas et al., 1982) used two photographs of female faces as stimuli. One larger-than-life and one smaller-than-life photograph were presented sequentially at the same distance from 5- and 7-month-old infants. With binocular viewing, both groups showed the same frequency of reaching to the two displays. With monocular viewing, however, the 7-month-olds, but not the 5-month-olds, reached more often to the larger face. This pattern of results was interpreted as indicating that the larger face was seen as closer by older infants who viewed it monocularly. It seems possible that infants might tend to reach more for large objects apart from the cue of familiar size. Yonas et al. tested this idea using large and small checkerboard stimuli, presented sequentially at the same distance, and found equal reaching by both age groups under monocular and binocular viewing. The results suggest that the familiar size cue operates for face stimuli (and that infants of this age have not learned the true size of standard checkerboards).

An even more remarkable demonstration of familiar size was reported by Granrud et al. (1985). Infants were given 5 min to play with unfamiliar wooden toys, one smaller than the other. Following this familiarization phase the infants viewed two toys that were the same shapes and colors as during familiarization but that now were of equal size (and displayed at the same distance). Seven-month-old infants reached more for the toy that was small during familiarization, suggesting that they perceived this object as nearer.

Perception of distance from familiar size provides some evidence for the role of learning in infant space perception. Apparently, not only does familiar size operate in infancy, but relatively brief experience is sufficient to develop the necessary object representations. The Granrud et al. result also demonstrates that infants' object representations, formed from brief familiarization, contain information about absolute size.

Interposition
Figure 3.6 shows displays used to study the development of interposition (Granrud & Yonas, 1984). If infants perceive depth order from interposition, then in figure 3.6a the leftmost part of the display would appear to be nearer than the middle, which in turn would appear to be nearer than the rightmost part of the display. In figure 3.6b, all contours change direction at the intersections, and no depth order is specified. Finally, figure 3.6c provides a control display in which the three panels are separated but have areas identical to those visible in figure 3.6a.

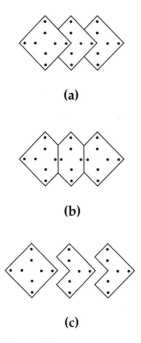

(a)

(b)

(c)

Figure 3.6
Displays used to study depth perception from interposition. a. Interposition display. b. Control display with no interposition information. c. Control display with no interposition but visible areas comparable to (a). Redrawn with permission from Granrud, C. E., & Yonas, A. (1984), Infants' perception of pictorially specified interposition, *Journal of Experimental Child Psychology, 37*, 500–511.

In the experiments, all parts of the displays were actually coplanar and equidistant from the observers. Subjects were 5- and 7-month-olds with one eye covered (to remove conflicting binocular information); their reaches to different parts of the displays were recorded. In the first experiment, both 5- and 7-month-olds were observed to reach significantly more often to the leftmost part of display in figure 3.6a than to the leftmost part of control display 3.6b. (The percentages were 61% to 3.6a and 50% to 3.6b for 7-month-olds, and 56 versus 47% for 5-month-olds). An alternative explanation of this initial result was that the relative size of visible areas, not interposition, influenced reaching. To test this idea, the interposition display in 3.6a was presented to another group of subjects along with the display in 3.6c. The results indicated that 7-month-olds reached reliably more to the leftmost part of the interposition display than this control display (63 versus 54%), whereas 5-month-olds showed no reliable difference (56 versus 54%). On balance, the results provide evidence for the use of interposition at 7 but not 5 months of age.

Figure 3.7
Example of surface topography specified by shading information. Cracks, protrusions, and orientation of local surface regions are indicated by luminance variations. Photograph © E. Christine Merritt.

Shading

Shading is a powerful cue to surface topography; figure 3.7 gives an illustration. In a study by Granrud, Yonas, and Opland (1985), 5- and 7-month-olds were presented with a surface containing a concavity and a convexity. They were also presented, under binocular and monocular viewing, with a photograph depicting a concavity and convexity. Classification of concavity and convexity from shading alone depends on the position of the light source; in some other species as well as in human adults, evidence suggests that illumination from above is assumed in perception of shaded regions (Hershberger, 1970). It was assumed that infants would reach preferentially to an area that appeared nearer than the rest of the surface. Both age groups reached preferentially for the real convexity in both monocular and binocular conditions. Seven-month-olds viewing the photograph reached preferentially for the area specified to be convex by shading information, but only when they viewed the display monocularly. When viewing binocularly, they showed no reaching preference. Five-month-olds showed no reaching preferences to the photographic display under either monocular or binocular viewing. The results suggest that shading alone provides depth information to 7-month-olds but not to 5-month-olds.

Overview of Pictorial Depth

Research on a variety of pictorial information sources are remarkably consistent in indicating an age of onset between 5 and 7 months of age. Because most studies have used reaching behavior as the dependent measure, we should consider the possibility that the observed differences reflect refinements in the control of reaching or the emergence of some perceptual-motor coordination. These hypotheses are vitiated by evidence that 5-month-olds do show clear reaching preferences to depth differences specified by binocular information (Granrud, Yonas & Pettersen, 1984; Granrud, 1986). Furthermore, in the case of at least one cue—familiar size—the same pattern of results has been found using an habituation method (Arterberry, Bensen & Yonas, 1991). The weight of the evidence favors the interpretation that these cues become functional en masse between 5 and 7 months.

The absence of pictorial depth sensitivity in the first half year and the apparent synchrony of the onset of various cues pose an interesting explanatory challenge. The similar timing of the appearance of the various cues has been cited as evidence that these cues arise from neural maturation of a general pictorial depth module (Granrud & Yonas, 1984). This interpretation is consistent with research on macaque monkeys indicating that sensitivity to several pictorial depth cues appears around 7 to 8 weeks of life (Gunderson, Yonas, Sargent & Grant-Webster, 1993). The timing is interesting because a variety of maturation-paced abilities seem to appear in the macaque monkey in about one-fourth the time it takes for them to appear in humans. Because these cues appear as a group in the macaque and because they approximately fit the 1 : 4 ratio, these data offer strong support for a maturational explanation.

Alternatively, pictorial depth sensitivity might be a product of learning. For example, infants may learn to use these cues after they begin to crawl at around 6 months of age. The importance of locomotion would be consistent with evidence in other species showing connections between self-produced locomotion and sensitivity to visual information about space (Held & Hein, 1963). Similarly, Bertenthal and Campos (1990) provided evidence that crawling experience correlates with human infants' avoidance of the deep side of the visual cliff.

Research aimed at directly assessing the locomotor hypothesis in relation to pictorial depth cues has been disconfirming, however. Arterberry, Yonas, and Bensen (1989) tested the relation of locomotor experience to sensitivity to linear perspective and texture gradients. Seven-month-olds at different stages of learning to crawl did not differ in their sensitivity to pictorial depth: infants in all locomotor groups showed preferential reaching to an object specified to be closer by perspective or textural gradients.

These findings are inconsistent with the notion that pictorial depth cues are learned in connection with crawling experience.

Other learning accounts for the onset of pictorial depth perception remain possible. Infants might, for example, learn relationships between static, monocular patterns and depth relations given by motion or stereopsis. Although the case for maturational origins is supported by cross-species comparisons, it is noteworthy that the depth cue of familiar size becomes useful around the same time as the other pictorial cues. Familiar size, as we noted, *necessarily* involves learning; it thus provides an existence proof for the operation of some learning in depth perception around this time.

Further empirical work will be needed to improve our understanding of the origins of pictorial depth perception. One experimental approach that might help to decide the roles of learning and maturation would be training studies, in which a new depth cue is presented along with already usable information about depth. Likewise, a longitudinal study that included tests for several different pictorial cues could address the hypothesis of a single maturational basis by showing how closely in time the various cues really come to operate. Such studies would be complex but useful undertakings.

Effects of Distance Perception on Object Perception

Besides its direct value, information about distance affects perception of object properties, such as size, shape, and motion. Conversely, studies of infants' perception of shape, size, and motion can provide windows into early spatial perception. In this section, we consider several findings of this sort that have important implications for the development of space perception.

Size Constancy

To detect an object's size requires relational information. A given object's projection on the retina varies as a function of its distance from the observer. The specific relation was shown back in figure 1.3. If S is the real size of the object, and D is the distance from the nodal point of the eye (where the rays cross), then

$$S/D = s/d, \tag{3.1}$$

where s is the projective size at the retina, and d is the depth of the eyeball from the nodal point to the retina. Since d is relatively fixed for a given eye, this relationship can be conveniently expressed as

$$S = sD/k, \text{ where } k \text{ is constant.} \tag{3.2}$$

It is even more convenient to think of the retinal projection in terms of visual angle. For viewing distances large relative to the object's size,[1] the visual angle Θ is given by

$$\operatorname{Tan}\Theta = S/D = s/d, \qquad (3.3)$$

and

$$S = D \tan \Theta. \qquad (3.4)$$

As (3.4) suggests, one way to achieve *size constancy* (perception of true size despite changes in projective size) is to combine projective size (visual angle) with information about viewing distance (Holway & Boring, 1941).

How size constancy develops is a classic topic in infant perception research. For constructivist views of perception, size constancy is a paradigm case. Because real size depends on distance information and projective size, size constancy illustrates the need for inference in perception. Furthermore, if distance perception itself must develop by learning, size constancy might be predicted to be an elaborate developmental construction. Learning to interpret projective size in relation to distance would require the scaffolding of learning to perceive distance in the first place. Against this background, the outcomes of research on infant size perception are nothing short of astonishing.

In some of the earliest work on this problem, Day and McKenzie (1981) found evidence that 18-week-old infants are capable of perceiving size by taking distance into account. They habituated subjects to an approaching and receding object. After habituation, infants were tested with the same size object at the same average distance and another object of a different size. By using a different average distance, this novel object's retinal projections during motion fell within the same range of visual angles as the habituation object. Infants dishabituated to the object of novel size.

More recently, Slater, Mattock, and Brown (1990) reported convincing evidence that newborn human infants have size constancy. Their conclusion rests on a pair of experiments, worth considering in some detail. In their first experiment, they measured newborns' visual fixation preferences to pairs of objects having identical shapes but different real sizes (cubes of 5.1 or 10.2 cm per side), positioned at several different distances (23 to 69 cm). In all cases in which projective size differed, infants showed clear preferences for the object of larger projective size. This experiment did not test size constancy but showed that infants' spontaneously look more at objects with larger projective sizes. In the second experiment, Slater et al. familiarized subjects with an object of constant size—either the large or the small cube—positioned at different distances over 6 familiarization trials. Then test trials were carried out in which the large and small cubes were presented and infants' looking preferences were measured. In these test trials, the large and small cubes were positioned so that they had equal projective sizes (that is, the cube that was twice as big was placed twice as far away). Moreover, the cube shown in familiarization was placed at a distance where it had not appeared earlier, making the retinal sizes of both test objects novel. If infants had detected the constant size of the object shown during familiarization, they were expected to look longer at the object of novel size during the test trials.

All 12 infants did exactly that: they devoted an average of 84% of total test trial looking toward the novel-sized object. Because the design was counterbalanced, the large and small cubes were each used as familiarization objects. Hence the large object was novel for half the subjects, and the small object was novel for the other half. An additional helpful feature of the experimental design was that the test pair in this experiment was identical to one presented in the earlier visual preference experiment, at which time it evoked no reliable preference. This comparison suggests that the strong preferences observed in the size-constancy experiment could be attributed to information gotten during the familiarization procedure.

This remarkable result is supported by other research (Granrud, 1987; Slater & Morrison, 1985). In Granrud's study, rates of habituation were examined to two kinds of sequences of objects in which retinal sizes varied identically. One sequence used an object of constant real size, whereas the other used varying object sizes. Infants showed slower habituation to the latter sequence, consistent with the idea that changing object sizes were detected in that case and sustained subjects' interest.

Apparently, size constancy is an innate visual capacity! No visual ability more directly addresses the classical arguments of Berkeley, Helmholtz, and whole generations of philosophers and psychologists about the need for learning in perception. The human infant is built to use the geometry of projection, combining projective size and distance information, from its earliest days. This finding alone militates a radically revised view of perceptual development.

The discovery of size constancy in newborns answers some very old questions but also raises some questions that have not yet been answered. Achieving accurate size perception in these experiments implies that at least one source of egocentric distance information (information indicating the distance of a target from the observer) is functional at birth. Studies to date have provided no direct evidence of what this source might be. We can make some inferences based on a process of elimination. In the experimental situation, projective size and viewing distance must combine to determine size. Relationships of size and texture occlusion (Gibson, 1950) were not available because objects in these studies were suspended in midair in front of homogeneous backgrounds. Only a few known sources of egocentric distance information are usable by newborns and were available in these experimental situations. In principle, accommodation of the lens could be used, but it may not have the required precision in newborns. In addition, it functions only weakly as a depth cue for adults, and there is no evidence that infants use it as a depth cue. Motion perspective would not appear to provide the information here either. Newborns require substantial head support and seldom make the lateral head movements needed to generate motion perspective. In Granrud's experiment, moreover, displays were moved back and forth to heighten subjects' interest. This procedure would complicate the recovery of distance from optical change. What remains is convergence as the most likely source of absolute distance information underlying size constancy. Its precision as a source of distance information in early infancy is unknown, as is the precision of newborn size constancy. How precisely must size be specified to produce the appropriate dishabituation patterns in the Slater et al. study? On the assumptions that newborns correctly register projective size and that an object will not be seen to change its size unless a change in its distance is registered, Kellman (1995) calculated that infants must locate the object in the experiment of Slater et al. with an error not exceeding 2.5 deg of convergence angle and not exceeding about 1.8 deg in Granrud's. This level of accuracy is consistent with recent work on convergence (Hainline et al., 1992) as we saw in chapter 2.

Shape Constancy
When a rectangle is slanted away from an observer (that is, rotated around a horizontal axis), its projection on the eyes will be trapezoidal. Likewise, if a trapezoidal object is slanted so that its physically larger side is farther away from the observer by just the right amount, its projection will be perfectly rectangular. Under ordinary viewing conditions, adults detect the true shapes of surfaces despite their three-dimensional orientations. This ability requires combining projective shape information with distance or orientation information. Without three-dimensional spatial information, recovering the shapes of planar objects slanted in depth should be impossible.

Twelve-week-olds showed evidence of shape constancy in a study by Caron, Caron, and Carlson (1979). Slater and Morison (1985) tested this ability with newborns (mean age: 2 days, 8 hours). Subjects were habituated either to a rectangle slanted in depth or a trapezoid slanted in depth. Both groups generalized habituation more to a frontoparallel object of the same real shape than to a frontoparallel object differing in real shape but matching the projective shape seen in the habituation period.

As in the case of size constancy research, these reports of planar shape constancy do not address the depth information underlying the observed performance. The objects were stationary, so motion perspective would be a possible source of information in principle, but newborns seldom make the required head movements, due to their poor neck strength (and the use of restrictive head and neck support). As we conjectured in our discussion of newborn size constancy, convergence is the likely source of distance information. Testing this hypothesis remains a priority for future research.

Position Constancy and Motion Perception

Another perceptual outcome dependent on distance information is seeing objects as remaining stationary (position constancy) or moving during motion of the observer (Gogel, 1982). Evidence suggests that infants as young as 8 weeks of age use distance information to determine which optical displacements indicate real object motion and which are consequences of stationary objects viewed during observer motion (Kellman & von Hofsten, 1992; Kellman, Gleitman & Spelke, 1987). The ability to discriminate moving and stationary objects was eliminated when infants viewed the displays monocularly, suggesting that convergence may also provide the distance information underlying this ability (Kellman & von Hofsten, 1992). We explore this topic further in chapter 6.

CONCLUSION

Views of the origins of space perception have been dominated by Berkeley's legacy, almost to the present. While varying in particulars, empiricist or constructivist positions have held that visual stimulation is inadequate to produce accurate depth perception and that reliance on other information, such as tactual sensations or action, is required to interpret vision. At the extreme, even the ability to detect spatial relations in two-dimensional images was sometimes theorized to arise from associative learning.

The emerging picture of early space perception renders all versions of these views obsolete. Neurophysiological findings indicate that the visual system is hardwired to preserve two-dimensional spatial relations from retina to visual cortex, and studies of pattern perception (see chapter 4) indicate that pattern sensitivity begins to operate very soon after birth. These discoveries alone might necessitate only minor repairs in the traditional view that space must be constructed from experience. But our revised picture is most revolutionary regarding the third dimension. The experimental evidence is clear in showing that human beings live in a three-dimensional perceptual world from birth. Not only do newborns perceive visually in three dimensions, but their perceptual systems appear organized to combine distance information with other information to determine important object attributes, such as size, shape, and motion. These findings require a new view of spatial perception as fundamentally based on inborn and rapidly maturing neural machinery for extraction of information about objects and arrangements in the three-dimensional environment.

Neither our description of early competence nor the mechanisms underlying it are complete, however. Some of the astonishing experimental demonstrations of infant spatial knowledge need to be followed up by research that makes clear what sources of information underlie infant performance. This is particularly true in the case of size and shape constancy. These spatial abilities require some degree of metric information about space, as opposed to merely ordinal depth information, and binocular convergence is emerging as the likely source of distance information in these cases. The case for convergence is largely circumstantial, however, and more direct evidence is needed. Berkeley may have been right in suggesting the importance in space perception of the muscular information from convergence. Its power to specify depth may be a result of inborn mechanisms and not learning, however. Motion-carried information about space appears to operate from the beginning, as shown, for example, by responses to kinematic information for approach. More study is needed here as well to uncover the origins of abilities to use the various kinds of kinematic information, especially motion perspective, which allows the newborns of some other species to perceive space. Perhaps our clearest developmental picture of the emergence of a depth-processing system is seen in stereoscopic depth perception. The rapid onset of stereoscopic acuity around 16 to 18 weeks of age, along with evidence for innate mechanisms for binocular vision in other species and knowledge of cortical maturation in humans, are all consistent with a mauturational account of this important depth perception ability in humans. Arising latest, sometime in the second half-year of life, are the pictorial cues to depth. Whether they depend on maturation, learning, or some combination is unknown.

The diversity of information sources contributes to the complexity of space perception. Adults use the full repertoire to comprehend spatial arrangements under varied circumstances, from viewing distant mountains to viewing a mosquito near the tip of one's nose. Our survey has revealed that the young infant perceives space three-dimensionally but uses only a subset of the tools available to the adult. Can we find any organizing theme in the progression of development? We raised earlier the idea that the infant perceives less comprehensively than the adult but must perceive *accurately*, so that early learning rests on a secure foundation. On this notion, the earliest-appearing sources of information might be those that have the highest ecological validity. This notion is consistent with the relatively early emergence of kinematic and binocular information (convergence and stereopsis). Because they are based on differences in the optical projection to different observation locations (a moving eye at two different points in time or the observer's two eyes at a single point in time), their ecological validity is high. In contrast, pictorial depth information is far more ambiguous and arises much later in development.

This attempt to connect developmental priority with ecological validity is conjectural. It is not clear how we might obtain definitive evidence for or against it. We might consider the conjecture to be strengthened if it fits the pattern of development in other perceptual domains having multiple sources of information. Object perception (chapter 5) is such a domain, and we revisit the ecological validity conjecture there.

Note

1. The exact formula, required when Θ is not small (that is, when distance is not large relative to object size), is

$$\Theta = 2\arctan(S/2D).$$

Chapter 4
Pattern Perception

Space as we have considered it so far is the container and arranger of objects and events. At smaller scales, spatial variation also defines objects and their properties, such as their shapes, textures, and local features. Spatial variation in the optical projections to the eyes also conveys the topography of surfaces. Figure 3.7 illustrates the power of fine-grained spatial variation. Even on a flat piece of paper, the impression of complex bumps and crevices in a surface is vivid.

We see a different function of pattern variation in figure 4.1a. Here similarities and differences of pattern elements lead to the grouping of elements into surfaces and their separation from adjacent surfaces. Such processes allow the *segmentation* of scenes into objects, beginning with the discovery of edges, where surface properties change in an abrupt manner. This kind of variation guides attention, as we can see in figure 4.1b. A single element "pops out" if it differs from surrounding elements. In such cases the time needed to detect the differing element does not increase with the number of surrounding elements (Neisser, 1964).

The difference between the target and background elements in this example lies in a spatial relationship. Both types of elements are composed of identical vertical and horizontal line segments, but their spatial arrangement differs. Perception of such configural relations is perhaps the defining idea of *pattern perception.*

In this chapter we examine the origins of human pattern perception abilities. Spatial structure in two-dimensional patterns has been the subject of many studies, and our inquiry must necessarily be selective. These studies have been conducted for many different reasons. Originally, much interest in two-dimensional pattern perception stemmed from a belief that three-dimensional object perception grows out of two-dimensional form perception. This idea turned out to be wrong, as we will see. Yet work on pattern perception has produced many interesting and useful results, some relevant to perception of objects and others informative about perception of surface texture, orientation, and other spatial properties. We treat sensitivity to two-dimensional pattern variables here and reserve for chapter 5 research that bears directly on three-dimensional object perception.

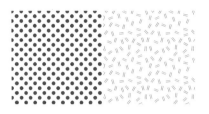

(a)

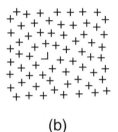

(b)

Figure 4.1
a. Surface segregation by texture. b. An illustration of attentional "pop out". The backward L is easily detected against the background texture of plus signs.

ECOLOGY OF PATTERN PERCEPTION

The ecology of pattern perception is multifaceted; important spatial relationships come in many varieties and contribute to many perceptual tasks. One unifying issue in the study of pattern perception involves the question of basic units or building blocks in perception. If we can perceive and represent an indefinitely large class of objects and patterns, these must somehow be constructed from sets of elementary constituents, limited in number. The key to understanding the flexibility and complexity of pattern and object perception might lie in the elementary pattern features and combination rules in early perception.

An early assault on this problem was Hebb's (1949) influential theory of cell assemblies and phase sequences. Complex perceptual structures were asserted to be based on neural connections built up from visual scanning of patterns in the outside world. The lowest level elements in this view were individual neural units coding specific locations. Basic features, such as an object corner, might emerge as eye movements along edges activate individual cells sequentially, causing them to become linked into *cell assemblies*.

Later visual scanning of a whole shape might lead to the formation of con-nections among these cell assemblies into a shape representation.

In the 1960s, neurophysiological work made it clear that the visual sys-tem starts out with a richer encoding of spatial variables (Hubel & Wiesel, 1962, 1965). Evidence that single neurons in the visual cortex are tuned to oriented edges, bars, and corners suggests that at least these spatial fea-tures need not be built through scanning or other experience. One inter-pretation of these findings was that they reveal innate building blocks of form perception. The possibility of such an elementary feature vocabulary was often embraced in models of pattern recognition for some time afterward.

As it turns out, the initial stage of visual filtering does not furnish directly the edges and corners of perceived objects. Instead, it appears to consist of an analysis, carried out in parallel across the visual field, of local orientation, contrast, spatial frequency, and motion. This analysis pre-serves spatial information but does not make it explicit. Indeed, the domi-nant view of this early stage of vision is that it performs in each local region a *Fourier* or *spatial frequency analysis* of the spatial luminance distri-bution. Any pattern of luminance can be uniquely analyzed as a combina-tion of sinusoidally varying luminance components of different frequencies (number of dark and light cycles per spatial unit), orientations, and ampli-tudes (contrasts). From these components, the original image could be re-constituted. Such a representation of the luminance distribution, however, could only be the input to perceptual analysis, not its result. A spatial fre-quency analysis does not make explicit objects, arrangements, or events in the external world.

Even the simple operation of locating object edges may not be accom-plished by the outputs of single units in V1, the first visual cortical area. The fact that the visual system samples independently at different spatial frequencies means that a single abrupt edge of an object activates several different frequency channels. Figure 4.2 illustrates the situation. Detectors of different frequencies will signal the transition from dark to light at the position and orientation of the edge. These several responses are excellent raw material for edge detection, but edge detection would seem to require a subsequent mechanism that integrates information from these multiple channels (Marr & Hildreth, 1980; Olzak & Thomas, 1991). An even more daunting problem is that early visual analysis furnishes positions and ori-entations in the two-dimensional image and not the positions and orienta-tions of features in the three-dimensional world. In short, the basic features needed for object perception or pattern recognition have to be synthe-sized further along in visual processing. The nature and origins of these mechanisms are not well understood.

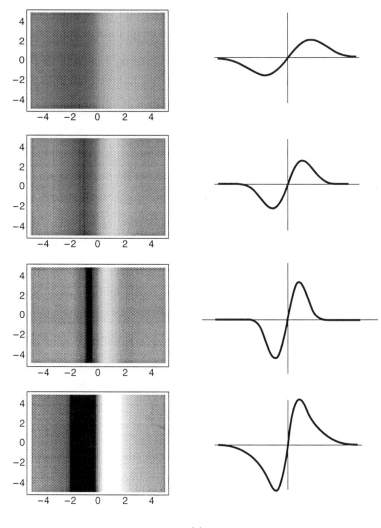

(a)

Figure 4.2
Relation of object edges, spatial frequency components, and spatial phase. The top three shaded panels in (a) and (b) show luminance profiles that would activate cortical detectors of sinusoidal variation at different spatial frequencies. To the right of each panel is a graph of its luminance profile. (Luminance is given on the y axis for horizontal positions given on the x axis.) The bottom panel shows the sum of the three luminance profiles above. a. Abrupt luminance edge shown at bottom is the sum of the three different spatial frequency com-

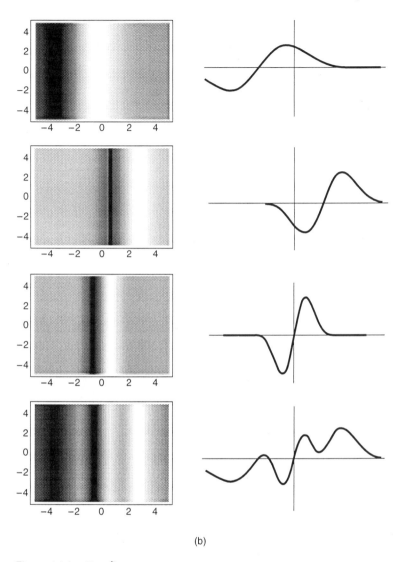

(b)

Figure 4.2 (continued)

ponents shown above it. The bottom pattern would maximally activate vertically oriented channels at different frequencies all having the same spatial phase (that is, positioning with respect to the edge). b. The same luminance components as in (a), shifted in phase. Their sum (bottom panel) does not show a sharp edge, and activation of the several channels in this case should not signal a sharp edge.

This background, although incomplete, gives us some useful ways of thinking about the development of pattern processing by human infants. On the one hand, we might find that infants start out with the basic filtering operations of early vision, indicated by sensitivity to orientation and spatial frequency. They may lack mechanisms of perceptual organization that allow processing of relations, such as configuration, symmetry, or depth. On the other hand, higher-level mechanisms for relational perception might come as part of the infant's initial vision package, in which case we should be able to find sensitivity to configuration, symmetry, and shape variables, and the infant would be much better equipped to process meaningfully the objects and structures in the outside world.

PATTERN PERCEPTION ABILITIES AND PROCESSES

Attention to Patterns

Infant attention is the means by which the experimenter accesses the infant's perceptual world. At minimum, an infant's attention must be attracted to the displays for most experimental methods to succeed. Beyond this, distinctive differences in infants' attention to various objects and events give us some idea of what game the infant is playing, so to speak. At any age, we can think of the infant as being involved with different perceptual tasks or having different priorities, determined by available perceptual capacities, knowledge (or lack of it), and motivation. We can gain some clues to these priorities and ask our own questions about perception by considering infants' attentional preferences.

Fantz, who developed the visual preference method (Fantz, 1958, 1961), conducted groundbreaking research on attentional preferences among patterns. He found that high-contrast stimuli were most effective in eliciting attention. Infants also preferred complex patterns and shapes. In descending order, infants most attended to a schematic face, newsprint, bull's eye, red circle, white circle with black outline, and a gray circle (see figure 4.3). In general, curved lines and edges attract greater attention than straight ones, and multiple concentric circles are especially attention attracting (Fantz et al., 1975). The effectiveness of a high-contrast bull's-eye has led some to speculate that this stimulus preference might reflect an innate mechanism for facilitating eye contact between the infant and other people.

Since Fantz's early work, a number of investigators have attempted to understand what underlies infant pattern preferences (see Fagan, 1979; Banks & Salapatek, 1983; and Olson & Sherman, 1983, for reviews). This work reveals important facts about infants' visual sensitivities and attention.

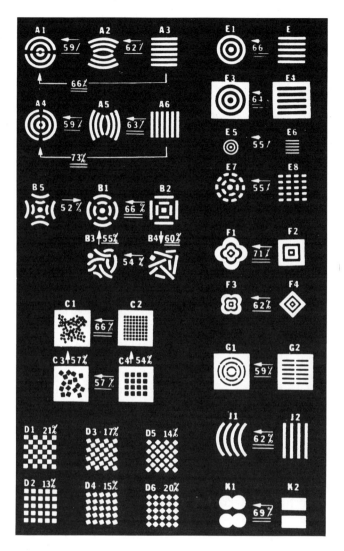

Figure 4.3
Stimulus patterns used by Fantz et al. (See text.) Reprinted with permission from Fantz, R. L.,
Fagan J. F., & Miranda, S. B. (1975), Early visual selectivity, in L. B. Cohen & P. Salapatek
(Eds.), *Infant perception: From sensation to cognition* (New York: Academic Press).

Pattern Complexity and Attention
Several studies have suggested that infants' attention varies with display complexity. In displays having multiple elements or repetitive features, such as checks in a checkerboard or turns in a random shape, attention increases with the number of features or elements up to some level and decreases with additional increases in complexity (Olson & Sherman, 1983). Preference for greater numbers of elements appears as infants get older. Likewise, in repetitive patterns, such as checkerboards, there may be an optimal size range or contour density that maximizes attentiveness (Karmel, 1974).

Studies of preferences related to pattern complexity provide rather indirect information about perceptual processes. An observed preference implies that the infant can see the difference between two stimuli; beyond that, it is hard to tell whether preferences reflect differences in activation of local sensory mechanisms or whether they indicate perceptual organization—that is, experience of the pattern as having a shape or configuration. What we would like to know is whether infants' responses reflect only the barest functions of early visual analysis or whether they reveal perception of configural relations. Several lines of research have sought to answer these questions.

Consider the patterns shown in the top half of figure 4.4, used by Fantz and Miranda (1975) to study newborns' pattern preferences. Members of each pair were equated in terms of several variables (black and white areas, total length of contours, element and angle numbers), except for the pair in column II. One-week-old infants preferred the curved member of each pair except for the pair in column IV, for which no reliable preference was shown. The investigators concluded that the preferences indicated form and contour discrimination by newborns.

Linear Systems Analysis
An alternative explanation is possible, however. Infants might distinguish the patterns based on any difference they pick up; perhaps there are differences between pattern pairs that do not require contour or form perception per se. Earlier we noted that a visual pattern may be analyzed as a set of sinusoidal luminance components having particular orientations, amplitudes, and frequencies. Moreover, it appears that the earliest cortical stage of visual processing may consist of this type of analysis (for a review, see DeValois & DeValois, 1988). There are some interesting features of such an analysis that make it a plausible candidate for what happens in early visual processing and that also make it interesting to determine the visual system's response to sinusoidal luminance patterns even if these were not explicitly encoded in our nervous system. It is worth

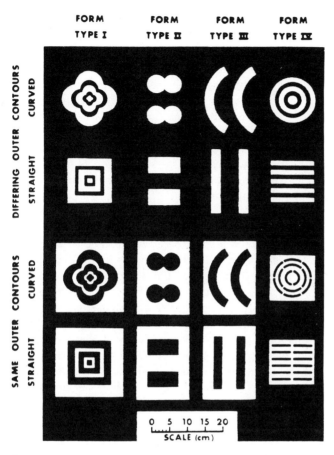

Figure 4.4
Curved versus straight-contoured stimulus pairs used to test newborn perception of form. Reprinted with permission from Fantz, R. L., & Miranda, S. B. (1975), Newborn infant attention to form of contour, *Child Development, 46,* 224–228.

spending a moment to describe these features, the elements of *linear systems analysis.*

A linear system is one that obeys two constraints, *superposition* and *homogeneity.* Superposition can be defined as follows. For any inputs *a* and *b* and outputs $f(a)$ and $f(b)$, the system satisfies the relationship

$$f(a + b) = f(a) + f(b).$$

In words, the response to a combination of two inputs equals the sum of the responses to each input separately. Homogeneity is the condition that

$$f(n * a) = n * f(a),$$

where *n* is any scalar (multiplier). That is, for an input multiplied by any quantity *n*, the system's response is the same as would be obtained by taking the system's response to the input alone and multiplying that output by *n*. Of the two conditions, superposition is more basic. (Except for some technicalities, homogeneity is derivable from superposition.)

An example of a linear system is a scale measuring weight. If two weights are placed on the scale at the same time, the measured weight should equal the sum of each measured separately. An example of a nonlinear system is a stack of some compressible items, such as lemon meringue pies. The height of twelve pies stacked on top of each other probably will not be twelve times the height of a single pie (and the whole experiment will make quite a mess).

The properties of linear systems make them easy to deal with mathematically. Moving from pies to visual displays we are concerned with patterns of luminance distributed across space. We assume that besides being linear, the system is *shift invariant*, which means that if the input is shifted in space or time by a particular amount, the output is shifted by the same amount (for details, see Wandell, 1995). If a system meets these criteria, then it has the interesting property that any sinusoidally varying input will produce a sinusoidal output of the same frequency. The action of the system can alter only the amplitude (intensity at that frequency) and phase (position of the beginning of a cycle). Now here is the reason (one reason, at least) that we are interested in sinusoidal patterns. The mathematician Fourier proved that any complex pattern can be broken down into a unique set of sinusoidal components. If a system is linear, therefore, we need only know how it affects sinusoidal components at each frequency to characterize the system completely. That is, we can know the system's response to any complex pattern if we know its response to sinusoidal inputs of different frequencies, called the *modulation transfer function* of the system. The procedure consists of mathematically analyzing any input pattern into its amplitude spectrum (how much contrast at each frequency) and then altering the amplitude of each frequency component as specified by the modulation transfer function. At this point, we would have the output amplitude spectrum—a representation of the magnitude of response of the system to the particular pattern for various orientations and spatial frequencies. (To reconstitute the image passed through the system we would also need the phase spectrum, which records the particular positioning of the amplitude components.)

To a reasonable approximation, human visual filtering through the first visual cortical area appears to satisfy the requirements of a linear system. This not only provides us with a powerful tool for understanding how an input pattern is encoded up to a certain point in visual processing but suggests an hypothesis about early pattern sensitivity. It is possible that early in development only the outputs of this first stage of processing are functional. Thus, a pattern viewed by a neonate may produce activations in a population of detectors sensitive to various orientations and spatial frequencies. Instead of perceiving an organized pattern and responding to its configural features, an infant's attention on this view might be guided by gross features of the amplitude spectrum, such as the sum of activations of the various detectors stimulated by a pattern.

Some evidence suggests that infant pattern vision starts out this way (Banks & Ginsburg, 1983; Atkinson et al., 1977a). Banks and Ginsburg (1983) investigated how a variety of experimentally observed infant pattern preferences might be explained by using simple measures based on the Fourier amplitude spectra of patterns, after filtering these in accordance with the infant's (estimated) contrast sensitivity function. Very simple indices, such as the maximum-amplitude component of a pattern and a total-energy measure (summing the squared amplitudes of the components) turned out to be good predictors of published data on pattern preference for 1- to 3-month-old infants.

Attention to patterns based on component amplitude information does not require locating object edges. It is important to note that the predictive variables used by Banks and Ginsburg (1983) included no phase information. *Phase*, the relative spatial positions of the pattern components, would appear to be essential to locating an edge rather than a collection of sinusoidal components. Figure 4.2 illustrated the role of phase relations in edge detection and showed that with different phase relations, patterns composed of the same spatial frequencies appear very different to adults. Direct tests of infants' discrimination of patterns having identical Fourier amplitude spectra but differing in phase were carried out by Braddick, Atkinson, and Wattam-Bell (1986). Before 2 months, they found no evidence of phase sensitivity. Both edge detection and classification would be hard to accomplish without some sensitivity to phase.

Sensitivity to Configuration

Behavioral evidence on edge and pattern perception in the first months of life is not entirely consistent. Although pattern preferences seem to be predicted to a large extent by general activation measures obtained from linear systems analyses, there are other clues that edges and forms are perceivable by newborns.

Looking again at figure 4.4, Fantz and Miranda (1975) found different results for the patterns in the bottom half of the figure. When all displays were enclosed by a white square, newborn pattern preferences disappeared. This effect appears to depend on the capture of attention by the outer contour of a pattern (Bushnell, 1979; Fantz et al., 1975; Haith, 1978).

Such an effect would not obviously be predicted by characteristics of the Fourier transforms of these patterns. Instead, it might indicate some processing of pattern organization per se. On the other hand, it might imply some simple scanning rules that govern infant fixation (Haith, 1978).

Configural Processing of Faces

Some of the most systematic research on configurational perception has centered on face perception. The emphasis is natural given the importance of faces and observations that infants show strong preferences for faces and facelike stimuli.

In studies of newborns by Fantz et al., facelike stimuli were among the strongest attractors of attention. But a display with scrambled face parts did not fare much worse. Maurer (1985) cites twenty-eight studies that investigated infants' preference for a normal face versus a face with the internal features rearranged or deleted. Before 2 months, infants do not show a preference for either type of display, but after 2 months of age, infants show a clear preference for a "normal" face over a "scrambled face." For truly configurational perception, an important change appears to occur around 2 months of age.

A deeper explanation of these early preferences has been suggested by several investigations applying linear systems analysis to early face preferences (Kleiner, 1987; Kleiner & Banks, 1987; Dannemiller & Stephens, 1988). The motivating question is whether observed preferences might be explained by the outputs of the earliest cortical stages of visual analysis— that is, the responses of units based on contrast, orientation, and spatial frequency. If so, early responses to faces would not imply social interest or even true pattern perception. Responses, as we described above, may be governed by some rule about the population of frequency detectors stimulated by the pattern.

An interesting method for testing this possibility was devised by Kleiner (1987). She used two stimuli, a face and a lattice (bricklike pattern). Using the Fourier transform, she obtained the amplitude and phase spectrum of each. She then generated two new images combining the amplitude spectrum of the lattice pattern with the phase spectrum of the face, and vice versa. These combinations have the effect of using the amplitudes (amount of contrast) for frequency and orientation components of one pattern but shifting their relative positions according to the phase relations taken from the other pattern (see figure 4.5). To adults, the displays "looked" like the stimulus whose phase spectrum was used. This occurs because the positional relations that create edges, corners, and other features are more crucial to pattern perception than having the correct amount of contrast for each amplitude component.

(a)   (b)

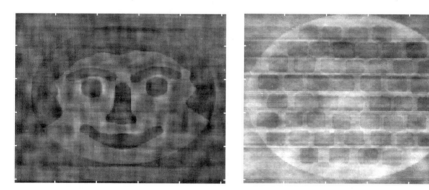

Figure 4.5
Stimuli used to test phase and amplitude information in infants' face perception. a. Amplitude and phase spectra of a face pattern. b. Amplitude and phase spectra of a lattice. c. Amplitude spectrum of the lattice and the phase spectrum of the face. d. Amplitude spectrum of the face and the phase spectrum of the lattice. Reprinted with permission from Kleiner, K. A. (1987), Amplitude and phase spectra as indices of infants' pattern preferences, *Infant Behavior and Development, 10,* 49–59.

These unique displays allowed Kleiner to test two competing hypotheses—that infants' preferences for faces are based on their structure (because they look like faces) or that infants' preferences depend on the high-contrast values generated by faces in their amplitude spectra. On the latter hypothesis, pattern preference might be predicted by simple rules, such as the total energy in the amplitude spectrum or the strongest single component in the amplitude spectrum. Kleiner and Banks (1987) called this idea the "sensory hypothesis" and contrasted it with the "social hypothesis" that infants have some built-in sensitivity to the structure of faces.

The specific predictions were as follows. On the sensory hypothesis that fixation preferences are governed by greater total amplitude of stimulation, patterns with the amplitude spectrum of the face (figure 4.5a and 4.5d) should be preferred to patterns having the amplitude spectrum of the lattice (4.5b and 4.5c) because phase should be irrelevant. On the social hypothesis that preferences involve facial structure, patterns 4.5a and 4.5c should receive the most attention because the phase relations in these patterns preserve the structural information characteristic of faces. Results with newborns (mean age = 1.7 days) were mixed. On one hand, pattern 4.5d was preferred to pattern 4.5c, a result interpreted as indicating the irrelevance of phase information (Kleiner, 1987; Kleiner & Banks, 1987; Dannemiller & Stephens, 1988). On the other hand, in preference trials pitting pattern 4.5a against pattern 4.5d, infants looked at pattern 4.5a 69% of the time, quite a lopsided result for a pattern preference study. On the sensory hypothesis, no difference was predicted.

These results have prompted a great deal of discussion (Badcock, 1990; Morton, Johnson & Maurer, 1990; Kleiner, 1990; Dannemiller & Stephens, 1988; Morton & Johnson, 1991). Badcock (1990) criticized Kleiner for a step used in stimulus preparation. After the amplitude spectra for the patterns had been obtained, they were subjected to "amplitude normalization," a procedure ensuring that a comparable range of gray values appears in the different displays. This procedure changes the amplitude spectra and may make the predictions unclear (Badcock, 1990). Mitigating this problem is the fact that the amplitude spectrum from the face, even after amplitude normalization, was always preferred in the results of Kleiner (1987).

More important, the results clearly show some sensitivity to phase information by newborns, evidenced by the preference for the normal phase stimulus over one with the same amplitude spectrum and differing phase information. This result may indeed indicate some innate visual attraction to human faces (Morton & Johnson, 1991), since it is otherwise unclear why one set of phase relations should be better than another. The failure of phase alone to induce a pattern preference (for pattern 4.5c over pattern 4.5b) suggests some limitation of early face processing. The results show an interaction in that newborns require both the amplitude and phase spectra of faces to display a face preference.

Kleiner and Banks (1987) tested 2-month-old infants with the same displays to see if the linear systems model predicts older infants' preferences. In contrast to newborns, 2-month-olds preferred the displays with the phase spectrum of a face—that is, the display that looks facelike to adults. A developmental shift was also found in a study by Dannemiller and Stephens (1988) on the role of contrast in infants' face preferences. They assessed infants' preference for a schematic face and the same face reversed in contrast. At 6 weeks of age, infants showed no preference, but at 12 weeks they preferred the face with the appropriate contrast.

In sum, research suggests that some preference for faces and facelike patterns is innate. Like a number of basic sensory abilities we considered in chapter 2, this tendency is weak and difficult to demonstrate in the first days of life. A more general and robust determinant of newborn pattern preferences appears to be the Fourier amplitude spectra of two-dimensional luminance patterns. Or, putting this more physiologically, it appears that overall activation levels in the cells of V1, where the earliest cortical visual processing occurs, strongly affect attentional preferences. By about 8 weeks, sensitivity to true pattern characteristics appears to become more dominant.

Symmetry

Well documented at least since the time of the Gestalt psychologists has been the special sensitivity of human visual processing to symmetry. Rubin (1915) noted symmetry as one factor influencing perception of ambiguous figure-ground displays (see figure 4.6). More generally, it has been argued that we tend to perceive the simplest, most symmetric organization consistent with the available information (Wertheimer, 1923/1958; Buffart, Leeuwenberg, & Restle, 1981). Some phenomena that seem to involve a tendency toward symmetric perception may be explained by the operation of more local mechanisms (Marr, 1982; Kellman & Shipley, 1991); thus, the status of symmetry as a causal variable in perceptual organization remains unclear. Yet it seems clear that symmetry is readily detected and that symmetric stimuli are more easily or quickly processed (Adams, Fitts, Rappaport & Weinstein, 1954; Garner & Sutliff, 1974; Pomerantz, Sager & Stoever, 1977). Even without knowing the exact mechanism, we can say that human vision exploits symmetry in detecting or encoding patterns.

Facility with symmetric patterns might be thought to arise from experience in perceiving and classifying objects. After all, animals are usually

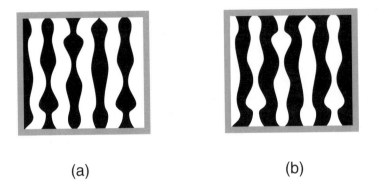

(a)   (b)

Figure 4.6
Symmetry in figure-ground organization. Symmetric black regions in (a) and white regions in (b) tend to be seen as figures rather than backgrounds.

bilaterally symmetric, and plants may have symmetry along more than one axis. There are indications, however, that sensitivity to symmetry is more deeply rooted in visual functioning, appearing quite early in infancy. Bornstein, Ferdinandsen, and Gross (1981) found that 4-month-olds habituated more quickly to a display having symmetry around the vertical axis ("vertical symmetry") than to a horizontally symmetrical or asymmetrical display. They also found that infants generalized habituation from one vertically symmetrical display to another, although they appeared less sensitive to horizontally symmetric displays. The advantage of vertical symmetry was explored further by Bornstein and Krinsky (1985). They recorded the number of 10 sec trials needed for 4-month-old infants' looking time to decline 50% from initial levels. For vertically symmetrical patterns (figure 4.7), they found a mean of 6.8 trials, as compared to 16 to 18 trials needed to habituate to the other patterns shown in figure 4.7.

The pattern of greater sensitivity to vertical symmetry shown by infants is also characteristic of older children and adults (Bornstein & Stiles-Davis, 1984; Mach, 1985/1959; Barlow & Reeves, 1979; Royer, 1981). It has been speculated that this advantage may be related to the bilateral symmetry of the visual system (Mach, 1885/1959). Another possibility is that an evolved sensitivity to vertical symmetry efficiently exploits informational redundancy in the natural world. In nature, vertical symmetry is most common—among plants, animals, and even the shapes of surfaces, such as hills and valleys. This predominance of vertical symmetry on the forms of nature is the handiwork of gravity, constraining biological priorities such as balance and locomotion, as well as as geological phenomena, such as erosion.

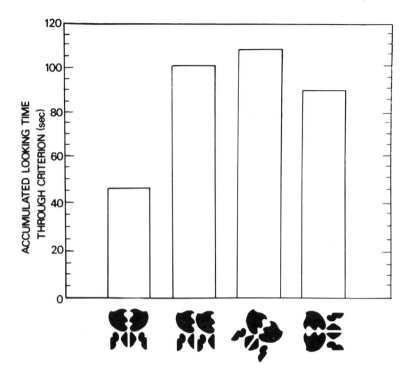

Figure 4.7
Habituation time for patterns varying in symmetry and orientation. Reprinted with permission from Bornstein, M. H., & Krinsky, S. J. (1985), Perception of symmetry in infancy: The salience of vertical symmetry and the perception of pattern wholes, *Journal of Experimental Child Psychology, 39*, 82–86.

Pattern Invariance

At the turn of the last century, Gestalt psychologists effectively criticized the dominant view of perception—that perceptions were aggregates of sensations. A cornerstone of their critique was the *transposition* argument: a form or pattern is not adequately defined as a set of sensations because the form can remain unchanged even if its constituent sensations change. Figure 4.8 illustrates several types of transposition. The "squareness" of the form remains despite changes in the retinal location of the form, whether it is large or small, whether it is made up of small circles or thin lines or changed in orientation.

Although the Gestalt critique came bundled with a nativist view of how the nervous system apprehends form, arguments about the nature of form and about its origins in perceptual development are two different things. Form may be an abstraction, but a process to do the abstracting

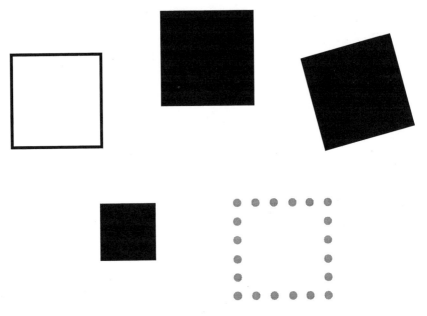

Figure 4.8
Examples of transposition. The form quality of squareness is preserved and easily seen, despite changes in size, location, and constitutent elements. (See text.)

may or may not be within the perceptual repertoire provided to humans by evolution. A notion of form might involve relating some more elementary inputs, such as pattern features or even the eye movements required to scan a form (Hebb, 1949; Sutherland, 1961; Salapatek, 1975). Infants do appear to scan forms in rather systematic ways, such as fixating angles and contours (Kaufman & Richards, 1969; for a detailed review of infant scanning patterns, see Haith, 1980).

Infant perception of form similarity across orientation was tested in a series of studies by Schwartz and Day (1979). Figure 4.9 shows the stimuli used in one experiment. Infants age 9 to 14 weeks were habituated to the figure shown in 4.9a and tested afterward for visual attention to the other three displays. Results in figure 4.10 are typical of those reported by Schwartz and Day. There was no reliable difference after habituation in looking times to 4.9a and 4.9b, identical patterns differing only in orientation. A pattern having similar constituents in a similar orientation (4.9c) received the most dishabituation, and pattern 4.9d also received more dishabituation than 4.9a. Results of their studies led Schwartz and Day to conclude that pattern invariance is perceived by infants by 9 to 14 weeks. Moreover, their results also indicated that infants detect orientation differences as well as pattern identity.

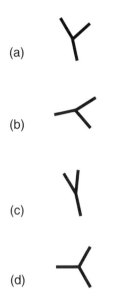

(a)

(b)

(c)

(d)

Figure 4.9
Displays used to test infants' perception of form similarity across changes in orientation. Redrawn with permission from Schwartz, M., & Day, R. H. (1979), Visual shape perception in early infancy, *Monographs of the Society for Research in Child Development, 44,* 63.

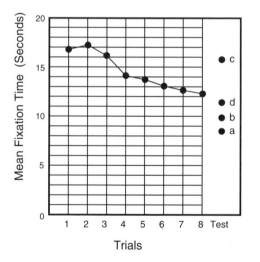

Figure 4.10
Mean fixation times during habituation and test trials in an experiment on orientation and form perception. Displays were those shown in figure 4.9. Infants were habituated to figure a and tested with figures a, b, c, and d. Redrawn with permission from Schwartz, M., & Day, R. H. (1979), Visual shape perception in early infancy, *Monographs of the Society for Research in Child Development, 44,* 63.

Subsequent research (Cohen & Younger, 1984) tested younger infants (6 weeks of age) with angle patterns made from two intersecting line segments (similar to the stimuli used in one of Schwartz and Day's experiments). After habituation infants viewed an identical pattern as well as two others, one of which had line segments of the same orientation in a different relation. With 12-week-old infants, they found evidence for pattern invariance. At 6 weeks, however, they found that infants responded to the orientations of particular line segments making up the patterns rather than the overall pattern itself. It appears that pattern invariance, at least for these angle stimuli, develops between 6 and 9 weeks.

The Externality Effect

Consider a display made of two shapes, one inside the other, such as a rectangle inside a circle. When infants younger than 2 months are presented with such a display, they seem to notice only the outer shape. This phenomenon was labeled by Milewski (1976) the *externality effect*. It was first identified in studies of infants' scanning by Haith, Bergman, and Moore (1977), Maurer and Salapatek (1976), and Salapatek and Kessen (1966, 1973). Infants at 1 month of age scan the external contour of a face, whereas 2-month-olds scan both internal and external features. Similarly, with simple geometric displays, 1-month-olds tend to restrict their fixations to the external edges of the display (Salapatek & Kessen, 1966, 1973).

Milewski (1976) investigated the externality effect using an operant paradigm in which visual displays were presented contingent on the infant's sucking on a nonnutritive nipple. One- and 4-month-old infants participated in three segments. In a baseline phase, infants' sucking rate was monitored in the absence of any visual stimulus. An amplitude criterion was set for each subject at approximately the median of his or her baseline sucking amplitudes. Following the baseline phase, infants were familiarized with a line drawing of a circle embedded in a square. Following familiarization, infants were presented with a test display that had either a novel external shape, a novel internal shape, both a novel external and internal shape, or no change. Four-month-olds responded to changes in all three change conditions with an increase in sucking amplitude. One-month-olds, on the other hand, responded only to the displays with novel external shape. Milewski suggested two possible explanations for this effect—attentional processes and poor acuity. To test for acuity limitations, Milewski presented another group of 1-month-olds with small and large single shapes. These were the same sizes used in the first study, but they were not compound figures. These infants responded to the changes in shape regardless of size. In another control study, Milewski tested for possible interference between contours of internal and external figures by increasing the separation between internal and external components. Still, with this increased separation, 1-month-old infants provided no evidence of discrimination of changes in shape.

Based on further studies showing that 1-month-olds fail to detect a *change* in a small object adjacent to a larger one, Milewski (1978) concluded that infants have an attentional bias toward larger figures.

To study further these attentional issues, Bushnell (1979) used displays in which the internal element *moved* independently. In a habituation of looking procedure, 1- and 3-month-old infants were presented with compound figures in which the internal element either oscillated or flashed. He found that both age groups responded to a change in the internal figure. In addition, no differences were found in responsiveness of the groups that viewed a flashing element or a oscillating element. In another study, infants viewed compound displays in which the whole array oscillated. Under these conditions, 1-month-olds provided no evidence of detecting a change in the shape of the internal element. Thus, it appears that relative movement of the internal element draws attention to its shape.

Bushnell's (1979) data are also consistent with an object segregation hypothesis. Perhaps infants attend to object edges rather than textural variations within an object. Enclosure by a contour may be used as information that an area consists of one object. Differential motion of an internal area, however, might be a more powerful determinant of perceived segregation (see chapter 5).

Ganon and Schwartz (1980) attempted to increase the salience of the internal target by making it more attractive without moving it. They used four compound figures—a bull's eye or a 2 × 2 checker board embedded within either a triangle or a square. Using a design similar to Milewski (1976), Ganon and Swartz found that 1-month-olds discriminated the internal target. These results suggest that target salience can overcome the normal effects of relative size and position on infants' attention.

Global versus Local Processing
Related to the effects of target size and position may be other results involving visual patterns made of smaller pattern elements. For example, a large letter A can be composed of small Ls with small spaces between them. A *global* response would be that the display is an A, whereas a *local* response would be that the display is a collection of Ls.

Ghim and Eimas (1988) investigated infants' responses to such stimuli. Three- and 4-month-old infants were presented with large squares, diamonds, Xs, and crosses made of small squares, diamonds, Xs, and crosses.

After familiarization with one shape, infants were tested for visual preferences for the familiar display and a novel display differing with respect to global form or constituent elements. Ghim and Eimas found that both age groups looked longer at the novel displays, suggesting that they are able to process and remember both local and global information available during familiarization.

To our knowledge this work has not been extended to younger infants. Given the parallels between the externality effect and the processing of global versus local properties, it is likely that infants younger than 2 months would respond to global but not local changes.

A progression from responding to outer contours or large objects to sensitivity to smaller or internal detail would be consistent with Eleanor Gibson's (1969) view of perceptual development and perceptual learning as a differentiation process, in which experience leads to extraction of finer detail. Given the maturational changes occurring around 8 weeks in attention and basic visual processing, however, it is hard to pinpoint differentiation learning as the cause of this progression.

CONCLUSION

Infant sensitivity to surface and pattern arrangements itself forms a clear pattern, consistent across the various lines of research. There is an early period, extending 6 to 8 weeks, in which pattern sensitivity can be documented but only by the most painstaking efforts of researchers. Following this period, infants exhibit a wide range of pattern perception abilities, including sensitivity to orientation, configuration, symmetry, and both internal as well as external features.

To this pattern of development, a maturational explanation is best suited. Various competencies that appear weak in newborns appear robustly after 6 to 8 weeks. The evidence seems incompatible with the idea that neural mechanisms for encoding configuration must be constructed from scanning or other associative operations, as has often been suggested (Hebb, 1949; Sutherland, 1961). Likewise, accounts based on learning by manipulation or locomotion cannot explain early pattern perception because infants in the first few months do not yet reach, crawl, or walk.

What do we know about mechanisms of change in the first 6 to 8 weeks of life? As we discussed in chapter 2, it has been argued that before about two months the human infant processes visual information only subcortically (Bronson, 1974, 1982; Johnson, 1990). Subcortical processing allows directing the gaze based on stimulation outside the fovea, but true pattern vision requires the maturation of the visual cortex around

2 months. Johnson (1990) has elaborated this hypothesis to account for some evidence that newborns respond to pattern information. He suggests that cortical processing is occurring in very young infants, but they cannot act on the information because connections between the cortex and motor systems are immature. At least some of the data we have considered indicate the newborn can act to some degree in deploying visual attention to patterns that are processed in the visual cortex and beyond. But the evidence is equally clear in indicating some deficit or bottleneck in such abilities.

The most frequently suggested bottleneck hypothesis is immaturity of visual cortical areas and of connections between cortical and subcortical structures (Johnson, 1990; Bronson, 1974; Atkinson et al., 1988). Improved processing at 6 to 8 weeks is thought to reflect myelination of the retinocortical pathway. Explosive growth of synaptic connections is also underway by two months of age (Huttenlocher, 1994). Particularly important might be myelination of connections between interacting areas. Casaer (1993, p. 106) hypothesized that "It is, however, not myelination as such which is important but rather whether centres in the brain which are intensively interacting are provided with fast signal-conducting pathways. The exciting developmental idea is the concept of myelination as highways connecting growing cities."

The evidence is on the whole consistent with idea that improvements in overall speed or processing capacity allow more sophisticated use of previously established mechanisms. This development would be analogous to a computer program that runs slowly or in limited fashion until a faster central processing unit (CPU) and more random access memory (RAM) are installed. It is telling that in each domain—orientation, faces, pattern invariance, and so on—experimenters have been able to detect in newborns the basics of later abilities. We saw in chapter 3 evidence that newborns perceive true object size despite differences in distance and planar shape despite different three-dimensional slants. These achievements require pattern processing of considerable sophistication. It is possible that future advances will allow us to identify particular information-processing components that are truly new at 8 weeks, but the current picture is consistent with the idea that a main effect of cortical maturation is to boost the power of abilities whose basic neural machinery is already in place. The human newborn is not merely a subcortical visual processor. Nor do configurational processing abilities appear *de novo* at 2 months as a result of learning or maturation. Rather, cortical maturation appears to provide the speed and capacity needed to make pattern processing more effective or, alternatively, to provide better voluntary control over visual attention that allows infants to demonstrate their abilities to experimenters.

One early motivation for studying two-dimensional pattern perception was that it would provide a window into the development of perception of three-dimensional space and objects. This goal has not been realized. There is no reason to believe that static two-dimensional displays are somehow simple or primary. In looking at results showing pattern discrimination, we can be confident that one pattern differs perceptually from another. We may be curious, however, as to whether a figure is seen as separate from ground or whether a single two-dimensional view can evoke a percept of a three-dimensional object, as in adult perception. Little progress on these questions has come from studying pattern perception. These are different questions, and they must be asked in different ways. We turn next to these issues of object perception.

Chapter 5
Object Perception

It is an interesting exercise to glance around a room, close one's eyes, and then attempt to remember what one has seen. In a certain room, one may remember a lamp, television, sofa, some small pillows, a notepad, and a pair of shoes. It is striking that our inventory of the environment consists primarily of *objects*. Object perception reveals the physical units in the environment—where the world comes apart. It enables predictions about interactions and events. When the two-year-old daughter of one of the authors tugs at her father's elbow, his hand is sure to follow, but the cup he is holding may not stay with his hand, and the coffee inside will surely not remain with the cup.

In obtaining knowledge about units in the physical world, vision is most important. The visual system is specialized for the extraction of spatial detail, and the interactions of light with surfaces allow us to gain precise and detailed knowledge from a distance. The packaging of much of this knowledge in terms of objects gives both a reasonable account of the physical world and an efficient vocabulary for cognition.

Any attempt to understand how object perception comes about quickly reveals that it is a complex and remarkable achievement. The physical linkages and three-dimensional arrangements of visible areas are not given by simple or obvious properties of reflected light. Rays of light do not cohere or connect to each other as do the parts of objects that reflect them. How we recover the structure of the environment from information in the light is the focus of studies of object perception.

ECOLOGY

The Relativity of Objects

From a great distance, the planet earth appears as an object, but ordinarily we experience it as an extended surface, not a bounded object. At the other extreme, a single molecule of a substance may be composed of a number of atoms, but neither the molecules nor the atoms are objects of ordinary perception. It appears that being an object depends on the observer and her attributes and purposes. Are objects, then, physical units, psychological units, or somehow both?

Objects are *ecological* units (cf. Gibson, 1966, 1979): they depend on both the organism and the environment. Specifically, objects are physical units that exist in restricted niches in terms of spatial extent, temporal duration, and their coherence relative to physical forces. The relevant ranges of extent, duration, and cohesion depend on the organism's (in this case, human) capacities and behavior.

- *Spatial scale*   Spatially, objects, such as rocks, leaves, chairs, and shoes, are bounded volumes of matter pertinent to the size and manipulative abilities of humans. In general, things that are large relative to the human body tend to be represented as surfaces rather than objects. It is interesting to consider that the objectness of certain things may change with growth and development. To an infant, a sofa may be large enough to be more or less a terrain feature, like a hill. The sofa is more objectlike to adults large enough to lift and carry it.

- *Temporal scale*   The philosopher Nelson Goodman suggested that "An object ... is an event with a relatively long temporal dimension" (Goodman, 1951, p. 129). When we characterize an object as functionally coherent, we mean that during events, such as moving or lifting, the entity retains its unity. But this coherence is conditioned on duration. The coffee mentioned earlier coheres momentarily with the flying cup before making its dramatic exit. At the other extreme, it is unlikely that over centuries the ceramic cup will remain intact as a unit. What counts as an object is thus tied up with events: an object is a physical unit whose persistence in time is long relative to the duration of human actions.

- *Forces*   The coherence of an object is considered relative to the forces involved in events. It is not an object if small biomechanical forces easily break it up; a clump of mashed potatoes is not an object. On the other hand, a ceramic cup is a perfectly good object because it survives ordinary human manipulation, even though it does not withstand being dropped on a hard floor. The relevant range of physical forces seems inescapably ecological. Perceived objects are the physical units that cohere through ordinary human activities.

- *Partial objectness*   There are ambiguous cases. A tree rooted in the ground is neither freely moveable nor fully integral with the earth. Touching a countertop with quick-drying glue on one's fingertip, the fingertip and countertop may now cohere as strongly as the fingertip and the rest of the finger. These cases might suggest that our description of the environment in terms of objects is somewhat arbitrary. Many ambiguous cases nevertheless have a physical basis, in terms of homogeneity of composition, the nature of the forces producing cohesion, and so on. It would be a mistake not to consider the tree and its roots a coherent object, since for many purposes (such as planting) it is one. And with the right solvent, your finger may be unglued from the countertop.

We have not exhausted the issues involved in defining objects and their ecological basis, but we have created a serviceable framework. Objects are physically cohering, bounded volumes of matter at a scale and across the transformations relevant to human activity.

The Task of Object Perception in Infancy

Parallel to our remarks about the ecology of space perception, the functions of object perception early in life differ from those that emerge later. This difference in the functions of object perception in infancy and later on may have consequences for the emergence of object perception abilities (Kellman, 1993). Adults perceive objects from a variety of sources of varying ecological validity. The diversity of information sources may allow adults to act adaptively under the widest range of situations. In a given situation, some sources of information may not be available, but others will be. Some information may be tentative or somewhat uncertain, but the perceiver's need to make a rapid response may require using what is available. Moreover, ongoing perceptual activity may allow the adult to correct errors. For the infant, the situation is the opposite. There is little capability for split-second action and less opportunity for active exploration. Consequences of erroneous perception might be greater in infants, whose general knowledge is limited. These consequences will involve not ineffective action but inaccurate data for the infant's developing comprehension of the world. The infant may not correct errors as well because its options for moving and exploring are limited. Evolutionarily, a premium may be placed on an ontogenetic sequence in which information of highest ecological validity comes to function earliest (Kellman, 1993). As we will see, the order of emergence of object perception abilities is consistent with this conjecture.

Information and Constraints

Defining objects is one thing; perceiving them is quite another. The facts of object perception are remarkable and challenging. Following our definition, we might imagine that objectness is determined by acting on candidate objects. Does it hold together as we move it? Does it separate from adjacent things? It is striking that these sensible tests for discovering objects play a negligible role for adult perceivers. We need not manipulate objects to perceive them. This faculty broadens our horizons of action and knowledge unimaginably. But it is mysterious. How are we able to partition the world accurately from information in reflected light (and in some cases from information in other ambient energy)? Perhaps this faculty depends on an earlier developmental stage in which objectness is determined by direct manipulation. On the other hand, at maturity, this faculty must be based on information of some sort, available when the perceiver views a scene at a distance. If there is information out there, might its use be hardwired in the nervous system rather than learned?

Multiple Components of Object Perception

Understanding object perception and its origins involves understanding multiple achievements. Light reflected to the eyes does not explicitly indicate the physical linkages and three-dimensional arrangements in a scene. The optic array does contain information, but much must be done to make this information explicit. As a revealing example, consider the standard representation of an image used in computer graphics. Such a *digitized image* consists of numbers for each location (pixel) indicating a gray-level value or three spectral component values (for a color image). Imagine poring over a printout of these values trying to determine the separate objects in the scene, their shapes, sizes, spatial arrangements, and so on. It is obvious that the pixel map contains no explicit information whatsoever about objects. The representation is silent about whether any two pixels come from the same or different objects in the scene.

To get the kinds of representations—of objects—we obtain perceptually, we must accomplish several different tasks. As we examine these components of object perception, we will see that each, in turn, can be based on multiple sources of information. With this profile in hand, we can determine the young infant's status with regard to various object perception abilities. Infants, it turns out, get an early start down the road of object perception, but their vehicle is a stripped-down model compared to what adults' drive. The picture of early competence and late-appearing abilities, moreover, reveals an intelligible overall pattern.

Edge Detection, Edge Classification, and Boundary Assignment

Projections to the eyes, and pixel maps as well, must contain information, or we could not perceive. What must be done to make that information explicit—to reach a representation that features objects, their boundaries, shapes, and so on? *Edge detection* is the first step. Which locations in the optic array might be object boundaries? Edge detection is based on locating various kinds of discontinuities in the optic array. Since objects are often made of different materials, luminance, color, and texture tend to be homogeneous or smoothly varying within a single object but often change abruptly from one object to another. Boundaries are also given by discontinuities in depth and in motion (Julesz, 1971; Gibson et al., 1969; Shipley & Kellman, 1994).

Not all discontinuities, however, correspond to object boundaries. In the case of luminance discontinuities, some are textural markings or shadows on surfaces. Depth and motion discontinuities may occur within a unitary object, when it is partly self-occluding. Edges once detected must therefore be classified into these functionally different categories, a process called *edge classification*. Next there is *boundary assignment*. Visible contours most often correspond to a boundary of one object, whereas the surface on the other side of the contour continues behind (Rubin, 1915; Koffka, 1935). When one sees a tree in front of a house, the contour between the tree and house bounds only the tree; the house continues behind. If there were a tree-shaped hole in the surface of the house, the boundary assignment would be reversed—that is, the house would be bounded, and an interior wall seen through the hole would pass behind. Boundary assignment is crucial to perceiving objects; it is an important part of the answer to Koffka's (1935) classic question: Why do we see things and not the spaces between them?

Depth and motion discontinuities at boundaries are some of the best specifiers of boundary direction. Of the two surfaces whose optical projections meet at the contour, the one whose points have greater depth values (that is, whose points are farther away) are on the surface that passes behind. During object or observer movement, accretion and deletion of texture specifies depth order, and once again, it is the nearer surface that "owns" the boundary.

UNIT FORMATION AND THE FRAGMENTATION PROBLEM

Spatial Fragmentation   Solving the riddles of edge detection and classification would be a great achievement but only a small step toward a full account of object perception. We have not yet introduced the hardest problem, what might be called the *fragmentation problem*. The spatial continuity and temporal persistence of objects contrasts with their fragmentary effects on our senses. Most objects are partly *occluded* by other objects. This problem was implicit in our description of boundary assignment. At each location where a boundary bounds one surface, another surface slips behind to destinations that are optically unspecified. A glance at the scene around you reveals how pervasive these effects are. For every object boundary you see, part of another object or surface is hidden at that location. How can the observer recover the structure of three-dimensional

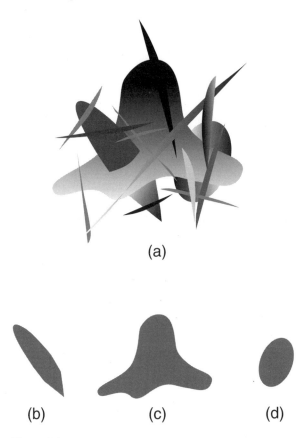

(a)

(b)   (c)   (d)

Figure 5.1
Example of perceptual unit formation despite spatial fragmentation. The unoccluded objects shown in (b), (c), and (d) are readily perceived in (a) despite the numerous instances of partial occlusion and luminance variation. Reprinted with permission from Kellman, P. J. (1996), The origins of object perception, in R. Gelman & T. Au. (Eds.), *Handbook of perception and cognition: Cognitive and perceptual development* (New York: Academic Press).

objects from optical input when virtually every boundary in the input specifies a location at which some part of an object or surface goes out of sight?

Somehow we manage. Consider the display shown in figure 5.1. Without special effort or reflection, the display in 5.1a may be seen to contain three large objects. Their shapes are shown in 5.1b, 5.1c, and 5.1d. Intermingled with these objects are a number of thin objects resembling blades of grass. Each of the grasslike objects is also seen as a bounded object. With effort we can count them and find that there are 12. Far more daunting is the task of counting the number of homogeneous regions that connect to form each object. The shape in 5.1c as it appears in 5.1a is formed by combining 11 regions separated by occluding surfaces; object 5.1d is formed from 8 regions; and object 5.1b from 5 regions. It is a revealing fact about the function of human visual perception that its outputs are complete objects and not the shapes of visible regions.

We have only scratched the surface of the perplexities in figure 5.1a. Here are a few more. The regions we have been referring to as homogeneous are really not in any simple sense; most have gradients of luminance (changing shades of gray). As is common in ordinary environments, widely separated and differently colored visible regions may belong to a single object. The perception of whole objects, rather than such separate regions, cannot be explained by familiarity; the shape shown in figure 5.1c, for example, was designed to be unfamiliar and could hardly be considered more familiar than many smaller regions in the image. Not all areas of similar luminance are seen as connected. In the figure there are several examples of object boundaries that traverse areas identical in luminance; these are *illusory contours*. One example is the midsection of the "blade of grass" at the top of figure 5.1a. An even more curious phenomenon occurs for the object in figure 5.1b. As it appears in figure 5.1a, this object passes through the surface of another object. Seeing it as one object requires linking separated parts into a unit that pierces the other object.

The ubiquity of partial occlusion derives from very basic facts: light moves in straight lines, most objects are opaque, and environments usually contain objects at different distances from the observer. Luckily, human perceivers possess visual processes equal to the physical demands of occlusion: in figure 5.1a, they turn the chaos of 45 projected regions into 3 objects and some stray foliage.

Temporal Fragmentation So far, we have described spatial fragmentation, but fragmentation occurs across time as well. As we move through an environment, the bits and pieces of objects that reflect light to the eyes and the occluded parts constantly change. Because visual acuity is relatively poor outside of the fovea, we also sample stationary environments over time with frequent changes of gaze. We may have a particular view of an object for 100 or 200 milliseconds, or perhaps as long as several seconds, but seldom much longer. Human perceivers recover objects' continuity despite temporal fragmentation. Understanding how visual processes accomplish this poses a great challenge.

Information for Unit Formation What information is available about connected objects in the world? Valuable types of segmentation and grouping information come from motion. Motion is closely related to the notion of an object (Spelke, 1988); to be an object is to maintain coherence during movement. A connected entity's parts are constrained; they may move only in certain ways while remaining connected. For three-dimensional rigid objects, projective geometry allows us to precisely characterize what optical changes can occur as the objects move through space (Braunstein, 1976; Johansson, 1970; Ullman, 1979). Nonrigid objects produce a greater variety of projective changes, but the class of transformations is still limited by the connectedness of the object. Conversely, certain optical transformations are not consistent with the possibility that two viewed areas are part of the same object.

A number of other stimulus relationships that play a role in perception of object unity were articulated by the Gestalt psychologists, who were the first to seriously wrestle with problems of unit formation (Wertheimer, 1923/1958; Koffka, 1935; Michotte, Thines & Crabbe, 1964). Motion's role was expressed as a principle of *common fate*: things are grouped together if they move together. Other principles applied to stationary arrays. The principle of *good continuation* holds that a straight or smoothly changing contour comprises a unit, whereas an abruptly changing one may not. *Good form* suggests that optical input is organized so that simple, symmetrical objects are perceived. Similar parts are unified according to the principle of *similarity*, and nearby things are grouped by *proximity*. These principles were explicitly applied to the problem of recovering unity of partly hidden objects by Michotte et al., (1964).

The Gestalt descriptive principles do not permit precise or quantitative predictions, and most of the key terms in the Gestalt laws resisted formal definition for most of this century. These include the "good" in good continuation and good form, and the notions of simplicity, common fate, and similarity. Nevertheless, the principles contained important insights, most of which could readily be illustrated.

Two Processes in Unit Formation   Some contemporary work has made progress in giving more precise form to the Gestalt principles. Kellman and Shipley (1991) proposed dividing information for unity into two categories—the *rich* or *edge-sensitive* (ES) process and the *primitive* or *edge-insensitive* (EI) processes.

The latter process elaborates Wertheimer's (1923/1958) idea of *common fate*. Visible areas that share certain geometric classes of motion relationship are grouped together. The class of rigid motions (motions that preserve interpoint distances in three-dimensional space) is certainly included, but certain nonrigid motions might be included also. The process is edge insensitive because the positions and orientations of the edges of visible parts play no role in determining their completion behind the occluding object. This information does not specify the exact form of the hidden parts under occlusion. For this reason Kellman and Shipley (1991) labeled it the "primitive process" (cf. Hebb, 1949).

Partly Occluded Objects   Illusory Objects

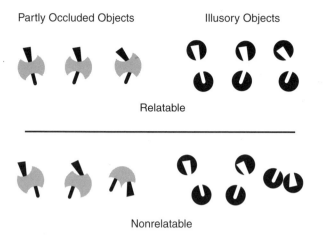

Relatable

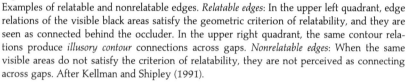

Nonrelatable

Figure 5.2
Examples of relatable and nonrelatable edges. *Relatable edges*: In the upper left quadrant, edge relations of the visible black areas satisfy the geometric criterion of relatability, and they are seen as connected behind the occluder. In the upper right quadrant, the same contour relations produce *illusory contour* connections across gaps. *Nonrelatable edges*: When the same visible areas do not satisfy the criterion of relatability, they are not perceived as connecting across gaps. After Kellman and Shipley (1991).

The ES process depends on edge positions and orientations, both in stationary and moving displays. Many of its formal properties, and some of its neural mechanisms, have been elucidated in recent years (Kellman & Shipley, 1991; Shapley & Gordon, 1987; von der Heydt, Peterhans & Baumgartner, 1984; Field, Hayes & Hess, 1993; Polat & Sagi, 1993). The input-output relations in this process may be thought of as a mathematical formalization of the Gestalt principle of good continuation—that is, that segmentation and connection of parts depend on straight lines and smooth curves. Detailed models of the ES process may be found elsewhere (Kellman & Shipley, 1991, 1992; Grossberg, 1994). For our purposes, two points are most important. First, for adults, certain edge relationships support object completion (such edges are termed *relatable*), whereas others do not. Figure 5.2 gives some examples of relatable edges and nonrelatable edges. The definition of edge relatability is a mathematical one, but it can be understood intuitively as expressing the constraints that boundaries constructed by the visual system are smooth (that is, they contain no sharp corners), are monotonic (they are singly inflected), and do not bend through more than 90 deg (Kellman & Shipley, 1991). Second, the boundary interpolation process at work in occlusion cases is the same as in illusory figures (Shipley & Kellman, 1992a; Ringach & Shapley, 1996;

Kellman, Yin & Shipley, in press). This identity allows us to obtain converging evidence on the developmental origins of the ES process.

Experimental evidence supports the relatability criterion as a description of the ES process (Kellman & Shipley, 1991; Shipley & Kellman, 1992a; Kellman et al., in press), although there may be additional constraints on unit formation. This account of unit formation emphasizes local edge tangents and their relations, rather than more global processes, such as overall symmetry of resulting objects or familiarity of objects, in the process of boundary perception. It thus differs from both Gestalt accounts and empiricist or associationist accounts. In contrast with rather open-ended inference or hypothesis-testing accounts (Gregory, 1972; Rock & Anson, 1979), the process appears to be governed by more autonomous mechanisms, consistent with evidence that completion and illusory contour formation are based on early visual processing (von der Heydt et al., 1984).

Three-Dimensional Form Perception
Once unit formation is complete, objects are segregated from surrounding surfaces, and remaining aspects of object perception have to do with their specific properties. Of these, *three-dimensional form* is especially important, since much of what we do with objects depends on their forms. Even in cases where some object property other than form, such as edibility, is most important, it is by means of form that we recognize objects.

Adults perceive three-dimensional form from at least three different sources of information, and each of these stands as the canonical example for a theory of form perception. We often perceive—or recognize—the whole form of a familiar object from a single, static view. From past experience, we may know what a certain three-dimensional object looks like from a particular viewpoint. This means of perceiving form illustrates John Stuart Mill's (1865/1965) definition of an object as "the permanent possibilities of sensation." On this view, the object's three-dimensional reality consists of its various retinal projections from different viewpoints. With experience associating the various views, each comes to evoke the set of possible views (as well as other object properties, such as the feel of the object).

The Gestalt theorists also emphasized form perception from a single view, but for radically different reasons. Even unfamiliar objects could be perceived this way because the two-dimensional stimulation sets in motion organizational forces in the nervous system that lead to perception of simple, regular, three-dimensional forms. The proposed neurophysiology connected to these ideas seems implausible today, but we might still argue that form perception depends on unlearned organizational tendencies. On the other hand, Brunswick (1956) suggested that these tendencies might be acquired by experience with object regularities.

Despite the centrality of form perception in perceptual theorizing over two hundred years, a wholly different kind of information has been discovered and analyzed just in the past several decades. This is the information given by continuously changing optical projections, often called *structure from motion* (Ullman, 1979) and originally called the *kinetic depth effect* (Wallach & O'Connell, 1953). As an object rotates or as an observer walks around an object, the projection to the eyes deforms. The observer does not see a deforming two-dimensional projection, however. Rather, the transformations are seen as a three-dimensional object of unchanging shape that is rotating in space. As we noted above, for a rigid object, the particular set of transformations received at the eye can be deduced using projective geometry from the structure of the object and the relative motion between object and observer. (This is the basis for generating three-dimensional computer graphics and television commercials in which household products seem to fly through outer space.) However, the task of vision is the reverse—to recover the object's three-dimensional structure from the optical transformations received. Under reasonable assumptions, these transformations in principle allow recovery of three-dimensional object structure (Gibson, 1966, 1979; Johansson, 1970; Ullman, 1979).

Size Perception
Detecting the physical size of objects requires relational information. The projected size of a given object varies as a function of its distance from the observer. Thus, a straightforward way of detecting physical size would be to combine projected size with information about viewing distance. As we considered in chapter 1, another source of information for objects resting on a ground surface might be relationships between projected size and ground texture.

Perception of Tangibility and Substance
We have saved for last one of the most important properties of all—perception of the *tangibility* or *substance* of objects. The study of perceived tangibility is not far advanced. J. Gibson (1966, 1979) made a number of insightful observations on this topic. Ordinary rigid surfaces tend to have visible surface texture; detecting these surfaces is important because they offer support for locomotion. Homogeneous surfaces, such as the glassy surface of a quiet lake, often do not offer support for standing or walking. Likewise, rigid relationships hold between elements on a surface of support, but nonrigid motions, such as those given by an undulating surface, can provide information that walking is not feasible.

We now have in hand a sketch of the components of object perception and of the information and constraints that makes each possible. Our taxonomy looks something like this:

1. Edge detection
2. Edge classification
3. Boundary assignment
4. Unit formation
5. Three-dimensional form perception
6. Size perception
7. Perception of substance

This breakdown is helpful in appreciating the multiple tasks involved in extracting objects and their properties from optical information. It does not represent a linear sequence of operations performed in perceiving objects. Although some steps logically precede others (for example, edge detection precedes edge classification and boundary assignment), others may have a more complex relationship, such as unit formation and boundary assignment (Kellman & Shipley, 1991). Still others are listed in no particular order, such as size and substance. Breaking object perception into these components does not constitute a sequential model but equips us to usefully examine the origins of object perception, which we now proceed to do.

ABILITIES AND PROCESSES

Edge Detection

There have been virtually no developmental studies directly concerned with edge detection or edge classification abilities. We can, however, make some reasonable inferences about the early status of these abilities from other research.

In chapter 4, we reviewed infant sensitivity to differences among two-dimensional shapes and patterns. Taken at face value, discrimination between two shapes might be interpreted as implying at least edge detection and possibly edge classification. To define shape, it might be argued, an edge must be classified as a surface boundary rather than a shadow or textural marking. This conclusion is not obvious, however. Recall our discussion of linear systems analysis. A pattern could be detected in terms of its Fourier components, and any detectable difference in the amplitude spectra of two patterns might be a sufficient basis for distinguishing them.

Other research, however, suggests an early capacity for perceiving object edges and much more. Previously, we discussed the findings of

Slater and Morison (1985) and Slater, Mattock, and Brown (1990) on new-born shape and size constancy. These abilities strongly imply that new-borns can detect and classify edges under at least some circumstances. If the planar shape of an object is perceived despite its three-dimensional slant, the perceiver must represent that object as bounded and situated in three-dimensional space. A similar argument can be made from the size constancy results. If real object size is perceived across a range of distances and projective sizes, as the newborn results suggest, the object's boundaries must be registered.

What is the basis for early edge detection? Both luminance edges and depth discontinuities (between object and background) were available in the Slater et al. studies. In other research suggesting edge detection, such as some studies of face perception, only luminance differences were present. Kinematic information also appears to specify edges as early as tested. Kaufmann-Hayoz, Kaufmann, and Stucki (1986) habituated 3-month-old infants to a shape specified only by accretion and deletion of texture. Their subjects dishabituated to a different shape, also specified by accretion and deletion.

There is currently little information on the limits of early edge detection abilities. Pattern perception research has typically used high-contrast boundaries. We can guess from our discussion of contrast sensitivity in chapter 2 that much of the fine detail and many low-contrast edges perceptible by adults are not detectable by infants. On the other hand, adult sensitivity far exceeds the minimum required for normal perception of objects and events, and infant sensitivity improves quickly from birth to about 6 months.

Edge Classification

Early shape perception may imply edge detection, but edge *classification* is less clearcut. Infants do appear to have an early capacity for classifying edges as object boundaries when depth or motion discontinuities exist at those edges. The newborn shape and size constancy results are probably as convincing for edge classification as for edge detection because the results appear to presuppose that detached objects (having shapes and sizes appropriate to their three-dimensional positions) were perceived. Regarding motion, accretion and deletion of texture allows shape perception (Kaufmann-Hayoz, Kaufmann & Stucki, 1986). This result does not necessarily imply edge classification, but other research indicates that 5- and 7-month-olds reach preferentially for the edges of objects specified by accretion and deletion.

Strikingly, there is a possibility that luminance and chromatic edges do not specify object boundaries until a relatively late age. When a shape of one color (and lightness) is seen against a background of differing color, adults ordinarily see the (projectively) enclosed area as figure and the surrounding surface as ground (Rubin, 1915). It is not clear that this is the case for infants. Instead, they may see the shape as a differently colored region on a continuous surface rather than as a separate object.

Some observations made by Piaget (1954) may be the earliest indications of this perceptual limitation. When Piaget's child Laurent was 6 months, 22 days old, Piaget noted that

> Laurent tries to grasp a box of matches. When he is at the point of reaching it I place it on a book; he immediately withdraws his hand, then grasps the book itself. He remains puzzled until the box slides and thanks to this accident he dissociates it from its support. (pp. 177)

Piaget concluded that Laurent did not segment the array into separate objects when it was stationary. In other words, visible luminance edges may not be classified as object boundaries. Piaget estimated that such segmentation abilities may not arise until around 10 months of age.

Piaget's observations might be subject to other explanations. Later experiments, however, have supported his account. Adjacent object displays were studied by Spelke, Breinlinger, Jacobson, and Phillips (1993). Some displays were homogeneous in that adjacent parts had identical luminance, color, and texture, and the parts' boundaries were continuous at their intersection points. Other displays were heterogenous: two adjacent parts differed in luminance and color, and they had discontinuities (T junctions) at their points of intersection. Infants were familiarized with a display and then viewed an event in which either both parts together or only the top part of the array was lifted. Longer looking time, relative to a baseline condition, to the event in which only the top part moved was interpreted as evidence for perception of the original array as a single, connected object. Three-month-old infants responded as if they perceived both the homogeneous and heterogenous displays as connected. Five- and 9-month-olds' results were ambiguous but consistent with some use of luminance or boundary discontinuities as information about object boundaries. Other research (Yonas & Arterberry, 1994) indicates that 7-month-olds discriminate differences in line ends that mark surface boundaries from line ends that occur as textural markings within a surface.

Von Hofsten & Spelke (1985) addressed similar issues using infants' reaching behavior. Five-month-old infants were presented with displays consisting of a small, near object, a larger, farther object, and an extended background surface. In some conditions the larger object moved, either rigidly with the background surface or with the smaller object. It was assumed that reaches would be directed to perceived boundaries of graspable objects (usually the one perceived as nearest in an array) (Yonas & Granrud, 1984). Spatial and kinematic relations between the objects were varied, and infants' reaches were recorded. Much as Piaget (1954) had observed, when the array was stationary and the objects were adjacent, infants reached more to the edges of the larger, farther object. This result suggests that infants perceived the two objects as a unit and distinguished the unit from a large extended background surface (as Piaget had also noticed). Separating the two objects in depth, however, led infants to reach more to the nearer, smaller object. Motion also produced object segregation: when the larger object moved differently from the smaller object, more reaches were directed to the smaller object. This clever manipulation excluded the possibility that infants merely reach for visible moving surfaces: motion of the larger, farther object increased reaching for the smaller, stationary one. The results support the idea that discontinuities in motion or depth segregate objects, whereas luminance discontinuities and overall shape variables do not. Other research has also confirmed the role of motion-carried information in infant object segregation (Granrud, Yonas, Smith et al., 1984).

Functionally, these results make sense. Some sources of object boundary information have higher ecological validity: they more accurately indicate physical separation in the environment. Depth and motion discontinuities are less ambiguous than luminance and color changes. The latter may arise from object boundaries but also from textural variation on continuous surfaces. Early edge classification appears to fit the theme that more valid information sources arise earlier in perceptual development.

If we are correct in hypothesizing an early stage in development in which luminance or color edges do not mark object boundaries, when adjacent objects begin to be parsed based on their surface qualities and what brings about this developmental advance remain important questions for future research.

Boundary Assignment

If an object is seen in front of another object or background, boundary assignment has occurred. The bounded object "owns" the visible contour; the other visible surface continues behind. Evidence that infants distinguish shapes, or figures from grounds, might indicate that they compute boundary assignment. A perceived shape may demarcate an aperture or hole rather than an object, however, making conclusions about boundary assignment difficult.

We may consider the Slater and Morison (1985) shape constancy result as suggesting both edge classification and boundary assignment, probably from discontinuities in depth at object edges. Accretion and deletion of texture also looks like a good candidate; in the Granrud, Yonas, Smith, et al. (1984) study, infants reached for the surface specified to be nearer by accretion and deletion. Of course, the youngest infants in this study were five months (a necessity with a reaching method because directed reaching emerges at 4 to 5 months); infants of this age may have had considerable opportunities for learning.

Studies of infants' defensive responses to approaching objects might offer a window into earlier boundary assignment capabilities. Even very young infants have been reported to show head withdrawal, eyeblinks, and hand raising to approaching objects (Yonas, 1981; Schiff, 1965). There have been interpretive controversies (see chapter 3), but on balance the evidence indicates that some observed responses, especially blinking, indicate defensive behavior (Yonas et al., 1979). Defensive responding to a looming object may imply boundary assignment. The infant might be defending against a substantial object approaching, whereas if boundary assignment were reversed, it would be an approaching aperture. Carroll and Gibson (1981) explored just this issue. They presented 3-month-old-infants with arrays in which all surfaces were covered with random dot texture. In one condition a textured object approached the infant, whereas in the other condition, an aperture (opening in the surface) approached. This difference in physical events was specified by different accretion and deletion effects at the boundaries, which would signal an approaching object or aperture to adults. Infants showed defensive behavior more frequently to the approaching objects than to apertures, suggesting they can perceive boundary ownership from accretion and deletion of texture at this early age.

Unit Formation

At this point, we know that from certain kinds of information, such as depth or motion, young infants parse the world into visible pieces. Each such piece may "own" some of its boundaries but be enclosed at others by occlusion boundaries—that is, boundaries belonging to some nearer object. What abilities do infant perceivers possess to sew together these visible pieces behind their occluders and arrive at representations resembling the real three-dimensional objects in the world?

To study infant's perception of unity under occlusion, Kellman and Spelke (1983) developed a method using habituation and recovery of visual attention. Suppose a partly occluded object such as the one at the top of figure 5.3 is shown on repeated trials during an habituation period. If infants perceive this display as containing a complete object continuing behind the occluder, then they should generalize habituation more to an unoccluded complete object than to an unoccluded display containing separate pieces (corresponding to the visible areas of the object present in the occlusion display). The two test displays are shown at the bottom of figure 5.3.

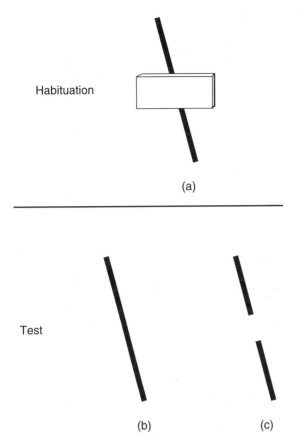

Figure 5.3
Habituation (a) and test stimuli (b) and (c) used to test infants' perception of partly occluded objects. Reprinted with permission from Kellman, P. J., & Spelke, E. S. (1983), Perception of partly occluded objects in infancy, *Cognitive Psychology, 15*, 483–524.

Using this method, perception of object unity and boundaries from both the edge-insensitive and edge-sensitive processes was studied in 16-week-old infants. At 16 weeks maturation of basic visual sensitivities has occurred, but skilled reaching and self-locomotion have not yet begun. Accordingly, unit formation abilities that depend on learning by association of touch or action with visual information should not yet be present.

Common Motion and Edge Relatability
One experiment maximized the information available by providing common motion (which should be usable by the EI process) and edge

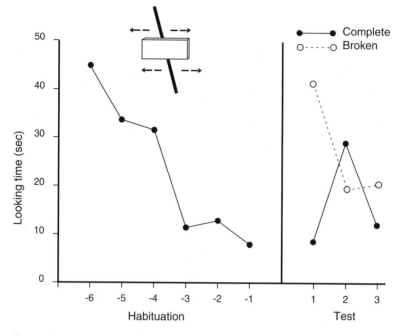

Figure 5.4
Results of experiment testing unity perception from common motion and relatable edges. Infants were habituated to two aligned, visible parts sharing a common lateral translation (pictured at top). Looking times are shown for the last six habituation trials (with the final one labeled −1) and the test trials. Test trials consisted of successive presentations of unoccluded complete and broken displays, with half of the subjects seeing the complete display first. Reprinted with permission from Kellman, P. J., & Spelke, E. S. (1983), Perception of partly occluded objects in infancy, *Cognitive Psychology, 15*, 483–524.

relatability (which should be usable if infants have the ES process). The occlusion display consisted of two visible, aligned parts of a rod that shared a common lateral translation. Infants were habituated to this display and tested afterward with two unoccluded test displays, presented in alternation. The *complete* test display contained a moving complete rod and the *broken* test display consisted of two moving rod pieces separated by a gap where the occluder had been. Results are shown in figure 5.4. After habituation, subjects showed the pattern that would be expected if the occlusion display had been perceived as a unified object: they dishabituated markedly on the first test trial to the broken display but not to the complete display. This study indicated that some unit formation ability operates by 16 weeks of age but did not distinguish the EI and ES processes because information usable by both was presented.

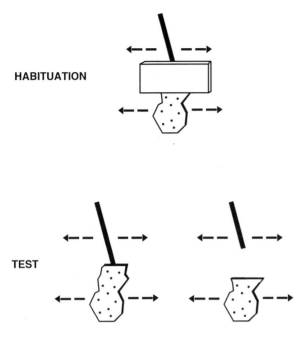

HABITUATION

TEST

Figure 5.5
Habituation and test stimuli used to test infants' perception of unity based on motion relationships apart from edge relatability. Reprinted with permission from Kellman, P. J., &
Spelke, E. S. (1983), Perception of partly occluded objects in infancy, *Cognitive Psychology, 15,*
483–524.

Isolating the Common Motion (Edge-Insensitive) Process

To specify which class of information determines infant unit formation,
Kellman and Spelke (1983) used displays like those shown in figure 5.5.
Protruding from behind the occluder was a black rod at the top and a red
blob-shaped piece with black textural markings. The visible edges of these
two parts were not relatable, nor were they linked according to similarity
or any other Gestalt principle. During habituation, they were moved back
and forth with a common lateral translation. Results were similar to the
first study: infants responded as if the two visible parts were connected
behind the occluder (see figure 5.6). The broken test display, which included only the parts previously visible in the occlusion display, produced
strong recovery of visual attention, especially on the first test trial after
habituation. The complete test display, constructed by continuing the rod
halfway down and the random blob halfway up, induced little recovery
from habituation.

The EI process appears to operate at 16 weeks: common motion alone
specifies object unity. An interesting sidelight of these results is that they

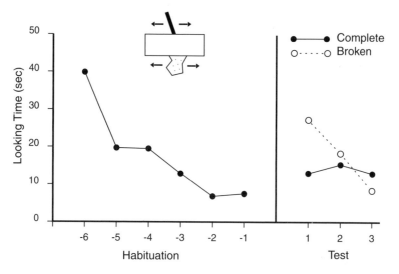

Figure 5.6
Results of experiment testing unity perception from common motion alone. Infants were habituated to two dissimilar, misaligned visible areas that shared a common lateral translation (pictured at top). Looking times are shown for the last six habituation trials (with the final one labeled −1) and the test trials. Test trials consisted of successive presentations of unoccluded, complete, and broken displays, with half of the subjects seeing the complete test display first. Reprinted with permission from Kellman, P. J., & Spelke, E. S. (1983), Perception of partly occluded objects in infancy, *Cognitive Psychology, 15,* 483–524.

occur despite the fact that the specific form of the connection between the two differing visible parts is unspecified in the occlusion display. (The EI process indicates unity but not the specific form of the occluded region.) The complete test display must have contained some novel contours in the region that had been occluded; yet this display evoked little dishabituation. It seems that visual attention in this situation is controlled more by unity or connectedness than by specific form, a conclusion also reached by Craton and Yonas (1990).

What Motion Relationships Support the Edge-Insensitive Process?
Subsequent research (Kellman, Spelke & Short, 1986) sought to specify what motion relationships underlie the edge-insensitive process. They found that rigid translations along any axis (including translations in depth, which are given by quite different stimulus variables) lead to infants' perception of unity.

The use of projective geometric information in rigid translations in object perception is consistent with ecological theories of how perception works and how it gets started (Gibson, 1966, 1979; Johansson, 1970). An even more elegant story would be one in which infant perception utilized the full class of rigid motions—that is, rotations as well as translations. Interestingly, the EI process does not appear to work with rotations in the frontal plane or most combinations of rotation and translation (Kellman & Short, 1987a). Evidence for unity perception was obtained in one condition in which rotation and translation were combined to have the same frequency and phase so that the top and bottom generally moved in the same direction (looking much like a windshield wiper). An incidental and unexplained finding was that infants were totally enraptured by all of the combined rotation and translation displays. Most infants fixated them for the maximum 2 min per trial for 10 to 20 consecutive trials (while the experimenters waited for habituation to occur). This is an enormous amount of visual attention for a young infant, and several parents offered to purchase the experimental apparatus!

It appears that the class of motions engaging the EI process in the early months is not the full class of rigid motions. In particular, common direction of visible parts seems to be required. For adults, the full class of rigid motions, as well as many nonrigid ones, support object unity. When rotations become effective for infants, and whether any nonrigid relations support perceived unity under occlusion, is not yet known.

The Nature of Motion in Unit Formation

In studies of motion in unit formation we have considered so far, the objects have moved. Optical events similar to those given by moving objects can arise from another source—movement of the observer. When a stationary observer views a rightward translating object, its image moves on the observer's retina. The same optical displacement can arise if the observer views a stationary object and moves to the left. This leads us to wonder whether the information for perceived unity is real motion of objects or merely optical displacement, which can arise from either object or observer motion.

This question raises another. Can infants tell the difference between optical changes given by moving objects and moving observers? This discrimination is an important perceptual ability in its own right. Separating optical changes given by observer motion from real object motions is crucial to perceiving the world as remaining stable when the observer moves—an ability called *position constancy*. Many perceptual theorists have suspected that achieving position constancy requires extensive learning. Prior to experience, events of object and observer motion may be confused with each other (Helmholtz, 1885/1925). William James thought this was one reason the newborn's world must "bloom" and "buzz." He believed that for neonates, "any relative motion of object and retina both makes the object seem to move, and makes us feel ourselves in motion"

(James, 1890, vol. 2, p. 173). From experience the observer becomes able to interpret particular optical changes as motion of an object or of the self. Helmholtz suggested that a useful source of information might derive from the fact that observer-induced optical changes tend to be reversible. One can make an object (optically) slide to the left by moving one's head to the right. A moment later one can put everything back in place by moving one's head to the right. When objects move, the changes are not reversible by the observer's action.

Another possibility exists, however. J. Gibson (1966, 1979) noted that the object and observer motion have different optical properties. Object motion produces changes between the object and its background that are in general different from what happens when the observer moves while viewing a stationary array. Given the ecological importance of distinguishing object and observer motion, it is possible that perceptual mechanisms sensitive to such differences exist even in young infants.

These questions—whether infants distinguish optical information for object and observer motion and, if so, which of these provides information for unit formation—were investigated by Kellman et al. (1987). Infants sat in a moving infant chair that was moved back and forth along a wide arc. In a *conjoint motion* condition, shown in figure 5.7a, the infant's chair and a partly occluded object were rigidly connected beneath the display table, so that they rotated around a vertical axis in between. This condition contained real motion of the object in space but no physical displacement relative to the subject. If real object motion underlies unit formation, and if it is detectable by a moving observer, this condition was expected to lead to perceived unity. In the *observer movement* condition, shown in figure 5.7b, the infant was moved in an arc while viewing a stationary occluded rod. If optical displacement alone can specify unity, infants were expected to perceive a complete object in this condition. Unit formation was assessed, as in earlier studies, by dishabituation patterns following habituation to the occluded displays. In the test trials, motion characteristics of the object parts were the same as in habituation—that is, moving in the conjoint condition and stationary in the observer movement condition.

In the conjoint motion condition, marked dishabituation was observed to the broken display, indicating that the occlusion display had been perceived as complete. The effect was consistent across subjects: 15 of 16 infants looked more than twice as long after habituation at the broken test display. In contrast, infants in the observer movement condition showed no evidence of unit formation: they dishabituated equally to the two test objects. Separate analyses, based on looking time differences to moving and stationary displays, suggested that conjoint motion infants perceived

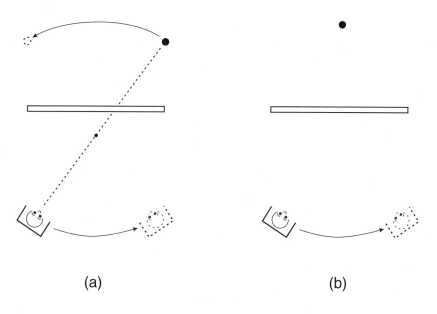

Figure 5.7
Top view of arrangement used to test infants' perception of unity under conditions of observer and object motion. a. Conjoint motion condition. b. Observer motion condition. From Kellman, P. J., Gleitman, H., & Spelke, E. S. (1987), Object and observer motion in the perception of objects by human infants, *Journal of Experimental Psychology: Human Perception and Performance, 13,* 586–593. Copyright © 1987 by the American Psychological Association. Reprinted with permission.

object motion during their own motion, whereas observer movement infants accurately perceived their occlusion display as stationary.

The results indicate that real object motion, but not optical change given by observer motion, supports the EI process. The reliance of unity perception on real motion, not optical displacement in general, makes sense in terms of the ecological validity of the two kinds of information. When two visible parts move through space with an unvarying relationship, they are virtually certain to be connected. Such a rigid relationship between moving objects would not occur by chance for very long. Thus, rigid motion of object parts has very high ecological validity as a specifier of unity. Contrast the information of common motion on the retina as an observer moves. This may occur for any parts of the environment that happen to be at about the same distance from the observer. Although such regions may sometimes be connected, it is hardly guaranteed. Common optical displacement from observer motion does not have high validity in indicating object unity.

The results also provided the first indication that young infants can distinguish optical changes from object and observer motion and that they can perceive moving and stationary objects during their own movement. We have more to say about these aspects of motion perception and position constancy in the next chapter.

Unlearned Foundations of Object Perception?

It is plausible that the edge-insensitive process comprises an unlearned foundation of object perception. It operates early in life. Specific proposals that object perception derives from action- or touch-based learning are disconfirmed because the EI process is detectable before the onset of skilled reaching or crawling. Moreover, common motion of visible areas has very high ecological validity as a signifier of object unity (Kellman, 1993); it rests on basic constraints that have held true throughout evolutionary time, namely the geometry of rigid motion and the fact that unconnected things hardly ever undergo rigid motions. That the EI process emerges earliest in unity perception (see below) also fits our conjecture that early perception should be based on information of highest validity.

Some research, however, suggests that the EI process is not present in newborns. Slater, Morison, Somers, Mattock, Brown, and Taylor (1990) replicated the findings of Kellman and Spelke (1983) with 16-week-olds, but their tests of newborns under identical conditions led to a different result. After habituation to an occlusion display, newborns showed a greater preference for the *complete* object than a broken display.

Because the displays used with 16-week-olds had relatively small depth separations, it was possible that newborns' responses were different because of difficulty in detecting the depth relations in the displays. Subsequent research, however, indicated similar results in several studies in which depth separation of the occluder and partly occluded object were varied (Slater, Johnson, Kellman & Spelke, 1994).

These findings may have two very different explanations (Slater et al., 1994). First, it is possible that newborns lack some basic visual sensitivity needed to detect common motion. We saw in chapter 2 that basic sensitivity to motion direction seems to be lacking before 6 to 8 weeks of age, probably due to immaturity of cortical visual areas (Wattam-Bell, 1991, 1992, 1996a, 1996b; Johnson, 1990). In occlusion situations, a newborn may detect motion but not the directional coherence of separate parts. If so, the visible areas may be perceived as separate, bounded fragments. In other words, the fact that some parts of the array move and others do not may be detectable and may be used to *segregate* objects. Without perception of common motion direction, however, unit formation may not occur.

The second possibility is that infants begin life with an incorrect perceptual rule, assigning occlusion edges as object boundaries (Slater et al., 1990). The "perceptual inference" (Slater et al., 1990) for connecting visible parts based on common motion might have to be learned.

There are reasons to favor the former hypothesis. First, there is evidence that the EI process does function as early as two months of age (Johnson & Aslin, 1995). This timing is right for the directional sensitivity hypothesis because sensitivity is estimated to arise at 1 to 2 months of age. If the EI process is unlearned, it should operate as soon as directional sensitivity operates adequately. On the alternative account, the onset of directional sensitivity would mark the beginning of a learning process. Some time period would be needed in which motions of the separate areas could be accurately encoded so that learning about the motion relations useful for unity perception could proceed. If the EI process is in place by 2 months, the learning process would have to be very rapid.

There are two other problems with a learning account given what is known. One is what constitutes the "truth data"—that is, if visible areas are originally seen as separate, what leads them to be seen as connected and allows induction of the common motion principle? Neither reaching nor crawling is available at this age for explorations of object connectivity. Purely visual learning might be possible, however, as in seeing that two regions are connected when they move out from behind an occluder. Another problem is more vexing. It involves the consequences of starting out with an incorrect perceptual rule. In the studies by Slater et al. (1990), newborns appeared to treat the visible areas as two separate pieces. This outcome is different from that of other circumstances in which infants do not perceive a complete object in occlusion displays. In those cases, as in the case of rotation treated earlier, infants consistently show equal looking times after habituation to complete and broken test displays. This outcome has been interpreted as indicating an "agnostic" perceiver (Kellman & Spelke, 1983). The infant may detect that something is occluded but does not know what goes on behind the occluder. (Pieces may either connect or not connect.)

The difference between an initially agnostic perceiver and one with the wrong perceptual rule is fascinating. With no knowledge about how two pieces continue behind an occluder, a learner might be able to learn relationships that indicate when the pieces connect. The perceiver who starts with an incorrect perceptual rule (things that translate rigidly are separate) needs learning ability and learning experiences plus something more. She must have a capacity to detect and correct errors. Correction requires that the initial rule be *modifiable*. Detecting errors requires assuming an interesting constraint about the physical world: separate pieces do not merge over time. Suppose a partly hidden object is seen as two separate pieces. It then moves out from behind its occluder, and the object's unity is perceived. For this experience to have any force in overturning the initial rule, it must be considered impossible (or unlikely) for the boundaries of objects to have changed over time. Otherwise, there would be no conflict between the initial percept of two objects and the subsequent percept of one.

Available evidence is consistent with the idea that the EI (common motion) process is unlearned, awaiting only the maturation of directionally sensitive mechanisms to operate. The similar timing of the appearance of directional sensitivity and the EI process, along with the difficulties involved if infants begin with an incorrect perceptual rule, both cast doubt on, but do not exclude, a role for learning in the development of the EI process.

The Edge-Sensitive Process
Perceiving unity under occlusion in stationary arrays depends on the edge-sensitive process, based on edge relatability (Kellman & Shipley, 1991). Considerable evidence suggests that relatable edges do not evoke perceived unity for infants in the first half year of life. After habituation to a stationary, partly occluded rod whose visible parts are collinear, for example, infants look equally to complete and broken test displays (Kellman & Spelke, 1983). What do equal looking times, with some dishabituation to both test displays, mean? If the visible rod pieces in the initial display were perceived as two separate objects, we would expect greater dishabituation to a complete display. Equal dishabituation to both test stimuli, as we mentioned above, suggests that the broken and complete displays are equally consistent with the initial display. It is also consistent with a lack of attention to those parts during habituation. In an experiment designed to test this possibility, Kellman and Spelke (1983) found evidence that the visible parts are detected; a broken test display with pieces too small to have been the visible parts in habituation evoked clear dishabituation. Given that infants detect the parts of the display in habituation, equal dishabituation to the broken and complete test displays suggests that both are equally consistent with the representation of the habituation display (Kellman & Spelke, 1983). As we argued above, if the rules about object interpolation are to arise later, perhaps by learning, it would seem far better that the perceiver start out "agnostic" rather than use an incorrect perceptual rule.

Infants' inability to use the ES process extends at least through the first half year (Schmidt & Spelke, 1984; Spelke, Breinlinger, Jacobson & Phillips, 1993; Bertenthal, Campos & Haith, 1980). Recall that the ES process, responsible for perception of partly occluded objects, has been implicated as the process underlying illusory contours and figures as well (Kellman & Shipley, 1991; Ringach & Shapley, 1996; Kellman et al., in press). Thus, studies of illusory contours can be used to provide convergent data about the origins of the ES process. Bertenthal et al. (1980) reported evidence of sensitivity to illusory contours at 7 months of age but not at 5 months. Similar results have been reported for kinetic illusory contours (which depend on relatable edges given sequentially in time) by Kaufmann-Hayoz, Kaufmann, and Walther (1988).

A possible exception to this convergence of evidence is a report by Ghim (1990), in which he suggested that illusory contours can be perceived by 3- to 4-month-olds. Using a familiarization and preference paradigm, he predicted that if infants perceived subjective contours, novelty preferences would be greater between a subjective contour display and a display without subjective contours than between two displays with no subjective contours. Some results were consistent with the hypothesis, but at least one outcome predicted by it failed to occur in each of 5 experiments. Results that were in line with the hypothesis of illusory contours perception have plausible alternative explanations. Ghim used an illusory square display made from 4 partial circle-inducing elements. Control (no illusory contour) displays were made from the basic display by changing the orientation of 2 or all 4 elements. The virtue of this manipulation was that it allowed experimental and control display pairs to differ by the same local feature contrasts. Unfortunately, the illusory contour and control stimuli differed in several global properties that could produce easier discrimination between illusory contour and control displays. For example, the outer perimeter of the illusory contour displays contained exclusively smooth contours, whereas all control displays had either 4 or 8 sharp corners and 2 or 4 deep concavities around their outer perimeters. Not only are these salient display features, but evidence suggests that young infants' attention is disproportionately governed by the outer contours of complex displays, as we saw in chapter 4. Given the inconsistencies in the results and difficulties inherent in the control stimuli, these data do not clearly conflict with the generalization that the ES process is absent in the first half year.

Origins of the Edge-Sensitive Process   How does the edge-sensitive process develop? Both maturation and learning are possible contributors. An interesting possibility is that edge-sensitive mechanisms for boundary interpolation might be related to pictorial depth cues. In particular, the depth cue of interposition is closely connected to boundary interpolation under occlusion (Kellman & Shipley, 1991). As we saw in chapter 3, pictorial depth cues seem to become useful around 5 to 7 months of age and may depend on common neural mechanisms maturing at that time. We also noted that studies by Gunderson et al. (1993) with macaque monkeys are consistent with phylogenetic origins of these abilities. The little available data on when the ES process does appear in infants put the onset around 7 months (Bertenthal, Campos & Haith, 1980).

Some suggestion about the origins of the ES process invoke the traditional empiricist view that it arises inductively from experiences with objects (Spelke et al., 1993; Nakayama & Shimojo, 1992; Wallach & Slaughter, 1988). There is no direct evidence for this idea, but it remains possible.

Several considerations favor the competing hypothesis that the ES process depends on modular perceptual mechanisms and not on recognition processes. For one, the ES process is innate in newborn domestic chicks. Regolin and Vallortigara (1995) used a filial imprinting technique to test newborn chicks' perception. Newborn chicks will follow and treat as a social partner the first moving thing they see after birth. In one experiment, newborn chicks were imprinted on a red triangle and tested after 3 days with two displays. In one, unoccluded, separated parts of the triangle were shown. In the other, the same parts were shown partly occluded. Chicks consistently chose to affiliate with the occluded triangle, rather than the fragmentary display. In a second experiment, the procedure was reversed. Chicks were imprinted on either a partly occluded triangle or unoccluded fragments and tested afterward with unoccluded complete or fragmented displays. Chicks imprinted on the fragments consistently associated with the fragmented test display. Chicks imprinted on the partly occluded triangle consistently associated with the complete display. All the results support the hypothesis that the ES process is innate in chicks. These results in another species do not decide the origins of the ES process in humans, but they do make it plausible that the process could be the result of neural maturation.

Other considerations fit this hypothesis as well. Neurophysiological data from primates suggest that boundary interpolation processes are carried out surprisingly early in visual processing, certainly as early as V2 and possibly V1 (von der Heydt et al., 1984). It is imaginable, of course, that effects in V2 or V1 reflect some unknown feedback from higher levels, but there is no evidence that this is the case. Numerous psychophysical results indicate the operation of the ES process in cases where no familiar objects are involved (Field, Hayes, & Hess, 1993; Kellman & Shipley, 1991).

Other indications that edge-sensitive unit formation is a perceptual module (cf. Fodor, 1983) come from evidence indicating that illusory contours and occluded contours are processed by the same mechanisms (Kellman & Shipley, 1991; Kellman et al., in press; Ringach & Shapley,

1996), that local edge relationships override familiarity (Kanizsa, 1979), and that the process obeys certain quantitative relationships (Shipley & Kellman, 1990; Lesher & Mingolla, 1993). If object completion depended on familiarity, these findings would all be unexpected. As one example, equivalent strength of boundary completion in illusory and occluded figure cases would be surprising because occluded boundaries are orders of magnitude more common in ordinary visual experience than illusory ones. (Illusory contours in ordinary scenes require a visual match of luminance, color, and texture between an object and parts of its background, a situation that is not common.)

In short, characteristics of the ES process in adults seem more consistent with a maturationally given perceptual mechanism than one derived from experience. On the other hand, the ES process is nowhere to be seen early in infancy, leaving its origins somewhat mysterious. Further research is needed to give us a clearer understanding of how the ES process arises.

Summary: Unit Formation
Unit formation in adult visual perception appears to be governed by two separate processes, which we have labeled edge insensitive and edge sensitive. The EI process utilizes motion, not edge, relationships and begins to operate in the early weeks of life. The ES process is richer in specifying not only connectedness of objects but the forms of hidden boundaries, but it is long delayed in development relative to the EI process. The developmental sequence of the two unit formation processes parallels their differing ecological soundness. If detected with precision, motion relationships are highly diagnostic of unity. Smoothness of object boundaries and connectedness of pieces that bear certain edge relations, are common but not nearly universal characteristics of our physical environment. Accordingly, the ES process, sensitive to edge relations given simultaneously or over time, is a robust and useful perceptual process but is not of the highest ecological validity. The development of unit formation, then, fits our characterization of perceptual development as beginning with the most secure information sources and progressing toward other useful but somewhat less trustworthy sources.

Three-Dimensional Form Perception

Each theoretical idea about the basis for three-dimensional form perception can be closely tied to a developmental account (Kellman, 1984). If an object's three-dimensional form is really a collection of stored two-dimensional views, then perceivers may initially have no notion of three-dimensional form at all. Form would develop from associated experiences of different views, perhaps closely connected to active manipulation of the object (Piaget, 1954). On this account, three-dimensional form perception awaits the results of a fabrication process that must take place for each object separately. An altogether different origin is possible if perceived three-dimensional form is a direct response to certain optical transformations. This view is often linked to the hypothesis of evolved neural mechanisms specifically sensitive to this kind of information (Fodor, 1983; Gibson, 1966; Shepard, 1984). The reason is that optical transformations and three-dimensional form are connected by physical and geometrical facts that have been unswervingly true and available throughout evolution. This kind of information does not depend on the particular types of objects that happen to be present in a particular setting or culture. It depends on the optics and geometry of projection of rigid objects. These are the kinds of regularity that evolution might have exploited in the adaptation of perceptual systems for mobile organisms (Gibson, 1966; Shepard, 1984). If so, sensitivity to this kind of information might be a basic property of the human visual system and not a product of learning.

A third developmental story, or actually two different stories, can attach to the idea that we use general principles to derive complete three-dimensional form from a single view of an object. On the Gestalt view, form can be perceived this way due to unlearned, organizational processes rooted in basic neurophysiology. A different account of the rules of perceptual organization was clearly articulated by Brunswik (1956) and anticipated by Helmholtz (1885/1925): the rules might be abstracted from an individual's experience with many objects. We noted above that the idea of generating three-dimensional form by collecting various two-dimensional views has the unappealing consequence that the learning process must operate specifically for each object. Yet adults often encounter unfamiliar objects and perceive their shapes, even from stationary views. The ability to extract general principles from one's experience with objects might provide a viable account of some perceptual organization phenomena. Obviously, this account would predict that three-dimensional form perception would not be present initially, whereas the organizational processes postulated by Gestalt theorists should operate as soon as the relevant brain mechanisms are mature.

Kinematic Information in Infant Three-Dimensional Form Perception

Which account of the origins of three-dimensional form perception is correct? Wallach (1985) theorized that in every perceptual domain, such as form, depth, or motion perception, there is one primary source of information, usable innately and not modifiable by experience. Other cues are acquired later, through correlation with the innate process. In form perception, he hypothesized that motion-carried information might be the innate process. This possibility motivated Wallach and O'Connell's classic (1953) studies of the *kinetic depth effect*. Specifically, Wallach and O'Connell wondered how knowledge of three-dimensional form can be available to congenitally monocular (stereoblind) observers despite their lacking binocular information about form. Pictorial information might specify three-dimensional form via learning, but what might guide the learning process? In other words, where could the *initial* notion of three-dimensional form come from? Thus, Wallach and O'Connell hypothesized an unlearned process of three-dimensional form perception based on the optical changes given by motion.

That motion-carried information about form is most basic has been claimed on other theoretical grounds. Adult speed and precision in detecting structure from motion (Johansson, 1975; Braunstein, 1976; Ullman, 1979) suggests dedicated neural machinery, especially given the complexity of the information itself. Another argument is more rooted in developmental considerations: kinematic form information has the highest ecological validity. Mathematically, perspective transformations contain sufficient information to specify uniquely an object's three-dimensional form under reasonable assumptions (Ullman, 1979).

For a stationary object viewed by a stationary observer, whole form may be predicted on the basis of simplicity, symmetry, or similarity to previously viewed objects. Such predictions depend on probabilistic facts about typical shapes of objects and vantage points that occur. It is hard to quantify the validity of this information, but it does not approach the validity of kinematic information. If early perception is based on the the most accurate information sources, we would expect kinematic information to be the original source of perceived form.

Evidence from infant research suggests that kinematic information does indeed play this role. The earliest competence for perceiving overall form appears to be based on kinematic information (Kellman, 1984; Kellman & Short, 1987b; Owsley, 1983; Arterberry & Yonas, 1988; Yonas, Arterberry, & Granrud, 1987a).

Testing infants' three-dimensional form perception presents a problem. A viewed three-dimensional object is seen from a particular vantage point or a set of such points. Each vantage point gives a particular two-dimensional projection to the eyes. To assess whether three-dimensional form is perceived, responses to these two-dimensional projections must be disentangled from responses to three-dimensional form. Suppose, for example, we habituate infants to a stationary three-dimensional object from a particular vantage point. If after habituation infants generalize habituation to this same display but dishabituate to a novel three-dimensional object, it may indicate that they detected the original three-dimensional form and discriminated it from the novel one. But responses might instead

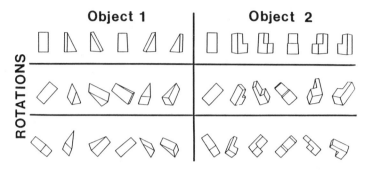

Figure 5.8
Objects and rotations used in experiments on infant three-dimensional form perception. The two columns contain views of the same three-dimensional object. Rows indicate different axes of rotation. Reprinted with permission from Kellman, P. J. (1984), Perception of three-dimensional form by human infants, *Perception and Psychophysics, 36*, 353–358.

be based on differences in the two-dimensional projections between the original and novel object.

This problem can be circumvented by exploiting the geometry of form and motion. Three-dimensional form information can be provided by rotation around various axes, so long as there is some component of rotation in depth. One can therefore test for perception of the same three-dimensional form across rotation sequences that vary and that have much different two-dimensional appearances.

An experiment of this type (Kellman, 1984) tested 16-week-olds using the two objects depicted in figure 5.8. The purpose of the experiment was to assess early form perception from kinematic information and also from information in single and multiple static views. In the kinematic condition, infants were habituated to videotaped displays of a single object rotating in depth. Two different axes of rotation alternated over the habituation trials; the only constant throughout was the three-dimensional form. After habituation, subjects were tested on alternating trials with the same object, moving around a novel axis of rotation and a different object, rotating around the same new axis. Changing the axis of rotation for the test trials ensured that the particular two-dimensional views and transformations were novel for both objects. Generalization of habituation to the same object would thus reflect extraction of three-dimensional form and not a response to particular two-dimensional views.

For adults, even the line drawings of static views of the objects shown in figure 5.8 are sufficient for perception of three-dimensional form. If infants were able to detect form from single views or sequences of static views, successful performance in the kinematic condition might indicate merely the use of one or more static views. To check this possibility, two other groups were presented with sequential stationary views taken from the rotation sequences. These two groups differed in the number and spacing of these views. (One group had twenty-four views spaced 15 deg apart in the rotation sequence, shown at a rate of 1 sec per view; the other had six views spaced 60 deg apart, shown for 2 sec per view.)

In the kinematic condition, infants showed evidence that they perceived three-dimensional form. They generalized habituation to the same object in a new rotation but dishabituated to the new object. This pattern occurred regardless of which object and axes of rotation were used in the habituation and test trials. By contrast, there was no evidence of three-dimensional form perception in the static condition. Infants did not discriminate between new views of an old object and views of a new object.

This basic profile of early form perception—young infants perceive three-dimensional form from continuous optical transformations but not from static information—has been confirmed in subsequent research, using a variety of methods (Kellman & Short, 1987b; Owsley, 1983; Yonas, Arterberry, Granrud & 1987a; Ruff, 1978). The research has also produced a more precise understanding of what appears to be a basic perceptual capacity.

Motion Perspective in Form Perception   In infants' perception of object unity from motion, we saw that real motion of the object was needed for unity perception. The situation is different for the optical transformations that specify three-dimensional form. As an observer walks through an environment, *motion perspective* information provides the same optical transformations, relevant to three-dimensional form, that occur if the object rotates while the observer is stationary. If these transformations are the basis of early form perception, we would predict that there is nothing special about having the object move: information could be given in principle by either object or observer motion. Kellman and Short (1987b) tested the prediction that three-dimensional form should be perceivable by moving infants viewing stationary objects. Using the apparatus sketched in figure 5.9 and the same objects as in Kellman (1984). They found that 16-week-old infants did indeed perceive objects' three-dimensional forms from motion perspective.

Isolating Edge Transformations   Mathematical analyses of structure-from-motion information have focused on the positions of identifiable points (such as corners) at different times (Ullman, 1979; Braunstein, 1976; Johansson, 1975) or spatiotemporal changes in length and orientation of object edges caused by the object's rotation (Todd, 1982). However, the transforming optical projection of a rotating (solid) object also contains changes in brightness and texture gradients (Pentland, 1990). Infant

Figure 5.9
Apparatus used in testing form perception from motion perspective. Observers were passively moved in an arc while viewing three-dimensional objects. From Kellman, P. J., & Short, K. R. (1987b), Development of three-dimensional form perception, *Journal of Experimental Psychology: Human Perception and Performance, 13,* 545–557. Copyright © 1987 by the American Psychological Association. Reprinted with permission.

experiments using solid objects present both kinds of information, and they do not allow us to know the basis of performance. It might be possible that changes in brightness and texture are necessary for young infants to detect form (Shaw, Roder & Bushnell, 1986).

Projective transformations of edges in the absence of surface gradients were tested by Kellman and Short (1987b). Figure 5.10 shows the wire objects, similar to those introduced by Wallach and O'Connell (1953), that were used in the study. Such objects contain thin edges but no surfaces connecting them. In rotation, the objects provide the same geometric transformations of surface boundaries as do solid objects but without transformations of surface brightness and texture. Lighting was arranged to eliminate visible shading changes even along the thin edges of the figures.

The stimulus objects also allowed a strong test of the notion that infants' performance depends on perception of three-dimensional form and on continuous transformations, not on two-dimensional similarities across axes of rotation or on three-dimensional information given in any static view. The two test objects were designed so that static, two-dimensional information could not give away three-dimensional form. A theorem of projective geometry states that all triangles are projectively equivalent:

95° Object   165° Object

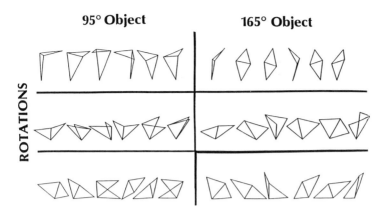

ROTATIONS

Figure 5.10
Objects and rotations used in experiment on three-dimensional form perception from edge transformations alone. The two columns, labeled "95° Object" and "165° Object," contain views of the same three-dimensional object. Rows indicate different axes of rotation. From Kellman, P. J., & Short, K. R. (1987b), Development of three-dimensional form perception, *Journal of Experimental Psychology: Human Perception and Performance, 13*, 545–557. Copyright © 1987 by the American Psychological Association. Reprinted with permission.

any two-dimensional projection of one triangle could be the (polar) projection of any other triangle in some three-dimensional orientation and distance. By constructing each three-dimensional figure from two triangles, the two-dimensional features of the two objects were largely interchangeable. The success of this manipulation was validated in an experiment with adults, who were unable to sort static views of the two three-dimensional objects accurately.

The pattern of data in figure 5.11 suggests that these 16-week-olds perceived the three-dimensional forms of the wire objects. Two groups are shown, each habituated to one of the wire objects, in two different axes of rotation. Each group generalized habituation to the same three-dimensional object tested in a novel rotation and dishabituated to the new object. These findings do not rule out the possible informativeness of transformations of shading and texture in other situations but show that these are not necessary for early three-dimensional form perception.

Although adults could not sort the two-dimensional views into their three-dimensional objects of origin, infants were tested with static views anyway. As expected, they showed no evidence of detecting three-dimensional form from the static views. These data disconfirmed both the idea that three-dimensional form was perceived from static views and the idea that similarities across rotations of the images of a single three-dimensional object could account for infants' dishabituation patterns.

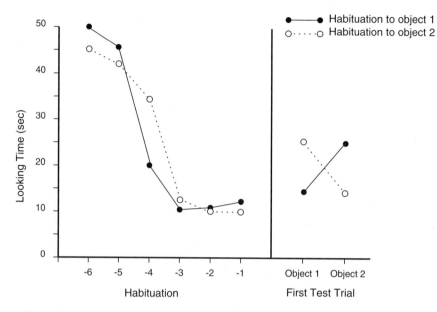

Figure 5.11
Data from experiment on three-dimensional form perception from edge transformations alone. Looking times are shown for the last six habituation trials (with the final one labeled −1) and the test trials. Test trials consisted of successive presentations of the two objects in a novel axis of rotation. (See text.) From Kellman, P. J., & Short, K. R. (1987b), Development of three-dimensional form perception, *Journal of Experimental Psychology: Human Perception and Performance, 13,* 545–557. Copyright © 1987 by the American Psychological Association. Reprinted with permission.

Static Three-Dimensional Form Perception

In our discussion of kinematic information about form, we noted several control groups whose data suggested that infants do not extract three-dimensional form from static views of objects. This finding has emerged consistently (Kellman, 1984; Kellman & Short, 1987b; Ruff, 1978). It is as striking in its own negative way as the finding of early competence with kinematic information. Recall that adults readily perceive form from single or multiple static views. It would seem that we use this ability ubiquitously. Walk into a room and note the objects present. How few are rotating as we watch! Although we get some motion perspective information about objects as we move, we need not. We can see form by just glancing through the doorway of a room.

The early lack of static form perception has been shown with both photographic slides and stationary views of three-dimensional objects. The earliest report was by Ruff (1978), who found that 6-month-old infants failed to apprehend three-dimensional forms from stationary views of rather complex solid objects. Some work suggests the problem persists at 8 months (Kellman, 1993). The sole exception to this pattern of results is that binocular, static views of objects may allow recognition of three-dimensional forms that have previously been given kinematically (Owsley, 1983; Yonas et al., 1987a). There is no evidence that infants form an *initial* representation of form from static, binocular views.

What might be the problem for infants in extracting three-dimensional form from static information? Clearly, infants have some abilities that might be relevant to this task. Recall Slater and Morison's (1985) findings that newborns detect invariant planar shape despite variations in three-dimensional slant. Such an ability should allow the accurate perception of the facets of a three-dimensional object. By 6 months of age, virtually all infants have stereoscopic depth perception, which should provide accurate information about surface slant. Given these abilities, infants' failure to perceive static three-dimensional form at 6 months and beyond is mysterious. Our best guess is that the obstacle is developing a global three-dimensional representation from single or successive views. The latter process is not fully understood with adults but seems to involve symmetry or simplicity in representing unprojected object surfaces (Buffart, Leeuwenberg & Restle, 1981). For infants, the three-dimensional forms of stationary objects viewed from a stationary position are apparently indeterminate. How and when infants become able to apprehend form is not yet known.

Nonrigid Unity and Form

Some of the most important objects in the infant's world are nonrigid. A person walking or a hand opening, a pillow or the nipple of a baby bottle bending, are examples of such objects. Perceiving nonrigid objects presents special challenges. We now take a look at what we is known about early unity and form perception in nonrigid objects.

We can define nonrigid objects as those having points whose separations in three-dimensional space change over time. If we manipulate a rock, all of its points remain in a constant relationship, despite the object's rotating or translating in space. A human hand is different. When a closed fist opens, the point-to-point distance from a fingertip to the base of the wrist changes a great deal. Human movements can be considered *jointed* motions because changes are caused by operation of joints between relatively rigid segments. Elastic motions, such as bending, stretching, or squeezing of a rubbery substance (or a jellyfish) are quite different nonrigid transformations. Analytically, it has been harder to describe processing constraints that allow recovery of nonrigid motions from optical information than is the case with rigid motion (Bertenthal, 1993; Cutting,

1981; Hoffman & Flinchbaugh, 1982; Johansson, 1975; Webb & Aggarwal, 1982).

Perceptual systems are undeterred, however. Form perception includes nonrigid objects, even if these present more analytical challenges. These objects paradoxically retain identity despite form changes. Is it meaningful to say that some aspect of form is preserved for nonrigid objects? It is. A jellyfish does not have the same form as a walking person, for example. What is preserved across nonrigid motions are not metric properties, such as inter-point distances, but topological ones, such as the adjacency of points.

Since the pioneering work of Johansson (1950, 1975), most research on nonrigid motion has used displays comprised of separated points of light in a dark surround. Johansson (1975) showed that the human form and events in which it participates can be detected from motion information alone. He constructed films of people moving in which the only visible information came from small lights attached to the main joints of the body. Viewing these films, observers rapidly and effortlessly detect a person walking, a couple dancing, and various other events. Inverting the display hampers recognition of a human form (Sumi, 1984).

Infant perception of the human form from motion relationships has been investigated programmatically by Bertenthal, Proffitt, and their associates (Bertenthal, Proffitt & Cutting, 1984; Bertenthal, Proffitt, Spetner, & Thomas, 1985; Bertenthal, Proffitt, & Kramer, 1987; Bertenthal, Proffitt, Kramer, & Spetner, 1987; Bertenthal, 1993). When 3- or 5-month-old infants were habituated to motion sequences of an upright walking person, they dishabituated to an inverted walker (see figure 5.12). Static views taken from the motion sequences did not support discrimination performance. These results do not indicate whether infants actually perceived a person walking in either display. Some evidence suggests that infants do detect the familiar form of a person in point-light displays beginning around 5 months of age (Bertenthal, 1993). This conclusion comes from two stimulus manipulations that disrupt the appearance of a walking person for adult perceivers—inversion and phase shifting. *Phase shifting* means staggering the starting locations in the periodic motions of particular point lights. Both 3- and 5-month-olds discriminate normal from phase-shifted displays when they are upright. When inverted, however, only the 3-month-olds discriminate the two display types (Bertenthal & Davis, 1988). A group of 7-month-olds also showed poorer discrimination with the inverted displays than with upright displays. The inference, albeit somewhat indirect, is that superior sensitivity to phase information with upright displays might be due to the fact that upright displays are perceived as a person walking and phase shifts disrupt that percept. Since inverted displays are not perceived as a person walking, proper phase re-

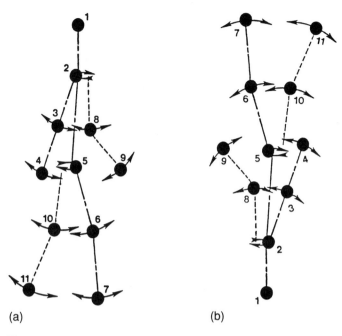

Figure 5.12
Array of 11 point-lights corresponding to the head and joints of a person walking. The motion vectors drawn through each point-light represent the relative motions of the points: (b) is the inverted version of the display in (a). From Bertenthal, B., Proffitt, D., & Kramer, S. (1987), Perception of biomechanical motions by infants: Implementation of various processing constraints, *Journal of Experimental Psychology: Human Perception and Performance, 13,* 577–585. Copyright © 1987 by the American Psychological Association. Reprinted with permission.

lations are less salient. Following this inference, the results are consistent with the idea that these nonrigid motions are encoded as biomechanical motion by 5 months but not at 3 months.

All of the findings to date are consistent with the idea that the infant's visual system is specially attuned to motion relationships. The task of recognizing a walking person requires not simply detecting unity and structure in a display of moving points but also making some sort of match to memories of a walking person. This matching process might be a fairly advanced skill and clearly one that depends on encoding relevant experiences. The basic sensitivity that allows detection and encoding of motion relations may begin much earlier than the point at which recognition performance is measurable. Fox and McDaniel (1982) demonstrated greater attention by 2-month-olds to animate motion patterns given by point lights, including a person walking and a hand opening and closing, than to displays with similar motion components whose relationships did not preserve animate motion.

It is important to realize that a point-light stimulus is ecologically bizarre. Whereas physical objects are ordinarily continuous, a point-light object is made of sparse, discontinuous points. Whereas normal objects have surface color and texture, point-light objects do not. Unless a visual system is built to process motion relationships, it is not obvious that these point-light collections should be encoded other than as noise. The recognition performance that may occur at 5 months presupposes that without any special training, normal events, such as a person walking, are encoded in terms of motion relationships that can be matched to the point-light displays. This is truly remarkable in the first half year or any other time, for it says that the human visual system is built to be a device for extracting structure from motion.

Summary: Three-Dimensional Form Perception
Research on the development of three-dimensional form perception supports an ecological view (Gibson, 1966, 1979; Shepard, 1984). Recovery of object structure from optical transformations appears to depend on mechanisms present very early. Accounts attributing three-dimensional form perception to learning seem implausible given the developmental order in which kinematic and static information become useful. Can one argue that infants initially encode two-dimensional optical transformations and later learn their meaning in terms of three-dimensional form? Since three-dimensional form is not recoverable from static views, and infants perceive three-dimensional form from optical change before they attain skilled reaching and manipulation abilities, it is hard to see where initial information about three-dimensional form might come from (Kellman, 1984; Wallach & O'Connell, 1953).

Size Perception

In the last chapter, we reviewed evidence that perception of real object size can be demonstrated in human newborns. The possibility of accurate size perception in infancy no doubt simplifies learning about the world compared to imaginable alternatives in which size is indeterminate or perceived to change with projective size. The fact that size perception in newborns depends on information in stationary arrays is remarkable, given the lack of facility shown with static information in unity and form perception. Allowing ourselves to speculate, perhaps size perception from static information appears early because the information is sound. Barring large illusions of distance, the combination of projective size with distance information to arrive at real size is a highly valid indicator of real size and one based on enduring properties of the physical world. The relative lag in the use of static information about unity and form may reflect their lesser ecological validity, especially in comparison with kinematic sources of information for those object properties. Size-distance computations may appear early in perception for the same reason kinematic information for unity and form does: both allow determination of some important object properties with high ecological validity.

Perception of Substance

Some might consider our discussion of object perception so far to have omitted the most basic property: objects are tangible. They take up space and resist penetration. Ecologically, perception of tangible objects is a priority of high order. Besides the basic determination of tangibility, there are particulars: is an object rigid, spongy, droopy, or elastic? These questions of substance are important for determining what or how objects can be grasped or manipulated, and what functions they might serve.

Some considerations of substance are implicit in what we have said already. Classifying a boundary as belonging to one surface and not another may be said to involve substance, since we are in effect determining where the tangible surface lies—whether a certain shape is a thing or a hole, for example.

There is more to be discovered about early perception of substance, however. Only a small amount of research has been done to date, mostly by E. Gibson and her colleagues. As in other domains, important carriers of information about substance are *events*. An object made of wood or steel or hard plastic will move rigidly, whereas one made of flesh or rubber will deform in certain characteristic ways as it moves. Gibson, Owsley, and Johnston (1978) tested 5-month-olds' sensitivity to substance from motion information. Infants were habituated to an object undergoing three different rigid motions and tested afterward with a fourth (new) rigid motion and a nonrigid (elastic deformation). Subjects generalized habituation to the novel rigid motion but dishabituated to the nonrigid deformation. Subsequent research (Gibson, Owsley, Walker & Megaw-Nyce, 1979) showed a similar pattern of results at 3 months of age. A separate experiment (Walker, Owsley, Megaw-Nyce, Gibson & Bahrick, 1980) produced a complementary result: when habituated to two deforming motions, infants generalized habituation to a new deformation but dishabituated to a rigid motion. These results are consistent with the interpretation that infants perceived a consistent object substance (rigid or nonrigid) in habituation in each case. An alternative interpretation is possible, however; infants might simply categorize the viewed events themselves as rigid motion or nonrigid motion, without attributing some consistent characteristic to the object.

CONCLUSIONS

As in the case of space, our view of early object perception has been conspicuously revised by research in recent years. Whereas Piaget believed that infants begin with incorporeal visual images devoid of meaning, we now believe that even the newborn begins on a much more solid footing.

Viewed with a wide-angle lens, the pattern of early infant object perception abilities fits an *ecological* view: perceptual systems evolved to provide meaningful contact with the environment and not to provide initially meaningless sensations (Gibson & Gibson, 1957; J. Gibson, 1966, 1979; E. Gibson, 1969, 1984; Johansson, 1970). Highlighted in early object perception are sources of information that go beyond spatial relationships present in a single, static retinal image. Kinematic information given by moving observers and objects specifies three-dimensional objects and their arrangements better than any classical cues, such as pictorial information.

Shifting from a wide-angle to a telephoto lens, we see that neither the ecological perspective nor the traditional learning-oriented view captures the nuances of infant object perception. In every component of object perception, there are multiple sources of information, such as information carried by motion, information related to perceived depth, and information in static spatial (two-dimensional) relationships. Infants in every case respond to a subset of the information usable by adults. They show sensitivity to some information as early as tested, but they lack competence to use other sources until well into the second half of the first year. The pattern of competence and incompetence is not random. In most domains, kinematic information appears early, whereas information carried in two-dimensional spatial relationships appears later.

Initial stages of visual processing in the human visual system appear to be specialized for edge extraction (Marr, 1982; DeValois & DeValois, 1988). Although subject to maturation, there is little doubt that edge detection is an unlearned ability. Evidence, direct and indirect, suggests that newborns detect edges from discontinuities in luminance and color, motion, and depth. But limitations are obvious. For example, stereoscopic depth information is unavailable in the first few months.

Edge classification in early infancy is accomplished from information carried by motion, such as accretion and deletion of texture, and from depth discontinuities. Early boundary assignment also appears to be based on motion and depth. Object boundaries seem not to be perceived initially from luminance and chromatic differences: infants detect these but do not *classify* them as object boundaries until considerably later.

A similar combination of early capacities and limitations applies to perception of unity. The edge-insensitive process (dependent on motion relationships) appears soon after birth, perhaps awaiting only the maturation of direction sensitivity in the visual cortex. But during this same period, unit formation from the edge-sensitive process (dependent on spatial relations of edges) is conspicuously absent.

Kinematic information is preeminent in three-dimensional form perception. For much of the first year, in fact, it appears to be the sole source of three-dimensional object representations (from vision). Perception of form from single, static views of objects seems routine for adults but outside of the young infant's repertoire. Considering both unity and form, we may conclude that stationary environments often appear indeterminate to young infants. A disproportionate share of learning about objects' connections and three-dimensional forms must come from events in which objects or observers move.

Finally, we have conjectured that the order of appearance of perceptual abililies closely parallels their ecological validity. This claim snugly fits early object perception. Adult perceptual systems exploit multiple sources of information for most object properties, but for infants, perceiving comprehensively is not nearly so crucial as perceiving accurately.

Chapter 6
Motion and Event Perception

Perceptual systems are the property only of mobile organisms. It is an individual's motion through the environment, and the purposes served by moving, that make perceptual knowledge crucial. Guiding this locomotion is perhaps the first priority of perception. Another is to detect and classify other moving things: some of these may afford danger, some comfort; some may be nutritious, but others may be hungry.

Particular patterns and sequences of motion define *events*. Events involve objects, motions, and changes that are connected in *time*. They are coherent temporal sequences analogous to objects, which are spatially coherent units persisting across time. An event may involve patterns of change in a single object, such as a person walking, or complex sequences involving many objects. We do not attempt here a definitive characterization of events as ecological units, although such an attempt might be useful. Instead, we note a few common characteristics that should be sufficient to guide our discussion.

For an object, physical coherence of parts in space is defining. What links the momentary changes that comprise a unitary event? One link is physical momentum. The flight of a ball through the air is a single event, although the flight may last for many seconds. The ball's trajectory is caused by the initiating force, and it continues on a smooth path, subject to the influence of gravity. Momentum also connects separate objects. When a bowling ball collides into a set of pins, they fly in many directions, all caused by collisions with the ball and each other. Not all events are organized strictly in terms of physical causality. Social interactions, for example, may be partitioned into events in sensible ways. Actions united by a common purpose, such as eating dinner, may be events, although they may in turn be comprised of many constituent events. Some interesting research on the partitioning of activities into events has been carried out by Newtson (Newtson & Engquist, 1976; Newtson, Engquist & Bois, 1977).

Perceptual events are scaled ecologically, as are objects. A long, slow happening such as the movement of a glacier will not be a perceived event, nor will the vibrations of atoms, due to their size and speed.

It hardly needs to be said that these criteria and examples are heuristic in nature. Ambiguous cases can be generated easily. Such ambiguities should not obscure the fact that perceptual experience often does come packaged into events, whose parts cohere with each other but are clearly separable from other events. A compelling case for coherence and selective attention in event perception was made by Neisser and Becklen (1976). They produced videotapes of two superimposed events. In one event, three people tossed a ball to each other, and in another event, two pairs of hands played a hand-slapping game. Although the events appeared simultaneously on the same screen, viewers instructed to report particular occurrences in one event sequence (such as each throw of the ball) were unaware of the other event sequence. In one experiment, a third event—a girl carrying an umbrella, indoors, walking across the screen— was also shown. Although seemingly a conspicuous and striking event, it was seldom noticed by observers monitoring one or the other of the ongoing event sequences.

The idea of event perception has also been important in understanding the information available for perceiving. As we saw in chapters 1, 3, and 5, ecological views of perception and empirical research both suggest that information carried by motion or change plays an important role in perception of objects and space. Some theorists have gone so far as to argue that event perception is paradigmatic in perception (Johannson, 1975; Gibson, 1979). A motionless perceiver, receiving a stationary glimpse of the environment, is a degenerate or limiting case. Normal perception is inextricably bound up with ongoing *action*, and interactions among objects are of primary importance in our comprehension of the environment. Gibson (1966) pointed out a particularly interesting aspect of events, what he called *dual specification*: Events provide information concurrently about *changes* occurring in the environment and *persisting properties* of objects and the spatial layout. We have seen in earlier chapters examples of how information carried by events specifies persisting properties of the world, such as object unity and form, depth, and spatial arrangement. In this chapter, we focus on the other part of dual specification: perception of moving things, including motion of the self. We will emphasize vision, because it provides our most detailed access to motion and events.

Ultimately, abilities to perceive motion and events serve to support action in the world. For the young infant, however, *responding* to events is not primary. An infant's rapt attention to motion and events must serve a different function, helping her to develop an understanding of the physical and social worlds.

ECOLOGY OF MOTION PERCEPTION

Information and Constraints

Motion has a controversial history in perceptual theory. In structuralist psychology, motion was considered an inference from sensations of qualitative similarity, position and time (e.g., Titchener, 1902). For example, a red circle seen at one place at one moment and then seen at another place, might be inferred to have moved.

Researchers began to assault this view around the turn of the last century. Exner (1875), performing experiments on perceived succession of two sparks, discovered that at short succession intervals, subjects lost the ability to perceive two separate sparks and instead reported a single entity moving. Exner argued that the ability to perceive motion below the threshold at which position and time could be distinguished indicated that motion was a perceptual primary and was not computed from registering position and time. The argument gained greater support from Wertheimer's (1912) stroboscopic motion experiments. With discrete flashes separated by a certain spatial interval, smooth motion of a single object was seen for time intervals between about 30 to 60 msec. If motion were a more general inference from positions of time and position, there would be no reason to expect it to be confined so rigidly. Wertheimer offered an additional argument. One kind of motion, which he labeled *phi* motion, had a curious character. At temporal intervals longer than those required for smooth motion, observers reported a dual percept. On one hand, they saw each light as being stationary and separate. At the same time, however, they saw something moving between them. Although the movement was clear, nothing in particular was seen as moving. For this reason, Wertheimer dubbed *phi* motion "objectless" motion. That motion can be perceived apart from moving things suggests that it is perceptually basic.

In the modern era, there seems to be little dispute over motion as a perceptual primitive, detected by dedicated mechanisms rather than constructed from other sensory products. This change in default assumptions about motion may be related to discovery of individual cortical cells whose firing is selectively influenced by location, direction, and speed of motion on the retina (e.g., Hubel & Wiesel, 1970) and by a particular visual cortical area, medial temporal cortex (MT), that seems specially dedicated to processing motion signals (Allman, Miezin & McGuinness, 1985; Mikami, Newsome, and Wurtz, 1986).

Multiple Stimuli for Motion Perception

Several types of situations can give rise to perceived motion.

• For a stationary observer, a target translating perpendicular to the line of sight produces a continuously changing projective location, or *optical displacement*.

• A target that moves only parallel to the line of sight (toward or away from the observer) produces a different projective change— *optical expansion* or contraction.

• Motion can also occur for a moving target without retinal displacement, if *optical pursuit* is engaged. In this case, although the visual input remains essentially unchanging, motion is signaled by the muscle commands controlling eye movements.

• *Stroboscopic motion* occurs, as we have noted, when discrete stimulus events have certain spatial and temporal relations.

• Finally, *induced motion* of a stationary target may be perceived when its surrounding visible context is moved (Duncker, 1929).

Systematic study of the development of motion perception is a relatively recent enterprise. Only some of the basic questions about the scope and limits of motion perception, and the effectiveness of particular stimuli, have been answered.

MOTION PERCEPTION ABILITIES AND PROCESSES

Motion and Attention

If you want to attract an infant's attention, move something in front of its eyes. From the earliest days, infants, orient to moving stimuli using head and eye movements (e.g., Fantz & Nevis, 1967; Haith, 1980; Kremenitzer, Vaughan, Kurtzberg & Dowling, 1979; White, Castle & Held, 1964). This power of motion to attract attention has been exploited by researchers who have added motion to their displays even when studying other aspects of perception (Atkinson, Braddick & Moar, 1977a, 1977b; Fox et al., 1980; Manny & Klein, 1985; Shimojo, Birch, Gwiazda & Held, 1984).

It is not clear whether infant attention to motion reflects a response to motion per se or attention to what is most informative. From an earlier sensation-based perspective on perceptual development, the former idea—that infants are hardwired to attend to movement—would be more plausible. Such a tendency would facilitate learning about objects and events. The alternative is that information, not motion, attracts attention. As we have already seen, infant perception of objects utilizes a subset of adult abilities; specifically, information carried by motion provides the earliest knowledge of object unity, three-dimensional form, and so on. As we see below, infants also have early capacities to extract complex, functionally important relations from events, such as causal connections. Infants may attend to motion and events because these furnish the richest informaton about the environment. Which of these accounts of infant attention to motion is correct is not known.

Motion Characteristics

A moving object has a velocity, comprised of a direction and speed of position change over time. Both characteristics are important to observers. Research on early motion perception has been concerned with capacities and limits in perceiving these characteristics of motion, as well as the underlying mechanisms that make motion perception possible.

Directional Selectivity

Recall that we considered in chapter 2 research suggesting that the ability to detect motion direction may not appear in infants' perception until 6 to 8 weeks of age (Wattam-Bell, 1991, 1992, 1996a, 1996b). Before this time, infants may be "direction-blind" (Wattam-Bell, 1996b). There are indications that infants do distinguish motion (or temporal modulation) from static displays even before direction can be extracted from moving displays. It remains possible that some directional sensitivity exists prior to 6 weeks. Perhaps the random dot motion displays used in these studies are not optimal for early direction sensitivity. This possibility would be difficult to test, given that displays showing moving objects or edges contain information, other than motion, that might affect responses in a variety of ways.

Velocity Sensitivity

A number of researchers have tried to characterize infants' motion perception abilities in terms of the range of velocities that can be detected. Most studies have focused on the slowest movement that evokes perception of motion, and these estimates have varied with other stimulus variables. In an early study by Volkmann and Dobson (1976), a horizontally oscillating checkerboard pattern and a similar stationary pattern were shown in a visual preference procedure. One-month-olds showed weak preferences for the moving display, whereas 2- and 3-month-olds clearly preferred the moving display even at 2 deg/sec, the slowest velocity tested. To get an idea how slow this speed is, consider that when one views a computer monitor from 18 inches (about 46 cm) away, an ant crawling across the screen at 2 deg/sec will move about .3 inches (8 mm) in one second and would take 40 sec to traverse a 12 in (30 cm) wide screen. This is a slow motion but well above velocity thresholds for normal adults. An even lower threshold was found by Kaufmann, Stucki, and

Kaufmann-Hayoz (1985) using rotary motion, about 1.4 deg/sec at one month and .93 deg/sec at 3 months.

Somewhat higher threshold estimates have come from studies designed to distinguish different mechanisms underlying responses to moving patterns. Using vertical grating (dark and light striped) stimuli and a 75% preference as the threshold criterion, Aslin and Shea (1990) found velocity thresholds of about 9 deg/sec at 6 weeks and 4 deg/sec at 12 weeks. Dannemiller and Freedland (1989) estimated thresholds at about 5 deg/sec for 16-week-olds and about 2.3 deg/sec for 20-week-olds. However, they found no reliable motion preferences at 8 weeks. Dannemiller and Freedland (1991) studied *differential* velocity thresholds—the minimum difference in velocity that could evoke a reliable looking preference. They assumed that infants would preferentially fixate the display appearing to move faster. Twenty-week-old subjects reliably distinguished a velocity of 3.3 deg/sec from 2.0 deg/sec but not from 2.5 deg/sec. Although it is difficult to compare stimulus conditions and measurement techniques, these threshold estimates are much higher than velocity thresholds for motion detection in adults; the latter can be as small as 1 to 2 min of arc/sec when stationary reference points are visible (Kaufman, 1974). At 2 min/sec, the ant crossing the 12 inch screen would take 40 minutes.

Isolating Mechanisms Sensitive to Motion

Although the notion that motion is a perceptual primitive detected by specialized mechanims is generally accepted, we may still question which particular responses by infants implicate motion mechanisms, such as detectors tuned to particular velocities. One complication in pinpointing such mechanisms is that the physical event of a continuously moving object produces multiple changes in a spatial array. It is possible that apparent detection of motion does not rely on motion sensing mechanisms per se. Preferential attention to a moving pattern might indicate motion detection, but there are other possibilities. Positional change of the display or some part of it might be detected. If periodic stimuli are used, such as the checkerboard pattern used by Volkmann and Dobson (1976), the luminance at any point will change periodically. Responses might be based on this *flicker* rather than on motion per se.

Distinguishing mechanisms sensitive to velocity, position, and flicker in infant perception is possible due to research by Aslin and Shea (1990), Freedland and Dannemiller (1987), and Dannemiller and Freedland (1989). Using several combinations of temporal frequency and spatial displacement with random black-and-white check patterns, Freedland and Dannemiller (1987) found evidence that preference for a moving pattern over a static one is influenced both by spatial displacement and temporal frequency. The influence of temporal frequency is consistent with a velocity-sensitive mechanism but also with a flicker-sensitive mechanism. Aslin and Shea (1990) used vertically moving luminance (square wave) gratings to distinguish velocity- and flicker-sensitive mechanisms. These may be separated experimentally using stimuli of several spatial frequencies and velocities. A response based on velocity, for example, might be expected to change if velocity is doubled and spatial frequency halved. A flicker-sensitive mechanism, however, should remain unchanged by this manipulation because the temporal frequency (rate of dark-light changes at a single location) remains the same. Aslin and Shea's results indicated that the motion preferences of 6- and 12-week-old infants depended on velocity. Dannemiller and Freedland (1989) tested 16- and 20-week-olds using a display that eliminated the flicker in particular spatial positions that is characteristic of spatially repeating, moving stimuli. Their display contained a single moving bar flanked by stationary reference bars. Velocity of this moving bar, not the extent of displacement, best predicted infants' visual preferences, suggesting that infants' preference patterns were best explained by a velocity-sensitive mechanism. These result converge reasonably well in indicating true motion-sensitive (that is, velocity-sensitive) mechanisms in the infants' visual system. These are present as early as 6 weeks of age.

A Lower, or Different, Threshold for Motion Detection

Von Hofsten et al. (1992) suggested that threshold estimates obtained in visual preference studies of motion perception may greatly underestimate infant motion detection abilities. One concern is that a reliable difference between a moving and stationary display in the visual preference method requires both that infants distinguish the displays and also that the moving display attracts more attention. Very slow velocities might be detectable but not interesting. Another concern involves motion perspective. As we saw in chapter 3, the evidence is a bit thin, but there are indications that infants extract depth information from motion perspective. This would not be possible, however, given the differential velocity thresholds suggested by Dannemiller and Freedland (1991). Von Hofsten et al. (1992) calculated that for a lateral head movement at 4 cm/sec, an observer with this threshold would not be able to distinguish a target at 69 cm (3.3 deg/sec) from one at 92 cm (2.5 deg/sec).

Using observer-contingent motion, von Hofsten et al. (1992) tested 14-week-olds for sensitivity to smaller velocities. Subjects showed sensitivity to a differential velocity of .32 deg/sec, much lower than earlier estimates. Subjects were also shown to be sensitive to the contingency of the motion with their own motion. Besides the results, there are two interesting differences, one methodological and one conceptual, between the studies of von Hofsten et al. (1992) and earlier motion threshold experiments. First, von Hofsten et al. used an habituation procedure, which might have overcome the detection versus interest problem we described in connection with preference measures. The second concerns the use of observer-contingent motion. It is possible that the smaller, observer-contingent motions studied by von Hofsten et al. are processed by a different perceptual system from larger, noncontingent motions. Contingent motions might be used by a motion perspective system to specify depth positions of stationary objects, while noncontingent motions (or larger motions) specify object motion. Further research is needed to explore the possibility of separate systems for processing optical change related to object motion and to depth.

Velocity Perception and Reaching
An interesting application of infants' velocity perception is their anticipatory reaching for moving objects. Research by von Hofsten (1980, 1983) indicates that infants reach in a predictive way for objects moving through their field of view. This behavior appears at about the same time (around 4 months of age) as directed reaching for stationary objects (von Hofsten, 1980). In these experiments, the moving object was attached to a 74 cm rod that rotated in a horizontal plane around a fixed point. At its closest point to the infant, the object was 14 cm away. Starting points and velocities were varied, and infants were scored for touching or grasping the object. Careful analysis of the timing and spatial properties of reaches suggests that infants reached with precision of about .05 sec and no systematic timing error. Accurate reaching was observed for even the fastest-moving objects in the study (60 cm/sec); additional observations on several subjects showed accurate reaching for objects moving at 120 cm/sec. For various reasons, it is difficult to work back from these remarkable results to specific conclusions about the precision of infant velocity perception. But the capacity to utilize spatial and motion information in this task is impressive. Assuming that the development of reaching to stationary objects depends on maturation in the motor system (Field, 1990), the findings also support the idea that accurate three-dimensional and event perception abilities precede skilled motor behavior. Given that predictive reaching and reaching for stationary objects appear at about the same time, the ability to perceive objects and events with considerable precision must already be in place.

Origins of Multiple Stimuli for Motion Perception

Wallach (1985) suggested that only optical displacement—the change in position of an object's projection to the retina—provides innate information for motion. Other cues, such as perceived motion during pursuit eye movements, might be learned by correlation with optical displacement.

His argument was based on the adaptability of cues other than image displacement under conflict conditions. In experiments with adults, when different motion cues gave conflicting indications, other cues were recalibrated, whereas optical displacement was not. These findings offer useful insights into perceptual adaptation processes, but they may not provide evidence about which cues arise from learning. Some useful clues, however, are available from studies of infants.

Optical Displacement

Our discussion of direction- and velocity-sensitive mechanisms above is relevant to a consideration of the origins of optical displacement. All the stimulus conditions used in the studies we discussed could plausibly produce optical displacement. Thus, the results may plausibly be taken to describe the development of motion perception from this stimulus. At the same time, none of the experiments controlled infants' fixation position. Thus, the subjects may have tracked a particular moving feature in these displays.

Optical Pursuit

There is evidence that infants detect and attempt to follow moving stimuli from the earliest ages. When an observer fixates a repetitive display—for example, a pattern of alternating black and white stripes, moving continuously—there is a characteristic, indeed involuntary, response, called *optokinetic nystagmus* (OKN). In the "slow" or tracking phase, the observer follows, with some lag, a feature of the display up to some extreme point; then, in the "fast" phase, the gaze jumps back to about the center of the field, and the cycle begins again. In adults and children, this response is virtually always accompanied by perceived motion.

Several studies have demonstrated that the OKN response to motion is innate (Brazelton, Scholl & Robey, 1966; McGinnis, 1930; Gorman et al., 1957; Dayton et al., 1964; for a review see Maurer, 1975). In these studies, the moving pattern ordinarily surrounds the subject—that is, the subject is placed within a moving cylinder. In the Gorman et al. study, 93% of infants, all younger than 5 days old, showed the response. Infants' following responses tend to be saccadic—that is, made up of small jumps rather than continuous smooth pursuit eye movements.

The existence of the OKN response is consistent with detection of motion by neonates, since OKN is ordinarily accompanied by perceived motion in children and adults. (This is true even in cases of motion sickness, where the perceived motion is illusory.) On the other hand, OKN may be a reflexive response mediated subcortically. Thus, it is conceivable that OKN exists in neonates unaccompanied by perceived motion.

Similarly, perception of motion is suggested by the fact that smooth pursuit eye movements can sometimes be detected in infants younger than 2 months of age (Shea & Aslin, 1990) and can readily be found in infants older than 2 months. Especially in the younger group, these eye movements have low gain but appropriate direction. One might infer perception of motion based on optical pursuit, but the inference is indirect.

Optical Expansion
We considered in chapter 3 research investigating whether infants detect and respond to the approach of objects from optical expansion, sometimes called *looming*. The weight of the evidence supports the notion that optical expansion signals object approach to infants. This conclusion is also consistent with psychophysical and neurophysiological indications that particular cortical cells exist that have maximal sensitivity to optical expansion or contraction (Regan & Cynader, 1979).

Stroboscopic Motion
Stroboscopic motion in infant perception has been studied using the OKN response. Tauber and Koffler (1966) reasoned that if infants could perceive stroboscopic motion, then they might exhibit an OKN response to a stroboscopic motion pattern. They arranged a display of stripes in which positions of black and white stripes shifted stroboscopically and found that infants viewing this display showed a clear OKN response. The displays in the Wattam-Bell (1992) studies of motion sensitivity, described in chapter 2, used dots displaced by differing amounts per frame in different conditions; the data across conditions may be taken as some indication of the ability of the limitations of the infant's motion system to integrate successive frames into a motion signal. Available data are thus consistent with perception of motion in stroboscopic motion displays from an early age.

Conclusion: Motion Perception

A variety of information sources appear to support perceived motion in infancy. These include optical displacement, pursuit eye movements, optical expansion or contraction, and stroboscopic motion. In some of these categories, the evidence is a bit sketchy. Part of the problem is that showing a response to particular stimulus conditions is easier than proving that the response implies perception of motion (as opposed to position change and so on). One stimulus for motion perception in adults—induced motion—has not yet been tested in infants, as far as we know.

During the early months of life, infants do not perceive motion with the sensitivity of adults. In fact, infants' ability to perceive direction of motion is weak or absent until about 8 weeks. Motion detection can be demonstrated earlier, but infants' thresholds for detecting velocity appear much higher than those of adults. Nevertheless, the infant at 6 weeks of age and onward can detect all but the slowest motions of nearby people and objects. Moreover, experiments using displacements contingent on motion of the observer suggest that velocity thresholds may be much lower than reported in other paradigms. It is not yet clear, however, whether these small displacements feed into a motion-perception system or a depth-perception system.

We have seen two reasons motion is fundamental in perception. It plays an important role in perception of persisting properties of objects and the spatial layout. It is also important because we often need to perceive particular motion characteristics of moving objects, such as trajectory and velocity. We have said little so far of the most important reason motion perception is fundamental: it is an integral part of perceiving *events*.

ECOLOGY OF EVENT PERCEPTION

It has been a long time since perceptual theorists debated whether motion was a product of perception or inference. In the meantime, the scope of perception has expanded. In ecological and computational views, perception's products are not sensory but abstract. The outputs of perception may include abstract descriptions of relationships in the physical world, as basic as where a moving observer is heading or as complex as causal relations between objects.

This is a radical idea. Functional descriptions of the environment—not just abstract representations of solid objects, surfaces, and spatial relations but descriptions of their actions and relations over time—may come from perception. Some of the earliest insights along these lines appeared in Michotte's (1963) book *The Perception of Causality*, in which he marshaled theoretical and empirical evidence supporting the notion that causal impressions were produced by perceptual mechanisms sensitive to particular spatial and temporal relationships. Another well-known example is Johansson's (1975) demonstration that a person walking, or other events, such as two people dancing, could be perceived rapidly and compellingly from a motion picture showing only the motions of tiny lights attached to the persons' main joints. Here, the local sensory inputs are impoverished. The points of light are not connected; the images contain nothing with any surfaces or volume, much less the sensory information that would normally be available from a person involved in an action in a well-lit environment. The relations in the point-light motions, in as little as two motion picture frames (Johansson, 1975), however, give striking and immediate impressions of persons and their actions.

Abstract properties of physical objects may also be products of event perception. Consider notions related to substance, such as solidity and weight. These might seem to be haptic or kinesthetically known properties of objects. According to a sensation-based view, in fact, it might seem impossible that such properties could be perceived visually from reflected light; not so, however, according to an event perception view. Runeson (1977) argued that kinematic patterns available when events are viewed specify the properties of objects. For example, subjects in his experiments viewed other people lifting a covered box containing varying weights and estimated the weight on each trial. Results showed that subjects' estimates were as good when they viewed someone else lifting the box as when they lifted it themselves! Complex relationships in the viewed biomechanical event of a person lifting something can specify material properties such as weight (Runeson & Frykholm, 1981).

Further work by Runeson and Frykholm (1983) extended these ideas to social perception. In their experiments, professional actors lifted covered boxes and attempted to convey the impression that the boxes contained either more weight or less weight than they really did. Subjects in this study viewed the actors and the lifting events. On the whole, subjects correctly detected both the true weights in the boxes, the deceptive intention of the actors, *and* the intended weight. Again, the authors explain their data in terms of information about physical (and social) dynamics available in visually perceived events.

Each of these examples of perceiving abstract physical properties from relationships in the input could be the subject of a long discussion. For example, we might ask whether the studies done so far show these abilities to be truly perceptual. These are empirical questions. The crucial point is that nothing in the definition or processes of perception rules out this possibility. Perception is often a response to higher-order relationships. Far from being incidental, the dependence of perception on relationships and on information given over time may be fundamental (Gibson, 1966, 1979; Johansson, 1970; Shepard, 1984). Related to this view is a particular idea about what *results* from perceiving: perception yields knowledge about objects and events and not merely swatches of color, high-pitched sounds, or other sensory data. This idea stretches ordinary conceptions of perception's limits. The idea that the human nervous system has mechanisms that take sound frequency information as input and produce experiences and representations of pitch is uncontroversial. The idea that the human nervous system may take patterns of motion as input and produce experiences and representations of causation, animacy, or social intention is a newer idea and far more controversial. From an ecological point of view, however, the idea that organisms have evolved mechanisms that extract important and abstract properties of objects and events from patterns in energy is fundamental.

The boundary between what is perceived and what is conceived or reasoned is difficult to resolve on philosophical grounds; it is probably an empirical issue (Fodor, 1983). We might ask what criteria can be used to establish that events are perceived. Among criteria that have been proposed for perceptual mechanisms are their strict dependence on particular stimulus relationships (Wertheimer, 1912; Michotte, 1963; Fodor, 1983), their speed, automatic engagement, dependence on specific neural mechanisms, and *information encapsulation*—that is, insulation of processing from general knowledge and beliefs (Fodor, 1983). Studies of infants may be among the most important sources of data for deciding these issues. Finding that some ability is tied to specific information and operates in early infancy raises the possibility of a perceptual account. We now examine several topics in event perception. In each, the data suggest that early capacities use stimulus patterns to obtain descriptions of functionally important environmental events. With these findings as perspective, we reexamine the boundaries between perception and cognition in chapter 11.

EVENT PERCEPTION ABILITIES AND PROCESSES

Object and Observer Motion

We begin with a complex of events closely related to perception of motion itself. How does the observer determine when he is moving through the environment and also determine which objects are stationary and moving during the event of self-motion?

Optical displacement is commonly considered the primary stimulus for motion. In the last chapter we encountered the fact that optical displacements always have two potential causes—object motion or observer motion. The same is true of other stimuli for motion perception, such as optical expansion or contraction. Optical expansion occurs when an object moves toward the observer but also when the observer moves toward the object.

Distinguishing optical changes caused by object motion from those produced by self-motion would seem to be a basic requirement for perceiving a stable, coherent reality. We saw in the last chapter one piece of evidence that infants distinguish object and observer motion, using only the former as information about the unity of partly occluded objects. Some other research has tested moving infants' perception of motion and

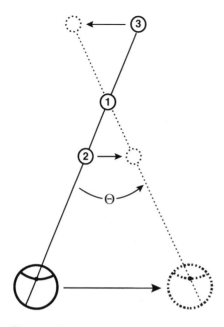

Figure 6.1
Geometry of object and observer motion. Observer movement is depicted by the eye at the bottom. When the observer moves, a stationary target at (1) changes visual direction by the angle Θ. The same optical change can be given by a nearer object moving in the same direction as the observer (2) or by a more distant object moving in the opposite direction as the observer (3). In this situation, distance information may be required to detect object motion or constant position during the observer's motion. Redrawn from Kellman (1995).

stability more directly (Kellman & von Hofsten, 1992). Their paradigm may be understood by reference to figure 6.1, which shows the basic geometry of object and observer motion, following the analyses of Gogel (1980, 1982). When the observer moves (shown as the moving eye in figure 6.1), a stationary target at one distance (1) produces a given optical change (Θ). The same optical change can be produced by a nearer object that moves in the same direction as the observer (2) or by a more distant object that moves in the opposite direction (3). In the absence of other information, detection of whether a viewed target is stationary or moving requires information about the target's distance (Gogel, 1982). In the experiments, the observer was moved laterally in an infant seat while viewing two or more objects. On any trial, one object moved a short distance along a path parallel to the observer's. The moving object appeared equally often on the left and right sides of the display area. A stationary object was placed on the side opposite to the moving one, at a distance chosen to produce the same optical change during the subject's motion.

Object size was also adjusted for distance so that the corresponding moving and stationary objects had the same projective sizes. The subject thus saw on each trial objects to the left and right having similar optical projections and displacements. Detecting the moving one required information about target distance. Based on other research, it was assumed that if infants could distinguish moving from stationary objects under these conditions, they would preferentially attend to the moving object.

At both 16 and 8 weeks of age, infants showed reliable preferences for the moving object when the object and observer movement were in opposite phase, whereas only 16-week-olds showed the preference when the object and observer moved in the same direction (Kellman & von Hofsten, 1992). The reason for the asymmetry in the younger group's data is unclear. When infants were tested monocularly (using a patch over one eye), motion preferences were eliminated. The results suggest an early ability of moving observers to perceive object motion and stability, and implicate the use of binocular information. It appears that binocular convergence provides the absolute (egocentric) distance information needed. Stereoscopic vision is present in about half of 16-week-olds but virtually never in 8-week-olds (Held et al., 1980). Moreover, binocular disparity alone specifies only depth order, not egocentric distance (Wallach & Zuckerman, 1963). Combined with some source of information about absolute distance, such as convergence, disparities can specify very precise depth intervals (Wallach & Zuckerman, 1963). It is likely that the combination of convergence and disparity underlies the better performance found at 16 weeks in these studies.

That young infants distinguish object motion and stability during observer motion is remarkable. Information of different kinds must be integrated to accomplish these tasks. The character of this integration is revealing. Motion (or stability) perception depends not merely on certain stimulus variables but also on perceived distance. This dependence of one perceptual outcome on another—what has been called *percept-percept coupling* (Epstein, 1982)—illustrates that sophisticated computations underlie perceptual processing even in early infancy.

Interrelations of Motion and Distance

The relationships of motion and distance, and their role in perception, suggest a paradox. Earlier we described the depth information called *motion perspective*. In motion perspective, optical changes given by stationary objects to a moving observer provide information about distance. Extracting this information depends on the assumption that objects are stationary: given this assumption and the extent of observer motion, distance can be determined. On the other hand, detecting whether an object is moving or stationary when the observer moves depends on the same geometry with different known and unknown quantities. In this case, some independent source of distance information, information about the extent of observer motion, and registered optical displacement determine whether the object is moving or stationary. Apparently, the geometry of motion and distance can be used in two ways—to extract distance, assuming that the object is stationary, or to extract target motion, if distance is known. An important challenge for both infant and adult vision research is to determine the conditions under which these relationships are used to determine motion from distance or distance from motion.

The event of observer motion is basic to perception and action. When moving, perceivers need to detect their own motion through the environment, the stability of stationary objects, and other things that move. These priorities appear to be reflected in processes that effectively exploit the projective geometry of motion and distance from an early age.

Perceiving Object Permanence

Theories that focus on events in perception open the possibility that more of human knowledge is perceptual than has previously been assumed. Few would quibble with the idea that extracting information about the movement or stationary positions of objects is part of *perception*. But consider *object permanence*. Human adults appear to have several core beliefs about physical objects, including the belief that an object experienced at different times has continued to exist in the interim. Stated this way, the principle appears to be part of our cognitive structure, not a product of perception.

The view of object permanence as a cognitive achievement is a cornerstone of Piaget's account of development. For Piaget, the ability to represent an object as enduring when it is outside of sensory contact is an important benchmark of a changing representational system, one that appears at about 9 months of age. This age fits with certain highly replicable observations made by Piaget. Young infants who readily reach for a certain object will not search for it when it is hidden, for instance, if it is covered by a cloth. At about 9 months, the child will search for the hidden object (Piaget, 1954).

Many researchers have questioned Piaget's interpretations. Infants' lack of active search when an object is hidden may be due to limitations in planning and carrying out action (Diamond & Goldman-Rakic, 1983) or in problem-solving abilities (Baillargeon, Graber, DeVos & Black, 1990).

These criticisms are especially important in light of a different analysis of object permanence proposed by Gibson (1966) and Gibson et al. (1969). The continued existence of a viewed object that goes out of sight may not be a matter of assumptions or inferences but a matter of *percep-*

(a)

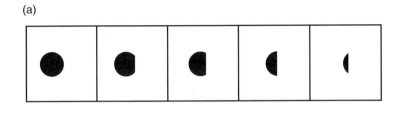

(b)

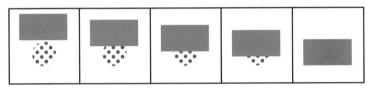

Figure 6.2
Progressive occlusion and accretion and deletion of texture. a. Example of progressive occlusion. When the frames shown are viewed in a motion sequence, an unchanging disk is seen slipping behind the surface through a slit (after Michotte, Thines & Crabbe, 1964). b. Accretion and deletion of texture. As the occluder covers the object, visible texture of the object is deleted, specifying that the object persists and goes behind the occluder (after Gibson, Kaplan, Reynolds & Wheeler, 1969).

tion. Certain optical transformations occur when an object passes behind another object; specifically, there is a progressive shrinkage of the visible area (Michotte et al., 1964), and there is deletion of the object's texture at the occluding edge (Kaplan, 1969; Gibson et al., 1969). Perceptual mechanisms may map these transformations into representations of object persistence. Figure 6.2 illustrates these two forms of information. Figure 6.2a, after Michotte et al. (1964), shows a sequence of frames that when shown to subjects, give the impression of an object slipping behind the surface through an unseen slit. Figure 6.2b illustrates the information of accretion and deletion discovered by Gibson et al. (1969). Different transformations specify an object going out of existence. Three examples are an object shattering into pieces on impact with a surface, an effervescent tablet dissolving in water, and a sandwich being eaten bite by bite. Although for convenience we have described the events and not their optical consequences, each of these events produces optical changes unlike the case of progressive occlusion.

To avoid possible limitations of young infants' abilities to plan and execute searches for hidden objects, researchers have designed tasks that assess infants' expectations in other ways. Baillargeon, Spelke, and Wasserman (1985) habituated infants to a screen, hinged to the display case floor, that rotated toward and away from the observer through 180 deg. After habituation, with the screen down in the forward position, a box was placed in its path. Two test events were then shown. In the "possible" event, the screen rotated back gradually occluding the box until the box was no longer visible; the screen continued backward and stopped where it would have been obstructed by the box, resulting in a 112 deg rotation of the screen. In the "impossible" event, the screen continued back through the space in which the box would have been (180 deg rotation). (Habituation and test events are diagrammed in figure 6.3.) Infants looked reliably longer at the impossible event, suggesting that they were surprised by the action of the screen in this event. A control experiment, in which the box was placed to the side of the screen, verified that the main result was not due to an intrinsic preference for the 180 deg

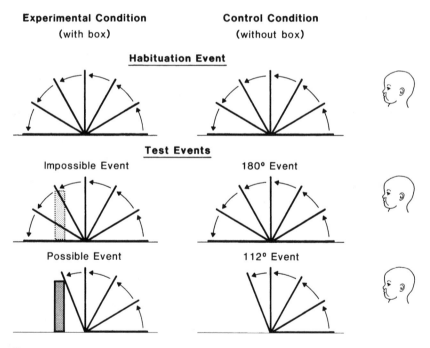

Figure 6.3
Habituation and test events used in an object permanence experiment. From Baillargeon, R. (1987), Object permanence in 3 1/2- and 4 1/2-month-old infants, *Developmental Psychology*, 23, 655–664. Copyright © 1987 by the American Psychological Association. Reprinted with permission.

event over the 112 deg event. Similar results were found in other experiments with infants as young as 3.5 months (Baillargeon, 1987).

These findings suggest an early capacity to represent the existence of an object that is out of sight. What is less often mentioned is that the persistence of the object may be *perceived*, at least initially. The optical transformation of gradual covering, as well as accretion and deletion of any visible texture on the hidden object, specifies the continuation of the object behind a nearer object (Gibson et al., 1969). To the best of our knowledge, all of the studies showing a capacity for object permanence early in life use this sort of optical transformation (see Baillargeon, 1993 for a review; Craton & Yonas, 1990; Van de Walle & Spelke, 1996). (Gibson et al., 1969, identified others that result, for adults, in perceived annihilation of the object, but no study seems to have employed these transformations with infants.) The studies of early object permanence may be interpreted in an event perception framework as indicating the early appearance of perceptual mechanisms that produce representations of persistence from certain optical transformations.

According to this view, is there any cognitive (nonperceptual) component to representing a fully hidden object? We believe there is. It seems to us likely that a perceptual mechanism produces a representation of an object that persists as it is being covered and momentarily afterward. If we leave for two days, return, and expect the object to be still under the cover, we are reasoning rather than perceiving. *Time* may be one important dimension separating representations resulting from perception from those requiring additional cognitive apparatus. We consider further the issue of separating perception from cognition in chapter 11.

Perceiving Causality

Earlier we mentioned Michotte's (1963) proposal that causal impressions are products not of inference but of perception. From a more sensation-oriented perspective, apprehending a causal event—such as when one object collides with another causing it to move—must be a cognitive act. One could register color, position, and motion of two objects, but their causal relation is not given in sensations. In Hume's classic analysis of causation, he claimed that recurrent experiences of succession produce causal expectations. If we have previously seen one billiard ball roll up to another and the second one move immediately afterward, we come to expect that the movement of the second ball will reliably follow the first, and we attribute a causal power to the first ball.

One of Michotte's (1963) arguments against Hume's account is that we need not experience recurrent successive events to get a causal impression; we get one on the very first exposure if certain spatial and temporal relations hold. The results of Michotte's many experiments are consistent with the idea that impressions of mechanical causality are produced by a perceptual mechanism tuned to particular spatial and temporal relationships.

Research on human infants has produced evidence of perceptual mechanisms sensitive to causality. This possibility fits with ecological views, which have hypothesized the importance of events and perceptual mechanisms attuned to them. Leslie and Keeble (1987) reported evidence of causal perception in 6.5-month-olds. Infants in one group were habituated to a film showing *launching*, the term Michotte used to designate the causal impression between two objects when an object is set into motion immediately on being contacted by a moving object. Another group was habituated to a similar film that would not give adults a causal impression; it had a delay between the stopping of the first object and the movement of the second. After habituation, both films were reversed. Because the objects and motions in the forward and backward films were similar, the experimenters hypothesized that there should be little dishabituation between them. If a causal interaction was perceived, then reversing the roles of the objects might be a more significant, attention-getting change. The results supported this hypothesis. Infants in the launching group dishabituated more than the delayed-reaction group to the reversed film. Leslie and Keeble (1987) interpret their results as consistent with the notion of an input module (autonomous perceptual mechanism) that delivers information about "the spatiotemporal and causal structure of appropriate events" (p. 286).

Other research suggests that this ability is somewhat fragile and is found consistently only in relatively simple situations (Oakes, 1994; Cohen & Oakes, 1993). Cohen and Oakes (1993) further suggest that causal perception may not be a modular ability, as suggested by Leslie and Keeble (1987). Their argument rests on variations in outcomes of causality studies due to changes in objects during the experiment. In one example, subjects who viewed events involving objects that changed from trial to trial distinguished causal and noncausal events less clearly than subjects in an earlier experiment with unchanging objects. Cohen and Oakes (1993) propose that a more general "information processing view" can encompass these variations more easily than a perceptual module. Other interpretations are just as plausible, however. The causal descriptions produced by a modular perceptual mechanism might well be about specific objects rather than about the general presence of causality across trials. Moreover, responses to novelty surely involve object characteristics other than causal relations. In the absence of more quantitative models, it is not clear what predictions about responses to confounded sources of novelty should be made from either an information-processing view or a modular-perceptual view.

On balance, the evidence supports the idea that infants visually extract causal relationships as early as 6.5 months of age. The dependence of infants' causal perception on particular spatial and temporal relationships is consistent with the account proposed three decades ago by Michotte (1963)—namely, that causal impressions arise perceptually. Whereas Michotte's hypothesis, applied to infants, remains plausible regarding the rudiments of causal knowledge, it is likely that these early appearing abilities undergo elaboration later in infancy (Oakes & Cohen, 1990) and beyond.

Conclusion: Event Perception

Our discussion of event perception has been necessarily brief and selective. Two generalizations are nevertheless obvious. First, infants from the early months of life possess startling competencies to extract and represent important functional relations from perceived events. Second, the very notion of event perception, especially in combination with its early beginnings, stretches our conceptions about the nature of perception and its relation to the rest of cognition. We return to these important matters in chapter 11.

Chapter 7
Intermodal Perception

It matters not through which sense I realize that in the dark I have blundered into a pigsty.
—von Hornbostel (1927, p. 83)

A young child drops a vase. She both sees and hears it shatter. The sound causes her mother to turn, expecting, then seeing, the worst. Ordinary incidents like this one illustrate the coordination of our several senses and reveal some of its most important aspects. A physical event—in this case, the transformation of a unitary object into multiple, intricately shaped pieces—comes to us through more than one sense. The event of shattering is seen and heard. The microstructures of the event as it appears in each sense coincide: at the same moment the child sees the object contact the floor, she hears the first sound of impact, and the bouncing fragments come to rest just as the last jingle subsides. The sounds alone alert the mother and also signal the nature of the event and its location; on looking, she confirms visually what she has already heard.

How do our separate senses come to furnish information about the same events and objects in the world? Why do the inputs to one sense give us expectations about what information will be available to other senses? How do our senses cooperate, and how do they diverge? How does the existence of multiple sensory channels allow us to learn about, and function within, the world? These are the questions of *intermodal* perception and its development.

ECOLOGY OF INTERMODAL PERCEPTION

No topic in perceptual development raises disagreements more fundamental than the origins of intermodal perception. To discuss the task and information of intermodal perception, we must begin with two radically different conceptions. For one view, the starting point is this: The world available to our senses consists of various kinds of energy—electromagnetic, acoustic, mechanical, chemical, thermal, and so on. To apprehend this energy, we have separate sensory channels, each special-ized to receive one kind of energy—for the eyes, light; for the ears, sound; for different receptors in the skin, pressure and temperature. We can follow the activity in our senses from these physical inputs to their mental outputs. On receiving its special energy, each sensory system gives rise to unique sensations. Vision gives us brightness and color. Tac-tile senses give us sharp contact or deep pressure, warmth or cold. Our chemical senses offer up tastes and smells, and audition renders loudness and pitch. Each sense has its own unique language in which its outputs are expressed. At the crossroads of these sensory products, the mind must at first be a Tower of Babel. A sensation of bright red is not translatable into a high pitch or a feeling of sharp contact. Given these facts, the central task of development must be *integration*: we must somehow learn to co-ordinate and integrate our separate senses.

The other view begins with the objects and events in the world. These interact with various forms of energy. The interactions produce patterns in the energy that reaches our receptor arrays. Our senses are best thought of as perceptual systems, specialized for extracting these patterns. Some of these patterns, termed *amodal*, are in fact the same in the different energy streams and can be apprehended by different senses. When one knocks on a door, the pitch and loudness of the sounds bear no sensory similarity to the colors and brightness of the hand and door. In an organism's internal framework of time, however, both of these events share the same begin-ning and end, and the same rhythm pattern of the knocking is both visible and audible. These temporal properties are amodal. The senses are unified in that they bring such information to us through different channels. Much of this information consists of abstract patterns available through more than one sense.

Should the newborn infant, like a newly hired worker, inquire as to her first assignment, she would, on these two perspectives of intermodal per-ception, be given completely different instructions. From the former per-spective, the assignment would be to learn relations between the unique products of the various senses. From the latter, the assignment would be to begin to learn about the unitary world that is manifest through the several sensory channels. Let us consider each perspective and its devel-opmental consequences in more detail, focusing on the earliest tasks and initial equipment. Subsequently, we will see how research over the past 20 years has helped to decide some of the basic issues and to determine the useful contributions of both perspectives.

Integrating the Senses

What could be more obvious than the separateness of the senses? Physio-logically, each sensory system has its own specialized receptors. Beyond the peripheral nervous system, our senses remain separate: we find distinct projection areas in the brain for sight, hearing, touch, and so on. Physically, each sense is specially designed to detect a particular form of energy. When acoustic waveforms, given by a person's voice, pass through the pupil of an observer's eye and contact the retina, there is complete indifference—no response. The same fate awaits light entering the nose or ear.

Starting from the view that the senses are distinct in their inputs and products, their physiology and their selective contact with the world, the question of intermodal perception must be: How do we learn to relate the separate senses?

The standard answer given by proponents of this perspective has been that learning occurs through the association of sensations that occur together in time or space (e.g., Titchener, 1902). Piaget's proposals (1954) modified this account somewhat, arguing that what glues together separate sensations is their connection with *action*. Separate streams of sensation are brought into correspondence by activity. When a child squeezes a doll, it deforms (sensed visually and tactually) and squeaks (sensed auditorily). The contingency of all of these sensory outcomes on the initial action, and their contiguity with one another, provide the basis for learning about intersensory relationships (Bushnell, 1994).

What are the requirements for associative learning? Classical views of the mind note spatial contiguity, temporal contiguity, and similarity as the bases for association (Hobbes, 1651/1974; Locke, 1690/1956; Aristotle, 1941). Regarding the inputs from separate senses, similarity would not appear to be much help, if sensory qualities are unique to each sense. This leaves contiguity in space and time. In order for activity in different senses to be related spatially or temporally, there must be a common space and time in which contiguity can be determined (cf. Kant, 1781/1902). Even with an integration view of intersensory development (Birch & Lefford, 1967), we might expect innate sensitivity to common timing, spatial location, or both, across the senses.

Perceiving the World through Multiple Senses

Turning to the second perspective, what is the meaning of von Hornbostel's (1927) graphic example about the pigsty? In this view of intermodal perception, the emphasis is on the physical world: the objects and events in it manifest themselves to us through several sensory channels. An event or object given through several senses remains one thing, not several things. This is a nice homily, but what might it mean? How does this sentiment overcome the physiological, physical, and phenomenological walls that separate our senses, one from the other?

We touched on the answer in chapter 1. To think of the senses as detecting energy and producing separate sensations is a seductive error. Instead, according to this alternative view, our senses detect *patterns* and produce representations of the *structure* of objects and events. The most important properties perceived may be those that are not specific to one sense. Rather, they are *amodal* properties (Michotte et al., 1964). Amodal properties invariably involve spatial, temporal, or spatiotemporal concepts. Of these, the simplest is location. An event specified visually comes from a certain direction relative to the perceiver; this same event and the same direction may be given auditorily. The events will also coincide in time. In the vase example, breaking glass gives visible and audible effects in the same location at the same time, leading to the perception of a unitary event.

Other amodal properties are given as patterns. The spatial array of spines on a porcupine may be detected visually or tactually. (Detecting visually may be wiser.) The rising and falling of a boat on rough seas is given to the passenger on deck visually and also by vestibular sensations. In these cases, the patterns in space or time do not differ across the sensory modalities; they are therefore referred to as *amodal invariants*.

The distinction between amodal properties is closely related to an older distinction, suggested by the philosopher John Locke, between *primary* and *secondary qualities*. In Locke's (1690/1956) words:

> primary qualities of things ... are discovered by our senses, and are in them even when we perceive them not: such are the bulk, figure, number, situation and motion of the parts of bodies; which are really in them, whether we take notice of them or no. Secondly, the sensible secondary qualities, which, depending on these are nothing but the powers those substances have to produce several ideas in us by our senses; which ideas are not in the things themselves otherwise than as anything is in its cause.... For to speak truly, yellowness is not actually in gold, but is a power in gold to produce that idea in us by our eyes, when placed in a due light.... Had we senses acute enough to discern the minute particles of bodies, and the real constitution on which their sensible qualities depend, I doubt not but they would produce quite different ideas in us; and that which is now the yellow colour of gold would then disappear, and instead of it we should see an admirable texture of parts, of a certain size and figure. (pp. 9–11)

Primary qualities—ideas about objects and events that correspond to real physical properties—are also *amodal* properties, in that they are not uniquely the province of only one sensory modality, and they may be detected in multiple sensory channels. Characteristically, amodal properties involve relationships in space or time. This is why we sometimes describe them as higher-order properties. Consider that the sweetness of a sugar cube is a *modal* sensory quality in that it is given only through a single sense—taste. The *form* of a sugar cube, on the other hand, may be detected visually or haptically. The property of form has to do with the arrangement of matter in space, not what the cube is made of. If we broke the cube into fragments, the pieces would still taste sweet, but the cube shape would be lost. A final way of giving the distinction between amodal and modal properties involves mental and physical predicates. Modal properties live in the world of our conscious experience: "sweetness" is not found in the vocabulary of physics. As Locke understood 300 years ago, it is an effect of physical stimulation on our sensory apparatus. Descriptions of the physical world do not invoke sweetness but do require arrangements in space and time; being cube-shaped is a meaningful idea in physics. (Explaining what physical stimuli taste sweet ultimately involves spatial arrangement as well, at very small scales.)

Amodal invariants open the door to a very different view of the task and information for intermodal perception. One task is to detect objects and events by means of amodal invariants. Another is to optimize behavior by using the differing advantages of the multiple windows onto the world afforded by separate perceptual systems.

From this perspective, what do we make of the separate physiology, physics, and phenomenology of the senses? The development of multiple sensory channels allows us to pick up patterns carried by different kinds of energy. But the patterns may be the same. Each receptor system, and each energy type, may have its uniquely helpful properties. Because light moves in straight lines and our visual apparatus preserves directional information, we obtain exquisite spatial detail visually. Sounds, given our auditory system, are less spatially precise but may more readily tell us about an event in the next room. Answering the question of whether the physical world is unitary or multiple depends on whether we focus on the separate streams of energy or the unitary objects and events about which they carry information.

Recent advances in neurophysiology show us that the separate senses are not so separate at certain levels of the nervous system. Some brain areas contain multimodal neurons—that is, single cells responsive to inputs from different modalities (Knudsen, Knudsen & Esterly, 1982; Knudsen, 1983, 1984; Meredith & Stein, 1986; Stein, Meredith & Wallace, 1994). Below we examine the implications of these findings for the notion that separate sensory channels are attuned to a unified, abstract spatial and temporal reality.

So far we have described amodal perception as underlying a single viewpoint about intermodal development. Actually, several different hypotheses have been proposed regarding the role of amodal invariants in development. One view (Gibson, 1969; Spelke, 1987; Bahrick, 1994) postulates that an innate sensitivity to amodal invariants forms the bedrock of early intermodal learning. Experience brings about finer differentiation of detail within and between modalities, but perception begins with a multichannel attunement to a common external world. A more modest version of the idea that intersensory coordination is built into the nervous system was suggested by Morrongiello (1994) regarding auditory-visual coordination. The infant begins with a mapping between modalities that controls some reflexive behavior. A sound may trigger head and eye movements to look in the sound's direction. This reflexive base promotes learning about auditory-visual relationships by getting the infant to look at what she is hearing.

Perhaps the most exotic notion of inborn sensory coordination was suggested by Bower (1974). The role of amodal information might be so extreme that initially an infant has no awareness of sensory modality at all. Information about spatial location, timing, or intensity might be picked up without any awareness that it has come from vision, audition, touch, and so on. As development proceeds, the infant would gradually become aware of the separateness of the sensory channels. A more restricted version of this hypothesis is that initially infants are most sensitive to stimulus intensity, regardless of modality (Turkewitz, Lewkowicz & Gardner, 1966; Schneirla, 1959). At an early stage, stimulus intensity may add or substitute across modalities to influence responding.

ABILITIES AND PROCESSES OF INTERMODAL PERCEPTION

We have described two sets of ideas that differ greatly in their implications for the development of intermodal perception. Although we have pointed out the fallacy in the idea that our senses *must* have as their outputs only sensations, the fallacy indicates not that the classical view is wrong but only that it cannot be established by logic. On the other side of the theoretical fence, it is clear that there is more than one specific way in which intermodal coordination might be built into the infant's nervous system or acquired by learning.

A question of high priority is whether amodal invariants support intermodal perception prior to specific experience. If they do, we might proceed to ask, how? Do they act through a few early reflexes, via true intermodal knowledge, or does the evidence suggest that the separate sensory channels themselves must be differentiated from an initial unity of experience?

Intermodal development involves other questions also. What about correlated properties of objects and events that are not supported by amodal invariants? One might learn, for example, that an apple is red and tastes sweet. Nothing about the common reality of space and time (or chemistry and optics, for that matter) guarantees this connection. It is imaginable that something red and apple-shaped could taste bitter. Yet learning of intersensory correlations that happen to be true in our world, such as that red apples taste sweet, is an important kind of knowledge. When do infants become able to learn such correlations? Are some kinds more easily acquired than others?

Development of Auditory-Visual Intermodal Perception

Links in Space and Time
In 1961, Michael Wertheimer reported that a newborn infant less than 10 minutes old would turn her eyes to look in the direction of a sound. A toy "cricket" was clicked next to one ear or the other, and although the infant made an eye movement on only about half of the 52 trials, when eye movements occurred they were almost always directed toward the sound.

This finding indicates some innate auditory-visual (or auditory-oculomotor) coordination. Such coordination may represent highly adaptive exploratory behavior. The central part of the visual field has greater acuity than the periphery. On hearing a sound from a particular location, newborns may turn to get a better look.

There are less expansive interpretations (Spelke, 1987; Clifton, Morrongiello, Kulig & Dowd, 1981; Morrongiello, 1994). The infant may be born with a reflex to turn in the direction of sound. Such a reflex could be guided by a simple mechanism. A discrete sound to one side reaches one ear before the other. A continuing sound reaches the two ears with a lower intensity and slight delay in its cycle (phase) at the far ear. These interaural differences may be wired into an eye movement reflex. The auditory information may not even have a spatial character at this stage: the direction of interaural differences might trigger visual orienting in the right direction but not to any particular location. Such a reflex may require no initial intermodal *knowledge* at all. Instead, it might be a simple mechanism that helps the infant to discover intermodal relationships.

We can separate two issues here. One is the issue of whether orienting is a reflex or an exploratory act. The other concerns the sophistication of intermodal mapping revealed by orienting. Do visual and auditory information feed into a common spatial coordinate system? Or is something much more rudimentary going on—for example, merely turning in the right direction, with no spatial metric?

Taking the second question first, there is evidence that orienting is sensitive to spatial location. Morrongiello, Fenwick, Hillier, and Chance (1994) presented newborn infants with a 20 sec recording of a rattle

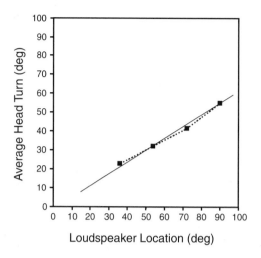

Figure 7.1
Extent of newborn head rotation (in degrees) as a function of sound displacement from midline (0 deg). Best-fitting (least-squares) linear function is shown: $Y = 0.62x - 2.2$, $R^2 = .992$. Data points from Morrongiello (1994).

sound from a loudspeaker displaced by varying angles from the midline. Figure 7.1 shows the average head turn plotted as a function of lateral position (displacement from midline) of a loudspeaker. The average head turn increased with increased angle in approximately linear fashion. Perfect accuracy would have produced a linear function with slope of 1 and intercept at 0; the data show the right intercept but a slope of around .7. Although the data show imperfect accuracy, they show an orderly relationship between auditory and visual information about space.

Returning to the first issue, several observations support a reflex interpretation of visual orienting in the newborn period. Newborns orient toward sounds in the dark and even when their eyes are closed (Mendelson & Haith, 1976; Turkewitz et al., 1966). Clifton et al. (1981) observed little habituation of orienting over trials when no visual target was present. Around 5 months of age, rapid habituation is observed when no visible target is present. These observations support the idea that orienting is not under voluntary control initially or at least is not very sensitive to the availability of visual information.

On the other hand, early auditory-visual coordination has properties that are not reflexlike. First, reflexes ordinarily involve specific, stereotypic sensory-motor combinations. Although Wertheimer (1961) measured eye movements, many subsequent reports have involved head-turning movements (Muir & Field, 1979; Clifton et al., 1981). Both seem appropriate in spatial direction. If these behaviors are reflexive, there are at least two reflexes here. (If newborns could twist their torsos with greater skill, perhaps there would be a third.) Second, auditory-visual orienting appears to violate the primary laws of reflex action, such as the intensity-magnitude law and the intensity-probability law (see Millenson, 1967, for discussion of the primary laws of the reflex). The former law states that as intensity increases, the magnitude of response increases. The latter states that as stimulus intensity increases, the probability of response increases. Experiments on early auditory-visual orienting have shown that soft sounds elicit eye movements in the direction of sounds but that loud sounds are more likely to produce looks away from the sound source. Studies on habituation of head turning have shown that newborns are sensitive to stimulus novelty. With repeated exposure, they will reliably begin turning away from a sound (Zelazo, Weiss & Tarquinio, 1991). A change in the sound reinstates head turning, even if that change is a decrease in stimulus intensity. These properties of infant orienting to sounds do not fit a reflex interpretation.

Other recent data indicate flexibility in ongoing responding that seems more like exploratory behavior than reflex action. In the experiments by Morrongiello et al. (1994), some trials were *shift* trials in which an initial sound location was used until the infant responded, after which the sound was shifted to a new location. Infants made compensatory responses in this situation, indicating that their monitoring of the sound's location is ongoing. Morrongiello et al. compared the situation to the updating of saccadic eye movements in adults when a target moves (Becker & Jurgens, 1979). On balance, neonate auditory-visual coordination does not appear to be a reflex. It looks more like rudimentary spatial exploratory behavior.

Neural Bases of Auditory-Visual Coordination
Exciting developments in neurophysiology give us important evidence from other species about the neural implementation of early auditory-visual coordination and how it changes with experience. The *superior colliculus* is a subcortical structure associated with attention and orienting functions. Some individual neurons in this region, at least in barn owls and cats, respond to *both* auditory and visual inputs. Specifically, each unit responds to sounds or visual events that come from the same spatial direction (Knudsen et al., 1982), and such units may be activated much more by simultaneous auditory-visual inputs than by either alone (Meredith & Stein, 1986). Sound localization in a variety of species, including humans, depends on intensity and phase differences in the sounds at two ears. An ear plug placed in one ear will attenuate sound intensity and produce a small phase shift at that ear, thus remapping the intensity and phase

differences for sounds originating from any direction. Knudsen (1983; Knudsen & Knudsen, 1985) raised young barn owls with one ear plugged and found that units in the superior colliculus had compensated so that they were receptive to sounds and sights from a single location. If the earplug was removed, discrepancies in the appropriate direction appeared (see figure 7.2). With experience, recalibration of receptive fields was possible so long as the owl had not reached adulthood. If the plug was removed after adulthood, the altered relations between auditory and visual locations remained permanent (Knudsen & Knudsen, 1985).

These neurophysiological findings suggest that at least the owl brain is wired to coordinate sights and sounds and to recalibrate the relationship (up to some point in development) as necessary. The existence of some intermodal orienting in human neonates suggests that at least a coarse matching of auditory and visual maps exists from the beginning. Each map must change somewhat because of growth (for example, changing separation between ears caused by growth alters intensity and phase differences), and the precision of the two spatial maps is not the same. The auditory map is less precise, whether measured in terms of neuronal receptive fields in animals (Knudsen & Knudsen, 1985; Meredith & Stein, 1986; Stein et al., 1994) or precision of localization performance (Morrongiello, 1994). But the amodal invariant of spatial location appears to provide in some form an innate foundation for intermodal perception.

Simultaneity

How far can we get in explaining intermodal perception by virtue of a common space in which sounds and sights occur? There are severe limitations. Different sounds and sights occur in a given direction at different times. Without a common *time* in which sensory experiences unfold, our cognition might remain incoherent despite a common space. Also, we may have mismatches in a given spatial direction between perceptible events. For instance, you may sit in a room and hear the sound of a car's motor outdoors. When you look in the direction of that sound, you may see only a stationary lamp and an opaque wall behind it. Intermodal development may require initial sensitivity to synchrony in time, and it may require some ability to match event structure. (The car sound and the stationary lamp should not be linked in intermodal learning, despite being in the same spatial direction at the same time.)

If temporal and spatial relationships figure in early intersensory perception, we might be able to discover the relevant properties by separating them. For example, detecting an event of similar temporal structure in vision and audition might lead to the expectation that the visually and auditorily given locations should match. An attempt to test infants' performance using this kind of reasoning was carried out by Aronson and

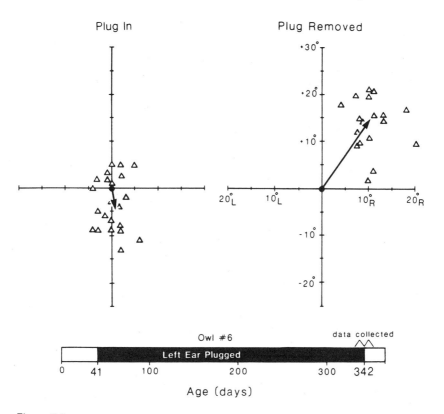

Figure 7.2
Shifts in the auditory spatial tuning of tectal units in an owl following monaural occlusion at 41 days of age. The centers of the auditory best areas (delta) of all bimodal units located in the rostral tectum are plotted relative to the centers of their visual receptive fields. The vectors represent the median auditory visual misalignment of these samples. The auditory history of this owl and the period over which the data were collected are indicated at the bottom. Reprinted with permission from Knudsen, E. I., & Knudsen, P., F. (1985), Vision guides the adjustment of auditory localization in young barn owls, *Science, 230,* 545–548. Copyright 1985 American Association for the Advancement of Science.

Rosenbloom (1971). Infants 1 to 2 months old viewed their mother talking with the soundtrack played through a loudspeaker. In the initial phase of the experiment, the sound and visual display were colocated (straight ahead). After either 2 or 5 min, the sound was played through a loudspeaker displaced by 90 deg around the infant (facing the right or left ear). The authors reported that infants showed visible distress at the locational discrepancy. Later research cast doubt on the reality of this phenomenon (Condry, Haltom & Neisser, 1977; McGurk & Lewis, 1974). In particular, distress reactions do not turn out to provide much of a window into intermodal perception.

A more sensitive measure for studying auditory-visual relationships in infancy was developed by Spelke (1976). It is based on the visual preference method and exploits infants' tendencies to look in the direction of a sound. Two side-by-side visual events are displayed, and sounds are played from a speaker centered between them. In the original experiments of this type, Spelke (1976) showed 16-week-olds two films—one showing percussion events between a baton, tambourine, and wooden block and the other a person playing peekaboo. When a sound track from one event was played, infants looked reliably longer at the appropriate visual event. Bahrick, Walker, and Neisser (1981) found similar results using a variety of event pairs.

Subsequent work sought to specify the bases of intermodal perception. Perhaps 16-week-olds had learned what kinds of sounds and sights go together, a possibility consistent with constructivist views of perceptual development. Alternatively, infants might have detected amodal invariants, such as synchrony of visual and auditory information for impact or identical rhythm patterns.

Studies by Spelke (1979) investigated these temporal relationships. Sixteen-week-olds viewed two stuffed animals that repetitively rose from and fell onto a surface. Two methods were used to test intermodal perception. One was the visual preference method described above. In 100 sec trials, looking preferences were measured to a pair of adjacent visual displays in the presence of a soundtrack consisting of discrete sounds. In a *search* method (Spelke & Owsley, 1979), the two visual displays first appeared without sound. Then the soundtrack occurred briefly, and several aspects of infant looking behavior were measured, including direction of first look and duration of looking to each visual display during a short period following the sound.

Two amodal invariants tested were synchrony and rate information. Synchrony was tested by equating the rate of the two bouncing animals but placing them in different phase. Sounds were synchronized to moments of surface impact in one of the visual displays. In the search procedure, infants reliably looked first at the visual display synchronized with the sound, whereas results from the visual preference measurements were equivocal. Sensitivity to rate information was tested using displays in which the two animals moved at different rates; the soundtrack always matched one or the other rate but was not synchronized with visual impacts. Here again, the search method, but not the preference method, indicated use of rate in intermodal matching.

The ecological "logic" of early intersensory perception may be revealed by the contrast of infants' behavior in these situations with others. Suppose two adjacent visual displays (such as checkerboard patterns) flash on and off at different rates while a pulsing sound is synchronized to one display. Studies using this paradigm (Lewkowicz, 1985, 1986) typically find little or no evidence of intermodal matching (Moore & Gibbons, 1988; Humphrey & Tees, 1980) as late as 10 months of age. When two flashing visual patterns are given with different *durations* as well as rates, 6- and 8-month-olds, but not 3-month-olds, look more at the visual display matched to the sounds. These findings suggest a later onset of sensitivity to amodal invariants than earlier research. One key to resolving this apparent conflict lies in the types of objects and events used (Walker-Andrews, 1994). Infants' competence seems clearest in cases where the amodal invariants arise from simple mechanics, such as a real object impacting a surface producing simultaneous sounds and sights. Static visual displays consisting of light sources that flash on and off in synchrony with pulsing sounds are somewhat anomalous ecologically; such events do not arise from simple mechanics in the ordinary environment. These events do not appear to engage the infant's earliest competence.

Interestingly, the details of the events used seem to affect not only infants' intermodal perception but also the effectiveness of different assessment methods. Most researchers agree that sensitivity to temporal synchrony is evident at 4 months of age (Spelke, 1976; Lewkowicz, 1992; Walker-Andrews, 1994), but it shows up in the original visual preference method only with distinctive and naturalistic stimuli, such as events like beating a drum, a person talking, hands clapping, and so on (Spelke, 1994). Even bouncing stuffed animals may give equivocal preference results (Lewkowicz, 1992; Spelke, 1979, 1994), perhaps because of the similar and repetitive nature of this event pair. Evidence for synchrony detection in cases where the preference method fails comes from search methods (Spelke; 1979; Spelke, Born & Chu, 1983) and habituation methods (Lewkowicz, 1992).

Sensitivity to higher-order temporal properties, such as rate, appears even more strongly affected by stimulus and procedural variables. Paradoxically, rate may be such a salient aspect of visual displays that it captures attention apart from auditory-visual relations (Lewkowicz, 1994). Visual preference measures with repetitive bouncing stimuli do not appear to be reliably affected by rate (Lewkowicz, 1992; Spelke, 1979), but search methods fare better (Spelke, 1979; Bahrick, 1987, 1992).

Single versus Multiple Objects

Another property that might be perceived intermodally is number. Bahrick (1987, 1992) tested infants' intermodal perception of single and multiple objects. One stimulus consisted of a large marble moving back and forth in a plastic tube (single stimulus). A second consisted of a group of small marbles moving in a tube (compound stimulus). The tubes' motions consisted of rotations around an axis perpendicular to the long axes of the cylinders, causing the marbles to fall downward (see figure 7.3). In a visual preference procedure, 4-month-old infants showed preferences based on synchrony of impact sounds with visual impacts. They did not show reliable preferences based on the temporal microstructure specifying single or multiple objects until 6 months of age (Bahrick, 1987). In a different procedure, Bahrick (1988) found evidence that learnability of sound and sight pairings by 3.5-month-olds was constrained by amodal invariants. In a habituation paradigm, only those infants habituated to visible and audible events corresponding in both global synchrony and temporal microstructure detected a change in auditory-visual relationships afterward. Infants habituated to sound-sight pairings that did not correspond in synchrony or microstructure showed no evidence of learning.

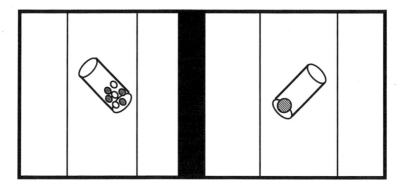

Figure 7.3
Stimuli used to test infants' ability to learn pairings of visual and auditory stimuli. The cylinders were rotated by the experimenter to produce the events used in the experiments. Reprinted with permission from Bahrick, L. E. (1987), Infants' intermodal perception of two levels of temporal structure in natural events, *Infant Behavior and Development, 10*, 387–416.

Substance

Can substance be perceived intermodally? On sensation-based accounts, notions of substance, such as solidity, rigidity, and elasticity, might be considered exclusively the province of tactile or haptic perception. On an ecological view, we might consider properties such as solidity and rigidity to be fundamentally abstract ones—that is, characteristics of physical objects that might be perceived via different perceptual systems. Bahrick (1983) studied 4-month-olds' intermodal perception of substance with visible and audible events. One visual display showed two wet sponges squeezing against each other, and the other showed two wooden blocks hitting together. One soundtrack played a "squishing" sound and the other a "clacking" sound. When the corresponding audible and visible displays were in synchrony, infants visually attended to the appropriate event. When the display of wooden blocks was synchronized to the squishing sound and vice versa, however, infants did not show this pattern. The results may indicate that both hearing and sight can pick up information about objects' substances, such as their rigidity and nonrigidity. As Bahrick notes, however, it is also possible that infants were sensitive to the noncorrespondence of certain subtle temporal patterns connected to these substances and events.

It is clear that at least some amodal invariants, such as synchrony, connect visual and auditory perception in 16-week-olds. Because many of the invariants have not been tested with neonates, it is difficult to say whether these results implicate unlearned sensory coordination or early learning experiences. One striking finding, however, points toward the former. In an experiment with two stuffed animals moving up and down, Spelke et al. (1983) tested two different conditions in which the sound was synchronized with one animal. In one condition, the sound occurred at the moment of impact between the animal and a surface. In the other condition, the sound was synchronized with the arrival of the animal at the top of its trajectory, the point at which it reversed direction to move downward. No surface was impacted at that point. Results showed that infants responded to intermodal synchrony in *both* of these conditions. It appears that infants at this age have an overly general rule about synchrony: the visual event of direction change can be matched to a sound event, even though such changes would produce impact noises only when a contact surface is present. A follow-up study showed that infants do not respond to synchrony when a sound occurs at a particular position in a continuous circular trajectory; only direction-reversal seems to work. Infants' use of an overly general rule indicates their use of amodal invariants more than the particulars that might be learned by observing objects. It would seem that contact would be a highly salient visual event correlated with sound production, yet contact is not necessary for intermodal responding. This intriguing finding is consistent with the idea that intermodal coordination begins with unlearned constraints that are somewhat overly generalized.[1]

Our tour of auditory-visual intermodal perception suggests several conclusions. First, at least some of the links across these two perceptual systems are hardwired. Early visual orienting toward a sound might conceivably be reflexive, but several of its properties are more compatible with the interpretation that it is a rudimentary system for exploration in a common auditory-visual space. Neurophysiological evidence in other species supports the idea of an abstract spatial representation that can be accessed through different sensory channels. A second conclusion is that besides colocation in space, synchrony in time allows young perceivers to detect the same event through sound and sight. Other amodal invariants also support early intermodal event perception under at least some circumstances, including rate and the temporal microstructure of collision events. Some of the latter variables appear to develop later than synchrony. Infants' abilities to utilize these invariants appear most readily in situations involving simple, mechanical events. Finally, it appears that from an early age, amodal invariants may constrain infants' learning about particular events.

Visual-Haptic Relationships

Coordination between seen and felt properties of objects is such a subtle aspect of skilled perception and action that we do not often reflect on it. Perhaps this is one reason that haptic perception has not been extensively studied in adult perception, although the situation is changing (Klatzky & Lederman, 1993; Lederman & Klatzky, 1987, 1990; Loomis & Lederman, 1986; Turvey et al., 1981). We might usefully distinguish *tactile* and *haptic* perception. Tactile perception—receiving information from contact of the skin with objects—has long been acknowledged as a basic sensory mode. The implicit idea that this mode functions by mere contact—stimulation of mechanoreceptors (or temperature receptors and so on) in the skin— provides only a limited view of what is possible through contact. For example, an object pressed into the hand is seldom recognizable (Gibson & Gibson, 1955). A more comprehensive concept is that of a *haptic perceptual system*. Tactile information is picked up in combination with systematic exploratory movement of the hand (or mouth), yielding much more information than passive contact. This kind of activity yields superior recognition of three-dimensional form, for example.

Haptic perception furnishes information about form, substance, solidity, temperature, texture, and other object properties. Research with adults suggests that we possess characteristic types of object exploration related to these different properties (Klatzky & Lederman, 1993). The combination with vision is especially powerful in underwriting skilled action. We see and reach toward an object, confirm our grasp by touch, maintain contact, and change the object's position (such as a steering wheel) while looking elsewhere to pick up information that guides an overall action (such as driving).

For adults, there are many varieties of haptic exploration (Lederman & Klatzky, 1987, 1990). For example, an object's temperature and solidity may be detected merely by grasping it, but a coordinated set of movements along object edges along with tactile feedback is required to detect three-dimensional form. Thus, the development of intermodal relationships between vision and touch depends not only on tactile receptivity but on selective and coordinated motor behavior that goes with it.

Oral-Visual Coordination
What are the roots of intermodal coordination between haptic and visual perception? Skilled reaching and manipulation of objects do not emerge until 4 to 5 months of age. Accordingly, the earliest visual-tactual coordination has been sought using a part of the motor system that seems to be more advanced in the early weeks of life—the mouth. Young infants will mouth an object in an exploratory manner. Meltzoff and Borton (1979) reported evidence that 1-month-old infants relate shape and texture information obtained orally and visually. After mouthing but not seeing a pacifier with either a small cube with nubs on it or a smooth sphere, infants were found to look longer at a visual display matching the one they had mouthed (Meltzoff & Borton, 1979). Information about substance was studied at about the same age by Gibson and Walker (1984). After oral experience with a rigid or nonrigid (deforming) cylinder, infants viewed a pair of events in which a hand manipulated either a rigid or nonrigid cylinder. Most infants looked longer at the object of novel substance.

These experiments suggest some relating of orally and visually given object properties. It is not entirely clear why these effects are sometimes manifest as familiarity preferences and sometimes as novelty preferences (as would be typical for habituation studies within a single modality). Interpreting a familiarity preference in a single experiment seems problematic. One might even be so perverse as to suggest that infants match tactual information for nonrigidity to visual information for rigidity and vice versa. Familiarity preferences, however, turn out to be common when transfer is tested cross-modally in humans (Bryant, Jones, Claxton & Perkins, 1972; Ruff & Kohler, 1978) and infants of other primate species (Dolgin, Premack & Spelke, 1980; Gunderson, 1983). Because modality change always produces substantial novel aspects in both members of a pair of test displays, cross-modal familiarity preferences may indicate the infant's recognition of commonality within a novel context. Whether novelty or familiarity preferences occur may depend on the degree of novelty of the test situation. In any case, the fact that familiarity preferences are common in cross-modal tests but not in intramodal ones tends to argue against the idea that very young infants are aware *only* of amodal information (Bower, 1974; Maurer, 1993; Lewkowicz & Turkewitz, 1980). Change of modality clearly makes a difference.

Visual-Manual Coordination
Evidence that infants relate information between eye and hand can be found quite early, but only in restricted situations. Streri (1987) familiarized 2-month-olds haptically or visually with one of two objects, either a ring or a disk of the same overall size. In the visual presentations, objects were suspended on an invisible string and rotated continuously. Subjects showed a novelty preference in visual testing after previously feeling an object. Haptic testing after visual familiarization turned up no reliable preference. Ironically, when 5-month-olds were tested in the same paradigm, they showed the *reverse* pattern: shape information transferred from visual familiarization to tactual testing but not vice versa.

These paradoxical data indicate that at least some information common to touch and vision can be extracted by the second month of life. They also give indications that visual-manual transfer follows a somewhat complex developmental course. One nice feature of the studies by Streri (1987) is that *intramodal* tests were carried out. These showed that both age groups responded to differences between the stimulus objects when tested within a single modality. Thus, the opposite patterns seen at 2 and 5 months do not derive from failures to detect object properties within each sense.

Other tests of visual-manual transfer have also yielded somewhat cryptic patterns. Rose, Gottfried, and Bridger (1981a, 1981b) found evidence for visual recognition of a previously felt object by 6- and 12-month-olds but no evidence of oral-visual matching at 6 months. A later study using similar methods and stimuli found no reliable evidence of visual-tactile matching at 12 months. Other studies have found tactile to visual transfer as indicated by familiarity preferences in 6-month-olds (Ruff & Kohler, 1978), in 8-month-olds who manipulated a toy that made noise (Bryant et al., 1972), as well as in nonhuman infant primates (Dolgin, Premack & Spelke, 1980; Gunderson, 1983).

Developments in the haptic system during the first half year might explain some of the patterns observed in visual-tactile intermodal studies (Streri & Molina, 1994). Two-month-olds tend to grasp objects; not until about 4 months do they develop the skilled interplay of hand movement and tactile feedback that allows detailed exploration of form (Rochat, 1989). Studies of adults indicate that grasping alone ("enclosure") can provide only vague information about form (Lederman & Klatzky, 1990). Infants may get only certain salient features from grasping. Visual information, on the other hand, can reveal overall three-dimensional form (Kellman, 1984; Kellman & Short, 1987; Yonas et al., 1987a). Haptic familiarization may allow infants to match some object parts or features with subsequent visual information. On the other hand, the global three-dimensional form representation derived from visual perception may not be well matched by the partial representation available in the tactile test (Streri & Molina, 1994).

A test of this hypothesis was carried out by Streri and Molina (1993). They reasoned that using two-dimensional silhouettes of objects for the visual presentations might increase the salience of local features, such as points or corners, while eliminating global three-dimensional information. After habituation to a silhouette of an object, infants were tested haptically with the corresponding solid object and a different solid object. Results showed that infants held the previously viewed object longer than the novel object. This outcome is consistent with the original hypothesis that the information extracted by the haptic system is somewhat fragmentary and more easily matched to basic contour information available visually in a silhouette than to a full-blown three-dimensional representation. On balance, evidence suggests that some intermodal transfer exists between hand and eye at least as early as two months, but it is subject to limitations throughout the first year of life that are not fully understood. At least some of these derive from age-related changes in haptic exploration (Streri & Molina, 1994).

Haptic Perception of Unity and Boundaries

As we have seen, many studies of haptic-visual coordination have centered on shape information. A different, perhaps more basic, question concerns perception of unity and boundaries. Under what conditions will parts of objects, separated in space, be perceived as connected? Visually, as we saw in chapter 5, infants in the first half year depend on common motion of visible parts, but not on surface or form similarities, to detect unity. Streri and Spelke (1988) studied infants' haptic perception to test whether this developmental pattern holds in haptic perception of objects. Infants of 4 to 5 months haptically explored two rings, one in each hand, that were either rigidly connected and moved together or were independently moveable. After habituation, infants were tested for looking time to two visual displays—one with two rings rigidly connected and the other with two rings separated by a gap. Relative to baseline looking performance, infants who habituated to the rigidly connected haptic display looked longer at the two disconnected rings; infants who habituated haptically to the independently moveable rings looked longer at the rigidly connected ring display. These results suggest that motion relationships given haptically lead to perception of unity or separateness in much the same way as visually given motion relationships.

Amodal versus Modality-Specific Unit Formation Mechanisms

Streri et al. (1993) argue from these results and others for amodal mechanisms in object perception. The argument is more than the claim that object representations are abstract. They assert that the *mechanisms* leading to object unity are amodal, taking their inputs from either visual representations of surfaces and motions or haptic ones. The idea is shown schematically in figure 7.4b. Figure 7.4a shows the alternative idea that unit formation mechanisms operate separately in visual and haptic domains. One argument put forth by Streri et al. for amodal mechanisms is that adults appear to use haptic and visual information differently in unit formation. The similarity in the haptic and visual relationships governing infant perception may be due to their reliance on a common mechanism early in life. Specifically, consider what happens when adults manipulate two grasped parts that move relative to each other in one dimension but remain rigidly connected in another. In tests by Streri et al. (1993), adults grasped two (unseen) parts that were either rigidly connected, moveable relative to each other vertically, or moveable horizontally. Subjects indicated on scales of -7 to 7 their impressions of connectedness and of unity. Results are shown in figure 7.5. The fact that all ratings were in the positive range was interpreted as indicating that both connectedness and unity were perceived in all of the conditions. In contrast, infants habituated haptically to nonrigid displays responded in subsequent visual tests as if they had perceived two independent objects. According to Streri et al., the infants differ from the adults because the former are relying on a common mechanism for haptic and visual unit formation, whereas the latter have acquired additional modality-specific information. The fact that infants show similar patterns for the same kinds of information presented visually or haptically may indicate the operation of an amodal object perception mechanism.

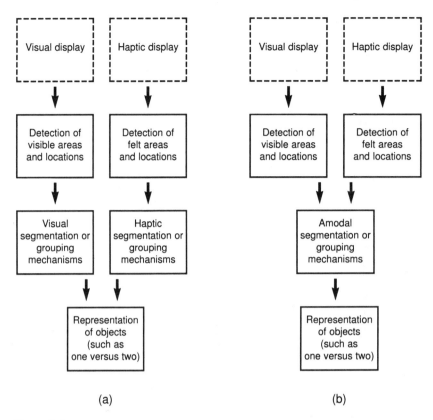

(a)   (b)

Figure 7.4
Two possible accounts of intermodal matching. a. Processes in each perceptual system (such as vision and touch) perform segmentation and grouping and produce object representations in a common format. b. Outputs of each perceptual system consist of unsegmented representations of surfaces and movements. An amodal mechanism parses these into units. Outputs of this amodal mechanism are connected or separate objects.

While fascinating, it is not clear how strong a case these results make for amodal mechanisms. To begin with, the claim that adults perceive relative motion in one dimension as specifying two separate objects visually but one object haptically is oversimplified. Adults can visually perceive constrained relative motions as belonging to a single nonrigid object (e.g., Bertenthal, Banton & Bradbury, 1993). There is also ambiguity in adults' impressions in the haptic tests carried out by Streri et al. (1993). Although constrained relative motion produced consistently high impressions of connectedness, *unity* ratings were much lower than for a rigid object. In other words, adults who manipulated the two pieces were sure they were

Connectedness ratings

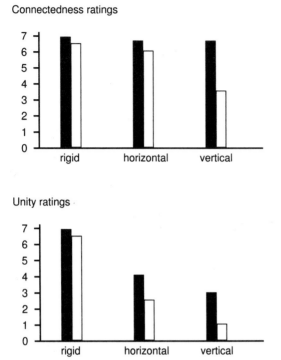

Unity ratings

Figure 7.5
Adults' judgments of the connectedness and the unity of objects presented under conditions of active (black bars) and passive (open bars) manipulation. Reprinted from *Cognition*, 47, Streri, A., Spelke, E., & Ramiex, E., Modality specific and amodal aspects of object perception in infancy: The case of active touch, pp. 251–279, 1993, with kind permission of Elsevier Science–NL, Sara Burgerhartstraat 25, 1055 KV Amsterdam, The Netherlands.

connected but were more equivocal about whether they formed a single unified object. This uncertainty may depend on the conflict between the information for rigid connectedness in one dimension and relative motion in another. There is a third factor: the relative motion had limits—that is, the pieces could be moved only so far apart before hitting a stop. In short, the situation is complex in terms of competing sources of information. The divergence of adult and infant results may show only differences in the relative salience of some of the conflicting information for adults and infants. This differential salience could be caused by limitations on haptic exploratory behavior by infants at 4 to 5 months (Streri & Molina, 1994). For example, movement along a single dimension may overshadow perception of the stops and the rigidity in other dimensions.

Parallellism in the information leading to perception of unified objects in infant vision and touch may indicate analogous, rather than common, mechanisms (Kellman, 1988). Basic physical facts make common and relative motion information of high ecological validity, more so than form similarity, contour alignment, and other static features (Kellman, 1993; see also chapter 5). These ecological facts may be related to the mechanisms that appear earliest in each perceptual system. It is difficult to decide between this account and the idea of a suprasensory mechanism based on existing data. Streri et al. point out that changes between birth and 4 months in visual unit formation abilities (Slater et al., 1994) might be expected to appear simultaneously in haptic unit formation, if both depend on the same mechanism. They suggest that appropriate longitudinal studies might help distinguish these two notions about intermodal object perception.

In this section we set out to discover whether visual-tactile coordination originates with mechanisms sensitive to amodal invariants. We found evidence indicating this is indeed the case, with connections between oral and visual exploration documented earliest, and coordination between visual and manual exploration appearing as early as two months. These early achievements may represent only the proverbial tip of the iceberg. They may contribute to, but not fully explain, the remarkable phenomenon of imitation of facial expressions by newborn human infants. We take up this stunning example of intermodal coordination of perception and action in chapter 10.

Although we emphasize infants' successes because of their theoretical interest, we note also the spottiness of early manual-visual matching. Two factors that may account for various limitations are the slow development of skilled haptic exploration and the domination of certain haptic tendencies, such as object transport (to eye or mouth) when skilled reaching begins.

CONCLUSION

Our treatment in this chapter has concentrated on auditory-visual and visual-haptic perception of events. The research we have considered hardly does justice to the many creative and informative contributions of workers in these areas. It suffices to give us some perspective, however, on the development of intermodal perception. Intermodal coordination begins at birth and rests heavily on amodal invariants, as theorized by ecological theorists of perception. There are strong reasons to believe that perceptual systems are attuned to a common physical environment and that their outputs are abstract representations of objects and events in that environment. Not all amodal information is found to be usable in the early months of life, and infants' intermodal coordination shows limitations that are not fully understood but that may rest on changing attentional dispositions as well as maturation and learning within each perceptual modality.

Associating sensory information from separate senses, predicted to be the main developmental agenda from traditional views of perception, plays a different role. Guided by amodal information that unifies our separate sensory channels, correlations among sensory attributes that are not based on amodal properties can be learned, allowing the developing child to discover and remember that apples are sweet and to anticipate the face that will appear momentarily when particular footsteps are heard.

Note

1. It is also possible that the rule used by infants is one that has been abstracted from early experience, according to a flawed learning heuristic. One might argue that infants encode visual impacts as direction changes and associate these with impact sounds. Then direction changes occurring without visual impacts might be connectable to impact sounds. The problem with this reasoning is that direction changes without impacts must be fairly common in the infant's visual world; they are extremely common for people moving, for example. Thus, the infant would be exposed to a large number of negative cases—visual direction changes without impact sounds. If these experiences did not lead to differentiation of visual impacts from nonimpact cases, they should hamper formation of any association between visual impacts and sounds.

Chapter 8
Auditory Perception

Much of our focus in this book has been on visual perception. This emphasis is reasonable in one way and unfortunate in another. It is reasonable because vision is preeminent among perceptual systems in giving us detailed representations of spatial arrangements and events. It is unfortunate if we are misled into underestimating the richness and importance of other sources of information, such as sound. For some other species, such as bats, auditory information is primary in perceiving objects and navigating through space. We need not travel to the world of the bat, however, to uncover the informativeness of sound and perceptual systems for extracting information from it. Auditory perception provides human perceivers with a rich array of properties of objects and events.

ECOLOGY OF AUDITORY PERCEPTION

Recall the vase we heard crashing to the floor in chapter 7. Our concern then was intermodal perception. As a result, we passed quickly by some rather striking features of the event. For one thing, the news and location of the event arrived first through hearing. Unlike vision, which requires the observer to look in the right direction, auditory perception allows us to monitor our surroundings without restrictions. Vision does not go around corners, but hearing does. We not only detect events but locate them in space. We have seen that infants are born with some of these localization abilities, and we explore them further below.

In an experiment, a subject is likely to hear a single sound source against an otherwise quiet background. In ordinary situations, we are exposed to a cacophony of superimposed auditory events. The sound of the vase shattering may have to be disentangled from vibrations arriving at the same two ears from traffic on a street outside, conversation in the next room, and voices from the television set. We possess a remarkable ability to parse such complex inputs to the ears into separate streams that derive from separate physical events. Bregman (1990) has carried out groundbreaking work on this problem of auditory stream segregation and has identified many of the physical determinants of this ability.

Now consider material substance. When we hear the vase shatter, we can tell that it is made of glass. When the morning newspaper flies out of a car and hits the sidewalk, it makes sounds different from those that would occur if a wooden block had been tossed and also different from a sheet of aluminum. It is unremarkable that the auditory signals from these events vary, but it is striking that we glean from them such clear classifications of *paper, wood,* or *metal.* There is more. We gain some information about form and size (or mass): it is the (flat) newspaper, not paper crumpled in a ball; it is a metal sheet, not a metal block; a wooden block, not a sheet. Auditory perception is a rich source of information about what things are made of and what forms they have. Perhaps most intriguing, we usually gain this information about material from events that involve contact between two objects or an object and a surface. We apprehend the substance of one or both colliding surfaces from such events. Whereas we earlier emphasized temporal synchrony as a glue for identifying unitary events across the senses, we now notice that the synchronous sounds, as with the visible array, must be parsed into separate objects and their material composition.

One limitation in assessing the development of auditory perception is that many of these informative properties of sound have barely been noticed, much less researched, in either adult or infant perception. The study of *ecological acoustics*—the analysis of what information environments make available for perceivers—is a scientific challenge waiting to be tackled. There are beginnings in cognitive science and in some engineering applications. Besides stream segregation, auditory localization—that is, perception of radial direction to a sound source—has been seriously studied. In recent years, some studies of auditory distance perception (Ashmead, Davis & Northington, 1995) and exciting work on the interaction of the pinnae (external ears) with sound to determine perception of events (Oldfield & Parker, 1986) have appeared. Bahrick (1983, 1992), as we saw in the last chapter, has investigated the use of sound to specify properties such as numerosity and rigidity, a striking foray into ecological acoustics. More work is needed, however, in defining the acoustical patterns that underlie our perceptions of object properties such as substance and number, as well as events such as bouncing and shattering. One reason we draw attention to the richness and significance of auditory information is the hope of stimulating further explorations in these areas.

Our present task, undertaken in the first part of this chapter, is to consider what we do know about auditory perception in infancy. In the second part of the chapter, we take up a specialized form of auditory perception, one with enormous implications for development of our cognitive and social natures as human beings—perception of speech.

ABILITIES AND PROCESSES OF AUDITORY PERCEPTION

Auditory Localization Abilities in Infancy

Localizing a sounding object requires determining its direction and distance. Information for localization comes from several sources. When a sound-producing event occurs to the hearer's left, the leading edge of the wave form produced in the air reaches the left ear sooner than the right. This difference in sound onset is zero for a sound directly in front of or behind the observer and greatest when the sound lies on a line connecting the two ears. Often we do not hear the onset of a sound but hear it as ongoing. Information similar to onset differences at the two ears is available for relatively low-frequency sounds in terms of phase differences at the two ears. (The differing time of arrival of the waveform at the two ears causes the positions in the cycle of the soundwaves at the two ears to be different at any moment.) As sound frequency exceeds about 1,000 Hz, this information becomes less helpful because the phase differences become large relative to the period of the soundwave, making the determination of which ear is getting the earlier information impossible. At high frequencies, information is provided by intensity differences at the two ears. Sound power drops with the square of distance traveled, and the loss is greater for higher frequencies. Interaural differences in intensity are small at low frequencies because the wavelength is long in comparison to the head. The shorter wavelengths of higher frequencies can result in interaural differences as large as 20 dB (Moore, 1982). There are other sources of information that resolve ambiguities in onset, phase, and intensity differences, including head movements and interactions of high-frequency sounds with the peculiarly shaped pinna (external ear).

    In chapter 7 we saw that newborns turn in the direction of sounds and that this early ability may be a result of an intermodal mapping of space. Throughout the first year of life, infants' precision in locating sounding objects in space improves. One way to test precision of localization is to assess the *minimum audible angle* (MAA). MAA is the smallest detectable angle of movement of a sound source. To assess 7-month-old infants' MAA, Ashmead, Clifton, and Perris (1987) presented infants with sounds that shifted from a center to a side loudspeaker. If subjects turned their heads in the right direction, they received visual reinforcement. Ashmead et al. found an average MAA of 19 deg, with a range of 13.6 to 24.4 deg. Adults tested with the same stimuli showed a MAA of 1 to 2 deg (typical for adults, e.g., Mills, 1958). Slightly better MAAs were found by Morrongiello (1988). Six-month-olds reliably detected 12 deg shifts, and this ability improved to 4 deg by 18 months. Similar threshold estimates were found by Ashmead, Davis, Whalen, and Odom (1991) in 20-, 24-, and

28-week-olds using the observer-based psychoacoustic procedure (OPP, described in chapter 2), ruling out the possibility that the high thresholds were an artifact of requiring infants to execute a head turn. Recall that with OPP, naive observers can use any behavior on the part of the infant to judge on which side the sound was presented. In this case, even a simple eye movement could be used by the observer making a judgment regarding whether the sound was to the left or to the right.

There are several possible explanations for the large difference in localization precision between adults and young infants. One factor could be age-related changes in head size. All binaural differences in sounds are smaller for smaller heads. It is also possible that the auditory system is calibrated for adult head sizes and as a result infants' localization abilities are imprecise until head size reaches adult levels. Several lines of evidence render this explanation unlikely (Clifton, Gwiazda, Bauer, Clarkson & Held, 1988; Held, 1955). Another possibility is that infants may be relatively insensitive to interaural time differences. When these differences are small, as when an object is located close to midline, infants may have difficulty localizing the sound source. This possibility, although intriguing, was ruled out by Ashmead et al. (1991). They showed that 16- to 28-week-old infants are sensitive to interaural time differences even though infants at this age showed poor auditory localization. In several experiments, infants wearing headphones were cued to look 30 deg to the left or right based on interaural time differences (a tone was presented in one ear before the other). Using the observer-based psychoacoustic procedure, naive observers judged whether the infant was cued to look to the left or to the right. Ashmead et al. (1991) found surprising sensitivity to interaural time differences; thresholds were on the order of 50 to 75 microseconds. A third possibility is maturation of the auditory cortex. Improvement in the ability to localize objects in space over the first two months of age may reflect refinement of cortical mechanisms mediating auditory localization.

Indirect evidence about the role of the auditory cortex in localization comes from studies of the *precedence effect*. The precedence effect, first investigated by Wallach, Newman, and Rosenzweig (1949), describes how the auditory system copes with echoes in a reverberant environment. Sounds bouncing off surfaces create reflections that in turn enter the auditory system. Generally, we hear only one sound coming from a particular location, suggesting that some suppression or matching must occur to avoid hearing echoes as separate sound sources. The precedence effect can be produced in the laboratory by presenting two brief clicks 1 to 5 msec apart. The two sounds will be heard as fused into a single sound emanating from the location of the first sound (hence the *precedence* effect). The effect is clearly a binaural phenonenon as the interaural difference between the two sounds allows for the localization of the sound source. Research with cats implicates the auditory cortex in the localization of precedence effect stimuli (Whitfield, Cranford, Ravizza & Diamond, 1972). Research with human infants found that the precedence effect, shown by directional responding to sounds emanating from a single source, was present in 3- and 5-month-olds but not in 2-month-olds (Clifton, Morrongiello & Dowd, 1984; Muir, Clifton & Clarkson, 1989). These results in conjunction with animal research suggest that improvements in auditory localization within the first 6 months of life may be due to maturation of the auditory cortex.

Auditory Distance Perception

Perceiving the direction of a sound source does not fix its location in three-dimensional space because the cues that specify direction do not indicate distance. Do infants pick up distance information auditorily? The question can be asked by using reaching measures with auditory targets.

Seven-month-old infants reliably reach for a sounding object that they cannot see, even when they cannot see their own hands (Perris & Clifton, 1988). Interestingly, when allowed to look, infants will reach for a nearby glowing object in the dark, not the sound source (that is, not the speaker placed above the object; Clifton, Rochat, Litovsky & Perris, 1991). Capitalizing on the fact the infants will reach for sounding objects in the dark, Clifton, Perris, and Bullinger (1991) tested infants' perception of direction and distance of objects specified by auditory information by presenting them with sounding objects located either within reach or beyond reach. They found significantly more reaching to the object when it was within reach.

Summary: Auditory Space Perception

The research on auditory space perception abilities in infancy suggests that some ability to localize objects based on sound is present at birth. Newborn infants know in which direction a sounding object is located, and by 7 months infants know how far away an object is (at least whether it is reachable or not). Future work might address whether younger infants perceive distance auditorily. Reaching as a measure is useful with infants 5 months of age or older, but it is not reliable with younger infants (Yonas & Granrud, 1985b). One approach to finding a suitable method is to consider the role of auditory localization in eliciting visual attention. Just as a head-orienting response serves the purpose of placing the image of an object on the retina, it is possible that observers make anticipatory convergence adjustments related to sound. That is, after hearing a sound, observers might adjust binocular convergence so that the object will be appropriately imaged in the two eyes when it comes into view. This idea might prove useful in testing infants' auditory distance sensitivity.

As to the rich array of other spatial, object, and event properties that adults derive from sound, such as knowledge of object composition and form and the structure of events, not much work has addressed their development. Uncovering the informational bases for these achievements and their developmental courses remain frontiers for perception and perceptual development research.

SPEECH PERCEPTION

Most perceptual abilities produce knowledge about objects, events, and the layout of space. The perception of speech often leads to knowledge about the world, but in quite a different way. Apart from their meanings, which the infant perceiver ultimately learns to extract, speech signals have little significance as physical events. As the gateway to language, however, the origins and development of speech perception are crucial.

Young infants are confronted at birth with the challenge of discriminating speech sounds from other environmental sounds (such as garbage disposals, music, coughs, and sneezes). To succeed at this task is remarkable, because the acoustic signals for speech are varied and complex. Infants are also challenged to recognize sounds across different speakers as equivalent, to parse the signal into meaningful units (that is, words and syllables), to recognize these units, and if possible to give an appropriate communicative response. How much of speech perception relies on specifically linguistic mechanisms as distinguished from generalized auditory ones is controversial. We return to this issue following our discussion of the development of speech perception.

We begin by asking about the earliest beginnings of speech perception. When are infants first exposed to speech, and what do they perceive? We will see that recognition of properties of speech signals begins surprisingly early. We then examine features of the child's linguistic environment that may assist her in coming to comprehend speech. How infants actually parse the speech stream is addressed next. We then examine the origins of perceptual constancy in speech perception—how the perceiver categorizes items having the same significance linguistically despite their physical variation. Finally, we conclude with the general question of whether the processes underlying speech perception are specifically linguistic or the result of general auditory capacities.

The Beginnings of Speech Perception

When do infants first attend to speech and begin to extract useful information from it? Researchers investigating the origins of infants' preferences for their mothers' voice over that of another female (e.g., Mills & Melhuish, 1974) have suggested that infants hear the voice of their mother while in utero. After birth very young infants prefer their mothers' voice to other females' voices (De Casper & Fifer, 1980) and prefer female voices to male voices (Brazelton, 1978), but they do not prefer their fathers' voices to those of other males (De Casper & Prescott, 1984).

Infants' processing of auditory information in utero was studied in elegant fashion by De Casper and Spence (1986). Pregnant women were asked to read a target story to their unborn children twice a day during the last 6 weeks of pregnancy. Three target stories were used: *The King, the Mice, and the Cheese*, the first 28 paragraphs of *The Cat in the Hat*, and the last 28 paragraphs of *The Cat in the Hat* in which salient nouns were changed to create a story named *The Dog in the Fog*. Mothers' made recordings of themselves reading each story before they began reading to their children regularly. After birth, 16 infants (average age: 55.8 hours) were tested for their preferences between the target story and a novel story. De Casper and Spence found that the preexposed infants showed a preference for the target story regardless of whether it was read by their mother or another female. Subjects who had not been exposed to the stories did not show a preference for either story. De Casper and Spence concluded that infants remembered something about the acoustic cues that specified their particular target passage.

What characteristics of sound might allow matching between sound events presented before and after birth? The frequency range for ordinary speech is 400 to 3,000 Hz and its intensity is approximately 60 dB (Goldstein, 1989). In utero, sounds above 1,000 Hz are attenuated, and the level of ambient noise is estimated to be 25 dB when the mother is not in labor (Querleu, Renard, Versyp, Paris-Delrue & Crepin, 1988). Against this background noise maternal voices are audible, but the situation approximates a low-pass filter. As would be predicted, newborn infants prefer a 500 Hz low-pass filtered sample (frequencies above 500 Hz are removed) of the maternal voice over another low-pass filtered female voice (Spence & Freeman, 1996). This suggests that infants have access to prosodic characteristics of speech (such as frequency contours and temporal patterning), which are available at low frequencies, but not to information conveyed by high frequencies. One prosodic feature that infants may use to recognize their mothers' voice is the fundamental frequency. When we whisper, the fundamental frequency of our speech is not available. Newborn infants can discriminate samples of whispered speech but do not recognize their mothers' speech when she whispers (Spence & Freeman, 1996).

Footholds for Learning

As we are reminded when we listen to fluent speech in a language we do not understand, the tasks of speech perception are immensely complicated. Several features of the infant's linguistic environment may assist the infant in coming to parse the speech stream and to recognize particular words, relations between utterances and situations, and communicative intents. We now consider two interesting sources of information, apart from the content of speech itself. First, we look at auditory-visual correspondence between the sounds heard and the moving faces in the infant's environment. Second, we examine infant sensitivities to the ways adults modify their speech when addressing infants and small children.

Intermodal Perception of Speech

The perception of speech is more than what meets the ear; visual information also plays a role. It is common knowledge that adults find speech to be more easily understood when they are watching the speaker, especially in noisy environments or when the listener is hard of hearing (e.g., Sumby & Pollack, 1954). In fact, a normal hearing observer may be strongly influenced by the articulatory movements of the speaker resulting in an illusory percept. For example, McGurk and MacDonald (1976) presented adults with auditory information specifying the sounds /baba/ and visual information specifying /gaga/. Subjects reported perceiving neither; they heard /dada/. Apparently, the discrepancy between visual and auditory information (which differed on the dimension of *place of articulation*) resulted in a resolution that resembled a compromise: the place of articulation for /dada/ lies between /baba/ and /gaga/.

Visual information is not necessary for the perception of speech, but it can contribute to our perception of speech. Understanding the development of auditory-visual relations in speech perception begins with the question of whether young infants are sensitive to the visual-auditory match of speech stimuli. Given our discussion in the previous chapter on infants' intermodal perception, the suggestion that young infants are able to identify a correspondence between lip movements and vowel sounds should not be surprising (Kuhl & Meltzoff, 1982, 1984). In one study, 4-month-old infants viewed a film of two faces, one mouthing the sound /a/ as in *pop* and one mouthing the sound /i/ as in *peep*. A speaker located between the two faces presented a soundtrack of either /a/ or /i/. The infants looked significantly longer at the /a/ face than at the /i/ face when the /a/ sound was played, and they looked significantly longer at the /i/ face than the /a/ face when the /i/ sound was played. Similar results were found using /i/ and /u/ (Kuhl & Meltzoff, 1988). These findings suggest that by 4 months of age, infants perceive the correspondence between lip movements and vowel sounds and have some knowledge of which movements produce which sounds.

Yet there is more information besides a correspondence between lip movements and vowel sounds to which infants may have responded. The displays contained temporal patterns that may have furnished information including the contingency between the onset and offset of the auditory information and lip movement. Infants may have matched the visual and auditory displays based on this information rather than on the appropriate vowel sound. To investigate whether infants were responding to spectral or temporal characteristics of the auditory stimulus, Kuhl and Meltzoff (1984) presented 4-month-olds with two faces (/a/ and /i/) and a pure-tone stimulus that preserved the duration, amplitude envelope, and onset/offset characteristics of the original vowels but removed the formant frequencies (or the sound's "vowelness"). Infants, when hearing pure tones, did not show a preference for the matching face. Instead, infants in both the /a/ and /i/ conditions preferred the /a/ face. Thus, infants did not merely respond to temporal features; instead they represented the vowel both visually and auditorily.

Whether cross-modal matching of speech stimuli is a fundamental ability present at birth or one that develops from the experience of watching lips and hearing speech is unknown at this point. It is likely that infants do not have to make the sounds themselves before being able to make a cross-modal match. By 4 months infants have begun to babble; they most likely have produced /a/ but not /i/ (Lieberman, 1980).

Because infants and adults are able to match visual and auditory information for vowels does not necessarily prove that speech perception is based on amodal invariants. Several aspects of speech fit better with the idea that amodal properties provide some support, but speech perception is primarily based on auditory properties. Visual information for speech is not as rich as the auditory information. Individuals with hearing impairments need extensive training and must rely on context in order to lipread (Massaro, Thompson, Barron & Laren, 1986). Moreover, some aspects of speech are not available at all visually—for example, manner of articulation, such as the voice-onset time that differentiates /da/ and /ta/.

Infant-Directed Speech
Another assist infants may get in coming to comprehend speech involves special characteristics of the acoustic signal when speech is directed to infants. Adults and older children speaking to infants modify their speech in surprisingly consistent ways. German mothers (Fernald & Simon, 1984), Chinese Mandarin mothers (Grieser & Kuhl, 1988), French, Italian, Japanese, British English, and American English mothers and fathers (Fernald, Taeschner, Dunn, Papousek, et al., 1989) alter their speech somewhat

when speaking to infants. This type of speech, initially termed *motherese*, is now referred to as *child-directed* or *infant-directed speech*. It is characterized by high pitch, exaggerated intonation contour, short sentences, phrases with longer pauses between them, and prosodic repetition (e.g., Snow, 1977; Snow & Ferguson, 1977; Fernald & Mazzie, 1991).

In addition to possibly signaling to infants that certain speech is intended for them, this type of speech may serve three related functions (see Fernald, 1984; Pegg, Werker & McLeod, 1992). First, it may be effective in eliciting and maintaining infants' attention. Adults can sustain communication with an infant for longer periods of time by modifying their speech in this way. Second, this type of speech may contribute to the positive affective interaction between parents and infants. Depending on the features of the speech, adults can communicate pleasure, ambivalence, or frustration. Finally, infant-directed speech may aid the infant in determining the linguistic units of their native language. These three functions are explored below.

Attentional Effects of Infant-Directed Speech   As discussed earlier, infants' initial preference for their mother's voice is likely due to perception of features of this sound before birth. Yet infants' preference for infant-directed speech is not limited to the speech of their own mother. Infants from birth to at least 10 months of age prefer infant-directed speech to adult-directed speech from unfamiliar females (e.g., Cooper & Aslin, 1989; Fernald, 1984, 1985; Fernald & Kuhl, 1987), and this preference generalizes to male speakers (Pegg et al., 1992). The preference for child-directed speech may be due to the increase in *frequency modulation* (variation in pitch) rather than an absolute elevation in pitch (Fernald & Kuhl, 1987). Infants did not show a preference for infant-directed speech over adult-directed speech when duration and amplitude characteristics of infant-directed speech were presented without frequency modulation. In other words, in the absence of pitch changes, loudness or rhythm of the speech does not affect infants' attention.

Affect and Infant-Directed Speech   Speech directed to infants conveys more than what the words mean; it conveys affective messages. In several experiments Fernald (1993) presented 5-month-old infants with approval ("Good!") or disapproval ("No!") speech samples. She found that 5-month-old infants raised in American English homes looked longer to neutral faces placed on speakers emitting German and Italian approvals than disapprovals. In addition, infants showed more positive affect to approvals and more negative affect to disapprovals in German, Italian, nonsense English syllables (in which the fundamental frequency was matched in range and variability), and natural English infant-directed (as opposed to adult-directed) speech samples. This pattern did not hold for Japanese approvals and disapprovals; infants did not show differences in looking or emotional responses to approvals and disapprovals in Japanese. Fernald explained this finding in terms of the reduced level of emotionality in Japanese facial and vocal expressions. These findings suggest that auditory information in the absence of visual information (that is, facial expressions) can provide information of affect for infants 5 months of age and it may be present as early as 7 weeks (Pegg et al., 1992).

Infant-Directed Speech and Parsing   Infant-directed speech may also help infants learn important things about the structure of their native languages and thereby facilitate language development. Many studies have documented the preference by infants for simpler exaggerated speech. From a functional point of view we have to ask why this developing organism comes equipped to prefer a type of speech that is atypical in the general linguistic environment. Does infant-directed speech have a functional significance in facilitating language learning?

Infant-directed speech may help the young language learner in parsing the unfamiliar speech stream. Anyone who has tried to learn a foreign language knows the difficulty of parsing utterances into words and phrases. Infant-directed speech may aid the parsing process because it contains longer pauses than adult-directed speech. In fact, infants *prefer* speech with pauses as long as they occur between clause units. Hirsh-Pasek, Kemler Nelson, Jusczyk, Cassidy, et al., (1987) and Kemler Nelson, Hirsh-Pasek, Jusczyk & Cassidy (1989) presented 7- to 10-month-old infants with two samples of infant-directed speech—one with pauses at the clause boundaries and one with pauses within clauses. Infants turned their heads and remained turned longer to the speaker who produced the sample with pauses between the clauses. In addition, Kemler Nelson et al. found no preference for pauses either within or between clauses in adult-directed speech. These investigators suggest that the exaggerated prosody of infant-directed speech increases the salience of acoustic cues to linguistic structure. Long pauses may help the infant parse the speech stream into meaningful and linguistically relevant units.

There is also evidence that features of infant-directed speech put new words into focus and that this process may facilitate word learning. Fernald and Mazzie (1991) found that mothers reading a picture book to their 14-month-old children gave exaggerated prosodic emphasis to new words. The focus words were more likely to occur at fundamental frequency peaks and at the end of the utterance. This pattern was not found when the same women were asked to teach a task that involved novel terminology to another adult.

Modified speech intended for infants appears to serve three functions— maintaining attention and extending the interaction, communicating affective information, and facilitating language learning. These findings are consistent with a conception of the infant as an active perceiver. The infant's behavior (such as paying attention more to infant-directed speech) reinforces this kind of speech on the part of the speaker and increases the probability that it will continue to be used. If this type of speech facilitates language learning, then infants are shaping the linguistic environment such that it maximizes meaningful information for them.

One caveat should be mentioned. Demonstration of a preference is not necessarily the demonstration of a process. Infants' preference for infant-directed speech does not by itself reveal much about how infants learn language. There is no evidence that infant-directed speech is a necessary condition for learning language. Cultures vary in the linguistic socialization techniques used with young children. For example, the Kakuli do not use child-directed speech with their children because they do not believe it is good to teach children childish forms of the language (Schieffelin, 1979, 1990). These infants are exposed to speech directed toward other adults, and they learn their native language on a timetable comparable to that of American babies.

Segmentation of Speech

An important step in learning language is breaking the continuous speech stream into meaningful units. Segmentation must in fact occur at multiple levels. Adults parse the speech stream into sentences and more finely into phrases within sentences, words within phrases, syllables within words, and phonemes (the smallest speech units that signal differences in meaning) within syllables. Some levels of segmentation have acoustic cues to aid in the process (such as pauses), whereas other levels do not have acoustic cues but may have more subtle information, like the combination of phonemes that cue word boundaries.

Parsing Phrases into Words

The previously mentioned work by Hirsh-Pasek et al. (1987) and Kemler Nelson et al. (1989) suggests that infants are sensitive to pauses delineating phrases. Yet to understand speech and to learn new words, one must be able to perceive the individual words that comprise a phrase. By 7.5 months infants are able to detect familiar words in fluent speech (Jusczyk & Aslin, 1995). How do they do this?

Prosodic cues, such as pauses, often do not help with this task because pauses occur inconsistently within words and between words. An example provided by Saffran, Aslin, and Newport (1996) illustrates this point. The stream *pretty baby* has a longer pause between the phonemes /pre/ and /ty/ than between /ty/ and /ba/. Instead, infants (and adults) must rely on more subtle cues to determine word boundaries. One cue is sensitivity to the statistical regularity of phonemes. Some phoneme combinations are highly regular and occur within words. Low-frequency phoneme combinations signal word boundaries. It appears that infants, at least by 8 months, are prepared to learn high- and low-frequency phoneme combinations quite easily. Saffran et al. presented infants with a continuous stream of four three-syllable nonsense words repeated in random order for 2 min. Following this familiarization phase, infants were presented with two types of test stimuli. One type contained items that were presented in the familiarization phase, and the second type contained novel sequences made from the same syllables. Infants listened longer to the novel-word stimuli, suggesting that they learned the regularities that distinguished the words in the short familiarization episode. Although younger infants were not tested, it is likely that this ability emerges between 6 and 8 months of age based on the work by Morgan and Saffran (1995).

Parsing Words into Syllables

Up to now we have reviewed research that suggests that infants are able to segment the speech stimulus into units at the level of phrase and word. Are they able to parse words into individual syllables? Researchers have studied infants' syllabic parsing abilities in the context of nonsense multi-syllabic strings. For example, Karzon (1985) tested 1- and 4-month-old infants' ability to discriminate multisyllabic sequences. Infants showed evidence of discriminating /marana/ from /malana/ when the second syllable was emphasized using intonation characteristics typical of infant-directed speech. Infants provided no evidence of discriminating the two sequences in adult-directed speech. Goodsitt, Morse, ver Hoeve, and Cowan (1984) tested infants' ability to discriminate /ba/ from /du/ when it was embedded in a three-syllable sequence that presented either a redundant context /ko, ko/ or /ti, ti/ or mixed context /ko, ti/. For example, after being trained to turn their heads toward a reinforcing stimulus when they heard /du/, 6-month-old infants were presented with /dukoko, koduko, kokodu/ or /dukoti, koduti, kotidu/. If infants are able to parse the speech stream into syllables and recognize /du/, they should turn their head to see the reinforcer. Goodsitt et al. varied syllable position (first, second, or third syllable location for target) and whether the target was placed within a redundant or mixed context. They found that 6.5-month-olds were able to discriminate the target syllable within the multisyllabic context regardless of location and that infants performed significantly better at discriminating the target within the redundant context than within the mixed context.

This work was extended by Goodsitt, Morgan, and Kuhl (1993) in a study that tested infants' perception of target syllables (such as /de/) that were embedded in a redundant context (such as /kokode, dekoko/), a context with an invariant order of syllables (such as /dekoga, kogade/), or a context with a variable order of syllables (such as /dekoga, gakode/). Goodsitt et al. found that infants were worse at detecting a change in a target syllable embedded in a variable context and concluded that infants were sensitive to the predicatability of elements within units. This strategy, referred to as a *clustering strategy* by Hayes and Clark (1970), involves the analysis of transitional probabilities between successive elements. Points of low transitional probability are identified as *boundaries between units*. These results seem closely related to those found by Saffran et al. (1996) in continuous speech.

Infants are able to parse speech at multiple levels. They treat phrases as units and are further able to break language down into smaller units—namely, words and syllables. The processes by which segmentation occurs may depend on the level. Two possible strategies are consistent with available data. The first strategy—bracketing—relies on prosodic information for determining the endpoints of a unit. Pauses are one such cue for the bracketing strategy because they can be used to determine the boundaries of phrases (in infant-directed speech). The second strategy—the cluster strategy—relies on probabilistic dependencies between elements.

Perceptual Constancy

Speech stimuli vary along a number of dimensions. Everyone has slight differences in the way they speak, yet listeners rarely have trouble understanding the meaning of an utterance. Some differences in speech, however, result in changes in meaning. For example, *voice-onset-time differences* distinguish /ba/ from /pa/, but whether /ba/ is spoken in a loud voice or a quiet voice or by a male or a female does not change the phoneme. These observations indicate the crucial importance of extracting relevant differences from speech signals and processing as equivalent physically varying inputs that do not differ in linguistically relevant ways. Some of these equivalence classes may derive from innate perceptual mechanisms, whereas others are learned via linguistic experience.

Categorical Perception

One example of perceptual equivalence is the phenomenon of categorical perception of phonemes. As we mentioned, the acoustic cue underlying the phonemic distinction between /ba/ and /pa/ is voice-onset time (VOT). To produce /ba/, there is a relatively short lag between the burst (from lip opening) and the onset of laryngeal voicing. In contrast, there is a relatively long lag in voicing to produce /pa/. (You can feel the difference in VOT by holding your fingers against your neck just under your chin and

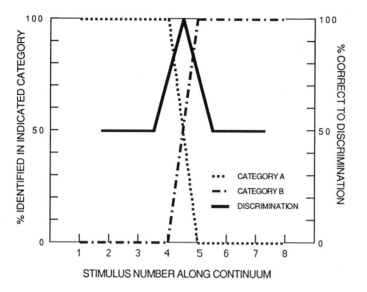

Figure 8.1

Schematic representation of categorical perception. Stimulus values above and below some critical value are classified as being in different categories with high probability. Discriminability (right ordinate) is better for stimuli on different sides of the category boundary than for stimuli having the same physical difference within a category. Redrawn from Studdert-Kennedy, M., Liberman, A. M., Harris, K. S., & Cooper, F. S. (1970), Motor theory of speech perception: A reply to Lane's critical review, *Psychological Review*, 77, 234–249. Copyright © 1970 by the American Psychological Association. Reprinted with permission.

saying /ba/ and /pa/ slowly.) In general, when onset of voice leads or follows the burst by less than 25 msec, adults perceive /ba/, and when voicing follows the release burst by more than 25 msec, they perceive /pa/ (see figure 8.1) Liberman, Cooper, Shankweiler & Studdert-Kennedy, 1967). Categorical perception simplifies the listener's task by grouping similiar but not identical sounds into the same phonemic category. Because of this grouping, the number of discriminable sounds is greatly reduced.

Many studies have investigated the degree to which infants' perception of speech is categorical (see Aslin, Pisoni & Jusczyk, 1983, for a review). In an early study, Eimas, Siqueland, Jusczyk, and Vigorito (1971) investigated 1- and 4-month-old infants' perception of the voiced-voiceless distinction using the stimuli /ba/ and /pa/. Infants were familiarized to one stimulus (such as +20 msec, perceived by adults as /ba/) and then tested for discrimination of two stimuli. Both contained a 20 msec difference, but one was from the same phonetic category (0 msec, perceived by adults as /ba/), and the other was from a different phonetic category (+40 msec, perceived by adults as /pa/). Eimas et al. found that infants showed a greater increase in responding to the cross-category stimulus than to the within-category stimulus. A given amount of change in the acoustic dimension was perceived by infants as a novel stimulus only when it crossed a phonemic boundary.

The paradigm of presenting infants with stimuli varying uniformly along a particular dimension and, at times, crossing a categorical boundary has been used to study several dimensions of speech. For example, it has been found that infants between 1 and 4 months of age categorically perceive speech sounds that are differentiated by information contained in formant transitions that signal distinctions between stop constants and semivowels such as /b-w/ along the voicing continuum (Aslin, Pisoni, Hennessy & Percy, 1981; Eimas & Miller, 1980a). Additionally, infants at 1 and 4 months differentiate manner of articulation, specifically the nasal-stop distinction in syllable initial consonants /ma-ba/ (Eimas & Miller, 1980b) and place of articulation /d/, /t/ versus /g/, /k/ versus /p/, /b/; /ma/ versus /na/ (Hillenbrand, 1983, 1984).

Equivalence across Speakers

Whereas the discrimination and classification of stimuli are important for the eventual understanding of language, speech stimuli also vary on dimensions that do not influence phonemic category inclusion. For example, different speakers (male, female, child) may produce an /a/ that varies in intonation contour or pitch. Moreover, there are regional differences in pronounciation of phonemes. For example, in the United States, a Boston native will pronounce car differently from a Los Angeles native. Yet adult listeners perceive all instances of /a/ as phonemically equivalent. Any speech recognition process must be able to extract invariance across widely differing basic parameters of the speech signal, and data suggest that this occurs within the first 6 months of life.

Kuhl and her colleagues (Kuhl, 1979, 1983; Kuhl & Miller, 1975, 1982; Hillenbrand, 1983; see Kuhl, 1987, for a review) conducted several studies investigating infants' ability to perceive vowel sounds (/a/ or /i/) that vary according to speaker or intonation contour as equivalent. In general, infants were either habituated to or trained to make a head-turn response to a vowel sound spoken by either a male or female with a particular contour. As the experiment progressed, infants were tested for discrimination of the training vowel from a novel vowel as the speaker or intonation contour changed. The results suggest that infants age 5 to 16 weeks can detect a vowel change within a context of random change in the pitch contour of the vowel (Kuhl & Miller, 1975). In a control condition, Kuhl and Miller (1975) determined that infants at this age can detect a change in pitch contour if the vowel is held constant. Moreover, 6-month-old infants, following training to a male speaker, recognize as similar the same vowel spoken by a female and a child (Kuhl, 1979). This work was extended to younger infants (5 to 16 weeks) in a study that varied pitch contour and speaker (Kuhl & Miller, 1982).

The fact that infants are able to perceive speech sounds from the same phonetic category as equivalent in the face of specific, nonlinguistically relevant transformations has implications for processes underlying learning to produce speech. Kuhl (1979) suggests that "it would be difficult, if not impossible, to learn to produce speech if the infant adopted the strategy of trying to imitate absolute formant frequencies produced by adult speakers" (p. 1677). If infants can detect and represent what is similar among vowels spoken by adult and child speakers, they will be on a good footing as they begin to produce speech sounds. Given the difference in size of the articulatory apparatus, it would be impossible for young infants and children to produce sounds that match exactly those sounds produced by adults.

Nonnative Speech Perception

Languages differ in phonemic contrasts. For example, the difference between /1/ and /r/ is meaningful in English but not in Japanese. As a result, native English speaking adults can discriminate these two sounds, whereas Japanese natives cannot.

Comparing infants' perception of contrasts that are and are not present in their linguistic environment is typically how researchers study the role of experience on speech perception. Infants are conditioned to make a head turn when a change in phoneme is heard. During conditioning, infants hear pairs of phonemes, or contrasts, that exist in their linguistic environment (adults can perceive the contrast). Following conditioning, infants are presented with contrasts that make no difference in their linguistic environment (and that adult native speakers cannot discriminate).

Cross-language studies have shown consistently that infants around 6 months of age make discriminations among speech samples that adults cannot make. As shown in figure 8.2, English infants discriminated contrasts from Hindi and Thompson (a language of a native Indian population spoken in central British Columbia), whereas English adults did not (Werker, Gilbert, Humprey & Tees, 1981; Werker & Tees, 1983, 1984). English infants discriminated an oral/nasal vowel distinction (/pa/ versus /pa ~ /, present only in French and Polish and the feature of stridency used by Czech speakers (Trehub, 1976). Spanish infants detected contrasts in Thai and English resulting from VOT differences in bilabial stop consonants in Thai and English, whereas adults did not (Lasky, Syrdal-Lasky & Klein, 1975). Kenyan infants approximately 2 months of age discriminated

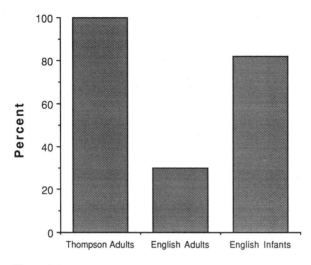

Figure 8.2
Percentage of subjects perceiving a glottalized velar or uvular (/ki/-/qi/) contrast in the Thompson language. Note that infants from English-speaking homes outperformed English-speaking adults in detecting this contrast. Redrawn with permission from Werker, J. F., & Tees, R. C. (1984), Cross-language speech perception: Evidence for perceptual reorganization during the first year of life, *Infant Behavior and Development, 7,* 49–63.

the English voiced/voiceless distinction, which does not exist in Kikuyu, the native Bantu language spoken in Kenya (Streeter, 1976).

The specialization of infants' speech perception occurs gradually across the first year of life. By 6 months of age infants do not perceive non-native vowel contrasts (Polka & Werker, 1994; Kuhl, Williams, Lacerda, Stevens & Lindblom, 1992), and by 11 months infants do not perceive nonnative consonant contrasts (Werker & Tees, 1984). Moreover, specialization of speech perception extends beyond phonemes. Nine-month-old American English infants prefer words that have sequences of sounds that exemplify native (English) rather than nonnative sound sequences (Dutch), but 6-month-olds do not (Jusczyk, Friederici, Wessels, Svenkerud & Jusczyk, 1993). Also, 9-month-olds prefer the stress pattern of English disyllabic words (strong-weak), whereas 6-month-olds show no preference (Jusczyk, Cutler & Redanz, 1993).

What process accounts for this shift from language-general to language-specific perception? In most perceptual domains, infants' performance improves with age. Here we have a case where infants' early competence is better than adults' competence and where infant competence declines with age. Aslin et al. (1983) and Burnham (1986) suggest similar processes to explain this phenomenon. They suggest that specific linguistic experience plays an attunement role in speech perception. Exposure to specific sounds, but not necessarily production of those sounds, maintains the discrimination capability, whereas lack of exposure leads to its loss.

There is controversy surrounding what form exposure must take. Some argue that infants may merely need auditory exposure (e.g., Burnham, 1986; Aslin & Pisoni, 1980). Thus, older infants' and adults' discrimination of nonnative contrasts declines as a result of the absence of certain sounds in the environment. An alternative account is that the changes are linguistic in nature (e.g., Eimas, 1978). With experience, infants organize sounds into phonemic contrasts relevant to their phonological system; nonnative contrasts are assimilated into existing contrasts. One argument for this viewpoint is that speech sounds that cannot be assimilated—for example, Zulu clicks—remain discriminable based on their acoustic properties (see Best, McRoberts & Sithole, 1988; Best, McRoberts, LaFleur & Silver-Isenstadt, 1995).

Is Speech Special?

By the end of the first year, infants possess remarkably mature speech perception abilities. This competence long precedes their own production of fluent speech. The rapid emergence of complex speech-perception skills, as well as the early presence of component abilities (such as categorical perception) have led many to wonder whether speech-perception abilities are modular in nature and specific to the human species. Eimas et al. (1971) suggested that categorical perception of phonemes was consistent with innate perceptual categorization mechanisms specifically geared to speech sounds. One argument in favor of this view is that when the same acoustic contrasts are used with nonspeech sounds, perception of the underlying acoustic dimension is not categorical (e.g., Eimas, 1974).

A variety of subsequent research efforts converge in suggesting that categorical perception is not unique to humans or to speech sounds. Jusczyk, Pisoni, Walley, and Murray (1980) showed categorical perception in human infants for complex nonspeech sounds differing in temporal onset characteristics. Studies have also documented categorical perception for human speech sounds by other species, including chinchillas (Kuhl & Miller, 1975) and macaque monkeys (Kuhl & Padden, 1982). Regarding the apparent differences in categorical perception for speech and nonspeech sounds, it now appears that the transformations of speech sounds to obtain the nonspeech control stimuli affected relational acoustic information used by auditory perceptual mechanisms (Aslin, Pisoni & Jusczyk, 1983). In sum, categorical perception of phonemes may reflect general properties of auditory processing in a variety of species and not a human specialization for language processing.

The fact the categorical perception turns out not to be unique to speech does not answer the general question about the modularity or species specificity of speech perception. Categorical perception of phonemes is a phenomenon involving the finest grain of speech-perception abilities, and other aspects of processing speech signals raise the issue of specialization and species specificity in their own right. Certainly, there are properties of mature speech processing that fit criteria for modular perceptual mechanisms (Fodor, 1983). The speed and automaticity of adult speech perception, however, as well as the operation of perceptual constancy, may be due to processes honed by perceptual learning and automatized by experience rather than by specialized speech processing mechanisms (Aslin, Pisoni & Jusczyk, 1983).

CONCLUSION

From the beginning of life, young infants obtain information from their environment through hearing. They localize and orient to events that produce sounds, and they pay special attention to some sounds, such as infant-directed speech. Long before uttering their first words, infants perceive phonemes categorically, they match visual and auditory displays on the basis of linguistic information, and they become attuned to the phonemic contrasts of their native language. From a surprisingly early age, they parse the speech stream into smaller, meaningful units and extract statistical regularities in sequences of these units.

That said, many questions remain to be answered about early auditory and speech perception. For example, research on infants' parsing abilities has found that 6-month-olds parse words into syllables, that 7-month-olds detect clause boundaries, and that 8-month-olds parse phrases into words. At first blush it might appear that parsing skills improve during this time period. Much of this research has used head-turning paradigms, however, that are ineffective with infants under 6 months. Accordingly, these research findings may not place a lower bound on certain abilities. It is unclear whether phrase, word, and syllabic parsing abilities emerge at the same time or at different times. Further research might reveal that infants begin parsing speech at a global level (that is, phrase) and then come to segment speech into smaller and smaller units (that is, words and syllables). Alternatively, infants may be able to parse speech at different levels at the same age depending on the demands of the task. Filling in the developmental picture will help us not only to better understand infants' abilities at different ages but also to identify underlying mechanisms for these abilities. While noting that the developmental story is incomplete, we can nevertheless marvel at the advances made over the last 20 years in describing early auditory abilities.

Chapter 9
Perception and Action

We must perceive in order to move, but we must also move in order to perceive.
—J. Gibson (1979, p. 223)

Perception and action are so interdependent that it is hard to imagine the evolution of either without the other already in place. Would some immobile, actionless organism ever have developed rudimentary perceptual ability? Doubtful. Knowledge without a capability for action seems useless. Did some ancient organism move about randomly, without information from the environment, to feed, escape, or reproduce? Perhaps.

The chicken-and-egg problems of perception and action in evolution are quite remote from us, but the same issues in the development of an individual are close by and fascinating. We have already encountered some of them. The young infant displays little coordinated action and for a long time was considered similarly inert perceptually. Methods to study infant perception have capitalized on a few subtle actions to reveal that the young infant can perceive far better than he or she can act. Unlike the case of our primordial immobile organism, perception without action for a developing individual makes functional sense because the infant can learn now and act later. We have also seen the importance of action in the service of perception, as in oculomotor activity and observer motion in the perception of objects and spatial layout. In this chapter, we focus directly on the relationship of perception and action, searching for general principles and elaborating specific examples.

ECOLOGY OF PERCEPTION AND ACTION

The ecology of any organism is conditioned by its capacities for action, just as it is conditioned by the information available for perception. How perception and action develop is a controversial matter, one that goes to the heart of traditional theoretical debates. In Piaget's view, reality itself is constructed by relating action to the pickup of sensory information. Initially, behavior consists of reflex reactions to specific stimuli along with some spontaneous movements. Later, sensory consequences of random actions are noted, and the actions tend to be repeated. Such sequences are referred to as *primary circular reactions* (Piaget, 1952). According to this account, neither perception nor action is well organized at first. The development of coordinated action structures and the emergence of perceived objects, instead of sensations or "interesting sights," occur together through the first two years of life.

The idea that perceptual reality must be constructed by action is not shared by ecological views. They assert a different, but equally close, coupling of perception and action. Human and animal behavior might in general be described in terms of *perception-action loops* (Gibson, 1966). Adjustment of active perceptual systems facilitates the extraction of information which is used in guiding action and additional seeking of information (Gibson, 1979; Mace, 1974; Turvey, et al., 1981). Extreme versions of this view deny that perception leads to memory representations. In lieu of stored descriptions and thought as the architects of action, the effects of the past on the future are conceived in terms of perception extended over time (e.g., Mace, 1974).

In the case of the human infant, a new view is called for (von Hofsten, 1990). The perceptual world is not, in general, constructed through action. The infant perceives a coherent environment and many of its important properties before the beginnings of directed reaching, crawling, or walking. The ecological view of perception-action loops does not seem quite right either. It may characterize much of adult human and animal behavior, but something is missing when this view is applied to human infants. The young infant does not usually perceive in order to act and is seldom engaged in complex perception-action loops. What we suggest is a new, lopsided perspective: perceptual skills develop ahead of action skills and form the foundation for their development.

On reflection, one might conclude it almost has to be this way. Piaget's vision of action and sensation mutually constructing reality is a profound and creative hypothesis. But it may have one too many degrees of freedom. If the infant begins by neither perceiving nor acting in an organized three-dimensional space, building reality would be a momentous task. Now add the problem of poor motor control; below we see that early in infancy, motor activity is undifferentiated and imprecise. (We cannot even consider the problem of perceptual error because perception on this account does not yet exist.) The Piagetian enterprise is to arrive at perceptual reality by attunement of action to sensation. But this process, once begun, would be fraught with mismatches due to errors in the motor system, the perceptual system, or both. Without a firm foundation in perception or action, how would development proceed? Perhaps with appropriate constraints and a great deal of time, such a learning situation might lead to coherent perception and action. But in chapters 4 and 6 we saw evidence that the infant perceives the positions, shapes, and sizes of objects in three-dimensional space *before* it has developed the ability of directed reaching. Now recall the following finding, which we considered in chapter 6. Around 4.5 to 5 months of age, when the infant first begins to reach for a stationary object in a directed fashion, the infant can be tested with a different stimulus—an object that moves in an arc passing briefly in front of the infant. The infant, on seeing this object, reaches not for where it is but for its anticipated position farther along in its trajectory. This anticipatory reaching leads to successful grasping of the object (von Hofsten, 1983). This example illustrates how perceptual competence may precede and guide emerging action systems.

We thus approach perception and action with a perspective derived from our observations of early perceptual ability. A major task of the first year of life may be the acquisition of motor skills under the guidance of maturation and information provided by perception (von Hofsten, 1990). In turn, new action systems make available new information and refine perceptual exploration.

ABILITIES AND PROCESSES

Perceptual Exploration

Some of the earliest actions performed by infants involve exploratory activity. In the classic visual cliff studies by Gibson and Walk (1960), the authors discovered that infants' actions (such as crawling over the deep or shallow side of the cliff) were dependent on visual and haptic exploration. According to Gibson and Walk, it was not uncommon for hesitant infants to pat the glass or put their face close to the glass to look into the deep side. Infants in this situation were using the information gained from exploration to decide whether the surface was traversable.

We might think of perceptual exploration as involving complicated actions such as reaching, crawling, or walking. But perceptual exploration can be accomplished with seemingly simple actions such as eye movements or mouthing that often go unnoticed. Most of the behavioral methods responsible for progress in infant perception research rely on infants' exploratory tendencies. These tendencies were observed in great detail by Piaget, who considered them perhaps the most crucial ingredients in the construction of reality. In light of infants' perceptual competencies that arise much earlier than Piaget anticipated, we can reinterpret infants' persistent exploratory behaviors. Rather than developing procedures to "make interesting sights last," infants are seeking information about objects and relationships in their environment.

Controlling Posture

We begin our study of perception-action relationships with a basic concern—the maintenence of posture. For adults, control of posture is crucial for standing and walking, and complex postural manipulations are required to perform actions, such as reaching, lifting, and throwing. For infants, postural control develops slowly. Not until 3 to 4 months does an infant possess enough neck strength to hold his head steady when upright. Around 6 months many infants become able to sit up without support.

Information for postural stability can be provided by kinesthetic, vestibular, and visual information. Kinesthetic information involves sensing one's own movement through receptors in joints and muscles. Vestibular information comes from gravity and accelerations. Much of our orienting and acting in the environment, however, depends on information gotten through vision. Gibson (1966) drew attention to the crucial role played by vision, coining the phrase *visual kinesthesis*. A standing observer will adjust posture every second or two without conscious awareness, based primarily on visual information (see Howard, 1982, for a review). The moving observer can discern important properties of her locomotion, such as heading, from *optic flow*, continuous optical changes given as the observer moves through an environment. Optic flow alone can induce the observer to perceive herself in motion, and this fact has been used in tests of the roles of visual and vestibular inputs in postural control with both adults and children.

Most often these studies use a "moving room." A chamber with three walls and a ceiling is either suspended from the ceiling or mounted on wheels such that the room can be moved to present flow fields to a stationary observer (the floor does not move). In this situation, the subject is presented with conflicting information for postural stability. Whereas kinesthetic information (from the legs and feet) and vestibular information indicate that the observer is stationary, visual information indicates that the subject is moving, usually forward or backward. Adults tested in this situation show effects of this informational conflict. For example, Lee and Lishman (1975) found, for a variety of stances, that subjects responded to the change in flow fields by adjusting their posture. Further work with adults identified the importance of the location of flow (e.g., Brandt, Dichgans & Koenig, 1973; Held, Dichgans & Bauer, 1975; Johansson, 1977; Stoffregen, 1985, 1986). Optic flow in the periphery is more effective in inducing the perception of self-motion and results in greater postural compensation.

At what point in development is optic flow information used in the control of posture? To answer this question Lee and Aronson (1974) studied infants who had just begun standing. Subjects ranging between 13 and 16 months of age were placed in a moving room. Lee and Aronson found that 82% of the responses (staggering or falling down) were directionally appropriate to compensate for the visually specified position change. Butterworth and Hicks (1977) extended this finding in a similar experiment in which they found that 11-month-olds who could sit independently, but could not stand, adjusted their seated posture in response to room movement. Children locomoting through a moving hallway show similiar patterns of postural instability (Schmuckler & Gibson, 1989). These findings suggest the early importance of visual information in maintaining posture. Visual information may dominate kinesthetic and vestibular information when these are in conflict. The magnitude of the response of postural change decreases with age; children fall down, whereas adults merely sway.

Recent developmental work has addressed the issues of location of flow, the effects of optical flow on a locomoting subject, and postural adjustments in infants who do not sit independently. Both Stoffregren, Schmuckler, and Gibson (1987) and Bertenthal and Bai (1989) found that, as in adults, flow in the periphery is more effective for specifying self-motion than centrally produced flow in standing infants. Stoffregren et al. (1987) and Schmuckler and Gibson (1989) also found that flow affected stability while the children (under the age of 2 years) were locomoting. Moreover, peripheral flow was more disruptive of locomotion than central flow.

Even before infants are able to sit independently, they adjust their posture in response to peripheral optic flow changes. This sensitivity develops between 5 and 9 months of age (Bertenthal & Bai, 1989). This conclusion comes from experiments in which infants were seated in a swinglike chair equipped with pressure transducers to monitor changes in pressure associated with postural adjustment. Measured adjustments to optic flow were dependent on age: 5-month-olds did not show significant appropriate responding in any of the movement conditions (peripheral, central, both), 7-month-olds showed a marginally significant response, and 9-month-olds responded appropriately in all movement conditions, with a lesser response when only central flow was present.

The answer to the question of when infants act on optical flow information to adjust their spatial orientation appears to be between 7 and 9 months of age, before most infants stand independently and not too long after they become able to maintain a sitting posture. The mechanism responsible for changes between 5 and 9 months is unknown. It is possible that infants need to learn the meaning of optic flow fields through their own self-initiated movements (Bertenthal & Campos, 1990). Research in other contexts, however, suggests earlier sensitivity to optical information for observer motion (e.g., Kellman et al., 1987), sensitivity that arises too early to be a result of learning based on crawling or even seated postural adjustments. Another possibility is that infants younger than 7 to 9 months are sensitive to optic flow information for orientation but lack the control over their trunk muscles to perform the relevant postural adjustments.

Development of Reaching

An important milestone in perception-action coordination is the development of reaching, around 4.5 months of age. Successfully reaching for and grasping an object requires perception of the object's location and appropriate generation of movements to that location. These movements involve the coordination of shoulder and arm muscles to move the hand toward the object and fine adjustments in hand orientation and grip size before a successful grasp can be made.

Prereaching Versus Visually Guided Reaching
Undoubtably, very young infants execute arm movements, but whether these arm movements constitute reaching movements has been debated. Traditionally, arm movements of infants between 0 and 4 months of age have been called *prereaching* (Trevarthen, 1975). Prereaching has been thought of as an early type of reaching that shares some of the characteristics of later visually guided reaching but that is qualitatively different. This conclusion follows from several pieces of evidence. First, prereaching is less accurate than visually guided reaching. Newborn infants show a hit rate—actual contact with the object—of only 9% (von Hofsten, 1982). In contrast, 17-week-olds typically show a hit rate of 93% to objects at the midline (Provine & Westerman, 1979). A second difference between visually guided reaching and prereaching is the nature of the trajectory of the reach. Prereaching has been thought to be ballistic in that, once the movement begins, no corrections are made. Visually guided reaching involves a continuous feedback process with trajectory adjustments made during the reach. A third difference between visually guided reaching and prereaching involves coordination between the target and the hand. In prereaching, the coordination is between a seen target and a felt hand. In other words, the infant executes an arm movement in response to seeing an object but does not monitor the arm or hand's progress visually as the movement continues. In visually guided reaching, the coordination is between a seen target and a seen hand. A final difference between prereaching and reaching is that prereaching is dominated by a synergy in which the fingers extend as the arm extends. As a result the fingers do not close around the object. With functional reaching, the reach ordinarily terminates in a grasp.

Recent research calls into question some of the apparent differences between prereaching and visually guided reaching. Neonatal reaching may be more similar to mature reaching than once thought. In a careful analysis of newborn reaching, von Hofsten (1982) found evidence that certain precursors of directed reaching are present in newborns' arm movements. Additionally, his research suggests that this reaching behavior may be under the influence of vision. In his study, infants ranging between 5 and 9 days of age were videotaped while a ball moved in front of them within reach. Infants' motor and visual behavior were recorded. Hofsten found that infants made more forward arm extensions while they were fixating the ball than when they were not. Furthermore, on the best-aimed reaches, the infants' hand slowed down as it neared the object and exhibited some hand opening, as if anticipating a grasp.

Von Hofsten and Ronnqvist (1993) further investigated the structure of newborn infants' reaching. They found that these early arm movements are subject to several sets of organizing principles. Neonatal reaching has a distinct temporal structure in that neonates change arm direction between movement units and show straight trajectories within movement units. This pattern of movement is similar to that found in more mature reaching. Older infants and adults typically show two movement units when executing a reach: the first movement is long, whereas the second movement is shorter and allows for correction (e.g., Ashmead, McCarty, Lucas & Belvedere, 1993). The change in direction found between movement units by von Hofsten and Ronnqvist indicates a means for correction of the trajectory of the reach in newborns. From these results, von Hofsten and Ronnqvist concluded that coordination between the eye and the hand does exist in newborns and that the precursors for mature reaching are present, even though this type of reaching is prefunctional, at best (see von Hofsten, 1990, for a review).

A second area of research suggests that neonatal reaching is influenced by visual information. Van der Meer et al. (1995) attached small weights to newborn infants' wrists and pulled the hands in the direction of their toes (see figure 9.1). Van der Meer et al. found that infants moved their arms to keep a seen hand in view. In a clever manipulation, infants were presented with a view of the hand that was *not* actually in the direction of their line of sight on a video monitor. In other words, infants looking to their left side saw their right hand on the video monitor. Even in this situation babies moved the seen hand more than the unseen hand. When neither hand was visible, infants did not show many arm movements. Thus, vision appears to play a role in activating arm movements. Because neonatal arm movements are not well coordinated, it is difficulty to evaluate whether vision plays a role in guiding these movements toward objects.

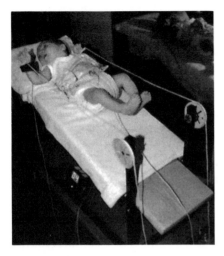

Figure 9.1
Apparatus used by Van der Meer et al. to tug infants' hands toward their feet. Reprinted with permission from Van der Meer, A. L. H., Van der Weel, R. R., & Lee, D. N. (1995), The functional significance of arm movements in neonates, *Science, 267,* 693–695. Copyright 1995 American Association for the Advancement of Science.

A third area of research questions the assumption that the onset of mature reaching is actually visually guided. Clifton, Muir, Ashmead, and Clarkson (1993) assessed whether sight of the hand was needed for the onset of mature reaching and grasping. In a longitudinal study, they tested 7 infants' reaching and grasping between 6 and 25 weeks of age. Infants were observed under two conditions—reaching for an object in the light and reaching for a glowing object in the dark. Results showed that the ages of onset for reaching and grasping did not differ between conditions. The mean age for reaching in the light was 12.3 weeks and 11.9 weeks for reaching in the dark. For grasping objects in the light and dark, mean age was 16.0 and 14.7 weeks (a nonsignificant difference), respectively. Because infants could not see their hands or arms in the dark, Clifton et al. concluded that infants did not use visual information to guide their reaching. Instead, they may have relied on kinesthetic or proprioceptive information. In this study vision did play a role in eliciting the arm movement but not in guiding it. These findings do not suggest, of course, that reaching is never visually guided. Vision may play an important role in the improvement in reaching accuracy.

What Accounts for the Onset of Accurate Reaching?
What accounts for the improvement in reaching that has been observed in the first 6 months of life is not known. Attentional changes and neuro-

physiological maturation have been advanced as possibilities (see Bushnell, 1985, for a review). Bower (1974) suggested that visually guided reaching is absent until 4 months because younger infants lack attentional capacities to attend to both target and hand. Alternatively, maturation of the motor system may be crucial. Kuypers' (1962, 1973) research suggests that arm and shoulder movements are governed by a proximal system (a subcortical system possibly tied to the extrapyramidal tract) whereas fine motor movements are governed by a distal system (a cortical system possibly tied to the pyramidal tract). In infant rhesus monkeys the proximal system develops earlier than the distal system. Within the first 3 months of life, for example, monkeys show arm movements to the location of objects but fail to execute hand and finger movements (Lawrence & Hopkins, 1972). Improvements in human reaching may also be due to the differential rates of maturation of these two systems. This suggestion might explain a number of developmental asynchronies in infant manual behavior (Lockman & Ashmead, 1983).

One seldom considered possibility is the role of spatial perception. Stereopsis emerges around 4 months of age (see chapters 2 and 3). Improvements in reaching accuracy appear at about the same time as the rapid onset of sensitivity to binocular disparity. Infants may be able to make fine motor adjustments as a result of their improved spatial perception. This possibility is supported by findings of Yonas and Hartman (1993). In their study, 4- and 5-month-olds were presented with an object that was either within or just beyond their arm lengths. Infants who could lean forward (not all can at this age) adjusted their behavior depending on whether the object was within or beyond reach. In other words, they reached and leaned to come into contact with an out-of-reach object. Yonas and Hartman concluded that 4- to 5-month-olds acted as if they had sensitivity to the absolute distance of an object and the length of their arm, as well as the effect that leaning forward had on their ability to make contact with a distant object. In chapter 3, we considered the findings of Granrud (1986) showing that infants at 4 to 5 months of age who were sensitive to binocular disparity reached more reliably to the closer of two objects than infants at these ages who showed no evidence of disparity sensitivity. Taken together, these results are consistent with the notion that the onset of stereoscopic depth perception plays some role in improvements in directed reaching.

Once mature reaching emerges, infants spend many waking hours reaching for objects. They readily distinguish targets within and out of reach (Field, 1976; McKenzie, Skouteris, Day, Hartman & Yonas, 1993), and they continue to refine their reaching to anticipate target orientation (Lockman, Ashmead & Bushnell, 1984) and other object properties (Pieraut-Le Bonniec, 1990; see von Hofsten, 1990, for a review). Especially intriguing are findings by von Hofsten (1983), discussed earlier, showing that as soon as infants become capable of directed reaching, they are skilled at catching moving targets. This achievement requires perceiving and anticipating trajectory. The display of anticipatory reaching at the time of onset of directed reaching provides a conspicuous example in which perceptual knowledge—in this case, perception of velocity—precedes and guides action skills as the latter emerge.

Perspectives on Reaching
Infants begin life with a repertoire of movements that include prereaching behaviors. Early arm movements share some similiarities to later, mature reaching. The prereaching versus visually guided reaching dichotomy may be somewhat misleading. At the same time, the changes in reaching frequency and accuracy that occur around 4.5 months are dramatic and abrupt enough to be considered a new phase. These improvements are most likely due to maturation within motor systems and possibly in attentional and planning abilities. The possibility that skilled reaching is obtained by gradual maturation and attunement of motor systems marks a departure from older ideas that perception and action develop by mutual interaction. In many respects, spatial and event perception abilities already in place guide the calibration of motoric, as well as attentional and planning, skills as these emerge. At the same time, continuing improvements on the perceptual side, such as the onset of stereoscopic depth perception, may contribute to the precision of reaching skills.

Exploring Objects

Once infants are able to make contact with objects, they have many new opportunities to explore. Infants who have just attained skilled reaching launch into a multimodal binge, picking up objects, manipulating them, looking at them, and mouthing them.

Oral exploration can be informative even before the advent of skilled reaching. When objects are placed in the mouth, infants are able to detect surface properties (Meltzoff & Borton, 1979) and object characteristics such as rigidity (Gibson & Walker, 1984; Rochat, 1987). These explorations becomes increasingly refined as infants develop control over their arms and hands. Rochat (1989) has documented eye-hand-mouth coordination in 2-month-olds, and this coordination becomes more sophisticated and differentiated through 12 months of age (Palmer, 1989; Rochat, 1989; Ruff, 1984).

Typically, infants' exploration is investigated in experiments in which babies are given an object or a series of objects for a specific time period and their actions are coded. Examples of actions are mouthing, banging,

Figure 9.2
A 12-month-old infant explores a novel object visually and manually (a) before exploring it orally (b).

fingering, scratching, squeezing, two-handed grasping, and waving. (See figure 9.2.) Some changes with age are (1) an increase in mouthing from 2 to 5 months and then a subsequent decrease between 6 and 12 months and (2) an increase in refinement of fingering between 2 and 12 months. Rochat (1989) suggests that there is coordination between vision and manipulation of the object with age; objects are increasingly brought into the field of view.

Infants also adapt their exploratory behavior to specific properties of objects. Three- to 4-month-olds exhibit flexibility in their manipulation when presented with two different objects, one mouthable and the other scratchable (Rochat, 1989). Similarly, infants between 4 and 8 months show different actions (mouthing or grasping), depending on object size and orientation (Whyte, McDonald, Baillargeon & Newell, 1994). Ruff (1984) documented the use of different repertoires of actions on objects with different surface characteristics. For example, 6-, 9-, and 12-month-olds more often fingered a bumpy object and more often mouthed a smoothly painted object. Palmer's (1989) work further supports this differentiation of actions based on object characteristics. Besides observing different exploratory actions related to different object properties, Palmer found that infants differentiated support surfaces (hard table versus foam surface) by the actions executed with the objects on those surfaces (for example, banging versus not banging). Thus, as early as 6 months infants not only are sensitive to object properties and the appropriate exploratory actions but also are aware of possible object and support-surface interactions.

As infants gain control over their motor systems, perception and action become intricately tied. The newborn baby who is limited to oral exploration grows into a 12-month-old who has developed an efficient and effective coordination of multiple perceptual and motor processes that allow discovery of information about objects and surfaces.

Surface Exploration and Locomotion

At about 6 months of age, infants begin to crawl, vastly expanding their possibilities for action in their environment. Although crawling is typical, some babies are quite adept at rolling or scooting in a sitting position. The onset of locomotion elevates to central importance information specifying surface characteristics such as support. Since the classic visual cliff studies by Gibson and Walk (1960), researchers have investigated perception and action with regard to surfaces in several related paradigms.

Gibson and her colleagues (Gibson et al., 1987) asked whether young locomotors are sensitive to surface characteristics specifying support and whether they adjust their actions to most effectively locomote. Crawling

Figure 9.3
Apparatus used in studies of infants' locomotion over different types of surfaces. From Gibson, E. J., Riccio, G., Shmuckler, M. A., Stoffregen, T. A., Rosenberg, D., & Taormina, J. (1987), Detection of traversibility of surfaces by crawling and walking infants, *Journal of Experimental Psychology: Human Perception and Performance, 13,* 533–544. Copyright © 1987 by the American Psychological Association. Reprinted with permission.

and walking infants were presented with walkways composed of either a rigid or a deforming surface. The rigid surface was composed of a piece of plywood covered with a textured cloth. The deforming surface was a waterbed (agitated by an experimenter) also covered with a textured cloth (figure 9.3). Most of the infants crossed both surfaces, and all crawled rather than walked across the waterbed. The walkers showed greater latency to cross than the crawlers and engaged in considerable visual and haptic exploration. When presented with a choice of traversing either a rigid or deforming surface (that is, when the two surfaces were placed side by side), walkers showed a strong preference for the rigid surface. Crawlers showed no preference.

Further experiments suggested that infants rely on haptic and visual information to different degrees when determining the traversability of a surface. When visual information conflicted with haptic information (the waterbed was covered with clear plexiglas), haptic information domi-nated. When visual information was reduced (by covering the plywood surface with a black velveteen cloth), infants suffered from indecision. Crawlers and walkers crossed both surfaces, but the latency to cross was greater for the untextured surface.

Surface properties other than rigidity have important implications for action. One such property is surface slope. Adolph, Eppler, and Gibson (1993a) investigated infants' locomotion up and down surfaces that sloped 10, 20, 30, or 40 deg. Walkers appeared to be sensitive to the surface slope and their own abilities: when presented with ascending surfaces, all infants proceeded. With descending surfaces of 30 and 40 deg, 11 out of 23 avoided at least one. Crawlers, in contrast, showed little sensitivity to their ability to negotiate slopes: most tried to locomote up and down slopes that were beyond their abilities. Adolph et al. attributed these dif-ferences to a refinement in exploratory behavior. Walkers often patted the slope with their hands or feet, rocked back and forth over their ankles, and explored alternative means of locomotion (e.g., crawling down a slope backward rather than walking forward). Crawlers explored less and did not investigate alternative means to descend the slopes; many started head first down the sloped and had to be rescued.

Research on surface traversability shows that infant locomotion is sensitive to surface-property information. The fact that walkers crawled across a deforming surface or down a steep descent indicated that they determined not only whether a surface afforded support but what type of locomotion was appropriate.

Perceiving Affordances

Perception of surface support or traversability has been claimed to illus-trate a particular idea about perception in general—that what is perceived are *affordances* (Gibson, 1979). Not only do we perceive an objects' shape or color, but we perceive what can be done with the object. Affordances relate to the needs and capabilities of the organism, but they are proper-ties of objects and surfaces in the environment, and they are there to be discovered by the perceiver. As J. Gibson (1979) put it, "An affordance is not bestowed upon an object by a need of an observer and his act of per-ceiving it. The object offers what it does because it is what it is" (p. 139). The sensitivity of infants' locomotor behavior to surface characteristics has often been interpreted in terms of affordances (Adolph et al., 1993a; Palmer, 1989). The concept is by no means universally accepted as a way of describing what is perceived. We may inquire about the value of this type of description and also how it may be possible to determine infants' perception of affordances. Infant researchers observe infants' actions with objects and infer that they have perceived specific object properties. Can it also be concluded that affordances have been perceived? How does one know the difference between perceiving an object property (such as, it is hard) and perceiving an affordance (such as, it is good for banging on a table)? Are there specific conditions that must be met to conclude that an affordance has been perceived?

A framework for studying the perception of affordances has been offered by Adolph, Eppler, and Gibson (1993b). They posit three conditions for claiming that infants (and adults) are responding to affordances. The first condition is a description of how an action is constrained by the fit between environmental properties and action capabilities. Thus, the researcher must identify the range of variation in action allowed by the affordance. As an example, they cite work on stairclimbing demonstrating that successful climbing depends on a fit between properties of the actor (such as leg and foot length) and properties of the stairs (such as riser height and tread depth). The second condition is that specific information must specify the affordance. The third condition is a close correspondence between perceived and actual actor-environment fit. Adolph et al. emphasize the need for quantitative methods to assess this link.

These criteria may prove useful in assessing how closely perception and action are coupled in particular domains. They capture the essence of the affordance notion—that perception supports the current actions and goals of the organism. It is not clear that these criteria alone distinguish the notion that what we perceive are affordances from the notion that perception furnishes descriptions of the environment. Representations of the environment produced by perception must be able to support immediate action, but they may also be more general, flexible, and enduring than required by the organism's immediate behavioral task. We return to this issue—how best to characterize the products of perception—in chapter 11.

Development of Action in Blind Children

Blind children provide a natural experiment to look at some relations between perception and action. If perceptual development—and vision, in particular—guides motor development, we might expect blind children's initial attainment of basic motor milestones to be delayed. Observations by Fraiberg (1968) and Bigelow (1986, 1992) confirm such delays in blind infants' motor development. The onset of reaching occurs from 1.5 months to 8 months later than in sighted infants. Moreover, the onset of self-produced locomotion—crawling and walking—is also delayed compared to sighted infants. In a sample of three children studied by Bigelow (1992), the age of onset of walking was 32, 17, and 36 months, considerably later than the average age of 12 months for sighted infants. Bigelow (1986, 1992) suggests that these delays stem from deficits in perceptual knowledge. Of course, the lack of visual input would be expected to affect action on almost any account of development. The fact that certain actions, such as reaching and walking, appear much later in blind children is nevertheless revealing. It suggests that the emergence of these abilities in sighted children depends upon information about the environment (and the self) already available through vision. This strong dependence appears to run counter to traditional notions, such as those of Piaget and Berkeley, that visual reality gains its meaning through action and locomotion.

Does Perception Precede Action?

The research presented in this chapter suggests that early in life perception and action are closely linked. In fact, this is a point on which all theories agree. Disagreement centers on whether action precedes and serves to construct meaningful perception, whether perceptual skill precedes and guides motor development, or whether both emerge together. Research we have considered in previous chapters suggests that perception of objects, surfaces, and events does not depend on motoric experiences such as reaching or locomoting, simply because the relevant perceptual abilities can be demonstrated before directed reaching and crawling begin. Even later-appearing abilities do not show these connections. For example, Arterberry, Yonas, and Bensen (1989) found that the onset of 7-month-olds' sensitivity to pictorial depth cues—the latest-appearing class of spatial information—was not predicted by locomotor status (precrawler, belly crawler, or hands-and-knees crawler).

Perception does not seem to be created from action, and in many cases it is relatively advanced when action begins. A possible exception we have noted is the contribution of spatial perception—specifically the emergence of stereoscopic depth perception—to the guidance of reaching. Often, however, advances in the motor system seem to be paced on their own timetable. When they do emerge, they benefit immediately from representations of the spatial layout given by perception. After beginning to reach, for example, an infant does not undergo protracted learning to reach for an object in motion, even though catching the object requires reaching not to where the object is seen but to where it will be when the reach is completed. This overview fits what we know of the timing of the emergence of many perceptual abilities and motor activity.

Other Relations between Perception and Action

Of course, this generalization about perception preceding action is only part of the story. Action brings about new opportunities for perceiving and leads to perceptual refinements. Some of these must include recalibration of perceptual information due to growth—such as information used in binocular vision changing as the eyes grow farther apart, or even more drastic remapping of visual space as retinal receptors migrate to new positions during the early months of life (Aslin, 1993). Although it is possible that some recalibration can be accomplished by comparisons among different sources of perceptual information, it is likely that perception-action loops provide much of the basis for recalibration. In fact, rapid remapping of space across senses as a result of action can be observed even in adults under conditions of changed input to one sense (e.g., Rock & Harris, 1967; Bedford, 1986).

There is some evidence for improvements in perception related to developing action systems. Bertenthal and Campos (1990) reported that some perceptual and cognitive developments in the second half of the first year benefit from the experience gained from self-produced locomotion (crawling). They suggested that "locomotor experience does not directly affect the emergence of any basic processing skill, but rather demands that the infant begin either to use information that was previously neglected or to use this information in novel ways" (p. 5). This view has notable antecedents (e.g., Held & Hein, 1963). Self-produced locomotion may enhance infants' use of visual-vestibular information for posture, sensitivity to emotional communication from others regarding ambiguous situations (called *social referencing*; see chapter 10), and sensitivity to heights, as on the visual cliff (Bertenthal & Campos, 1990). Before crawling, infants perceive depth; what may change with crawling experience is the coordination of depth and surface perception with their own motion in space.

Another domain in which the development of action may enhance perception involves haptically perceived object properties (Bushnell & Boudreau, 1993). Temperature, texture, and hardness require rather minimal exploratory activity; these properties are detected by infants at about 6 months of age. Weight and shape, on the other hand, required more sophisticated haptic activity, and these properties are not detected until 9 to 12 months of age. Bushnell and Boudreau claim that the emergence order is due to the development of specific hand actions that are optimal for perceiving these properties.

Some recent work emphasizes the importance of *prospective control* in the development and coordination of perception and action (von Hofsten, 1993; Bertenthal, 1996). Actions must be controlled prospectively to coordinate with events because of time lags involved in initiating and carrying out body movements. Consequently, predicting what will happen next is a central problem in perceptual and cognitive guidance of behavior. To some extent, perception appears to be adapted in certain ways to provide this information, as we saw in the case of anticipatory reaching. But prospective control in perception and action systems also improves with experience in particular perception-action relationships. It involves learning to seek the information that will be needed next along with coordinating action. Obviously, this is not a unitary ability; attunement to relevant information and accurate motor anticipation may develop separately for particular skills (Bertenthal, 1996).

Dissociations between Action and Knowledge

A number of findings in adult perception and action, neurophysiological research with nonhuman primates, and studies of patients with neurological deficits are consistent with the idea of multiple perceptual representations subserving separate functions. For example, observes show drastic foreshortening in *estimating* distances from visual information, but when asked to walk blindfolded to targets, they show excellent accuracy (e.g., Loomis, Da Silva, Philbeck & Fukusima, 1996). One generalization that may capture many of these facts was proposed by Goodale and Milner (1992). They suggested that we have distinct neural systems for perceptual control of action and for perception and recognition of objects and events. Sometimes these are labeled the *what* and the *how* systems, indicating that one performs object recognition and the other controls actions on objects. This dichotomy may turn out to be incomplete or inaccurate, but there is little doubt that perception leads to multiple representations that may be recruited for different tasks.

Not much is known about the origins of multiple perceptual representations in infancy. We do see some hints of dissociations, including some between action and knowledge. For example, infants by 4.5 months show considerable knowledge about the existence of hidden objects, but they do not search for a hidden object until approximately 8 months of age (e.g., Piaget, 1954; Harris, 1987). Moreover, this ability to search for a hidden object can be manipulated by time delays between the hiding and finding phases, but such delays do not interfere with infants' ability to remember the location of a hidden object if tested in a looking paradigm (Diamond, 1988; Baillargeon, DeVos & Graber, 1989). A second dissociation between cognition and action may imply competence in the action domain before competence in the cognitive domain. As we see in chapter 11, Spelke, Katz, Purcell, Ehrlich, et al. (1994) found little evidence that infants under 12 months of age reason about objects in accordance with an inertia principle, yet von Hofsten (1983) found that 5-month-old infants catch moving objects by anticipating their trajectories. Such prediction would be difficult without an implicit understanding of inertia. These observations may suggest that humans initially have separate representational systems for knowledge and action (Goodale & Milner, 1992; Bertenthal, 1996; Spelke, 1996).

CONCLUSION

Much remains to be learned about the development of action and its relations to perception. By the same token, much has been learned in just a few decades of active experimentation on these questions. Action does not appear to be the source of early perceptual reality, as Piaget (1969) suggested. The description of behavior in terms of perception-action loops may characterize much of skilled behavior later on, but it is not adequate to characterize young perceivers, whose perceptual abilities in general emerge earlier than their action skills. A tentative generalization about perception and action in the first year of life is that a gradual maturation and attunement of action systems occurs under the guidance of perception. As action systems mature, they lead to refinements in the pickup of information that in turn support more effective action. One emerging theme in perception and action is that perception may lead to the formation of multiple representations useful for different tasks. Representations for guiding action may be special, and even among these, the refinement of perception-action connections with experience may be quite task-specific. Distinguishing and tracing the origins of separable tasks and representational systems remain high priorities for research. Such efforts will lead to a better understanding of the connections between perception and action as well as the underlying mechanisms that produce both.

Chapter 10
Perceptual Foundations of Social Development

An organism's survival and well-being depend on action guided by perception. Often the individual acts directly on the physical world, as in reaching for an object or navigating around an obstacle. In a social species, however, direct action on the physical environment is not the sole means to survival and well-being. Much of the time we fulfill our needs and those of others by acting in the social world. Compare foraging for food to arranging by telephone to have pizza delivered. The balance between acting directly on the physical world and acting in the social world is even more lopsided for an infant. An infant's abilities to act usefully on the physical environment are modest, whereas abilities to influence caretakers are quite powerful from the start.

ECOLOGY OF SOCIAL PERCEPTION

This capsule view of the infant's situation points to some priorities of early perceptual activity. Perhaps the most basic is to distinguish social beings from other objects. Because the social and nonsocial worlds require different kinds of behavior, acting effectively depends first of all on sorting correctly. A further priority is to learn about the workings of the social world. Through it, the infant interacts indirectly with the physical world; thus, understanding the rules of the social world takes on great significance. This learning includes representing the roles and potentials of specific individuals and forming important generalizations and classifications about social phenomena.

The process will attain astonishing sophistication in a short time. A toddler shows obvious empathy in offering a crying child his teddy bear, yet feels none at all for a vase that falls from a shelf and shatters. Even such ordinary incidents require complex and subtle perceptual and cognitive achievements. In this chapter we probe some of the foundations and initial achievements of social perception.

ABILITIES AND PROCESSES OF SOCIAL PERCEPTION

When and how infants acquire knowledge of people and their interactions has been an intriguing question for researchers. According to Piaget (1981) the emergence of social cognition is tied to advances in other areas of cognitive development within the first two years. He claimed that infants begin life with instinctual behaviors and affective reactions, such as smiling or crying. These behaviors, while communicative in impact, are not intentionally directed toward people and do not reflect mature social-cognitive understanding. Between 1 and 6 months, infants begin to have feelings of pleasure, pain, and so on, which are acquired through experience. They also begin to differentiate needs and interests. Yet at this stage, feelings are still directed toward the self. According to Piaget, the child is undifferentiated, in that she does not yet understand the boundaries between herself, others, and the world. As she begins to differentiate between objects and people at around 6 to 8 months, feelings and actions become directed toward other people. People begin to be appreciated as separate objects which are localizable and which are autonomous sources of causality. In addition to the appearance of true exchange relationships, imitation of others appears. Thus, from a Piagetian perspective the foundation for social cognition, perception of other people as special objects, emerges in conjunction with differentiation of the self and advancing object knowledge in the second half of the first year of life. This understanding matures over the sensorimotor period. Stern (1985) also hypothesized a prolonged period of development in which infants come to differentiate themselves from others and acquire a sense of self.

Others have suggested that infants *begin* life as social beings (Trevarthen, 1979). As a result of observing face-to-face interactions between 6- to 8-week-old infants and their mothers or an object, Trevarthen concluded that infants at 8 weeks behaved very differently facing their mothers than they did facing a familiar object. Trevarthen claims that in order to be social participants, infants must possess subjectivity and intersubjectivity. Subjectivity is individual consciousness and intentionality, and it involves relating objects and situations to oneself. For example, infants focus their attention on objects, they manipulate objects with an interest in consequences, and they anticipate events with an intent to avoid or orient to them. Intersubjectivity occurs when interacting with other people. Infants fit their behavior with that of others, and they signal anticipation or avoidance of interaction with specific behaviors, such as orienting or looking away from others. Hence, Trevarthen proposes that social participation is founded on a differentiation of self from objects, including social objects, and the ability to mesh one's intentions with the intentions of others to regulate an exchange.

It is difficult to imagine that infant perception research will any time soon furnish a detailed account of how and when the several and subtle dimensions of self concepts arise. We take up a more modest task. Social development requires distinguishing social and nonsocial beings, as we have said. On many accounts, it also requires truly social interactions. By examining several lines of research, we can gain some idea of when social perception and interaction begin. We begin by examining newborn imitation.

ABILITIES AND PROCESSES OF SOCIAL PERCEPTION

Imitation

In 1977, Meltzoff and Moore published the first paper reporting imitation abilities in newborns. They claimed that babies between 12 and 21 days old imitated gestures. In this study an adult modeled a gesture (tongue protrusion, lip protrusion, mouth opening, or sequential finger movement), and observers coded the infants' responses (see figure 10.1). Infants were more likely to produce the gesture that was being modeled than any other action. Later work found similar effects in infants from 42 min to 32 hours old (Meltzoff & Moore, 1983). To rule out the possibility that infants were in some way matching the action based on a reflexive response, Meltzoff and Moore (1983) restricted the infant from responding immediately to the model's action. During the modeling phase in which an infant viewed the gesture (either tongue protrusion or mouth opening), a pacifier was placed in the infant's mouth. Following modeling, the pacifier was removed, the model assumed a passive face, and the infant's response was recorded. As in the initial study, infants imitated the two gestures. Further work suggested that infants' imitation was not limited to the above gestures. Newborns also widened their lips when viewing a smile, pouted when viewing a frown, and opened their mouths when viewing a surprised facial expression (Field, Woodson, Greenberg & Cohen, 1982).

These early findings on newborn imitation were hotly disputed, but the results have survived tests of numerous alternative explanations and at least 20 replications (see Meltzoff & Moore, 1989, 1994, and Meltzoff & Gopnik, 1993, for reviews). Imitation has been found in Israeli infants (Kaitz, Meschulach-Sarfaty, Auerbach & Eidelman, 1988) and Indo-Aryan infants of Nepal (Reissland, 1988). The work has also been extended to other gestures, such as imitation of head movements (full rotation of the head in a clockwise direction; Meltzoff & Moore, 1989) and subject populations, such as premature infants (Field, Woodson, Greenberg, Garcia & Collins, 1983).

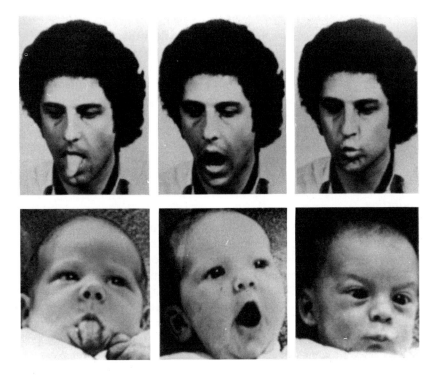

Figure 10.1
Examples of imitative responses by 2- to 3-week-old infants to an adult protruding his tongue, opening his mouth, and pursing his lips. Reprinted with permission from Meltzoff, A. N., & Moore, M. K. (1977), Imitation of facial and manual gestures by human neonates. *Science, 198*, 75–78. Copyright 1977 American Association for the Advancement of Science.

We can sympathize with critics, however, because newborn imitation is nothing short of astonishing. It seems to imply sophisticated capacities not just of perception but of representation and action, some of which have not previously been documented and some of which have been theorized to be impossible. On the face of it, to imitate a seen event, one must perceive the event as an event—not as patches of brightness and color or as a set of activations of orientation-sensitive cortical cells but as a representation of objects, surfaces, and changes occurring. Furthermore, this representation must be abstract; it does not live solely in the visual world because it must be able to connect to other representations—in particular, those that produce action. The infant does not see his or her own face when imitating. To imitate tongue protrusion requires making some kind of match between a tongue that is seen and one's own tongue that is felt and moved by motor commands. Finally, it is possible that imitation involves true social awareness (see below). The infant may realize he is involved with a social being and perhaps resembles it, that this being and he both have tongues, that both are protruding their tongues, and so on.

Mechanisms of Imitation

If imitation implies all or even part of this array of abilities, it is impressive indeed. None of it is remotely possible for newborns or infants of several weeks—or months—according to Piaget's view of development or traditional constructivist accounts of perception, representation, and action. Perhaps it is no wonder that despite evidence to the contrary, some have maintained that imitation is a reflex or *fixed-action pattern* (FAP) (Abravenel & Sigafoos, 1984; Bjorklund, 1987). Such a hypothesis would not require any intermodal matching mechanism, any representational capacity, any capacity for voluntary action, or any social awareness. The stimulus event "releases" an innately determined action pattern because the infant's nervous system is wired this way. The explanation for such a wiring pattern, as for others studied by ethologists, might be sought in the adaptive value of such behavior. Imitation FAPs might serve to foster social interaction with conspecifics.

This approach appears to be stretched in accounting for the variety of responses—mouth movements, tongue protrusion, finger movements, and head rotation—that young infants have been found to imitate. The number of FAPs proliferates on an ad hoc basis. Nevertheless, newborn imitation is surprising, and explaining it requires making some new assumptions. Proliferating FAPs may appear to some to be the simplest and most plausible explanatory strategy.

Recent research, however, helps to clarify the ongoing controversy. Meltzoff and Moore (1994) tested several hypotheses about early imitation relevant to the FAP hypothesis and their own *active intermodal matching* (AIM) view. Six-week-old infants were tested on three consecutive days. Each infant was assigned to a treatment group in which the adult model produced tongue protrusion at the side of the mouth, tongue protrusion in the middle of the mouth, mouth opening, or no oral movement. Infants' responses were recorded during 90 sec test trials. During these periods, the model displayed the gesture for 15 sec periods alternating with 15 sec periods of no gesturing. After one 90 sec test trial on the first day, infants were tested on the second day in a memory trial in which the adult model presented a neutral face for the entire period. This was followed by another 90 sec trial of the same sort as the day 1 imitation trial, using the same facial gesture. Day 3 testing was the same as day 2.

Results showed that infants imitated the modeled gesture reliably more than the other gesture (the two types of tongue protrusions were not distinguished for this analysis). Remarkably, this was true for the memory trials as well. Infants' behavior while viewing the passive model included markedly higher frequency of the facial gesture it had seen on the previous day! This finding indicates that imitation performance at 6 weeks rests on a representational capacity that can preserve information for long periods of time and is presumably abstract enough to mediate the connections among situations, perceived events, and actions. Meltzoff and Moore (1994) also looked at the detailed topography of responding over trials to the gesture of tongue protrusion to the side. They found evidence that infants made progressively better approximations to this gesture over trials.

These findings add some new considerations to interpreting early imitation. Specifically, a fixed-action pattern account would have difficulty in explaining imitation over a 24 hour delay. Also, FAPs are ordinarily stereotyped behaviors. The gradual changing of the response to conform more to the model suggests a very different interpretation of what infants are doing, according to Meltzoff and Moore (1994). As they put it "The capacity to organize actions based on a stored representation of perceptually absent events is a starting point in infancy, not its culmination" (Meltzoff & Moore, 1994, p. 95). According to the AIM proposal, early imitation involves an active intention to match the model.

Some conjectures about infants' motivation for imitating were also offered by Meltzoff and Moore (1994). After a full day's delay, infants viewing the passive model may produce the gesture seen earlier as a means of identifying and querying the person, perhaps to determine whether this is the same person or whether the social encounter will work today as it did yesterday. This hypothesis is consistent with the notion that infants use their perceptual and action abilities from an early time to explore, learn about, and classify objects and events in the social world.

Should imitation be viewed as an example of social interaction? The AIM hypothesis could be consistent with infants' imitating a perceived physical event that is not social in nature. Protrusion of the model's tongue could be seen by the infant as an interesting event in which an object appears between two surfaces. Imitation may occur as a means of attempting to comprehend or motorically encode the event. It is hard to draw firm conclusions about a social component in early imitation, but some data support the idea that imitation is truly social. First, imitation is limited to the actions of live models; it does not generalize to inanimate objects simulating gestures such as tongue protrusion and mouth opening (Abravanel & DeYong, 1991; Legerstee, 1991b; but see Jacobson, 1979). When infants were shown a tube with a red cylinder appearing and disappearing from the tip, they failed to produce a tongue-protrusion action

(Legerstee, 1991b). Second, imitation may involve turn taking (e.g., Meltzoff & Moore, 1983). Early imitative interactions include a balance of actions and pauses that are tied to the actions and pauses of others. This coordination of the infants' actions with those of others may demonstrate a rudimentary understanding of intersubjectivity.

Imitation and Learning in Infancy

For our conceptions of perception and development, infant imitation phenomena have profound significance. For the infant, imitative abilities may be equally profound in their importance for learning. We can glimpse the possibilities in two types of imitation that emerge beyond the newborn period—vocal imitation and imitation of object manipulation. Imitation of vowel sounds has been found in 3- and 4-month-olds (Legerstee, 1990; Kuhl & Meltzoff, 1988), a finding relevant to learning about language and linguistic interactions. Imitation of object manipulation has been documented at 6 months of age for simple actions, such as waving an object to make it rattle (von Hofsten & Siddiqui, 1993). At 9 months of age, infants imitate more complex actions, such as pressing a button on a box to make a beeping sound or breaking a novel toy into two pieces (Meltzoff, 1988c). Nine-month-olds immediately imitate novel object manipulations modeled by a person and also imitate after a 24-hour delay between modeling and imitation (Meltzoff, 1988c). Fourteen-month-olds imitate a live model after a one-week delay (Meltzoff, 1988b). Infants at this age also imitate models on television (Meltzoff, 1988a) and other 14-month-old models (Hanna & Meltzoff, 1993). Imitation occurs despite changes in context (such as moving to a different room) and object features (such as changing object size or color; Barnat, Klein & Meltzoff, 1996). Not only do infants learn how to perform new actions by watching others in their environment, but they also learn something about intended actions. Meltzoff (1995) asked whether 18-month-olds would produce an action the model intended but did not perform. In one study, for example, infants viewed an adult attempting to pull apart a toy that looked like a dumbbell. On three attempts the adult's hand slipped off one of the ends so the infants never saw the toy in two pieces. When infants were given the toy, they produced the intended action: they grasped the two ends of the dumbbell and pulled it apart. A second study suggested that infants were in fact responding based on a psychological understanding of the actor's intentions. When infants were presented with a mechanical device that slipped off the ends of the dumbbell, failing to pull it apart, infants did not imitate the "intended action." By this age, and perhaps much earlier, infants' imitation may involve considerable social understanding.

Human infants' imitative abilities beginning at birth are striking. The unlearned connections between event perception and action evident in newborn imitation are among the most compelling phenomena in revamping our notions of early perception and representation. It is difficult to account for the data without a view of perception as producing meaningful representations suitable for supporting action. Some nuances also suggest that infant imitation is truly social and that infants are predisposed to engage in social interaction. The consequences for development are enormous. Given their generality and flexibility, infant imitative abilities appear to comprise a key foundation, specially adapted to a social species, for learning about the physical and social worlds.

Distinguishing People from Other Objects

Earlier we described the ability to discriminate people from objects as the beginning of social cognition. Piaget's (1981) observations of his own children led him to conclude that not until 8 months do they recognize people as different from objects. A number of other observations fit this developmental timetable. Infants in the second half of the first year point at both objects and people but seem to expect a response only from people, such as a comment about the object, action on the object, or a change in direction of gaze of another person to look at an object (e.g., Harding & Golinkoff, 1979; Sugarman, 1978). Observers of spontaneous infant behaviors can judge when 10-month-old infants are interacting with their mothers as opposed to objects but cannot do so with 3-month-olds (Frye, Rawling, Moore & Myers, 1983). In addition, between 8 and 12 months infants come to distinguish differences in agency between social and nonsocial objects (Poulin-Dubois & Shultz, 1990). For example, 13-month-olds look longer at an event in which a chair moves autonomously than at an event in which a person moves autonomously. They look longer at an event of a ball appearing to roll itself across a table than a ball pushed by a person. These examples are a few of many that support Piaget's contention that the distinction between people and objects emerges around 8 months of age.

Our discussion of infant imitation may already lead us to suspect, however, that the distinction between people and objects arises earlier. Recall that imitation seems specific to human models and tends not to occur for mechanical events. Other research converges on this point (e.g., Field, 1979; Klein & Jennings, 1979; Legerstee, 1991a). For example, Legerstee conducted several studies in which she compared infants' interactions with people and inanimate objects. In a longitudinal study beginning at 3 to 5 weeks of age, infants were observed while viewing their mother, an unfamiliar female, or a doll. Each object was either active (interacting with the infant in the case of the people or moving in the case of the doll) or passive. By 9 weeks of age, infants showed evidence of distinguishing the people from the doll. For example, infants produced melodic, speechlike, vocalizations more frequently to the active mother and active stranger than to the doll (Legerstee, 1991a). Even at 7 weeks, infants vocalized positively (laughed and cooed) and smiled more in the presence of a person than a doll (Legerstee, Pomerleau, Malcuit & Feider, 1987), and their arm and hand movements differed depending on whether a person or a doll was present (Legerstee, Corter & Kienapple, 1990). These findings suggest that infants can distinguish between people and objects earlier than 8 months of age. In fact, this ability may emerge by 8 *weeks* of age. Infants respond to people using a constellation of distinctive behaviors including vocalizations, facial expressions, and arm movements. It is not clear why infants' different behaviors to social and nonsocial stimuli are not readily detectable by some measures, such as adult judgments of infants used by Frye et al. (1983). Perhaps the relevant differences discovered in experimental studies are not particularly salient ones to adult observers.

On what basis do babies make the distinction between social and nonsocial objects? One possibility is that animate objects initiate their own movements, and their movements are sometimes contingent on the infant's behavior. For example, when an infant points and gazes toward an object, an adult will often turn to look at the object and possibly will name the object. Perhaps infants are sensitive to such contingencies. Legerstee (1991a) studied this possibility by linking a doll's movement to the infant's action. When the infant fixated the doll, it moved and jingled. In this study, infants still produced more speechlike vocalizations and more emotional sounds facing their mother and facing a stranger than facing a doll, and Legerstee found no difference between responses to an active and passive doll. Thus, rudimentary contingency of movement is not enough for distinguishing between people and objects.

Auditory information may play a role in distinguishing between people and objects. Several researchers compared infants' behaviors to sounding objects and speaking people (e.g., Klein & Jennings, 1979; Legerstee, 1991a) and found that infants responded differently to them. The types of sounds emitted by the objects may be important. In particular, speech sounds may be an important distinguishing feature of social objects. For example, speech has been found to aid 6-month-olds' success in finding hidden objects: infants were more successful in finding their hidden mother when she talked than they were in finding a hidden sounding object (Legerstee, 1994).

In sum, by 2 months of age infants exhibit different behaviors toward people and objects. The informational bases of these abilities have been studied but remain unclear. The emergence of infants' distinguishing between people and objects is consistent with Trevarthen's observations that infants at 2 months behave very differently with people than they do with objects. Less clear from this work is when infants truly possess inter-subjectivity. Intersubjectivity entails more than distinguishing people and objects; it requires sensitivity to the intentions of others. There is little evidence from early infancy on the development of this important component of social knowledge.

Perceiving Faces

In chapter 4 we saw that it is possible to demonstrate a preference for faces over other stimuli in newborns. The tendency is weak at first but robust by two months. This change in sensitivity, like others in the early weeks of life involving basic visual variables, seems likely to be caused by cortical maturation, including a probable subcortical to cortical shift in the control of attention (Bronson, 1974; Morton & Johnson, 1991). Here we take a more socially inspired look at face perception abilities, including infants' abilities to recognize individuals.

Sensitivity to Facial Configuration

In the research by Kleiner (1987), discussed in chapter 4, we noted that between two patterns both having the amplitude spectrum of a face, newborns preferred to fixate the one that also had the phase spectrum of a face. There are other results that also suggest innate sensitivity to facial configuration. When supine newborn infants are shown a display of a schematic face or a scrambled face straight ahead and the display then moves to one side or the other, infants reliably track the face stimulus more than the scrambled stimulus (Goren, Sarty & Wu, 1975; Johnson, Dziurawiec, Ellis & Morton, 1991; see figure 10.2). In addition, 5-week-old infants reliably track a schematic face stimulus, but they do not show a preference for such a stimulus when tested in a habituation of looking procedure (Morton & Johnson, 1991).

It has been suggested that two independent processes may function in early face-perception tasks (Morton & Johnson, 1991; Johnson & Morton, 1991). One process is an innate subcortically mediated process that allows infants to recognize members of their own species. This process might produce the tracking behavior described above. As cortical maturation proceeds, infants develop a second process that underlies their ability to identify specific faces. This process makes possible learning about features of faces in general and the specific features of individual faces. As a result, by 2 months infants begin to show greater attention to schematic than scrambled faces, and with age, infants' perception of faces becomes more precise. By 5 months infants recognize individual faces (e.g., de Schonen & Mathivet, 1990; Deruelle & de Schonen, 1991), by 5 to 6 months

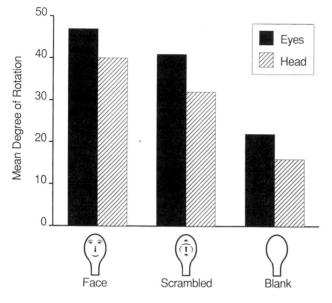

Figure 10.2
Newborn face-tracking data. Reprinted with permission from Morton, J., & Johnson, M. H.
(1991), CONSPEC and CONLERN: A two-process theory of infant face recognition, *Psychological Review, 98*, 164–181. Copyright © 1991 by the American Psychological Association.
Reprinted with permission.

infants discriminate faces varying in gender and age (e.g., Lasky, Klein,
& Martinez, 1974; Walker-Andrews, Bahrick, Raglioni & Diaz, 1991),
and by 12 months infants discriminate attractive from unattractive faces
(Langlois, Roggman & Rieser-Danner, 1990).

Unfortunately, this coherent framework has been upset by studies suggesting that newborn and 1-month-old infants recognize their mothers
(Bushnell, Sai & Mullin, 1989; Pascalis, de Schonen, Morton, Deruelle &
Fabre-Grenet, 1995; Sai & Bushnell, 1988). In a paired-preference task,
infants discriminated their mother from a stranger who was matched in
complexion and hair color even when olfactory cues were masked. Findings of Pascalis et al. suggest that this ability is not based on internal facial
features alone. When the hairline of the mother and stranger were masked,
the visual preference for the mother's face disappeared. These findings
suggest that infants in the earliest weeks of life possess the ability to
encode and discriminate specific faces. This learning is more than a tendency to attend to generic facial configurations characteristic of one's conspecifics (Morton & Johnson, 1991). The finding may also imply better
cortical function than previously supposed because recognition memory is
thought to be under cortical control (de Schonen & Mathivet, 1990;

Deruelle & de Schonen, 1991). The specific developmental change that makes face preferences easier to detect at 6 to 8 weeks remains somewhat vague. As with several visual abilities we considered in chapter 4, however, the evidence suggests that face encoding and preferences for faces are rudimentary, but not absent, in newborns.

Obtaining Information from Faces

Faces, in addition to being interesting and complex stimuli that signal the presence of a person, also signal emotional states. As we watch someone eat a novel food, we monitor their facial expression to communicate whether it is tasty or not. By watching facial expressions, infants have the opportunity to learn about the feelings of others, and through this knowledge they may also come to know much about nonsocial objects and events. When do infants become able to extract the information in facial expressions and use it to guide their behavior?

Sensitivity to Emotional Expressions   If you smile at a baby, the baby may smile back. This is the case even for some newborns. As we have seen earlier, newborns imitate facial expressions, and this imitation is not limited to smiles; they also open their mouths when viewing a surprised face, and they pout when viewing a sad face (Field et al., 1982). Imitation of facial expressions by newborn infants is suggestive evidence that young babies discriminate the expressions of happiness, surprise, and sadness. At a minimum, imitating infants are discriminating mouth positions that accompany different facial expressions.

Between 4 and 10 months, infants discriminate a range of facial expressions, although some expressions are more easily discriminated than others (Ludemann & Nelson, 1988; Serrano, Iglesias & Loeches, 1992; see Nelson, 1987, for a review). They may also distinguish moderate from extreme exemplars of the same expression (Ludeman & Nelson, 1988), and they categorize facial expressions across different models (Nelson & Dolgin, 1985; Ludeman & Nelson, 1988). Some evidence suggests that infants' categorization of facial expressions is not based on individual stimulus features, such as the presence of teeth in a smile, but on emotional expression configurations (Kestenbaum & Nelson, 1990).

Although studies suggest that infants discriminate among facial expressions, it is more difficult to determine whether infants understand their meanings. When do infants know that a smile means positive affect, a frown means negative affect, or a fearful expression means potential danger? Information about affect in a facial expression is often accompanied by auditory information. Infants between 3 and 5 months discriminate vocal expressions of happy and sad (Walker-Andrews & Grolnick, 1983) and match visual and auditory information for affect (Walker, 1982;

Walker-Andrews, 1986). Yet matching stimuli such as a smiling face with a happy vocalization does not mean that infants necessarily apprehend positive affect.

Research to date does not allow firm conclusions about when infants know that facial expressions are correlated with specific emotional states. It is interesting to ask how such knowledge may be acquired. One intriguing observation is that several basic facial expressions appear to be universal across cultures (Darwin, 1896; Eibl-Eibesfelt, 1989). The connection between felt emotion and facial expression may originate in innate links between the infant's own feelings and expressions. Being able to match one's own facial gestures with seen expressions is an additional step, but one that may be facilitated by early imitation abilities.

Social Referencing Emotional expressions provide the viewer with information regarding the internal feelings of a person. Yet these emotional states are often triggered by external events. For example, most people smile when they receive a gift and show fear when someone unexpectedly jumps out of a closet and yells. Infants have the potential to learn about events in their world by monitoring the emotional reactions shown by adults to these events. They may be able to use others' reactions to interpret novel situations and possibly guide action.

The monitoring of others' emotions is called *social referencing*. It has been defined as a process of emotional communication in which one's perception of another person's interpretation of events is used to form one's own understanding of that event (Feinman, 1982). In a typical study on social referencing, the infant and an adult are placed in an ambiguous situation (for example, on a visual cliff or in a room in which a novel toy appears). The adult is instructed to give a particular emotional expression (happiness, fear), and the infant's behavior is measured. Generally, it is found that babies around 12 months of age tailor their behavior to the emotional expression of their mother (Walden & Ogan, 1988; Source, Emde, Campos & Klinnert, 1985; Klinnert, 1984; Gunnar & Stone, 1984) or a friendly stranger (Barrett, Campos & Emde, 1996; Klinnert, Emde, Butterfield & Campos, 1986). For example, babies will not cross the visual cliff if their mothers give a fear expression but will if their mothers smile, and babies will approach a novel toy if their mothers smile but not if their mothers frown.

Recall that infants between 4 and 10 months of age discriminate and categorize facial expressions. Social referencing, however, does not appear until several months later. Two possible explanations for this delay appear plausible. First, the phenomenon of social referencing may indicate the onset of children's *understanding* of emotional expressions. It may be the case that infants do not learn the meaning of facial expressions until several months after they successfully discriminate the expressions.

Alternatively, infants may understand the meaning of facial expressions earlier than 12 months of age but come to comprehend that the expression of another person has meaning for their own behavior or well-being. For example, infants might have to learn that on witnessing their mothers' fear, they should behave cautiously. In particular, infants may need more experience with the facial expressions commonly used in social referencing experiments (specifically, fear). In their studies on categorization, Nelson and Dolgin (1985) found that 7-month-olds looked longer at a fear expression, indicating that it was perceived as novel, and Ludeman and Nelson (1988) found that babies could not categorize fear expressions or discriminate fear from happiness or surprise. Ludeman and Nelson suggested that fear is an expression infants see less frequently than expressions of happiness or surprise. Perhaps experience with particular emotions and observed behaviors is instrumental in developing social referencing behavior.

Shared Attention   Facial expressions, as we have seen, provide information about a person's internal state, and, at times, knowledge of this internal state can provide an observer with information about objects in the environment. If a mother shows a fearful expression, her 12-month-old is less likely to approach a strange object. Infants can obtain more subtle information about objects by attending to what others find attention deserving. By monitoring another's line of sight, infants can learn about objects and can engage in a shared interaction with the other person.

During most interactions, adults monitor where infants are looking (see Schaffer, 1984, for a review). But infants as young as 2 months are able to adjust their attention to match that of an adult (Scaife & Bruner, 1975; Butterworth & Jarrett, 1991; see Butterworth, 1995, 1996, for reviews). For example, in a study by Butterworth and Jarrett (1991), mothers of 6- to 18-month-old infants were asked to interact naturally with their babies. Following a signal, they were asked to shift their gaze to one of several objects in the room. Six-month-olds looked to the correct side of the room but showed no evidence of making the finer discrimination of fixating the correct target. Instead, infants were most likely to fixate the first object they encountered along their line of sight. Twelve- and 18-month-olds showed improvement in locating the correct target, regardless of its location along their scan path.

From these results, Butterworth and his colleagues suggest that infants at a very young age are able to enter into a "communication network with others through comprehension of an adult's direction of gaze" (Butterworth & Jarrett, 1991, p. 69). Such behavior suggests early mechanisms of social perception and a propensity to use them to learn about the physical and social environments.

CONCLUSION

Perceptual abilities are prerequisite for a human infant to begin social interaction and development. Conversely, in looking at social contexts, we have seen some of the most stunning examples of the sophistication of infant perception, as well as representation and action. We underscore just two of these. Newborn imitation demonstrates a complex constellation of abilities that come prepackaged, including the ability to perceive and represent functionally important events in an abstract format, suitable for guiding actions. Face recognition by infants from birth to one month is equally startling. These observations serve two purposes in the current context. First, they confirm and extend the picture of sophisticated perceptual abilities producing useful representations in the human infant. Second, they indicate that the infant begins on a firm footing in her explorations of the social world and in those learning endeavors that will make her a fully functioning member of the human community.

Chapter 11

Perceptual Foundations of Cognitive Development

The origins of knowledge through perception have concerned philosophers and scientists for centuries. Systematic scientific research on human infant perception has been with us for only decades. Preceding it and continuing until very recently was a dominant view of how reality emerges—that it is constructed by associating raw sensory impressions with each other and with action. According to this view, no external world, no three-dimensional space, and no people, objects, or events can be known until such constructions have been achieved. Gradually, meaning emerges as current impressions activate stored sensory and motor patterns, a process that extends well into the second year of life (Piaget, 1954).

This view must be discarded, for the evidence we have considered requires a radically different view of the origins of perception. It is more consistent with a view grounded in evolution, as are contemporary ecological and computational views of perception. Infants perceive an external world, its objects and events, from the beginning of life. This is made possible by perceptual mechanisms that respond to patterns in stimulation and produce abstract representations, rather than memory traces of sensory activations. These transformations from input patterns to abstract representations are made possible by constraints embodied in perceptual machinery. Perception improves with maturation; some abilities do not arise until later, and some may be learned. A rich endowment of perceptual competence, however, derives not from learning by the individual but from earlier evolution of the species.

We have seen numerous examples. Newborns respond to the real sizes of objects, taking into account their positions in three-dimensional space. Pattern information characteristic of the human face attracts infant attention from the start, and the ability to encode and later recognize specific faces may also begin at birth. Abstract temporal and spatial patterns are matched across different senses in the early months of life; some specify particular events in the world such as collision, substance, and numerosity. Amazingly, newborn infants see and imitate several facial gestures made by adults, an ability that requires abstract encoding and matching of perceived events in a form that traverses perceptual and action systems. Some evidence suggests that this early imitation involves true social awareness. From an early age, objects are perceived visually and haptically from information given over time, despite spatial gaps in the input. Infants detect objects using mechanisms that follow the laws of projective geometry to recover three-dimensional structure from transforming two-dimensional projections. Moving infants perceive which parts of the world move and which remain at rest during their own movements. As soon as they become able to reach in a controlled fashion, they anticipate in their reaches the future position of a moving object.

In this chapter, we consider the consequences of this relatively new picture of perception for views of cognitive development. We also draw out some implications about the nature of perception itself that are suggested by our knowledge of perception in infancy.

COGNITIVE DEVELOPMENT ON A NEW FOUNDATION

In Piaget's classic view of cognitive development, the first tasks are protracted ones. In a sensorimotor period, which itself encompasses six stages over 2 years, actions, beginning with reflexes, become encoded along with their sensory consequences as *sensorimotor schemata*. The gradual accumulation and coordination of schemata ultimately gives way to true internal representations of external reality during the preoperational period. Perception, action, and knowledge representation are inseparable in Piaget's sensorimotor stage.

But what if there is no sensorimotor stage? To most developmental psychologists, the suggestion sounds heretical. If the view of perception we have described is correct, however, the designation of initial development as *sensorimotor* is a mistake that must be corrected. This is hardly to suggest that Piaget, a remarkably keen observer, did not pinpoint important aspects of early development. Rather, his observations must be seen in a different theoretical light.

What we have seen is that the characterization of early infancy as sensorimotor will not do for perception. It is not possible, however, simply to add meaningful perceptual reality to the sensorimotor perspective and leave its views of knowledge and action otherwise untouched. We discussed some implications for action in chapter 9; here we focus on implications for knowledge and cognitive development.

What does perception give us? A straightforward answer is that it gives knowledge about the environment (and about ourselves). In computational views of perception, this knowledge takes the form of descriptions—that is, mental representations. These are the sorts of things that can be remembered, thought about, and so on. Some ecological theorists (E. Gibson,

1984; J. Gibson, 1979; Mace, 1974) prefer to think about the results of perception in a less representational way: what is perceived are affordances—that is, the functional possibilities an environment offers. Rather than producing representations, perception guides ongoing action, which in turn produces new requirements and opportunities for perceiving. These cyclic events are described as perception-action loops.

Some of perception surely works this way, but we prefer to think of perception as producing descriptions of the environment. These can support ongoing action, but they also can be stored and recruited for later thought and action. The rest of cognition—such as memory, categorization, thinking, and problem solving—requires representations obtained from perceiving.

We have seen that very young infants perceive objects, people, spatial relations, and events. In many studies, infants' perception was assessed by methods requiring encoding and comparison of stimuli over time. Some striking recent work suggests that representations of individuals, such as the infant's mother, form very early. Other studies point toward the abstractness of representations formed from perception, even at the beginning. Cognitive development begins with meaningful descriptions of external reality delivered by perceptual mechanisms.

THE SCOPE OF PERCEPTION

How far does perception go? When perception was thought to consist of the adding up of sensations, its ultimate products could not stray too far from concrete elements of sensation, involving brightness, color, pitch, loudness, and so on. With the Gestalt psychologists arose the realization that perceptual processes utilize abstract relationships as inputs and produce abstract outputs, such as perceived form, that are not explicable as sums of sensory qualities. This realization was developed further by Gibson, who argued that perceptual systems respond to higher-order relationships in stimulation, especially patterns given over time, and by others, such as Michotte (1963), who emphasized that perception has an amodal and functional character:

Its biological role is to initiate and direct the behavior of men and animals. It not only provides material for their contemplation, but invites them to action, and allows them to adjust this action to the world in which they live. The phenomenal world does not consist of a simple juxtaposition of "detached pieces," but of a group of things which act upon each other and in relation to each other. Thus the regulation of conduct requires a knowledge of what things do or can do and what living creatures (and ourselves in particular) can do with them. (p. 3)

This view of perception raises anew the question of how much of human knowledge might be perceptual. As we saw in chapter 6, event perception research suggests that some forms of knowledge that are abstract or that intuitively seem to involve inference and belief systems might actually be products of perception. Causality, object solidity, weight, biological motion, and even social intention may be perceived. It seems likely that the outputs of perception produce representations consisting of *basic physical descriptions*—static structure in the three-dimensional spatial environment and physical mechanics of moving things. Such descriptions of objects and surfaces and their relations in space and time are not the province of a single sense but abstract representations to which various sensory channels contribute.

Perceptual Descriptions as Knowledge

The understanding of perception as producing representations of the physical environment and ecologically important events is controversial. Many recent discussions of cognitive development acknowledge empirical findings about early perception but reject the idea that perception goes this far. Some, in fact, deny that perception produces true knowledge of any sort. Mandler (1988, 1992) believes that findings from infant perception experiments can be explained by what she calls "primitive recognition":

> To say that the starting parameters of the perceptual system produce object perception rather than patch perception does deemphasize one type of constructive activity that was a focus of Piaget's theory of sensorimotor development, but this approach does not require conscious access to such information on the part of the infant. Nor does it require a symbolic, or conceptual, form of representation or the ability to think about objects in their absence. (p. 118)

To move from the products of perception to true knowledge, Mandler proposed a mechanism of "perceptual analysis." This is "a symbolic process (probably conscious) by which one perception is actively compared with another" (Mandler, 1988, p. 126).

In this scheme, several criteria are proposed for distinguishing perceptual processes from accessible knowledge. One is *consciousness*: "the crucial aspect of sensorimotor procedures, whether motor or perceptual, is that much, if not most, of the information that is being processed is not accessible to consciousness" (Mandler, 1988, p. 115). Two others are the *ability to recall information* and the *ability to represent abstract information*.

Using any or all of these criteria, it is difficult to make the case that perception yields "protoknowledge" (Kellman, 1992)—that is, some precursor to real knowledge. Consciousness as a criterion seems problematic. Mandler (1988) argued that perception is different from accessible knowledge because we have little or no conscious access to the processing that allows us to recognize a face or detect the speed of an oncoming car. This is true, both for adults and presumably infants, but is it relevant? The issue about perception and knowledge concerns not the processes but the *outputs* of perception. Ordinarily, these are conscious for adults. We can find no reason to suspect that infants do not have conscious experiences from perceptions. None of the methods used in infant perception is capable of directly assessing consciousness, but the same is true, of course, about the methods we use in studying adults. In any case, a criterion based on consciousness does not seem to be very useful in making claims about infant knowledge.

What about the abstractness of knowledge and recall abilities? These would seem to be reasonable criteria for assessing the nature of representations. If the outputs of perception were always closely tied to particular actions or were never encoded in a long-term store, they would be qualitatively different from many of adults' perceptual representations. The evidence suggests, however, that much of infant perception produces representations that are abstract, as we have seen. To imitate viewed facial or manual gestures using one's own facial or manual movements, perception must produce abstract representations capable of supporting action. Imitation experiments, and others, also address the issue of recall. Meltzoff and Moore (1994) found evidence of imitation in newborns 24 hours after their exposure to modeled facial expressions. Indeed, Mandler's (1988) review concluded that there is clear evidence for recall processes as early as 3 to 4 months, with no data precluding the possibility that recall processes operate even earlier.

By these criteria, perception in infancy yields knowledge representations. Nevertheless, an idea that has become popular is that conceptual theories in particular domains must operate on perceptual data to produce abstract knowledge, such as knowledge of object solidity, causality, or animacy (Mandler, 1988, 1992; Carey & Spelke, 1994; Gelman, Durgin & Kaufman, 1995; Leslie, 1995). In most of these accounts, the reason for invoking nonperceptual mechanisms appears to be an assumption that descriptions coming from perception cannot represent abstract or functional information. For example, Leslie (1995) claims that visual perception must stop short of producing descriptions of mechanical causation, on the grounds that visual representations can contain only properties such as visible shape but not properties such as solidity, unity, cohesiveness, or attachment:

A purely visual object does not have to possess any degree of hardness. Imagine entering a room in which a superb three-dimensional hologram of a cup is displayed sitting upon a table. As long as one is restricted to examining it visually, one is convinced it is a cup. Those visual processes that recognize objects by shape, immediately recognize this apparition as a cup. However, when one tries to grasp it, one's fingers pass through the visible surfaces with no resistance whatsoever. Now one will say that, after all, there is "nothing there." However, the apparition will continue to be a perfectly good visual object. (Leslie, 1995, p. 134)

This view has eminent ancestors. It is a somewhat revised version of classical sensation-based notions critiqued by the Gestalt psychologists and by Gibson (1966, 1979), Michotte (1963), Johansson (1970, 1975), and others. (There are signs of progress: *visible shape* now counts as a visual notion, whereas Berkeley would have insisted that shape was a tactile notion and that visual qualities could include only brightness, color, and retinal location.) The view also appears to us to be a descendant of the seventeenth-century conundrum of how we can see an upright world when the retinal image is inverted. What is being rejected, more or less intuitively as far as we can tell, is the notion that perception can be a mapping between certain stimulus relationships and representations of abstract physical properties, such as solidity or causality.

Such a view leads to unnecessary burdens and paradoxes (Kellman, 1988). In this book, we have seen numerous examples of the abstractness of perceptual representations. In addition, we have mentioned that animals that locomote from birth demonstrate abstract perceptual knowledge, such as knowledge about the tangible physical world obtained by seeing. Based on seeing, a newborn goat will step onto a solid surface that offers support, but it will not step off a precipice. A newborn chick will locate and peck at a kernel of corn but not at a random location on the ground (Hess, 1956). The idea that visual information does not specify solidity—that vision gives some intangible representations that achieve tangibility only when worked on by cognitive theories of mechanics—seems specious in the case of the goat. The idea that the environment is carved into bits of corn by domain-specific cognitive theories seems overly glamorous for the chick. Why must we assume such processes for chicks, goats, or human infants?

Among its problems, this account leads to a paradox in explaining human infant data on causality (Leslie, 1982, 1984). Leslie showed that 6-month-olds responded to causal structure in visually perceived events and gave persuasive arguments that an object must possess solidity to participate in mechanical causal events. How might the solidity of the objects be known by 6-month-old infants perceiving causal events? Given the purported limits of vision, such solidity cannot be seen, and infants were given no other perceptual contact with the objects in these studies. If there is no information for solidity, why should the objects be seen as having causal powers?

This example is more easily explained in an event-perception framework. A number of visual attributes of a single object or surface, such as surface texture and rigid motion, may lead to perception of solidity, rigidity, or nonrigidity (E. Gibson et al., 1978), which is fortunate for the mountain goat. But these attributes may also be extracted from events involving object interactions. A collision event in which one object moves when struck by another specifies both the solidity of the objects and the event in which they participate. (Recall J. Gibson's, 1966, notion of *dual specification*, described in chapter 6: information given by events specifies both the events occurring and the enduring properties of objects.) If on "impact" one seen object passes through the other without disturbing it, this event would specify a ghostlike, intangible object without causal powers. The object's tangibility or ghostliness may be specified by information in visible events.

Perceptual versus Cognitive Processes

The examples of the goat and the chick above might be used to insist that vision informs viewers about the physical world and not merely about a visual world. Yet if we accept that perception can yield abstract knowledge, we still do not know what its limits are. Where do percepts stop and concepts begin? It is doubtful that we are going to get the concept of prime number out of perceptual mechanisms.

Of immediate concern are the claims about events and functional relations so basic to ecological views of perception. Are notions like causality and animacy really perceived? Perhaps perception stops with some representation of moving things, and concepts handle these more advanced notions (e.g., Gelman, Durgin & Kaufman, 1995). How can we tell?

There do not appear to be compelling logical grounds that indicate where the boundary between perception and cognition should be placed. (For a useful discussion, see Fodor, 1983, pp. 86–88.) The matter seems to be an empirical one. Fodor (1983) sets forth some useful criteria for distinguishing perceptual mechanisms (*input modules*, in his terminology) from more central cognitive mechanisms. Among the criteria are these. Input modules

- are domain specific, (we might expect, for instance, separate ones for visual perception of form and auditory localization of sound),

- operate quickly and their operation is often mandatory (you need not make an effort to hear from which direction a sound comes),
- appear to be associated with particular neural architectures,
- may exhibit specific breakdown patterns, and
- depend primarily on innate or maturationally given mechanisms.

One of the most important criteria suggested by Fodor (1983), and one of the most useful for perception researchers, is the notion that input modules are *informationally encapsulated*, meaning that their processing depends on certain characteristic sources of information and is not influenced by general knowledge, beliefs, and so on. A similar criterion has a long history in perception studies. A classic case was Wertheimer's (1912) argument (chapter 6) about the dependence of apparent motion on tightly constrained spatial and temporal relations.

Many examples we have labeled as *event perception* meet these criteria. We considered the idea that an object's persistence is specified visually as it passes behind an occluder. In this case, there are specific sources of information—namely, characteristic projective changes and deletion of texture—that control perceptual responses in both adults and infants (Granrud, Yonas, Smith et al. 1984; Gibson et al. 1969; Michotte et al., 1964). Many relevant experiments have been carried out on computer monitors. Information encapsulation is suggested by the fact that accretion and deletion of texture readily creates illusions of depth order and object persistence for adults whose general knowledge tells them that there is no depth order and no hidden object in the monitor. What about causality or animacy? We do not yet know of specialized neural architecture subserving causal or animate perception. Regarding the specificity of information, Michotte's research suggested that causality depends on highly constrained spatial and temporal relations and not on prior experience. Johansson (1975) showed that a compelling impression of animacy (and of a particular action, such as a person walking) was obtained from films of moving light points in as few as two motion picture frames. Evidence that infants in the early months of life are also sensitive to such relations (Leslie, 1988; Bertenthal, 1993) strengthens the case that animacy and causal descriptions could be the results of perceptual mechanisms.

A problem in distinguishing perceptual and cognitive explanations for infant performance is that cognitive mechanisms may also be endogenously determined (Spelke, 1988; Mandler, 1992). If cognitive mechanisms were hypothesized to arise later than and less stereotypically than perceptual ones, the empirical task of distinguishing them would be simpler. If a mechanism is nonperceptual, perhaps its processing should be susceptible to influences from general knowledge and reasoning—that is, it may not be informationally encapsulated. Perhaps experiments could be designed around this issue. Spelke (1988) notes, however, that some clearly cognitive processes appear somewhat encapsulated and gives examples.

We cannot now draw a definitive line between perception and cognition, but we can embrace two important conclusions. First, no argument or evidence of which we are aware rules out the possibility that perception produces abstract representations, such as seeing a physical object as solid, or "complex" classifications, such as seeing an entity as animate or an event as causal. Second, what we know about infant perception and perception in general is consistent with this possibility. Perception need not stop short of events; on the contrary, it may be fundamentally about events (Gibson, 1966, 1979; Johansson, 1970; Shepard, 1984, Michotte, 1963). Those who have suggested that perceptual descriptions fall short of "deeper" conceptual structures may have taken too narrow a view of perception. As Jones and Smith (1993) put it, "The perceptual properties that matter are ones that are highly relevant to causal beliefs about objects and their origins" (p. 122).

INTERACTING PERCEPTUAL AND COGNITIVE FOUNDATIONS

The discovery that coherent perceptual reality arrives without a protracted sensorimotor construction of reality reverberates throughout developmental theory. Other cognitive capacities might use the products of perception and might begin their ascent much earlier than previously believed. We turn now to some of these cognitive domains that benefit from perception and furnish other kinds of knowledge. Our goal is to highlight both the perceptual contributions to these cognitive developments and their own unique foundations. We examine domains of number, categorization, and physical laws of object motion.

Number

Understanding number may have its roots in infant perceptual and cognitive abilities, according to research over the past decade or so. Infants between birth and 12 months discriminate between two and three items in a display (e.g., Antell & Keating, 1983; Starkey & Cooper, 1980; Strauss & Curtis, 1981). This discrimination may reflect some type of numerical competence, such as an understanding that one is different from two. Alternatively, this behavior could merely be the result of a well-functioning perceptual system that is tuned to respond to proximal differences in stimulation, such as item density, complexity, or configuration. How best to interpret discrimination performance and the more general question of numerical competence in preverbal humans has been hotly debated. On one side of the debate are those who argue that early numerical skills are merely the result of pattern recognition processes (e.g., Davis, Albert & Barron, 1985).

Several pieces of evidence do not support the pattern recognition explanation. First, when infants were presented with comparisons (2 versus 3 or 4 versus 6) that have similar ratios in terms of perceptual features, such as contour, they discriminated small sets but not larger sets (Antell & Keating, 1983; Starkey & Cooper, 1980; Strauss & Curtis, 1981). For example, Antell and Keating found that newborns looked significantly longer at a display of 3 dots after habituation to displays of 2 dots than they did at a display of 6 dots after habituating to a display of 4 dots. If infants were making their judgments based on contour ratio, there should be no effect of display size. Second, infants' performance cannot be explained merely by static configural information (van Loosbroek & Smitsman, 1990). The possibility has been considered because small set sizes are generally tied to some spatial arrangement. When viewing a display of 2 items, the items form a line. When viewing a display of 3 items, the items form a triangle. Van Loosbroek and Smitsman presented infants with moving displays of 2, 3, and 4 items (thus eliminating static configural information). Five-month-olds discriminated displays of 3 items from those containing 2 and 4 items, and 8-month-olds discriminated displays of 4 items from those of 3 and 5 items. From this evidence it appears that infants respond to number per se.

Conceptions of Early Numerical Ability

If infants are not merely recognizing differences among patterns, then what is the best way to characterize this early numerical competence? There are several processes by which one can apprehend the numerosity of a set of items (see Davis & Perusse, 1988). Counting is the process that comes to mind, but there are ways to make numerosity judgments that are less sophisticated than counting. One such process is relative numerousness judgments. When infants discriminate 2- and 3-item displays, they might be noting an inequality between the displays rather than the absolute number of the set. Evidence against this possibility comes from the fact that infants' numerical competence appears to be limited to small sets. If infants were merely making judgments of more versus less, discriminating 4 from 6 items should be as easy as discriminating 2 from 3 items.

A second process that infants might use to determine numerosity is *subitizing*. Subitizing describes adults' rapid, confident, and accurate report of number for sets containing 6 or fewer elements (Kaufman, Lord, Reese & Volkmann, 1949). A subitizing process might explain why infants discriminate small sets but not larger sets, as this ability in adults is limited to 6 items; yet this process does not explain all the infant data. Infants may perceive the numerosity in sequentially presented displays and detect numerical correspondence across displays (Starkey, Spelke & Gelman, 1983, 1990).

If we conclude that infants are indeed counting in some sense, it must nevertheless differ from counting in older children and adults. True counting consists of several operations (Gelman & Gallistel, 1978) that are not mastered until well beyond the first year. To count, one must assign a number term to each item, and one must know that there is a one to one correspondence between items and unique numerical labels. Clearly, a preverbal infant is not assigning linguistic labels to individuated items but is able to discriminate and, more important, individuate the items in the array based on perceptual features such as surface texture, form, spatial location, and so on. In other words, some findings might be explainable if number is an implicit feature of perceptual representations, able to support discrimination performance even before explicit counting skills arise.

Can this kind of explanation stretch further? Wynn (1992) raised the debate about infants' numerical abilities to a new level by suggesting that 5-month-olds can add and subtract. In her experiment, infants viewed events, illustrated in figure 11.1, in which the number of objects either increased from one to two or decreased from two to one. For example, in one event infants viewed an object placed in a display case. Then a screen hid the object, and infants watched as a second object was added behind the screen. The screen was then removed, and infants viewed either two objects (a possible, or likely, outcome) or one object (an "impossible," or unlikely, outcome). Infants looked significantly longer at the impossible events, suggesting that they knew the number of objects was incorrect. In a second experiment, infants were presented with test events that contained two (possible) versus three (impossible) objects. Infants showed a significant increase in looking to the three-object event. Wynn concluded that infants possess true numerical concepts: "They have access to the ordering of and numerical relationships between small numbers, and can manipulate these concepts in numerically meaningful ways" (Wynn, 1992, p. 750).

One might attempt to explain these effects without explicit use of numerosity information. The observer might encode each object as it goes into the display case and expect to see it again when the barrier is removed. Object "files" that are left unmatched, or new object files that must be opened (if too many objects appear), may trigger surprise. The results might implicate object representations that are updated with new experiences. Counting, addition, and subtraction may not be explicitly involved in the generation of surprise. These early abilities to track individuals may nevertheless serve as the first step on a long trajectory of developing mathematical skills.

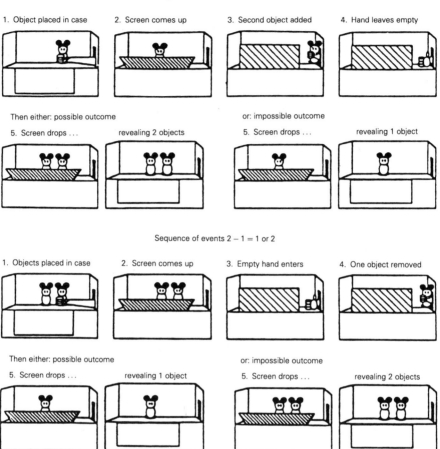

Figure 11.1
Sequence of events presented to 5-month-old infants to study infants' ability to add and subtract. Reprinted with permission from Wynn, K. A. (1992), Addition and subtraction by human infants, *Nature, 358,* 749–750. Copyright 1992 Macmillan Magazines Limited.

Expected Event

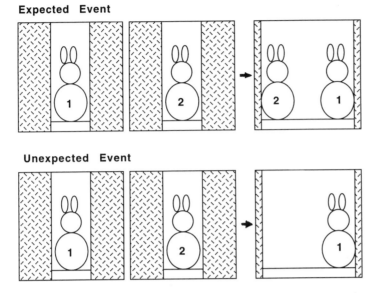

Unexpected Event

Figure 11.2
Expected and unexpected test events presented to infants to test their perception of object number across space and time. Reprinted with permission from Arterberry, M. E. (1995), Perception of object number through an aperture by human infants, *Infant Behavior and Development, 18,* 359–362.

Information Processing Limitations in Early Perception and Cognition

The topic of numerosity discrimination provides an opportune vehicle for making an important point about infant perceptual and cognitive abilities and research on these topics. Most experiments are designed to give infants the best possible chance to demonstrate some ability. When we find evidence of some early competence, we must keep in mind that such experiments do not tell us how generally, flexibly, or robustly the ability functions in ordinary situations.

In the domain of number, research by Arterberry (1995) illustrates this point. Eight-, 10-, and 12-month-old infants were presented with events in which two objects moved behind a gap created by two curtains (see figure 11.2). At no time could both objects be seen through the gap, but as the objects passed by both were revealed over time. Periodically, the curtains opened fully to reveal either the presence of two objects (an expected event), or the presence of only one object (an unexpected event). It was predicted that if infants could determine the number of objects behind the gap, they would look significantly longer to the unexpected test event, indicating that they detected a change in object number. In this study, 12-month-olds, but not 8- or 10-month-olds, looked significantly longer at the unexpected than at the expected test event.

At first glance, the task used by Arterberry seems to test abilities similar to those tested by Wynn (1992). Yet Wynn's subjects showed sensitivity to numerosity at 5 months, whereas Arterberry's subjects at 10 months did not. If there is a difference in these tasks, it would appear to be subtle. In a "1 + 1" task in Wynne's paradigm, one object was viewed in place before the barrier was interposed. Then another object was placed behind. In Arterberry's task, both objects were seen only as they passed behind an aperture. We can speculate that the exposure of at least one object in Arterberry's task was briefer than in Wynn's. Nothing in the research we have reviewed in this book has prepared us for data suggesting that such a minor task variable should produce a 7-month lag in infant's performance.

A related example does not involve number but reinforces the point. In another series of studies, Arterberry (1993) studied perception of the length of rectangles that passed behind a narrow aperture. Recall that we saw in chapter 5 that information given over time appears to be of primary importance in early object perception. Object length in Arterberry's study was specified by the time it took for the rectangle to pass back and forth behind an aperture. The objects had visible texture on them, so they produced accretion and deletion information at occlusion boundaries. Infants were habituated to a rectangle (for example, 24 cm in length) that moved back and forth in full view. Following habituation, infants viewed the same rectangle and a rectangle of a different length (for example, 8 cm in length) moving behind a narrow stationary aperture. Neither 8-month-olds nor 10-month-olds looked significantly longer at the novel rectangle. Control groups showed that even 4- and 8-month-olds discriminated rectangles of differing lengths when tested with no aperture present during the test trials (see figure 11.3.) In contrast to the 8- and 10-month-olds, 12-month-olds did look significantly longer at the novel rectangle (figure 11.3d), suggesting that they perceived the length of the rectangles as they moved behind the stationary aperture. In this task, information about length given over time was not effectively extracted until a comparatively late age.

The caveat arising from findings like these is clear. Most studies of perceptual development attempt to minimize attentional and memory limitations, distractions, task complexity, and other variables in testing particular abilities. Clearly, this strategy is most appropriate for making inferences about competence apart from potentially interfering performance variables. It has served us well in allowing inferences about the origins and processes of perception. We should not be misled, however, into thinking that infants' abilities as seen under optimal conditions function consistently under ordinary conditions. The study of performance limitations—attention, memory, situational complexity, and other variables—on infant perception and cognition in natural environments has hardly begun. Research in sterile settings has given us the broad outlines of perceptual competence, but we know relatively little of the microstructure of perceiving and thinking in development.

Categorization

Categorization involves creating representations that group together objects or events. Despite being discriminably different, the members are treated in some way as being the same. For certain purposes, the differences among members are much less important than what they have in common and how they differ from things outside the category.

Categorization produces cognitive economy. If you are told that lurking outside the door is a strange animal, a vorp, you can infer much about it despite never having encountered one before. Knowing the vorp is an animal, you have no doubt the vorp has a circulatory system and eats food, for example. The ecological trick in categorization is grouping and separating based on object properties so as to produce the greatest efficiencies in thought and behavior.

Some categorizations appear to be built into sensory mechanisms. Two examples are categorical perception of phonemes (chapter 8) and categorical perception of color (chapter 2). Even though the stimuli may vary continuously along a physical dimension, infants perceive them categorically. There are a number of similarities between these categorizations given by sensory mechanisms and categories of generic knowledge (Medin & Barsalou, 1987).

Studies investigating infants' categorization abilities have typically used versions of the habituation paradigm. Across habituation trials infants are presented with different exemplars from the same category (such as trucks). Following habituation infants view a new exemplar from the same category (a new truck) and an object from a different category (such as an animal). Infants demonstrating categorization look significantly longer at the object from the new category than at the new exemplar from the habituation category, even though the new exemplar is discriminably different from exemplars presented during the habituation phase.

Categorization has been tested with a wide variety of stimuli (see Quinn, & Eimas 1996, for a review). Within the first 6 months from birth, infants categorize dot patterns (Bomba & Siqueland, 1983; Younger & Gotlieb, 1988), orientation of lines (Bomba, 1984; Quinn, Siqueland & Bomba, 1985), the relations between lines (Cohen & Younger 1984), and the spatial relations *above* and *below* (Quinn, 1994). Categorization studies

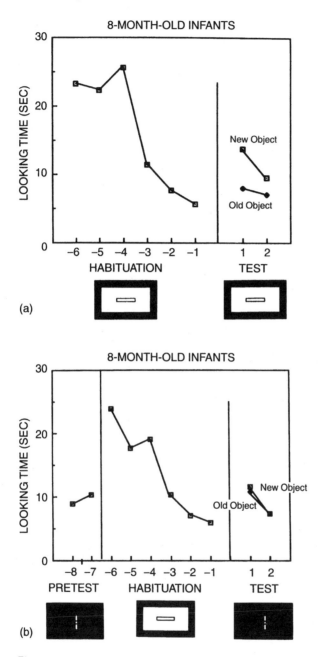

Figure 11.3
Habituation results. Results demonstrating that 8-month-olds can discriminate the length of objects presented in full view (a) but not when presented over time behind an aperture (b).

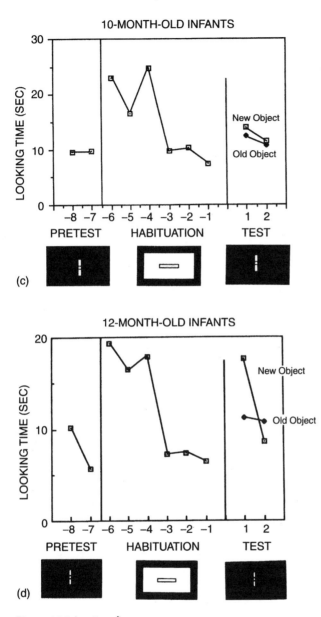

(c)

(d)

Figure 11.3 (continued)
Ten-month-olds also failed to discriminate the length of objects moving behind an aperture
(c). Twelve-month-olds did discrminate the length of the objects through the aperture (d).
Reprinted with permission from Arterberry, M. E. (1993), Development of spatiotemporal
integration in infancy in infancy, *Infant Behavior and Development, 16,* 343–363.

with generic knowledge categories have produced results of surprising specificity and abstraction. Eimas and Quinn (1994) showed that 3-month-olds presented with pictures of horses distinguished new exemplars of horses from zebras, giraffes, and cats. In studies by Mandler and McDonough (1993) infants 7 to 11 months distinguished animals from vehicles.

Perhaps the central issue in interpreting early categorization abilities involves the relative contributions of perceptual and conceptual processes (for excellent reviews, see Mandler, in press, and Quinn & Eimas 1996). The issue relates directly to the question we considered earlier about what kinds of outputs perception produces. Can abstract, functional properties of objects be extracted by perceptual mechanisms? Do perceptual processes produce outputs consisting of descriptions in some amodal vocabulary, such as physical structures and the mechanics of their interactions? Some have argued that the original bases of categorization are perceptual processes that pick out ecologically important properties of objects (e.g., Jones & Smith, 1993; Quinn & Eimas, 1996). Others claim that the outputs of perception must be redescribed or processed further in some manner for conceptual categories to be derived (e.g., Leslie, 1995; Mandler, 1988, 1992, in press). The claim appears to rest on a theoretical assumption and related empirical observations. Infants categorize using information apart from the surface similarity of the objects presented. For example, Mandler and McDonough (1993) emphasized that 7- to 11-month-olds who distinguished animals from vehicles did so despite the fact that some objects from different categories were similar, such as birds with outstretched wings and airplanes. The theoretical assumption is that perceptual categories must be sensitive to this sort of similarity, whereas use of more abstract criteria must implicate nonperceptual inputs, such as cognitive theories of natural kinds.

We have already considered and rejected this assumption about the limits of perception above. It is based on a cherished but flawed view of perception as being primarily or exclusively about sensory similarities. The assumption is quite explicit: As Mandler (in press) puts it: "The features of concepts are often functional, behavioral, or abstract properties, whereas the features of perceptual categories are typically shapes, colors and other perceptual properties". As we have seen, a strong case can be made that perception is about exactly what Mandler (in press) says of a concept: "It answers the question: what kind of thing is it?" Crucial to this view of perception is information given by events. If infants sort animals and vehicles, it may be because they have perceived that animals are self-moving and vehicles are not, or that animals display jointed or elastic motions and vehicles do not, or that animals seek food, whereas vehicles do not. Not only are all of these properties perceivable, they are the sorts of properties perceptual systems probably evolved to pick up. Why one would suspect that perceptual systems evolved to group together "all the red things" or birds and airplanes with similar overall shape but totally different body structures and modes of movement has not been made clear.

Ultimately, humans surely develop concepts that are more remote from ecological perceptual encodings of reality. The notion of an even number would be one example. Closer to our discussion, theories distinguishing animals from vehicles based on more subtle properties (such as animals have DNA) seem unlikely to be given by early perception. By the same token, we would assume that these properties are not what 11-month-olds' categories are about.

It seems likely to us that many of infants' categorization abilities in the first year of life, including those that use abstract, functional criteria, are based on properties encoded and made salient by perceptual mechanisms. At minimum, we can say that no existing data or theoretical considerations of which we are aware rule out this idea. Of course, our view relies in part on parsimony; we have given no argument that excludes the possibility that abstract category representations involve nonperceptual cognitive theories. Our argument merely rejects the usual rationale for invoking nonperceptual factors because that rationale is based on a misunderstanding of perception. In some domains, such as infants' understanding of the motions of physical objects (see below), there already may be evidence for constraints that may reflect innate cognitive structures. Discovering the origins of these nonperceptual bases of categorization early in life and understanding their relations to perceptually based categorizations remain important challenges.

One difficulty in making empirical progress on the issue of perceptual versus conceptual bases for categorization is methodological, specifically the use of artificial stimuli. In many categorization studies, experiments have shown infants pictures of objects. Other methods have been designed, in part due to reservations about pictorial stimuli. Oakes, Madole, and Cohen (1991) adapted an object examination task introduced by Ruff (1986) for studies of categorization. As in visual familiarization and preference procedures, infants are given one object at a time from a given category. After familiarization over several trials (and exemplars), test trials are given in which a new member of the old category and a member of a new category are presented sequentially, with examination time being the dependent measure. Mandler (in press) suggests that the object examination method is superior because "The conceptual system that guides attentive processing during object examination may not be fully engaged when young infants look at pictures."

But why stop there? Just as tests with static, two-dimensional pictures may not reveal much about infants' categorizations of real objects, tiny plastic replicas of animals and vehicles may not do so either. Infants no doubt perceive veridically that the stimuli are toy objects. Given even the best possible sculpting of an angry German shepherd, we would not expect the subject to show fear of this potentially vicious dog. What we should expect is that subjects might overweight static visual features that survive the transformation into hand-held objects. Responses to other features that may be in the subject's memory, such as the relative sizes of elephants and frogs, are at best being assessed in a cue conflict situation. By far the worst cue conflict is that the toy objects do not show the movement characteristics or participation in events characteristic of real objects. This problem does not seem severe for 7- to 11-month-olds who clearly invoked relevant, learned information to sort animals and vehicles. For studying the development of these sorts of categories at younger ages, however, more realistic displays (such as videotapes of moving objects or virtual reality displays of objects) would be preferable. Infants with less prior experience with real objects may appear to use surface similarities if presented with inert toy objects. On the other hand, with unfamiliar objects and realistic events, researchers might test whether very young infants tend to group objects by sensory properties, such as color, or event-relevant properties, such as self-initiated motion.

Physical Laws of Object Motion

Some research suggests that infants are born with cognitive abilities that organize the growth of knowledge about physical interactions of objects. Consider a situation studied by Spelke et al. (1992). An infant was habituated to the following event (see figure 11.4). A ball was dropped and passed behind an occluding surface. The occluder was removed, and the ball was seen resting on the floor surface. After habituation, a shelf was inserted above the floor while the infant watched. Then the occluder was reintroduced, and the ball was again dropped. Infants were tested for their looking times to two test events. In one, the occluder was removed, and the ball was shown resting on the upper shelf. In the other, the ball was shown resting on the floor. In the latter event, the ball's position was more similar to what had been seen repeatedly in habituation. In the former event, the object obeyed a principle that objects move on continuous paths and do not go through solid surfaces. Spelke et al. found that 3- to 4-month-olds dishabituated more to the event with the ball on the floor surface, suggesting that they were sensitive to constraints of continuity and solidity.

Experimental Events

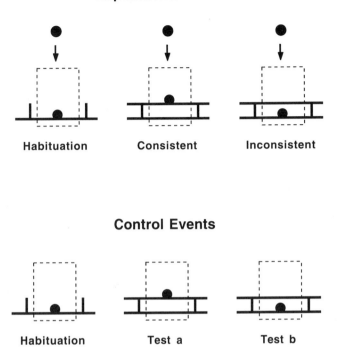

| Habituation | Consistent | Inconsistent |

Control Events

| Habituation | Test a | Test b |

Figure 11.4
Displays used to test infants' sensitivity to the constrainsts of continuity and solidity. (See text.) From Spelke, E. S., Breinlinger, K., Macomber, J., Jacobson, K. (1992), Origins of knowledge, *Psychological Review, 99,* 605–632. Copyright 1992 by the American Psychological Association. Reprinted with permission.

Perceptual and Cognitive Contributions

What aspects of this performance might be understood in terms of early perceptual processes, and what might lead us to suspect additional cognitive contributions? Perception contributes in several ways. Segmentation of the scene into objects, the spatial arrangement of the display, the solidity of the ball and shelf, and the trajectory of the object are all likely products of perception. At first glance, the experiment seems to provide evidence that infants' expectations are guided by some knowledge apart from what is perceived. Specifically, a belief that objects must move along continuous space-time paths could explain the data. When the path of the ball was hidden, there was no information about whether the ball did or did not follow a continuous space-time path. This seems to have the character of an assumption and not a percept. One could take a contrary view, however. The initial and final positions of the ball might engage perceptual mechanisms signaling path continuity, as in Michotte's tunneling effect. More generally, perceptual systems may incorporate the assumption of spatiotemporal continuity as a constraint on perceptual processing (cf. Marr, 1982). Phenomena of stroboscopic motion, in which continuous motion is perceived between discrete flashes of light, suggest some such constraint is indeed incorporated in perceptual processing. It appears to be very difficult to separate the knowledge gotten in two possible ways—by perceptual mechanisms that incorporate constraints about the way world works and by cognitive theories about mechanics. Given that both could arise from innate foundations (Spelke, 1988), deciding between them empirically is difficult at best.

The results of Spelke et al. (1992) and others nevertheless can be claimed to have a clear cognitive component, apart from how the constraint about spatiotemporal continuity is implemented. Perception might produce representations of the solid objects in the displays and might produce a representation of the path followed by the ball when it was occluded. Detecting a *conflict* between these representations seems to involve a process of comparison relating representations of different things (the ball's path through space and the structure of objects in that space). Comparisons are, of course, implicit in any habituation and recovery study, but ordinarily the change that produces novelty responding is a change in a particular object or event. In the case we are considering, something more synthetic is going on: novelty responding is based on a contradiction between two representations given by perception. Infants' performance may plausibly be interpreted as involving rudimentary reasoning processes in this example.

The study described above, and others, suggests that some reasoning about physical objects and events appears quite early, by 3 months. At least two core principles receive strong support as innate or acquired in the earliest weeks of life. One is spatiotemporal continuity. The other is a notion of object solidity—that objects do not ordinarily pass through each other or through solid surfaces. The latter is consistent with the results of Spelke et al. (1992) as well as earlier research, such as the object-permanence studies of Baillargeon et al. (1985) and Baillargeon (1987). In discussing that research in chapter 6, we focused on the infant's knowledge of the persisting object. Here we note that the result of infants' surprise at the event of a screen rotating through an object's location also presumes that the object is not totally compressible.

Later-Developing Principles

Other principles that are important to adults' comprehension of object motions probably do not form part of infants' core knowledge. One ex-

Condition A

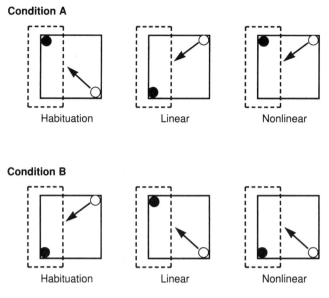

| Habituation | Linear | Nonlinear |

Condition B

| Habituation | Linear | Nonlinear |

Figure 11.5
Events used to test infants' sensitivity to inertia. (See text.) Reprinted from *Cognition, 51,* Spelke, E. S., Katz, G., Purcel, S. E., Ehrlich, S. M., & Breinlinger, K., Early knowledge of object motion: Continuity and inertia, pp. 131–176, 1994, with kind permission from Elsevier Science–NL, Sara Burgerhartstraat 25, 1055 KV Amsterdam, The Netherlands.

ample is the principle of inertia: freely moving objects do not abruptly change speed or direction. To test infants' sensitivity to the principle of inertia, Spelke et al. (1994) presented subjects with events of a ball rolling across a table (figure 11.5). During familiarization events, the ball rolled from one corner to the other. During the test phase, the ball rolled across the table under an occluder. The occluder was raised, and the ball was either in a location consistent with inertia or a location that was inconsistent with inertia. Infants 4.5, 6, 8, 10, and 12 months of age failed to provide a pattern of looking that was consistent with the inertia principle. Instead, if they showed any preference for one display over the other, they looked significantly longer to the display that contained a superficially novel object location and not to the display that was a violation of the inertia constraint.

Another important influence on an object's motion is gravity. Like inertia, gravitational effects are pervasive and have existed throughout evolutionary time. One might expect that perceptual or cognitive mechanisms have come to incorporate constraints related to gravity. Informal observations of young infants suggest that infants have an understanding of the principle of gravity at least by the time they are able to independently manipulate objects.

Perception of object motions in accordance with the principle of gravity show this understanding to emerge between 5 and 7 months of age. For example, Kim and Spelke (1992) showed infants events of balls rolling up or down inclines. In some of the events the motion was appropriate; a ball rolling up an incline slowed down. In other events the motion was inappropriate; a ball rolling down an incline slowed down. They found that 7-month-olds, but not 5-month-olds, looked significantly longer at the inappropriate events. Moreover, when 4-month-olds saw an event in which a ball was released and fell behind an occluder (similar to the events shown in figure 11.4), they did not look significantly longer when the ball appeared to be "resting" in midair than when the ball was resting on a supporting surface (Spelke et al., 1992). This finding suggests that the infants did not have the expectation that the ball should continue to fall until it was visibly supported.

Infants' understanding of support relations may be used to assess their understanding of gravity principle. For example, if we view a box sitting on top of another box and the lower box is moved, we would expect the upper box to fall. Studies of infants' understanding of support provide conflicting evidence about when infants understand support relations and, by extension, the principle of gravity. The emergence of an understanding of gravity between 5 and 7 months of age is supported by findings of Sitskorn and Smitsman (1995), who found that 6- and 9-month-old infants looked longer at an event in which a block appeared to be supported by an open box whose width was wider than the block. In contrast, 4-month-olds did not provide any evidence of perceiving the impossibility of this event. Other studies investigating infants' perception of support suggest an earlier understanding of gravity. Infants aged 6.5, 5.5, and 4.5 months looked significantly longer at events when the supporting object was moved and the previously supported object did not fall (Baillargeon & Hanko-Summers, 1990; Needham & Baillargeon, 1993).

Studies of physical principles in early infant cognition have produced startling results. Principles of object solidity and space-time continuity appear to guide infants' behavior within the first 6 months of life. Whether principles such as space-time continuity influence behavior because they are built-in constraints on the formation of perceptual representations or whether they are embodied as principles in intrinsic cognitive theories is an issue that cannot now be decided. What is clear is that comprehension of the physical world begins very early and that infants' behavior suggests early reasoning processes that compare representations obtained from perception.

CONCLUSION

Research on the development of perception places early cognitive development on a new foundation. There is no sensorimotor stage in which meaningful reality must be constructed from sensations and action. Perception delivers ecologically meaningful representations of objects, arrangements, and events to the new perceiver, coarsely at first and with greater precision later. These new foundations have many implications. That perception depends on relationships and produces abstract descriptions of reality opens the possibility that important aspects of knowledge traditionally considered conceptual may be obtained directly through perception. Notions such as solidity, animacy, and mechanical causality may be primitives in the vocabulary in which the outputs of perception are expressed. That meaningful perception begins early and need not be laboriously constructed implies that learning about the physical and social worlds can get underway much earlier than previously believed. These learning endeavors may be guided not only by ecologically meaningful perceptual descriptions but by distinctly cognitive contributions, in domains such as number, categorization, and physical knowledge, that also appear early in infancy.

Chapter 12
Trends and Themes in Perceptual Development

Research on the origins of perception has changed forever our conceptions of how human mental life begins. A harsh inheritance—the "blooming, buzzing confusion" envisioned by William James and generations of philosophers and psychologists—has given way to a coherent, meaningful reality furnished by perceptual mechanisms. Descriptions produced by perception make explicit abstract physical properties of objects and events, as well as functionally important relations. This birthright gives human infants a strong foothold for learning and developing in their physical and social environments. In this final chapter, we distill some general ideas that have emerged from our explorations into the development of perception and some priorities for future research.

COMPETENCE AND LIMITS IN INFANT PERCEPTION

Our celebration of infants' competence should not obscure the limitations of early perception and the importance of developmental changes. It is difficult to name more than one or two abilities of infants in the first half year of life for which the precision or speed of infants' perception is on a par with adults'. Although we have stressed the attunement of infants' visual perception to events, even the most optimistic estimates of infants' visual velocity thresholds are an order of magnitude higher than those of adults. Equally important, human infants' contact with reality, as we have seen, occurs through a subset of the perceptual abilities available later on. Recall, for example, that adults perceive three-dimensional form using either kinematic or static information but that infants appear to require kinematic information to perceive form until sometime late in the first year. Pictorial depth information and the edge-sensitive process in perceiving objects under occlusion are other examples. In short, our portrait of infant perception is a distinctive one and not merely a faint copy of the adult's profile.

THE RISK-AVERSE PERCEIVER

We can say more about the portrait. The strengths and weaknesses in early perception may conform to an intelligible pattern. Consider first that the omissions, numerous as they are, always involve information sources and not tasks. In surveying the gamut of infant perception, we did not find a single important perceptual task—such as object, depth, motion, or intermodal perception—for which the infant was not prepared in some manner. It never turned out that infants could perceive patterns but not depth or depth but not motion or that no links initially connected sounds and sights, and so forth. We have found no major aspect of the infant's environment marked "access denied."

What we do find is that in many domains, adults utilize a variety of information sources whereas infants have a more limited competence. In many domains, we observed the precocity of abilities based on kinematic information and the delay of abilities based on static spatial relationships. Much of object and space perception fits this description, for example. We could encompass these observations with the generalization that motion-processing mechanisms are prewired whereas others require maturation or learning.

A different generalization may be more apt, however (Kellman, 1993). Development may be described as risk averse in that early appearing perceptual skills are those using information of highest ecological validity—that is, those virtually guaranteed to produce accurate perception. Many examples of perception based on kinematic relationships fit in the category of high validity (Gibson, 1966; Johansson, 1970; Shepard, 1984), but they do not exhaust it. Relationships in static arrays that are high in ecological validity, such as size-distance invariance, also appear early in development. We recall Gottlieb's (1971) pronouncement that "evolution is a consequence of nature's more successful experiments in ontogeny" (p. 106). The key to this experiment may be the importance of accurate perception in the infancy period. As has been argued at several junctures in this book, the infant's motor capabilities do not support escaping from predators, foraging for food, or weaving among obstacles at high speed. Accordingly, the infant's priorities, unlike adults', do not require perceptual mechanisms that can deliver rapid descriptions of reality under the widest possible range of circumstances. For the infant, the priority may be on accurate rather than comprehensive perception. Indeterminacy or ambiguity of some aspects of the environment is less of a problem for an infant, who cannot *do* much, than for an adult, who can. Conversely, *errors* of perception may have far greater repercussions in infant development than later on. An adult may misperceive, out of the corner of an eye, a distant aircraft as a nearby insect. Turning to look directly, the mistake is realized at once. An infant possesses fewer capacities for error correction. Lower sensory resolution and less mobility may preclude further investigation. Worse, the infant may not know whether insects ever turn into airplanes! Instead of realizing perceptual errors, the infant may simply arrive at faulty beliefs.

We arrive at two conjectures, which we might call *access* and *risk aversion*. The infant is born with perceptual abilities giving access to most if not all major features of his environment (that is, objects, events, and spatial arrangements), albeit with less precision than will come later. Within each perceptual domain, however, access is based on a subset of adult abilities, and that subset tends to include those information sources of highest ecological validity. These are broad characterizations and are not subject to a single definitive test. Like many evolutionary arguments, they are perhaps unsatisfyingly post hoc. But we would be remiss not to point out how neatly these conjectures apply. Perhaps due to imperatives of successful development, infants' perception is broad in its access to aspects of the environment and narrow in its selective reliance on information sources of the highest ecological validity.

DESCRIPTION AND EXPLANATION IN PERCEPTION

From the beginning of the modern era of infant research to the present, much investigation has focused on discovering what infants perceive and when various perceptual abilities come to operate. These questions are obvious starting points for understanding perceptual development, and they have been pursued with notable success. Experimental findings have in many cases answered centuries-old questions and corrected enduring misconceptions about the origins of human knowledge.

Beyond discovering that infants can perceive a certain aspect of their environment at a certain age, much research has sought to specify the information that engages particular perceptual abilities. Understanding what information is used in a perceptual task is a key priority at the ecological level of analysis and one that opens the door to meaningful inquiry about the processes and biological mechanisms of perception.

A much smaller subset of research, however, has revealed in detail the computational processes or neurophysiological mechanisms of early perceptual abilities. Clearly, advancing our understanding of computational processes and neural mechanisms is the great challenge for the future of perception research at all ages. The tasks appear formidable (recall those 10^{14} neural connections!). The wave of research over the past thirty years that has described the course of perceptual development may appear to have surmounted less difficult tasks than those remaining. This perspective is to some degree a result of the success infant perception research has enjoyed in actually answering many of its key questions at the level of competence and information. To have in hand a reasonably clear description of perceptual development after about three decades of scientific research is remarkable. Such a description was certainly out of reach for hundreds of years, despite intense interest in the subject.

Perceptual Mechanisms

There is more to be done, however, to achieve complete explanations of how perception works. Some of it may call for new methods and new creativity. We have seen already, however, examples of research that illuminates not only the ecological level of task and information but process and mechanism as well. For example, findings that vision and hearing provide human infants with information for a common external space converge with neurophysiological findings in other species of neurons whose receptive fields cover a region of space, whether the input from that region is auditory or visual. These converging lines of research do not yet pinpoint specific neural mechanisms in humans, but we are dealing with data and hypotheses remarkably advanced from even twenty years ago. Research relating changes in a variety of visual abilities to maturation in the visual cortex around 6 to 8 weeks, or the separate maturation of stereoscopic depth perception at around 16 weeks, provides other examples. Such connections are based on convergent behavioral and electrophysiological methods. Ideal observer analyses have located limitations of early infant vision at particular levels of the nervous system; these efforts bring together computational, psychophysical, anatomical, and physiological data.

Perceptual Processes and Representations

Research in infant perception has also begun to shed light on the processes that extract information from the environment and produce perceptual descriptions. In fact, they allow us to comment on issues of process that have divided ecological and computational views of perception. For Gibson, Johansson, and other theorists of direct perception, an important theoretical tenet, (and a break with prior inferential theories) is that perception is a response to higher-order relations and not merely to first-order sensory dimensions. Computational theorists (e.g., Marr, 1982) also embrace the use of higher-order relationships but argue that perceptual computations are algorithmic, consisting of operations on intermediate levels of representation and involving constraints or assumptions that allow perceptual processes to reach determinate (and sensible) results.

From what we have seen, the answer is yes to both views. Infant perception has yielded many examples of perception as a response to complex spatial and temporal relationships, consistent with specialized neural mechanisms. Perceptual mechanisms in a number of domains appear to be attuned to extract relationships far more complex than anticipated prior to the emergence of ecological views. At the same time, some of the evidence clearly points to computational schemes involving intermediate representations (what might be called *interresponse* or *dependent variable coupling*, Epstein, 1982; Hochberg, 1974). Three examples are perceiving planar shape at a slant, the dependence of object unity on perceived motion, and the detection of object motion during observer motion.

The directness of perception is an empirical issue that may have differing answers in different perceptual domains. Researchers in infant perception have already met with some success in understanding perceptual processes, but much remains to be done. As Benjamin Franklin remarked, "The reward for good work is more work."

MECHANISMS OF CHANGE

Another area in which rewards await is in revealing the mechanisms of perceptual change. We have identified classes of information that do not influence perception in early infancy, and in some cases we know when they become effective. Little is known, however, about the causes of change. We have noted instances in which evidence indicates a linkage of neural maturation to certain sensory developments in the early months. What about other mechanisms of change? E. Gibson (1969, 1984) championed the idea of continuity in perceptual learning throughout the lifespan. Perceptual learning—improvements in processes of information pickup with practice in a given domain—certainly appears to underly much of adult expertise (Goldstone, 1994, Kellman & Kaiser, 1994). A number of studies of infants have been described in terms of differentiation of types of motion or of surface invariants, and so on. These studies show sensitivity to certain kinds of information, but so far specific demonstrations of a differentiation learning process in infant perception have been lacking.

The task is difficult because it is likely that improved precision of perceptual skills occurs during the first year due to both neural maturation and perceptual learning. And what about the kind of learning we called *enrichment*—the attachment of meaning to stimulus variables with experience? Not many aspects of infant perception appear to fit this conception, which is surprising in that associative learning has long occupied the preeminent place in conjectures about perceptual development. Such conjectures persist. Nakayama and Shimojo (1992), for example, suggested that experience with the probability structure of object views from different vantage points (*generic view* theory) might lead to certain tendencies in image interpretation. No evidence for this view has appeared in infant research. In fact, in its most likely applications, such as the edge-sensitive process in perception of object unity and in pictorial depth perception, available evidence is more consistent with maturational accounts, as we saw in chapters 3 and 5. One example that does implicate a role for learned information in perception is the depth cue of familiar size (see chapter 3). Infants by 7 months use remembered information about object size along with its projective size to compute its distance, at least when binocular information is excluded.

It thus remains possible that enrichment learning plays a role in other aspects of perceptual development; perhaps the kinds of experiments that would clearly demonstrate such learning in other perceptual domains have simply not been done. Efforts to formulate and test detailed hypotheses about mechanisms of change in perceptual development remain a high priority.

CONCLUSION

Systematic research on perception in the human infant is a relatively new venture, begun in the latter half of the twentieth century. From modest beginnings, this research has proceeded a great distance toward answering classic questions about human nature and producing a coherent picture of the origins of perceptual knowledge. This picture mandates a new account of the origins of the mind and human development, one in which a human being interacts from the start with a meaningful and coherent reality. It changes permanently our views of how perception works and how much of human knowledge derives from it. We have tried in this book to convey the nature and implications of these advances. We hope that what has been learned will provide a foundation for investigations leading to even deeper insights into the nature of perception and its development.

Appendix
Origins and Concepts of the Habituation and Dishabituation Method

---

Habituation and recovery of visual attention, along with its variants, is the most commonly used method in the study of infant perception and cognition. In this appendix we consider its origins and assumptions in greater detail.

The habituation method has its historical roots in investigations of animal learning. The basic interpretation of habituation and recovery data draws on Sokolov's (1963) studies of the *orienting reflex* (OR), a concept introduced by Pavlov (1910/1927). On presentation of a novel stimulus, a variety of changes occur, such as body and head movements as well as specific adjustments of perceptual systems, such as the eyes and ears. Autonomic effects include changes in heart rate and respiration. Sokolov also described changes in electroencephalographic activity and lowering of sensory thresholds as components of the OR.

Most important, Sokolov noted two general features of the OR. First, the OR is similar for any change in stimulation, and second, it undergoes extinction with repeated trials, and this extinction is *specific to the stimulus*. In both humans and animals, repeated presentation of a stimulus results in a gradually reduced OR. Presentation of a novel stimulus, however, reactivates the OR. Given these properties, the OR can be used to assess sensory and perceptual sensitivity. Repetition of a particular stimulus reduces the OR. A stimulus change is then presented. If the change is sufficiently large, the OR will recover, with magnitude of recovery increasing with the degree of discrepancy between the new stimulus and the old stimulus.

Sokolov theorized that repetitions of the same stimulus must produce a neural pattern to which later inputs are compared. Specifically, "the nervous system produces an exact model of the properties of external objects acting on the sense organs" (Sokolov, 1963, p. 286). Such an internal model is required to explain the selectivity of extinction of the OR.

HABITUATION AND THE ORIENTING REFLEX

The relation between habituation and dishabituation of visual attention and the properties of the OR is part analogy and part identity. The visual behavior measured in the habituation method—duration of visual attention—does not appear to meet the criteria for a reflex. The variability of looking onsets and durations from trial to trial is more consistent with voluntary exploratory activity than reflexive behavior, even allowing for the relatively variable responses observed with some reflexes in infancy. The departure from reflexive behavior is even more marked when looking time on a trial is measured with allowances for gaps—momentary breaks in fixation—so long as the gaps do not exceed some interval (for example, 2 sec). In this common variant, the patterns of target fixations and looks away may be highly variable.

On the other hand, the initial capture of attention by some displays, such as moving ones, may be reflexive. Moreover, visual (and other perceptual) exploration is precisely the kind of follow-up behavior that might be expected from a functional analysis of the OR. The function of the OR appears to be the attunement of the organism to receive important information from the environment (Sokolov, 1963; Jeffrey, 1968). Ongoing activity ceases, while perceptual and attentional mechanisms are alerted. Thus, it is not surprising that visual exploration, and other forms of sensory attunement, should follow the same course as the OR. When a stimulus is novel, exploration is activated; with repetition, attention decreases.

Habituation and dishabituation of visual attention, then, might be considered an extention of the behavioral pattern Sokolov described. Visual attention, however, turns out to be more useful for studying perception. Why should this be the case? If both the OR and subsequent visual attention are triggered by novelty, use of the OR as a dependent variable might be preferable. Reflexes occur with high-reliability, well-defined characteristics and in brief time periods, whereas looking durations are far more variable.

A problem is that many stimulus changes may be too subtle to evoke a discernible OR. A sudden loud noise or bright light will do so. A small change in the orientation or shape of an object may not because it does not radically change the ambient energy reaching the organism. Detection of such changes may also depend on where the subject is looking.

DIFFERING REPRESENTATIONS GOVERNING THE ORIENTING REFLEX AND VISUAL ATTENTION

A more general form of this hypothesis is that the OR and visual attention are both governed by novelty but often utilize differing representations. The representations or *models*, in Sokolov's terms, governing the OR appear to be sensory ones, closely tied to basic energy variables. A sudden noise may attract our attention without our determining what event has occurred. Pickup of many properties of objects and events may require the allocation of attention and further perceptual processing. Thus, sensory change alone may cause orienting, which results in further processing. Anatomically, there appear to be separate neural pathways in the visual system for carrying detailed pattern information (thalamic and cortical pathways) and for visual alerting and activation (superior colliculus) (e.g., Schneider, 1969).

In contrast to the OR, habituation and dishabituation of visual attention appear to be governed by more detailed and abstract representations (Cohen, 1969; McCall & Kagan, 1967). Complex structural information can determine whether attention is sustained or rejuvenated. Habituation and dishabituation patterns can be based on distal properties of objects that are specified by means of different proximal stimuli during different parts of the experiment. In fact, the design of habituation experiments to isolate abstract, perceived properties as the basis of response has become a mainstay of contemporary infant research.

Incidentally, these differences suggest an interesting hypothesis regarding the distinction between sensation and perception, which we discussed in chapter 1. Much work in perception suggests that *patterns* in ambient energy are used to determine the structure of objects, space, and events. In contrast, we obtain little information about the energy itself. For example, our ability to distinguish and recognize surfaces of varying reflectances is excellent, but our knowledge about how much light comes from a surface to our retinas is poor.

The emphasis on perception by means of energy, rather than perception of energy, has led many to discard the old notion that perceptions are built from sensations and led some to question whether sensations really exist at all (Cornman, 1975). Perhaps this newer idea that we are not really detectors of energy is too extreme. It appears that we have an orienting system based on sensing: it detects basic energy changes, and it produces largely uninterpreted experiences whose function is to activate and direct our perceptual systems. Once activated, these perceptual systems use patterns in incident energy to determine structure and events in the world.

PROCEDURAL VARIABLES

A significant practical advance in the use of the habituation method was the development of the infant control procedure (Cohen & Gelber, 1975; Horowitz, 1975). In this procedure, each trial's length is not fixed but is determined by the infant's looking behavior. Typically, a trial begins with some criterion look—say, .5 or 1 sec—and lasts until the infant looks away for two continuous seconds. Thus, the looking time observed on any given trial may be the cumulation of several fixations interrupted by brief breaks in fixation. The definition of habituation also can be geared to the infant's looking patterns. Whereas an *absolute criterion* of habituation might define habituation as occurring when looking times over several trials fall below some fixed value, a *relative criterion* defines habituation in terms of a percentage decline—say, 50 percent—from the looking times measured from that subject on the first several trials of the experiment.

The benefits of these infant control aspects are several. First, trials become more meaningful units in an experiment since they begin and end based on the subject's attention. Second, subject loss is reduced since neither single trials nor the habituation phase continue for long after the subject becomes bored. And finally, the use of a relative criterion also provides a more rational definition of habituation, since subjects vary in initial levels of looking. For example, three trials measuring 10 sec of looking time on each may represent persistent, strong interest from a subject whose initial trials were on the order of 12 sec but may indicate a drastic decline of interest in a subject whose initial looks averaged 60 sec. Research by Horowitz and her colleagues (Horowitz, 1975) suggested specific parameters for infant control procedures that have proven useful in many subsequent studies.

RESPONSES TO ABSTRACT ATTRIBUTES

Another useful innovation involves the stimuli used in the habituation phase of the habituation and dishabituation procedure. Whereas studies of the OR and early habituation procedures used an unchanging stimulus, it has proven possible to use changing stimuli in which some aspect is unchanging. An example, described in detail in chapter 5, concerns perception of three-dimensional form (Kellman, 1984). In this study, subjects habituated to a three-dimensional object rotating around two different axes of rotation and were then tested for dishabituation to that same object rotating around a new axis of rotation or to a novel object also rotating around a third new axis. Differing rotation axes in habituation and test phases were needed to test perception of three-dimensional form apart from particular two-dimensional projections to the observer. Given a constant habituation stimulus, however, subjects might have dishabituated during the test period either to a new three-dimensional form or to a new axis of rotation. The use of two different rotation axes in habituation served to decrease sensitivity to changing rotation; the only constant throughout habituation was the three-dimensional form. In this way it was possible to assess responses to form apart from particular rotations and two-dimensional projections (Kellman, 1984; Kellman & Short, 1987; Arterberry & Yonas, 1988). The use of changing habituation stimuli to focus habituation on a single stimulus attribute has been extended to even higher levels of abstraction—for example, in studies of categorization (e.g., Younger & Cohen, 1983; Younger, 1990).

LIMITATIONS OF THE HABITUATION AND DISHABITUATION PARADIGM

Despite its popularity and proven value, the habituation method has drawbacks. The major drawback is that because looking times are influenced by many factors, conclusions about the effects of certain display variables are necessarily based on group averages. Although a group pattern may show that infants detected a change in a certain stimulus dimension by looking longer to some test display, a particular infant's looking pattern may better reflect his momentary bout of hiccoughs or the time interval since his last nap. Variation due to chance factors and to individual subjects' looking tendencies tend to average out of group data but preclude clear interpretation of the individual's results. A related source of difficulty is subject loss due to fussing. In most cases, loss of subjects simply increases the work required by the experimenter to complete the study. In some instances, however, subjects who fail to complete a session may be a nonrandom subset of the subjects with respect to the ability under study. To imagine an extreme case, consider some stimulus attribute that might be upsetting to infants who detect it. In such a case, the abilities of the age group under study might be misconstrued, since the subjects who were dropped from the sample may ironically be those whose detection abilities are best. Many of the the problems encountered with the habituation method arise with other techniques as well. All methods must cope with the fact that human infants are nonverbal, relatively immobile, and only intermittently cooperative experimental subjects.

References

Abravanel, E., & DeYong, N. G. (1991). Does object modeling elicit imitative-like gestures from young infants? *Journal of Experimental Child Psychology, 52*, 22–40.

Abravanel, E., & Sigafoos, A. D. (1984). Exploring the presence of imitation during early infancy. *Child Development, 55*, 381–392.

Adams, O. S., Fitts, P. M., Rappaport, M., & Weinstein, M. (1954). Relations among some measures of pattern discriminability. *Journal of Experimental Psychology, 48*, 81–88.

Adolph, K. E., Eppler, M. A., & Gibson, E. J. (1993a). Crawling versus walking in infants' perception of affordances for locomotion over sloping surfaces. *Child Development, 64*, 1158–1174.

Adolph, K. E., Eppler, M. A., & Gibson, E. J. (1993b). Development of perception of affordances. In C. Rovee-Collier & L. P. Lipsitt (Eds.), *Advances in infancy research* (Vol. 8, pp. 51–98). Norwood, NJ: Ablex.

Allen, D., Banks, M. S., & Norcia, A. M. (1993). Does chromatic sensitivity develop more slowly than luminance sensitivity? *Vision Research, 33*(17), 2553–2562.

Allman, J., Miezin, F., & McGuinness, E. (1985). Direction and velocity specific responses from beyond the classical receptive field in the middle temporal visual area. *Perception, 14*, 105–126.

Ames, A. (1951). Visual perception and the rotating trapezoidal window. *Psychological Monographs, Series No. 324.*

Anand, K. J. S., & McGrath, P. J. (Eds.). (1993). *Neonatal pain and distress.* Amsterdam: Elsevier Science.

Andersen, G. J., & Cortese, J. M. (1989). 2-D contour perception resulting from kinetic occlusion. *Perception & Psychophysics, 46*(1), 49–55.

Antell, S. E., & Keating, D. P. (1983). Perception of numerical invariance in neonates. *Child Development, 54*(3), 695–701.

Aristotle (1941). *Basic works* (R. McKeon, Trans.). New York: Random House.

Aronson, E., & Rosenbloom, S. (1971). Space perception in early infancy: Perception within a common auditory-visual space. *Science, 172*, 1161–1163.

Arterberry, M. E. (1993). Development of spatiotemporal integration in infancy. *Infant Behavior and Development, 16*, 343–363.

Arterberry, M. E. (1995). Perception of object number through an aperture by human infants. *Infant Behavior and Development, 18*, 359–362.

Arterberry, M. E. (1997). Development of sensitivity to spatial and temporal information. In P. v. d. Broek, P. Bauer & T. Bourg (Eds.), *Developmental spans in event comprehension and representation: Bridging fictional and acutal events* (pp. 51–78). Hillsdale, NJ: Erlbaum.

Arterberry, M. E. (1997). Spatiotemporal integration in infancy. In C. Rovee-Collier & L. Lipsitt (Eds.), *Advances in infancy research* (Vol. 11, pp. 219–268). Norwood, NJ: Ablex.

Arterberry, M. E., Bensen, A. S., & Yonas, A. (1991). Infants' responsiveness to static monocular depth information: A recovery from habituation approach. *Infant Behavior and Development, 14,* 241–251.

Arterberry, M. E., & Yonas, A. (1988). Infants' sensitivity to kinetic information for three-dimensional object shape. *Perception & Psychophysics, 44*(1), 1–6.

Arterberry, M. E., & Yonas, A. (1995). Perception of structure from motion by 2-month-old infants. *Investigative Ophthalmology and Visual Science Supplements, 36*(4), 909.

Arterberry, M. E., Yonas, A., & Bensen, A. S. (1989). Self-produced locomotion and the development of responsiveness to linear perspective and texture gradients. *Developmental Psychology, 25,* 976–982.

Ashmead, D. H., Clifton, R. K., & Perris, E. E. (1987). Precision of auditory localization in human infants. *Developmental Psychology, 23*(5), 641–647.

Ashmead, D. H., Davis, D. L., & Northington, A. (1995). Contribution of listeners' approaching motion to auditory distance perception. *Journal of Experimental Psychology: Human Perception & Performance, 21,* 239–256.

Ashmead, D. H., Davis, D. L., Whalen, T., & Odom, R. D. (1991). Sound localization and sensitivity to interaural time differences in human infants. *Child Development, 62,* 1211–1226.

Ashmead, D. H., McCarty, M. E., Lucas, L. S., & Belvedere, M. C. (1993). Visual guidance in infants' reaching toward suddenly displaced targets. *Child Development, 64,* 1111–1127.

Aslin, R. N. (1977). Development of binocular fixation in human infants. *Journal of Experimental Child Psychology, 23*(1), 133–150.

Aslin, R. N. (1981). Development of smooth pursuit in human infants. In D. F. Fisher, R. A. Monty & J. W. Ser🔹rs (Eds.), *Eye movements: Cognition and visual perception* (pp. 31–51). Hillsdale, NJ: Erlbaum.

Aslin, R. N. (1987). Visual and auditory development in infancy. *Handbook of infant development* (2nd ed.) (pp. 5–97). New York: Wiley.

Aslin, R. N. (1993). Infant accommodation and convergence. In K. Simons (Ed.), *Early visual development: Normal and abnormal* (pp. 30–38). New York: Oxford University Press.

Aslin, R. N. (1993). Perception of visual direction in human infants. In C. Granrud (Ed.), *Visual perception and cognition in infancy* (pp. 91–119). Hillsdale, NJ: Erlbaum.

Aslin, R. N., & Pisoni, D. B. (1980). Some developmental processes in speech perception. In G. H. Yeni-Komshian, J. F. Kavanagh & C. A. Ferguson (Eds.), *Child phonology. Vol. 2. Perception* (pp. 67–96). New York: Academic Press.

Aslin, R. N., Pisoni, D. B., Hennessy, B. L., & Percy, A. J. (1981). Discrimination of voice onset time by human infants: New findings and implications for the effects of early experience. *Child Development, 52*(4), 1135–1145.

Aslin, R. N., Pisoni, D. B., & Jusczyk, P. W. (1983). Auditory development and speech perception in infancy. In M. M. Haith & J. J. Campos (Eds.), *Handbook of child psychology* (Vol. 3, pp. 573–687). New York: Wiley.

Aslin, R. N., & Salapatek, P. (1975). Saccadic localization of visual targets by the very young human infant. *Perception & Psychophysics, 17*(3), 293–302.

Aslin, R. N., & Shea, S. L. (1990). Velocity thresholds in human infants: Implications for the perception of motion. *Developmental Psychology, 26*(4), 589–598.

Aslin, R. N., Shea, S. L., & Metz, H. S. (1990). Use of the Canon R-1 autorefractor to measure refractive errors and accommodative responses in young infants. *Clinical Vision Science, 5,* 61–70.

Atkinson, J. (1984). Human visual development over the first 6 months of life: A review and a hypothesis. *Human Neurobiology, 3*(2), 61–74.

Atkinson, J., & Braddick, O. (1976). Stereoscopic discrimination in infants. *Perception, 5*(1), 29–38.

Atkinson, J. & Braddick, O. (1981). Development of optokinetic nystagmus in infants: An indicator of cortical binocularity? In D. F. Fisher, R. A. Monty, & J. W. Senders (Eds.), *Eye movements: Cognition and visual perception* (pp. 53–64). Hillsdale, NJ: Erlbaum.

Atkinson, J., Braddick, O., & Moar, K. (1977a). Contrast sensitivity of the human infant for moving and static patterns. *Vision Research, 17*(9), 1045–1047.

Atkinson, J., Braddick, O., & Moar, K. (1977b). Development of contrast sensitivity over the first three months of life in the human infant. *Vision Research, 17*(9), 1037–1044.

Atkinson, J., Braddick, O., Weeks, F. & Hood, B. (1990). Spatial and temporal tuning of infants' orientation-specific responses. *Perception, 19,* 371.

Atkinson, J., Hood, B., Wattam-Bell, J., Anker, S., & Tricklebank, J. (1988). Development of orientation discrimination in infancy. *Perception, 17*(5), 587–595.

Badcock, D. R. (1990). Phase- or energy-based face discrimination: Some problems. *Journal of Experimental Psychology: Human Perception & Performance, 16*(1), 217–220.

Bahrick, L. E. (1983). Infants' perception of substance and temporal synchrony in multimodal events. *Infant Behavior and Development, 6*(4), 429–451.

Bahrick, L. E. (1987). Infants' intermodal perception of two levels of temporal structure in natural events. *Infant Behavior and Development, 10,* 387–416.

Bahrick, L. E. (1988). Intermodal learning in infancy: Learning on the basis of two kinds of invariant relations in audible and visible events. *Child Development, 59*(1), 197–209.

Bahrick, L. E. (1992). Infants' perceptual differentiation of amodal and modality-specific audio-visual relations. *Journal of Experimental Child Psychology, 53*(2), 180–199.

Bahrick, L. E. (1994). The development of infants' sensitivity to arbitrary intermodal relations. *Ecological Psychology, 6*(2), 111–123.

Bahrick, L. E., Walker, A. S., & Neisser, U. (1981). Selective looking by infants. *Cognitive Psychology, 13*(3), 377–390.

Baillargeon, R. (1987). Object permanence in $3\frac{1}{2}$- and $4\frac{1}{2}$-month-old infants. *Developmental Psychology, 23*(5), 655–664.

Baillargeon, R. (1993). The object concept revisited: New directions in the investigation of infants' physical knowledge. In C. Granrud (Ed.), *Visual perception and cognition in infancy* (pp. 265–315). Hillsdale, NJ: Erlbaum.

Baillargeon, R., DeVos, J., & Graber, M. (1989). Location memory in 8-month-old infants in a non-search AB task: Further evidence. *Cognitive Development, 4*(4), 345–367.

Baillargeon, R., Graber, M., DeVos, J., & Black, J. (1990). Why do young infants fail to search for hidden objects? *Cognition, 36,* 255–284.

Baillargeon, R., & Hanko-Summers, S. (1990). Is the top object adequately supported by the bottom object? Young infants' understanding of support relations. *Cognitive Development, 5*(1), 29–53.

Baillargeon, R., Spelke, E. S., & Wasserman, S. (1985). Object permanence in 5-month-old infants. *Cognition, 20,* 191–208.

Ball, W., & Tronick, E. (1971). Infant responses to impending collision: Optical and real. *Science, 171*(3973), 818–820.

Banks, M. S. (1980). The development of visual accommodation during early infancy. *Child Development, 51*(3), 646–666.

Banks, M. S., & Bennett, P. J. (1988). Optical and photoreceptor immaturities limit the spatial and chromatic vision of human neonates. *Journal of the Optical Society of America A, 5*(12), 2059–2079.

Banks, M. S., & Crowell, J. A. (1993). Front-end limitations to infant spatial vision: Examination of two analyses. In K. Simons (Ed.), *Early visual development: Normal and abnormal* (pp. 91–116). New York: Oxford University Press.

Banks, M. S., & Dannemiller, J. L. (1987). Infant visual psychophysics. In P. Salapatek & L. Cohen (Eds.), *Handbook of infant perception*. Vol. 1. *From sensation to perception* (pp. 115–184). Orlando, FL: Academic Press.

Banks, M. S., Geisler, W. S., & Bennett, P. J. (1987). The physical limits of grating visibility. *Vision Research, 27,* 1915–1924.

Banks, M. S., & Ginsburg, A. P. (1985). Early visual preferences: A review and a new theoretical treatment. In H. W. Reese (Ed.), *Advances in child development and behavior* (pp. 207–246). New York: Academic Press.

Banks, M. S., & Salapatek, P. (1978). Acuity and contrast sensitivity in 1-, 2-, and 3-month-old human infants. *Investigative Ophthalmology and Visual Science, 17*(4), 361–365.

Banks, M. S., & Salapatek, P. (1981). Infant pattern vision: A new approach based on the contrast sensitivity function. *Journal of Experimental Child Psychology, 31*(1), 1–45.

Banks, M. S., & Salapatek, P. (1983). Infant visual perception. In M. M. Haith & J. Campos (Eds.), *Infancy and biological development* (pp. 435–572). New York: Wiley.

Banks, M. S., & Shannon, E. (1993). Spatial and chromatic visual efficiency in human neonates. In C. Granrud (Ed.), *Visual perception and cognition in infancy: Carnegie Mellon symposia on cognition* (pp. 1–46). Hillsdale, NJ: Erlbaum.

Bargones, J. Y., & Werner, L. A. (1994). Adults listen selectively; infants do not. *Psychological Science, 5*(3), 170–174.

Barlow, H. B., & Reeves, B. C. (1979). The versatility and absolute efficiency of detecting mirror symmetry in random dot displays. *Vision Research, 19*(7), 783–793.

Barnat, S. B., Klein, P. J., & Meltzoff, A. N. (1996). Deferred imitation across changes in context and object: Memory and generalization in 14-month-old infants. *Infant Behavior and Development, 19*(2), 241–251.

Barrett, K., C., Campos, J., & Emde, R. N. (1996). Infants' use of conflicting emotion signals. *Cognition and Emotion, 10,* 113–135.

Barten, S., Birns, B., & Ronch, J. (1971). Individual differences in the visual pursuit behavior of neonates. *Child Development, 42,* 313–319.

Bayley, N. (1969). *Bayley scales of infant development.* New York: Psychological Corporation.

Beauchamp, G. K., Cowart, B. J., Mennella, J. A., & Marsh, R. R. (1994). Infant salt taste: Developmental, methodological, and contextual factors. *Developmental Psychobiology, 27,* 353–365.

Beauchamp, G. K., Cowart, B. J., & Moran, M. (1986). Developmental changes in salt acceptability in human infants. *Developmental Psychobiology, 19,* 17–25.

Becker, W., & Jurgens, R. (1979). An analysis of the saccadic system by means of double step stimuli. *Vision Research, 19*(9), 967–983.

Bedford, F. L. (1989). Constraints on learning new mappings between perceptual dimensions. *Journal of Experimental Psychology: Human Perception & Performance, 15,* 232–248.

Berkeley, G. (1709/1910). *Essay towards a new theory of vision.* London: Dutton.

Bertenthal, B. I. (1993). Infants' perception of biomechanical motions: Intrinsic image and knowledge-based constraints. In C. Granrud (Ed.), *Visual perception and cognition in infancy: Carnegie Mellon symposia on cognition* (pp. 175–214). Hillsdale, NJ: Erlbaum.

Bertenthal, B. I. (1996). Origins and early development of perception, action, and representation. *Annual Review of Psychology, 47,* 431–459.

Bertenthal, B. I., & Bai, D. L. (1989). Infants' sensitivity to optical flow for controlling posture. *Developmental Psychology, 25*(6), 936–945.

Bertenthal, B. I., Banton, T., & Bradbury, A. (1993). Directional bias in the perception of translating patterns. *Perception, 22*(2), 193–207.

Bertenthal, B. I., & Campos, J. J. (1990). A systems approach to the organizing effects of self-produced locomotion during infancy. In C. K. Rovee-Collier and L. P. Lipsitt (Eds.), *Advances in infancy research* (Vol. 6., pp. 1–60). Norwood, NJ: Ablex.

Bertenthal, B. I., Campos, J. J., & Haith, M. M. (1980). Development of visual organization: The perception of subjective contours. *Child Development, 51*(4), 1072–1080.

Bertenthal, B. I., & Davis, P. (1988). Dynamic pattern analysis predicts recognition and discrimination of biomechanical motions. Paper presented at the annual meeting of the Psychonomic Society, Chicago, Ill.

Bertenthal, B. I., Proffitt, D. R., & Cutting, J. E. (1984). Infant sensitivity to figural coherence in biomechanical motions. *Journal of Experimental Child Psychology, 37*(2), 213–230.

Bertenthal, B. I., Proffitt, D. R., & Kramer, S. J. (1987). Perception of biomechanical motions by infants: Implementation of various processing constraints. Special Issue: The ontogenesis of perception. *Journal of Experimental Psychology: Human Perception and Performance, 13*(4), 577–585.

Bertenthal, B. I., Proffitt, D. R., Kramer, S. J. & Spetner, N. B. (1987). Infants' encoding of kinetic displays varying in relative coherence. *Developmental Psychology, 23,* 171–178.

Bertenthal, B. I., Proffitt, D. R., Spetner, N. B., & Thomas, M. A. (1985). The development of infant sensitivity to biomechanical motions. *Child Development, 56*(3), 531–543.

Best, C. T., McRoberts, G. W., LaFleur, R., & Silver-Isenstadt, J. (1995). Divergent developmental patterns for infants' perception of two nonnative consonant contrasts. *Infant Behavior and Development, 18,* 339–350.

Best, C. T., McRoberts, G. W., & Sithole, N. M. (1988). Examination of perceptual reorganization for nonnative speech contrasts: Zulu click discrimination by English-speaking adults and infants. *Journal of Experimental Psychology: Human Perception and Performance, 14*(3), 345–360.

Bigelow, A. E. (1986). The development of reaching in blind children. *British Journal of Developmental Psychology, 4*(4), 355–366.

Bigelow, A. E. (1992). Locomotion and search behavior in blind infants. *Infant Behavior and Development, 15,* 179–189.

Birch, E. E., Gwiazda, J., & Held, R. (1982). Stereoacuity development for crossed and uncrossed disparities in human infants. *Vision Research, 22*(5), 507–513.

Birch, H. G., & Lefford, A. (1967). Visual differentiation, intersensory integration, and voluntary motor control. *Monographs of the Society for Research in Child Development, 32*(2), 1–87.

Bjorklund, D. F. (1987). A note on neonatal imitation. *Developmental Review, 7,* 86–92.

Bomba, P. C. (1984). The development of orientation categories between 2 and 4 months of age. *Journal of Experimental Child Psychology, 37*(3), 609–636.

Bomba, P. C., & Siqueland, E. R. (1983). The nature and structure of infant form categories. *Journal of Experimental Child Psychology, 35*(2), 294–328.

Bornstein, M. H. (1975). Qualities of color vision in infancy. *Journal of Experimental Child Psychology, 19*(3), 401–419.

Bornstein, M. H. (1978). Chromatic vision in infancy. In H. W. Reese & L. P. Lipsitt (Eds.), *Advances in child development and behavior* (Vol. 12, pp. 117–182). New York: Academic Press.

Bornstein, M. H., Ferdinandsen, K., & Gross, C. G. (1981). Perception of symmetry in infancy. *Developmental Psychology, 17*(1), 82–86.

Bornstein, M. H., Kessen, W., & Weiskopf, S. (1976). Color vision and hue categorization in young human infants. *Journal of Experimental Psychology: Human Perception & Performance, 2*(1), 115–129.

Bornstein, M. H., & Krinsky, S. J. (1985). Perception of symmetry in infancy: The salience of vertical symmetry and the perception of pattern wholes. *Journal of Experimental Child Psychology, 39,* 82–86.

Bornstein, M. H., & Stiles-Davis, J. (1984). Discrimination and memory for symmetry in young children. *Developmental Psychology, 20*(4), 637–649.

Bower, T. G. R. (1974). *Development in infancy.* San Francisco: Freeman.

Braddick, O. (1993). Segmentation versus integration in visual motion processing. *Trends in Neurosciences, 16*(7), 263–268.

Braddick, O., Atkinson, J., French, J., & Howland, H. C. (1979). A photorefractive study of infant accommodation. *Vision Research, 19*(12), 1319–1330.

Braddick, O., Atkinson, J., & Wattam-Bell, J. R. (1986). Development of the discrimination of spatial phase in infancy. *Vision Research, 26*(8), 1223–1239.

Braddick, O., Wattam-Bell, J., & Atkinson, J. (1986). Orientation-specific cortical responses develop early in infancy. *Nature, 320,* 617–619.

Brainard, M. S., & Knudsen, E. I. (1995). Dynamics of visually guided auditory plasticity in the optic tectum of the barn owl. *Journal of Neurophysiology, 73,* 595–614.

Brainard, D. H., Wandell, B. A., & Chichilnisky, E. J. (1993). Color constancy: From physics to appearance. *Current Directions in Psychological Science, 2*(5), 165–170.

Brandt, I. (1979). Patterns of early neurological development. In F. Falkner and J. M. Tanner (Eds.), *Human Growth.* Vol. 3 *Neurobiology and nutrition* (pp. 243–304). New York: Plenum Press.

Brandt, T., Dichgans, J., & Koenig, E. (1973). Differential effects of central versus peripheral vision on egocentric and exocentric motion perception. *Experimental Brain Research, 16,* 476–491.

Braunstein, M. (1976). *Depth perception through motion.* New York: Academic Press.

Brazelton, T. B. (1978). The remarkable talents of the newborn. *Birth and the Family Journal, 5*(4), 187–191.

Brazelton, T. B., Scholl, M., & Robey, J. (1966). Visual responses in the newborn. *Pediatrics, 37,* 284–290.

Bredberg, G. (1968). Cellular pattern and nerve supply of the human organ of Corti. *Acta Otolaryngologica, 236* (Suppl.).

Bregman, A. S. (1990). *Auditory scene analysis: The perceptual organization of sound.* Cambridge, MA: MIT Press.

Bronson, G. (1974). The postnatal growth of visual capacity. *Child Development, 45*(4), 873–890.

Bronson, G. W. (1982). *The scanning patterns of human infants: Implications for visual learning.* Norwood, NJ: Ablex.

Bronson, G. W. (1990). Changes in infants' visual scanning across the 2- to 14-week age period. *Journal of Experimental Child Psychology, 49*(1), 101–125.

Brookman, K. E. (1980). Ocular accommodation in human infants. Doctoral dissertation, Indiana University.

Brown, A. M. (1990). Development of visual sensitivity to light and color vision in human infants: A critical review. *Vision Research, 30*(8), 1159–1188.

Brown, A. M., Lindsey, D. T., McSweeney, E. M., & Walters, M. M. (1995). Infant luminance and chromatic contrast sensitivity: Optokinetic nystagmus data on 3-month-olds. *Vision Research, 35*(22), 3145–3160.

Brunswik, E. (1956). *Perception and the representative design of psychological experiments.* Berkeley: University of California Press.

Bryant, P. E., Jones, P., Claxton, V., & Perkins, G. M. (1972). Recognition of shapes across modalities by infants. *Nature, 240*(5379), 303–304.

Buffart, H., Leeuwenberg, E., & Restle, F. (1981). Coding theory of visual pattern completion. *Journal of Experimental Psychology: Human Perception & Performance, 7*(2), 241–274.

Bull, D., Schneider, B. A., & Trehub, S. E. (1981). The masking of octave-band noise by broad-spectrum noise: A comparison of infant and adult thresholds. *Perception & Psychophysics, 30*(2), 101–106.

Burnham, D. K. (1986). Developmental loss of speech perception: Exposure to and experience with a first language. Special Issue: Language loss. *Applied Psycholinguistics, 7*(3), 207–239.

Bushnell, E. W. (1982). Visual-tactual knowledge in 8-, 9½-, and 11-month-old infants. *Infant Behavior and Development, 5,* 63–75.

Bushnell, E. W. (1985). The decline in visually guided reaching during infancy. *Infant Behavior and Development, 8*(2), 139–155.

Bushnell, E. W. (1994). A dual-processing approach to cross-modal matching: Implications for development. In D. J. Lewkowicz and R. Lickliter (Eds.), *The development of intersensory perception: Comparative perspectives* (pp. 19–38). Hillsdale, NJ: Erlbaum.

Bushnell, E. W., & Boudreau, J. P. (1993). Motor development and the mind: The potential role of motor abilities as a determinant of aspects of perceptual development. *Child Development, 64,* 1005–1021.

Bushnell, I. W. (1979). Modification of the externality effect in young infants. *Journal of Experimental Child Psychology, 28*(2), 211-229.

Bushnell, I. W. R., Sai, F., & Mullin, J. T. (1989). Neonatal recognition of the mother's face. *British Journal of Developmental Psychology, 7,* 3–15.

Butterworth, G. (1995). Factors in visual attention eliciting manual pointing in human infancy. In H. L. Roitblat & J. Meyer (Eds.), *Comparative approaches to cognitive science* (pp. 329–338). Cambridge, MA: MIT Press.

Butterworth, G. (1996). Pointing, joint visual attention and referential communication. In J. Georgas, M. Manthovli, E. Besevegis & A. Koffevi (Eds.), *Contemporary psychology in Europe* (pp. 144–152). Seattle: Hodgrefe & Huber.

Butterworth, G., & Hicks, L. (1977). Visual proprioception and postural stability in infancy: A developmental study. *Perception, 6*(3), 255–262.

Butterworth, G., & Jarrett, N. (1991). What minds have in common is space: Spatial mechanisms serving joint visual attention in infancy. *British Journal of Developmental Psychology, 9,* 55–72.

Carey, S., & Spelke, E. (1994). Domain specific knowledge and conceptual change. In L. A. Hirschfeld & S. A. Gelman (Eds.), *Mapping the mind: Domain specificity in cognition and culture* (pp. 169–200). New York: Cambridge University Press.

Caron, A. J., Caron, R. F., & Carlson, V. R. (1979). Infant perception of the invariant shape of objects varying in slant. *Child Development, 50*(3), 716–721.

Carroll, J. J., & Gibson, E. J. (1981). Infants' differentiation of an aperture and an obstacle. Paper presented at the meeting of the Society for Research in Child Development, Boston, MA.

Casaer, P. (1993). Old and new facts about perinatal brain development. *Journal of Child Psychology & Psychiatry & Allied Disciplines, 34*(1), 101–109.

Chapanis, A., & McCleary, R. A. (1953). Interposition as a cue for the perception of relative distance. *Journal of General Psychology, 48,* 113–132.

Chomsky, N. (1980). *Rules and representations.* New York: Columbia University Press.

Clarkson, M. G., Clifton, R. K., & Morrongiello, B. A. (1985). The effects of sound duration on newborns' head orientation. *Journal of Experimental Child Psychology, 39*(1), 20–36.

Clavadetscher, J. E., Brown, A. M., Ankrum, C., & Teller, D. Y. (1988). Spectral sensitivity and chromatic discriminations in 3- and 7-week-old human infants. *Journal of the Optical Society of America A, 5*(12), 2093–2105.

Clifton, R. K., Gwiazda, J., Bauer, J. A., Clarkson, M. G., & Held, R. (1988). Growth in head size during infancy: Implications for sound localization. *Developmental Psychology, 24*(4), 477–483.

Clifton, R. K., Morrongiello, B. A., & Dowd, J. M. (1984). A developmental look at an auditory illusion: The precedence effect. *Developmental Psychobiology, 17*(5), 519–536.

Clifton, R. K., Morrongiello, B. A., Kulig, J. W., & Dowd, J. M. (1981). Newborns' orientation toward sound: Possible implications for cortical development. *Child Development, 52*(3), 833–838.

Clifton, R. K., Muir, D., Ashmead, D. H., & Clarkson, M. G. (1993). Is visually guided reaching in early infancy a myth? *Child Development, 64,* 1099–1110.

Clifton, R. K., Perris, E. E., & Bullinger, A. (1991). Infants' perception of auditory space. *Developmental Psychology, 27*(2), 187–197.

Clifton, R. K., Rochat, P., Litovsky, R. Y., & Perris, E. E. (1991). Object representation guides infants' reaching in the dark. *Journal of Experimental Psychology: Human Perception & Performance, 17*(2), 323–329.

Cohen, L. B. (1969). Observing responses, visual preferences, and habituation to visual stimuli in infants. *Journal of Experimental Child Psychology, 7,* 419–433.

Cohen, L. B., & Gelber, E. R. (1975). Infant visual memory. In L. Cohen & P. Salapatek (Eds.), *Infant perception: From sensation to cognition* (Vol. 1, pp. 347–403). New York: Academic Press.

Cohen, L. B., & Oakes, L. M. (1993). How infants perceive a simple causal event. *Developmental Psychology, 29,* 421–433.

Cohen, L. B., & Younger, B. A. (1984). Infant perception of angular relations. *Infant Behavior and Development, 7*(1), 37–47.

Condry, S. M., Haltom, M., & Neisser, U. (1977). Infant sensitivity to audio-visual discrepancy: A failure to replicate. *Bulletin of the Psychonomic Society, 9,* 431–432.

Conel, J. L. (1939–1963). *The postnatal development of the human cerebral cortex.* (Vols. 1–7). Cambridge, MA: Harvard University Press.

Cooper, R. P., & Aslin, R. N. (1989). The language environment of the young infant: Implications for early perceptual development. Special Issue: Infant perceptual development. *Canadian Journal of Psychology, 43*(2), 247–265.

Cornman, J. W. (1975). *Perception, common sense, and science.* New Haven: Yale University Press.

Craig, K. D., Whitfield, M. F., Grunau, R. V., Linton, J., & Hadjistavropoulos, H. D. (1993). Pain in the preterm neonate: Behavioural and physiological indices. *Pain, 52*(3), 287–299.

Craton, L. G., & Yonas, A. (1988). Infants' sensitivity to boundary flow information for depth at an edge. *Child Development, 59*(6), 1522–1529.

Craton, L. G., & Yonas, A. (1990). The role of motion in infants' perception of occlusion. In J. T. Enns (Ed.), *The development of attention: Research and theory* (pp. 21–46). Amsterdam: Elsevier North Holland.

Crook, C. (1987). Taste and olfaction. In P. Salapatek & L. Cohen (Eds.), *Handbook of infant perception.* Vol. 1. *From sensation to perception* pp. 237–264. Orlando: Academic Press.

Crowell, J. A., & Banks, M. S. (1993). Perceiving heading with different retinal regions and types of optic flow. *Perception & Psychophysics, 53,* 325–337.

Cutting, J. E. (1981). Coding theory adapted to gait perception. *Journal of Experimental Psychology: Human Perception & Performance, 7*(1), 71–87.

Cutting, J. E. (1986). *Perception with an eye for motion.* Cambridge, MA: MIT Press.

Dannemiller, J. L. (1989). A test of color constancy in 9- and 20-week-old human infants following simulated illuminant changes. *Developmental Psychology, 25*(2), 171–184.

Dannemiller, J. L., & Freedland, R. L. (1989). The detection of slow stimulus movement in 2- to 5-month-olds. *Journal of Experimental Child Psychology, 47*(3), 337–355.

Dannemiller, J. L., & Freedland, R. L. (1991). Detection of relative motion by human infants. *Developmental Psychology, 27*(1), 67–78.

Dannemiller, J. L., & Hanko, S. A. (1987). A test of color constancy in 4-month-old human infants. *Journal of Experimental Child Psychology, 44*(2), 255–267.

Dannemiller, J. L., & Stephens, B. R. (1988). A critical test of infant pattern preference models. *Child Development, 59*(1), 210–216.

Darwin, C. (1896). *The expression of the emotions in man and animals.* New York: Appleton-Century-Crofts.

Davis, H., Albert, M., & Barron, R. W. (1985). Detection of number or numerousness by human infants. *Science, 228*(4704), 1222.

Davis, H., & Perusse, R. (1988). Numerical competence in animals: Definitional issues, current evidence, and a new research agenda. *Behavioral and Brain Sciences, 11,* 561–615.

Day, R. H., & McKenzie, B. E. (1981). Infant perception of the invariant size of approaching and receding objects. *Developmental Psychology, 17*(5), 670–677.

Dayton, G. O., Jr., Jones, M. H., Steele, B., & Rose, M. (1964). Developmental study of coordinated eye movements in the human infant. II. An electrooculographic study of the fixation reflex in the newborn. *Archives of Ophthalmology, 71,* 871–875.

De Casper, A. J., & Fifer, W. P. (1980). Of human bonding: Newborns prefer their mothers' voices. *Science, 208*(4448), 1174–1176.

De Casper, A. J., & Prescott, P. A. (1984). Human newborns' perception of male voices: Preference, discrimination, and reinforcing value. *Developmental Psychobiology, 17*(5), 481–491.

De Casper, A. J., & Spence, M. J. (1986). Prenatal maternal speech influences newborns' perception of speech sounds. *Infant Behavior and Development, 9*(2), 133–150.

Deruelle, C., & de Schonen, S. (1991). Hemispheric asymmetries in visual pattern processing in infancy. *Brain and Cognition, 16,* 151–179.

De Schonen, S., & Mathivet, E. (1990). Hemispheric asymmetry in a face discrimination task in infants. *Child Development, 61,* 1192–1205.

DeValois, R., & DeValois, K. (1988). *Spatial vision.* New York: Oxford Press.

Diamond, A. (1988). Differences between adult and infant cognition: Is the crucial variable presence or absence of language? In L. Weiskrantz (Ed.), *Thought without language* (pp. 337–370). Oxford: Clarendon Press.

Diamond, A., & Goldman-Rakic, P. S. (1983). Comparison of performance on a Piagetian object permanence task in human infants and rhesus monkeys: Evidence for involvement of prefrontal cortex. *Neuroscience Abstracts (Part I), 9,* 641.

Dobson, V. (1980). Behavioral tests of visual acuity in infants. *International Ophthalmology Clinics, 20*(1), 233–250.

Dobson, V., & Teller, D. Y. (1978). Visual acuity in human infants: A review and comparison of behavioral and electrophysiological studies. *Vision Research, 18*(11), 1469–1483.

Dodwell, P. C. (1983). Spatial sense of the human infant. In A. Hein & M. Jeannerod (Eds.), *Spatially oriented behavior* (pp. 197–213). New York: Springer-Verlag.

Dolgin, K., Premack, D. & Spelke, E. (1980, November). *Evidence of intermodal sensory transfer capacity in infant primates.* Paper presented at the Eastern Regional meeting of the Animal Behavior Society, Binghamton, NY.

Duncker, D. K. (1929). *Uber induzierte Bewegung (Ein Beitrag zur Theorie optisch wahrgenommener Bewegung).* London: Kegan Paul Trench Trubner.

Eibl-Eibesfelt, I. (1989). *Human ethology.* New York: Adline De Gruyter.

Eimas, P. D. (1974). Auditory and linguistic processing of cues for place of articulation by infants. *Perception & Psychophysics, 16,* 513–521.

Eimas, P. D. (1978). Developmental aspects of speech perception. In R. Held, H. W. Leibowitz & H. L. Teuber (Eds.), *Handbook of sensory physiology.* Vol. 8. *Perception* (pp. 357–374). Berlin: Springer-Verlag.

Eimas, P. D., & Miller, J. L. (1980a). Contextual effects in infant speech perception. *Science, 209*(4461), 1140–1141.

Eimas, P. D., & Miller, J. L. (1980b). Discrimination of information for manner of articulation. *Infant Behavior and Development, 3*(4), 367–375.

Eimas, P. D., & Quinn, P. (1994). Studies on the formation of perceptually based basic-level categories in young infants. *Child Development, 65,* 903–917.

Eimas, P. D., Siqueland, E. R., Jusczyk, P., & Vigorito, J. (1971). Speech perception in infants. *Science, 171*(3968), 303–306.

Eisele, W. A., Berry, R. C., & G Shriner, T. H. (1975). Infant sucking response to patterns as a conjugate function of changes in the sound pressure level of auditory stimuli. *Journal of Speech and Hearing Research, 18,* 296–307.

Elliott, L. L., & Katz, D. R. (1980). Children's pure-tone detection. *Journal of the Acoustical Society of America, 67*(1), 343–344.

Engen, T., & Lipsitt, L. (1965). Decrement and recovery of responses to olfactory stimuli in the human neonate. *Journal of Comparative and Physiological Psychology, 59,* 312–316.

Epstein, W. (1982). Percept-percept couplings. *Perception, 11*(1), 75–83.

Exner, S. (1875). Uber das sehen von bewegungen und dies theories des zusammengesetzen auges. *S. B. Akad. Wiss. (Wien), 72,* 156–190.

Fagan, J. F. (1979). The origins of facial pattern recognition. In M. Bornstein & W. Kessen (Eds.), *Psychological development from infancy: Image to intention* (pp. 83–113). Hillsdale, NJ: Erlbaum.

Fantz, R. L. (1956). A method for studying early visual development. *Perceptual & Motor Skills, 6,* 13–15.

Fantz, R. L. (1958). Pattern vision in young infants. *Psychological Record, 8,* 43–47.

Fantz, R. L. (1961). The origin of form perception. *Scientific American, 204,* 66–72.

Fantz, R. L. (1963). Pattern vision in newborn infants. *Science, 140,* 296–297.

Fantz, R. L., Fagan, J. F., III, & Miranda, S. B. (1975). Early visual selectivity as a function of pattern variables, previous exposure, age from birth and conception, and expected cognitive deficit. In L. B. Cohen & P. Salapatek (Eds.), *Infant perception: From sensation to cognition.* Vol. 1. *Basic visual processes* pp. 249–345. New York: Academic Press.

Fantz, R. L., & Miranda, S. B. (1975). Newborn infant attention to form of contour. *Child Development, 46*(1), 224–228.

Fantz, R. L., & Nevis, S. (1967). Pattern preferences and perceptual-cognitive development in early infancy. *Merrill-Palmer Quarterly, 13,* 77–108.

Fantz, R. L., Ordy, J. M., & Udelf, M. S. (1962). Maturation of pattern vision in infants during the first six months. *Journal of Comparative and Physiological Psychology, 55,* 907–917.

Feinman, S. (1982). Social referencing in infancy. *Merrill Palmer Quarterly, 28*(4), 445–470.

Fernald, A. (1984). The perceptual and affective salience of mother's speech to infants. In L. Feagans, C. Garvey & R. Golinkoff (Eds.), *The origins and growth of communication* (pp. 5–29). Norwood, NJ: Ablex.

Fernald, A. (1985). Four-month-old infants prefer to listen to motherese. *Infant Behavior and Development, 8*(2), 181–195.

Fernald, A. (1993). Approval and disapproval: Infant responsiveness to vocal affect in familiar and unfamiliar languages. *Child Development, 64*(3), 657–674.

Fernald, A., & Kuhl, P. K. (1987). Acoustic determinants of infant preference for motherese speech. *Infant Behavior and Development, 10*(3), 279–293.

Fernald, A., & Mazzie, C. (1991). Prosody and focus in speech to infants and adults. *Developmental Psychology, 27*(2), 209–221.

Fernald, A., & Simon, T. (1984). Expanded intonation contours in mothers' speech to newborns. *Developmental Psychology, 20*(1), 104–113.

Fernald, A., Taeschner, T., Dunn, J., Papousek, M., de Boysson-Bardies, B., & Fukui, I. (1989). A cross-language study of prosodic modifications in mothers' and fathers' speech to preverbal infants. *Journal of Child Language, 16*(3), 477–501.

Field, D. J., Hayes, A., & Hess, R. F. (1993). Contour integration by the human visual system: Evidence for a local "association field." *Vision Research, 33,* 173–193.

Field, J. (1976). The adjustment of reaching behavior to object distance in early infancy. *Child Development, 47*(1), 304–308.

Field, T. M. (1979). Visual and cardiac responses to animate and inanimate faces by young term and preterm infants. *Child Development, 50,* 188–194.

Field, T. M. (1990). *Infancy.* Cambridge, MA: Harvard University Press.

Field, T. M., Goldstein, S., Bega-Lahr, N., & Porter, K. (1986). Changes in imitative behavior during early infancy. *Infant Behavior and Development, 9,* 415–421.

Field, T. M., Woodson, R., Greenberg, R., & Cohen, D. (1982). Discrimination and imitation of facial expressions by neonates. *Science, 218,* 179–181.

Field, T. M., Woodson, R., Greenberg, R., Garcia, R., & Collins, K. (1983). Discrimination and imitation of facial expressions by term and preterm neonates. *Infant Behavior and Development, 6,* 485–490.

Fodor, J. A. (1983). *The modularity of mind: An essay on faculty psychology.* Cambridge, MA: MIT Press.

Fodor, J. A., & Pylyshyn, Z. W. (1981). How direct is visual perception? Some reflections on Gibson's "ecological approach." *Cognition, 9*(2), 139–196.

Fox, R., Aslin, R. N., Shea, S. L., & Dumais, S. T. (1980). Stereopsis in human infants. *Science, 207*(4428), 323–324.

Fox, R., & McDaniel, C. (1982). The perception of biological motion by human infants. *Science, 218,* 486–487.

Fraiberg, S. (1968). Parallel and divergent patterns in blind and sighted infants. *Psychoanalytic Study of the Child, 23,* 264–300.

Freedland, R. L., & Dannemiller, J. L. (1987). Detection of stimulus motion in 5-month-old infants. Special Issue: The ontogenesis of perception. *Journal of Experimental Psychology: Human Perception & Performance, 13*(4), 566–576.

Frye, D., Rawling, P., Moore, C., & Myers, I. (1983). Object-person discrimination and communication at 3 and 10 months. *Developmental Psychology, 19,* 303–309.

Ganon, E. C., & Schwartz, K. B. (1980). Perception of internal elements of compound figures by one-month-old infants. *Journal of Experimental Child Psychology, 30*(1), 159–170.

Garner, W. R., & Sutliff, D. (1974). The effect of goodness on encoding time in visual pattern discrimination. *Perception & Psychophysics, 16*(3), 426–430.

Geisler, W. S. (1984). Physical limits of acuity and hyperacuity. *Journal of the Optical Society of America, 1,* 775–782.

Geisler, W. S. (1989). Sequential ideal-observer analysis of visual discriminations. *Psychological Review, 96,* 267–314.

Gelman, R., Durgin, F., & Kaufman, L. (1995). Distinguishing between animates and inanimates: Not by motion alone. In D. Sperber, D. Premack, and A. J. Premack (Eds.), *Causal cognition: A multidisciplinary debate.* Symposia of the Fyssen Foundation (pp. 150–184). New York: Clarendon Press/Oxford University Press.

Gelman, R., & Gallistel, C. R. (1978). *The child's understanding of number.* Cambridge, MA: Harvard University Press.

Ghim, H. R. (1990). Evidence for perceptual organization in infants: Perception of subjective contours by young infants. *Infant Behavior and Development, 13*(2), 221–248.

Ghim, H. R., & Eimas, P. D. (1988). Global and local processing by 3- and 4-month-old infants. *Perception & Psychophysics, 43*(2), 165–171.

Gibson, E. J. (1969). *Principles of perceptual learning and development.* New York: Appleton-Century-Crofts.

Gibson, E. J. (1984). Perceptual development from an ecological approach. In M. Lamb, A. Brown, & B. Rogoff (Ed.), *Advances in developmental psychology* (Vol. 3, pp. 243–285). Hillsdale, NJ: Erlbaum.

Gibson, E. J., Owsley, C. J., & Johnston, J. (1978). Perception of invariants by five-month-old infants: Differentiation of two types of motion. *Developmental Psychology, 14*(4), 407–415.

Gibson, E. J., Owsley, C. J., Walker, A., & Megaw-Nyce, J. (1979). Development of the perception of invariants: Substance and shape. *Perception, 8*(6), 609–619.

Gibson, E. J., Riccio, G., Schmuckler, M. A., Stoffregen, T. A., Rosenberg, D., & Taormina, J. (1987). Detection of the traversability of surfaces by crawling and walking infants. Special Issue: The ontogenesis of perception. *Journal of Experimental Psychology: Human Perception & Performance, 13*(4), 533–544.

Gibson, E. J., & Walk, R. D. (1960). The visual cliff. *Scientific American, 202*, 64–71.

Gibson, E. J., & Walker, A. S. (1984). Development of knowledge of visual-tactual affordances of substance. *Child Development, 55*(2), 453–460.

Gibson, J. J. (1950). *The perception of the visual world.* New York: Appleton-Century-Crofts.

Gibson, J. J. (1966). *The senses considered as perceptual systems.* Boston: Houghton Mifflin.

Gibson, J. J. (1979). *The ecological approach to visual perception.* Boston: Houghton Mifflin.

Gibson, J. J., & Gibson, E. J. (1955). Perceptual learning: Differentiation or enrichment? *Psychological Review, 62*, 32–41.

Gibson, J. J., & Gibson, E. J. (1957). Continuous perspective transformations and the perception of rigid motion. *Journal of Experimental Psychology, 54*, 129–138.

Gibson, J. J., Kaplan, G. A., Reynolds, H. N., Jr., & Wheeler, K. (1969). The change from visible to invisible: A study of optical transitions. *Perception & Psychophysics, 5*(2), 113–116.

Gilchrist, A. L., Delman, S., & Jacobsen, A. (1983). The classification and integration of edges as critical to the perception of reflectance and illumination. *Perception & Psychophysics, 33*(5), 425–436.

Ginsburg, A. P. (1978). Visual information processing based on spatial filters constrained by biological data. Doctoral dissertation, University of Cambridge.

Gogel, W. C. (1977). An indirect measure of perceived distance from oculomotor cues. *Perception & Psychophysics, 21*(1), 3–11.

Gogel, W. C. (1978). Size, distance, and depth perception. In E. C. Carterette & M. P. Friedman (Eds.), *Handbook of Perception* (Vol. 9, pp. 299–333). New York: Academic Press.

Gogel, W. (1980). The sensing of retinal motion. *Perception & Psychophysics, 28*(2), 155–163.

Gogel, W. C. (1982). Analysis of the perception of motion concomitant with a lateral motion of the head. *Perception & Psychophysics, 32*(3), 241–250.

Goldstein, B. E. (1989). *Sensation and perception.* Belmont, CA: Wadsworth.

Goldstone, R. L. (1994). Influences of categorization on perceptual discrimination. *Journal of Experimental Psychology: General, 123*, 178–200.

Goodale, M. A., & Milner, A. D. (1992). Separate visual pathways for perception and action. *Trends in Neuroscience, 15*, 20–25.

Goodman, N. (1951). *The structure of appearance.* Cambridge: Harvard University Press.

Goodsitt, J. V., Morgan, J. L., & Kuhl, P. K. (1993). Perceptual strategies in prelingual speech segmentation. *Journal of Child Language, 20*(2), 229–252.

Goodsitt, J. V., Morse, P. A., ver Hoeve, J. N., & Cowan, N. (1984). Infant speech recognition in multisyllabic contexts. *Child Development, 55*(3), 903–910.

Goren, C., Sarty, M., & Wu, P. (1975). Visual following and pattern discrimination of face-like stimuli by newborn infants. *Pediatrics, 56*, 544–549.

Gorman, J. J., Cogan, D. G., & Gellis, S. S. (1957). An apparatus for grading the visual acuity of infants on the basis of opticokinetic nystagmus. *Pediatrics, 19*, 1088–1092.

Gorman, J. J., Cogan, D. G., & Gellis, S. S. (1959). A device for testing visual acuity in infants. *Sight-Saving Review, 29*, 80–84.

Gottlieb, G. (1971). Ontogenesis of sensory function in birds and mammals. In E. Tobach, L. Aronson and E. Shaw (Eds.). *The biopsychology of development* (pp. 67–128). New York: Academic Press.

Granrud, C. E. (1986). Binocular vision and spatial perception in 4- and 5-month-old infants. *Journal of Experimental Psychology: Human Perception & Performance, 12,* 36–49.

Granrud, C. E. (1987). Size constancy in newborn human infants. *Investigative Ophthalmology and Visual Science, 28* (Supp.), 5.

Granrud, C. E., Haake, R. J., & Yonas, A. (1985). Infants' sensitivity to familiar size: The effect of memory on spatial perception. *Perception & Psychophysics, 37*(5), 459–466.

Granrud, C. E., & Yonas, A. (1984). Infants' perception of pictorially specified interposition. *Journal of Experimental Child Psychology, 37*(3), 500–511.

Granrud, C. E., Yonas, A., & Opland, E. A. (1985). Infants' sensitivity to the depth cue of shading. *Perception & Psychophysics, 37*(5), 415–419.

Granrud, C. E., Yonas, A., & Pettersen, L. (1984). A comparison of monocular and binocular depth perception in 5- and 7-month-old infants. *Journal of Experimental Child Psychology, 38*(1), 19–32.

Granrud, C. E., Yonas, A., Smith, I. M., Arterberry, M. E., Glicksman, M. L., & Sorknes, A. C. (1984). Infants' sensitivity to accretion and deletion of texture as information for depth at an edge. *Child Development, 55,* 1630–1636.

Greenough, W. T., Black, J. E., & Wallace, C. S. (1987). Experience and brain development. *Child Development, 58*(3), 539–559.

Greenough, W. T., Volkmar, F. R., & Juraska, J. M. (1973). Effects of rearing complexity on dendritic branching in frontolateral and temporal cortex of the rat. *Experimental Neurology, 41*(2), 371–378.

Gregory, R. L. (1972). *Eye and brain: The psychology of seeing* (2d ed.). London: Weidenfeld and Nicolson.

Grieser, D. L., & Kuhl, P. K. (1988). Maternal speech to infants in a tonal language: Support for universal prosodic features in motherese. *Developmental Psychology, 24*(1), 14–20.

Grieser, D., & Kuhl, P. K. (1989). Categorization of speech by infants: Support for speech-sound prototypes. *Developmental Psychology, 25*(4), 577–588.

Grossberg, S. (1994). 3-D vision and figure-ground separation by visual cortex. *Perception & Psychophysics, 55*(1), 48–120.

Grunau, R. V., Johnston, C. C., & Craig, K. D. (1990). Neonatal facial and cry responses to invasive and non-invasive procedures. *Pain, 42*(3), 295–305.

Guillery, R. W. (1972). Binocular competition in the control of geniculate cell growth. *Journal of Comparative Neurology, 14,* 117–29.

Gunderson, V. M. (1983). Development of cross-modal recognition in infant pigtail monkeys (Macaca nemestrina). *Developmental Psychology, 19*(3), 398–404.

Gunderson, V. M., Yonas, A., Sargent, P. L., & Grant-Webster, K. S. (1993). Infant macaque monkeys respond to pictorial depth. *Psychological Science, 4*(2), 93–98.

Gunnar, M. R., & Stone, C. (1984). The effects of positive maternal affect of infant responses to pleasant, ambiguous, and fear-provoking toys. *Child Development, 8*(1), 25–33.

Hainline, L., Riddell, P., Grose-Fifer, J., & Abramov, I. (1992). Development of accommodation and convergence in infancy. Special Issue: Normal and abnormal visual development in infants and children. *Behavioural Brain Research, 49*(1), 33–50.

Haith, M. M. (1978), Visual competence in ealy infancy. In R. Held, H. Leibowitz and H-L. Teuber (Eds.), *Handbook of sensory physiology.* Vol. 8. *Perception* (pp. 311–356). Berlin: Springer-Verlag.

Haith, M. M. (1980). *Rules that babies look by: The organization of newborn visual activity.* Hillsdale, NJ: Erlbaum.

Haith, M. M., Bergman, T., & Moore, M. J. (1977). Eye contact and face scanning in early infancy. *Science, 198,* 853–855.

Hamer, R. D., Alexander, K. R., & Teller, D. Y. (1982). Rayleigh discriminations in young human infants. *Vision Research, 22*(5), 575–587.

Hamer, R. D., & Norcia, A. M. (1994). The development of motion sensitivity during the first year of life. *Vision Research, 34,* 2387–2402.

Hanna, E., & Meltzoff, A. N. (1993). Peer imitation by toddlers in laboratory, home, and day-care contexts: Implications for social learning and memory. *Developmental Psychology, 29*(4), 701–710.

Harding, C. G., & Golinkoff, R. M. (1979). The origins of intentional vocalizations in prelinguistic infants. *Child Development, 50,* 33–40.

Harris, P. (1983). Infant cognition. In M. M. Haith & J. J. Campos (Eds.), *Cognitive development* (pp. 689–782). New York: Wiley.

Harris, P. L. (1987). The development of search. In P. Salapatek & L. Cohen (Eds.), *Handbook of infant perception: From perception to cognition* (pp. 155–207). Orlando: Academic Press.

Harter, M. R., Deaton, F. K., & Odom, J. V. (1977). Maturation of evoked potentials and visual preference in six 45-day-old infants: Effect of check size, visual acuity, and refractive error. *Electroencephalography and clinical Neurophysiology, 42,* 595–607.

Hayes, J. R., & Clark, H. H. (1970). Experiments on the segmentation of an artificial speech analogue. In J. R. Hayes (Ed.), *Cognition and the development of language* (pp. 221–234). New York: Wiley.

Haynes, H., White, B. L., & Held, R. (1965). Visual accommodation in human infants. *Science, 148,* 528–530.

Hebb, D. O. (1949). *The organization of behavior.* New York: Wiley.

Heck, J., & Zetterstrom, B. (1958). Analyse des photopischen Flimmerelektroretinogramms bei Neugeborenen. *Ophthalmologica, 135,* 205–210.

Heinemann, E. G., Tulving, E., & Nachmias, J. (1959). The effect of oculomotor adjustments on apparent size. *American Journal of Psychology, 72,* 32–45.

Held, R. (1955). Shifts in binaural localization after prolonged exposures to atypical combinations of stimuli. *American Journal of Psychology, 68,* 526–548.

Held, R. (1985). Binocular vision: Behavioral and neuronal development. In J. Mehler & R. Fox (Eds.), *Neonate cognition: Beyond the blooming buzzing confusion* (pp. 37–44). Hillsdale, NJ: Erlbaum.

Held, R. (1988). Normal visual development and its deviations. In G. Lennerstrand, G. Von Noorden, & E. Campos (Eds.), *Strabismus and amblyopia* (pp. 247–257). London: Macmillan.

Held, R. (1989). Perception and its neuronal mechanisms. Special Issue: Neurobiology of cognition. *Cognition, 33*(1–2), 139–154.

Held, R. (1993). What can rates of development tell us about underlying mechanisms? In C. Granrud (Ed.), *Visual perception and cognition in infancy. Carnegie Mellon symposia on cognition* (pp. 75–89). Hillsdale, NJ: Erlbaum.

Held, R., Birch, E., & Gwiazda, J. (1980). Stereoacuity in human infants. *Proceedings of the National Academy of Sciences, USA, 77,* 5572–5574.

Held, R., Dichgans, J., & Bauer, J. (1975). Characteristics of moving visual scenes influencing spatial orientation. *Vision Research, 15*(3), 357–365.

Held, R., & Hein, A. (1963). Movement produced stimulation in the development of visually guided behavior. *Journal of Comparative and Physiological Psychology, 56,* 872–876.

Helmholtz, H. v. (1965). *Handbook of physiological optics.* Vol. 3. In R. Herrnstein and E. G. Boring (Eds.). *A sourcebook in the history of psychology* (pp. 151–163). Cambridge, MA: Harvard University Press. (Original Work Published 1885).

Hering, E. (1861–1864). *Beitrage zur physiologie.* Leipzig: Engelmann.

Hershberger, W. (1970). Attached shadow orientation perceived as depth by chickens reared in an environment illuminated from below. *Journal of Comparative and Physiological Psychology, 73,* 407–411.

Hess, E. H. (1956). Space perception in the chick. *Scientific American, 195,* 71–80.

Hickey, T. L., & Peduzzi, J. D. (1987). Structure and development of the visual system. In P. Salapatek & L. B. Cohen (Eds.), *Handbook of infant perception: From sensation to perception* (pp. 1–42). New York: Academic Press.

Hillenbrand, J. (1983). Perceptual organization of speech sounds by infants. *Journal of Speech and Hearing Research, 26*(2), 268–282.

Hillenbrand, J. (1984). Speech perception by infants: Categorization based on nasal consonant place of articulation. *Journal of the Acoustical Society of America, 75,* 1613–1622.

Hirsh-Pasek, K., Kemler Nelson, D. G., Jusczyk, P. W., Cassidy, K. W., Druss, B., & Kennedy, L. (1987). Clauses are perceptual units for young infants. *Cognition, 26*(3), 269–286.

Hobbes, T. (1651/1974). *Leviathan.* Baltimore: Penguin.

Hochberg, C. B., & Hochberg, J. E. (1953). Familiar size and subception in perceived depth. *Journal of Psychology, 36,* 341–345.

Hochberg, J. (1968). In the mind's eye. In R. N. Haber (Ed.). *Contemporary theory and research in visual perception* (pp. 309–331). New York: Holt, Rinehart & Winston.

Hochberg, J. (1971). Perception II. Space and movement. In J. W. Kling & L. A. Riggs (Eds.), *Woodworth and Schlosberg's experimental psychology* (pp. 475–550). New York: Holt, Rinehart and Winston.

Hochberg, J. (1974). Higher-order stimuli and inter-response coupling in the perception of the visual world. In R. B. McLeod & H. L. Pick (Eds.), *Perception: Essays in honor of J. J. Gibson* (pp. 17–39). Ithaca, NY: Cornell University Press.

Hochberg, J. (1978). *Perception* (2d ed.). Englewood Cliffs, NJ: Prentice-Hall.

Hochberg, J. (1981). On cognition in perception: Perceptual coupling and unconscious inference. *Cognition, 10*(1–3), 127–134.

Hoffman, D. D., & Flinchbaugh, B. E. (1982). The interpretation of biological motion. *Biological Cybernetics, 42*(3).

Holloway, R. L., Jr. (1966). Dendritic branching: Some preliminary results of training and complexity in rat visual cortex. *Brain Research, 2*(4), 393–396.

Holway, A. H., & Boring, E. G. (1941). Determinants of apparent visual size with distance variant. *American Journal of Psychology, 54,* 21–37.

Hood, B., Atkinson, J., Braddick, O., & Wattam-Bell, J. (1992). Orientation selectivity in infancy: Behavioural evidence for temporal sensitivity. *Perception, 21*(3), 351–354.

Horowitz, F. D. (Ed.) (1975). Visual attention, auditory stimulation, and language discrimination in young infants. *Monographs of the Society for Research in Child Development, 39,* 1–140.

Horsten, G. P. M., & Winkelman, J. E. (1964). Electroretinographic critical fusion frequency of the retina in relation to the histological development in man and animals. *Ophthalmologica, 18,* 515–521.

Howland, H. C. (1982). Infant eyes: Optics and accommodation. *Current Eye Research, 2*(3), 217–224.

Howland, H. C., Dobson, V., & Sayles, N. (1987). Accommodation in infants as measured by photorefraction. *Vision Research, 27*(12), 2141–2152.

Hubel, D. H., & Wiesel, T. N. (1962). Receptive fields, binocular interaction and functional architecture in the cat's visual cortex. *Journal of Physiology (London), 160,* 106–154.

Hubel, D. H., & Wiesel, T. N. (1965). Receptive fields and functional architecture in two non-striate visual areas (18 and 19) of the cat. *Journal of Neurophysiology, 28,* 229–289.

Hubel, D. H., & Wiesel, T. N. (1970). Stereoscopic vision in macaque monkey. Cells sensitive to binocular depth in area 18 of the macaque monkey cortex. *Nature, 225,* 41–42.

Hubel, D. H., & Wiesel, T. N. (1979). Brain mechanisms of vision. *Scientific American, 241*(3), 150–162.

Humphrey, K., & Tees, R. C. (1980). Auditory-visual coordination in infancy: Some limitations of the preference methodology. *Bulletin of the Psychonomic Society, 16*(3), 213–
216.

Huttenlocher, P. R. (1990). Morphometric study of human cerebral cortex development.
Neuropsychologia, 28, 517–527.

Huttenlocher, P. R. (1994). Synaptogenesis in human cerebral cortex. In G. Dawson & K. W.
Fischer (Eds.), *Human behavior and the developing brain* (pp. 137–152). New York:
Oxford University Press.

Ittelson, W. H. (1953). A note on "Familiar size and the perception of depth." *Journal of
Psychology, 35,* 235–240.

Jacobson, M. (1991). *Developmental neurobiology* (3rd ed.). New York: Plenum Press.

Jacobson, S. W. (1979). Matching behavior in the young infant. *Child Development, 50,* 425–
430.

James, W. (1890). *The principles of psychology* (Vol. 2). New York: Holt.

Jeffrey, W. E. (1968). The orienting reflex and attention in cognitive development. *Psychological Review, 75,* 323–334.

Johansson, G. (1950). *Configurations in event perception.* Uppsala, Sweden: Almkvist and
Wiksell.

Johansson, G. (1970). On theories for visual space perception: A letter to Gibson. *Scandinavian Journal of Psychology, 11*(2), 67–74.

Johansson, G. (1975). Visual motion perception. *Scientific American, 232*(6), 76–88.

Johansson, G. (1977). Studies on visual perception of locomotion. *Perception, 6*(4), 365–
376.

Johansson, G., von Hofsten, C., & Jansson, G. (1980). Event perception. *Annual Review of
Psychology, 31,* 27–63.

Johnson, M. H. (1990). Cortical maturation and the development of visual attention in early
infancy. *Journal of Cognitive Neuroscience, 2*(2), 81–95.

Johnson, M. H., Dziurawiec, S., Ellis, H., & Morton, J. (1991). Newborns' preferential tracking
of face-like stimuli and its subsequent decline. *Cognition, 40,* 1–19.

Johnson, M. H., & Morton, J. (1991). *Biology and cognitive development.* Oxford: Blackwell.

Johnson, S. P., & Aslin, R. N. (1995). Perception of object unity in 2-month-old infants.
Developmental Psychology, 31(5), 739–745.

Jones, S. S., & Smith, L. B. (1993). The place of perception in children's concepts. *Cognitive
Development, 8*(2), 113–139.

Julesz, B. (1971). *Foundations of cyclopean perception.* Chicago: University of Chicago Press.

Jusczyk, P. W., & Aslin, R. A. (1995). Infants' detection of the sound patterns of words in
fluent speech. *Cognitive Development, 29,* 1–23.

Jusczyk, P. W., Cutler, A., & Redanz, N. J. (1993). Infants' preference for the predominant
stress patterns of English words. *Child Development, 64*(3), 675–687.

Jusczyk, P. W., Friederici, A. D., Wessels, J. M., Svenkerud, V. Y., & Jusczyk, A. M. (1993).
Infants' sensitivity to the sound patterns of native language words. *Journal of Memory
and Language, 32*(3), 402–420.

Jusczyk, P. W., Pisoni, D. B., Walley, A. C., & Murray, J. (1980). Discrimination of relative
onset time of two component tones by infants. *Journal of Acoustical Society of America,
67,* 262–270.

Kaga, K., & Tanaka, Y. (1980). Auditory brainstem response and behavioral audiometry:
Developmental correlates. *Archives of Otolaryngology, 106,* 564–566.

Kaitz, M. K., Meschulach-Sarfaty, O., Auerbach, J., & Eidelman, A. (1988). A reexamination
of newborns' ability to imitate facial expression. *Developmental Psychology, 24,* 3–7.

Kajiura, H., Cowart, B. J., & Beauchamp, G. K. (1992). Early developmental change in bitter
taste responses in human infants. *Developmental Psychobiology, 25,* 375–386.

Kandel, E. R., Jessell, T. M., & Schwartz, J. H. (1991). *Principles of neural science* (3rd ed.). New York: Elsevier Science.

Kanizsa, G. (1979). *Organization in vision.* New York: Praeger.

Kant, I. (1781/1902). *Critique of pure reason* (F. Max Muller, Trans.) (2nd ed.). New York: Macmillan.

Kaplan, G. (1969). Kinetic disruption of optical texture: The perception of depth at an edge. *Perception & Psychophysics, 6,* 193–198.

Karmel, B. Z. (1974). Contour effects and pattern preferences in infants: A reply to Greenberg and O'Donnell (1972). *Child Development, 45*(1), 196–199.

Karzon, R. G. (1985). Discrimination of polysyllabic sequences by one- to four-month-old infants. *Journal of Experimental Child Psychology, 39*(2), 326–342.

Kaufman, E. L., Lord, M. W., Reese, T. W., & Volkmann, J. (1949). The discrimination of visual number. *American Journal of Psychology, 62,* 498–525.

Kaufmann, F., Stucki, M., & Kaufmann-Hayoz, R. (1985). Development of infants' sensitivity for slow and rapid motions. *Infant Behavior and Development, 8*(1), 89–98.

Kaufman, L. (1974). *Sight and mind.* New York: Oxford University Press.

Kaufman, L., & Richards, W. (1969). Spontaneous fixation tendencies for visual forms. *Perception & Psychophysics, 5*(2), 85–88.

Kaufmann-Hayoz, R., Kaufmann, F., & Stucki, M. (1986). Kinetic contours in infants' visual perception. *Child Development, 57*(2). 292–299.

Kaufmann-Hayoz, R., Kaufmann, F., & Walther, D. (1988). Perception of kinetic subjective contours at 5 and 8 months. Paper presented at the Sixth International Conference on Infant Studies, Washington, DC.

Kellman, P. J. (1984). Perception of three-dimensional form by human infants. *Perception & Psychophysics, 36*(4), 353–358.

Kellman, P. J. (1988). Theories of perception and research in perceptual development. In A. Yonas (Ed.). *Perceptual development in infancy: The Minnesota symposia on child psychology* (Vol. 20, pp. 267–281). Hillsdale, NJ: Erlbaum.

Kellman, P. J. (1992). Perception, conception, and infant self-awareness. *Psychological Inquiry, 3*(2), 121–122.

Kellman, P. J. (1993). Kinematic foundations of infant visual perception. In C. Granrud (Ed.), *Visual perception and cognition in infancy. Carnegie Mellon symposia on cognition* (pp. 121–173). Hillsdale, NJ: Erlbaum.

Kellman, P. J. (1995). Ontogenesis of space and motion perception. In W. Epstein & S. Rogers (Eds.), *Handbook of perception and cognition* (Vol. 5, pp. 327–364). New York: Academic Press.

Kellman, P. J. (1996). The origins of object perception. In R. Gelman, & T. K. Au (Eds.), *Perceptual and cognitive development. Handbook of perception and cognition* (2nd ed., pp. 3–48). San Diego: Academic Press.

Kellman, P. J. and Banks, M. S. (1997). Infant visual perception. In R. Siegler and D. Kuhn (Eds.), *Handbook of child psychology* (5th ed.), *Cognition, perception, and language* (Vol. 2, pp. 103–146). New York: Wiley.

Kellman, P. J., Gleitman, H., & Spelke, E. S. (1987). Object and observer motion in the perception of objects by infants. Special Issue: The ontogenesis of perception. *Journal of Experimental Psychology: Human Perception & Performance, 13*(4), 586–593.

Kellman, P. J., Hofsten, C. von, Vandewalle, & Condry, K. (1990, April). Perception of motion and stability during observer motion by pre-stereoscopic infants. Paper presented at the Seventh International Conference on Infant Studies, Montreal, Quebec.

Kellman, P. J. & Kaiser, M. K. (1994). Perceptual learning modules in flight training. *Proceedings of the 38th Annual Meeting of the Human Factors and Ergonomics Society,* 1183–1187.

Kellman, P. J., & Shipley, T. F. (1991). A theory of visual interpolation in object perception. *Cognitive Psychology, 23*(2), 141–221.

Kellman, P. J., & Shipley, T. F. (1992). Perceiving objects across gaps in space and time. *Current Directions in Psychological Science, 1*(6), 193–199.

Kellman, P. J., & Short, K. R. (1987a, June). Infant perception of partly occluded objects: The problem of rotation. Paper presented at the Third International Conference on Event Perception and Action, Uppsala, Sweden.

Kellman, P. J., & Short, K. R. (1987b). Development of three-dimensional form perception. Special Issue: The ontogenesis of perception. *Journal of Experimental Psychology: Human Perception & Performance, 13*, 545–557.

Kellman, P. J., & Spelke, E. S. (1983). Perception of partly occluded object in infancy. *Cognitive Psychology, 15*(4), 483–524.

Kellman, P. J., Spelke, E. S., & Short, K. R. (1986). Infant perception of object unity from translatory motion in depth and vertical translation. *Child Development, 57*(1), 72–86.

Kellman, P. J., & von Hofsten, C. (1992). The world of the moving infant: Perception of motion, stability, and space. In C. K. Rovee-Collier and L. Lipsitt (Eds.), *Advances in infancy research, 7.* (pp. 147–184). Norwood, NJ: Ablex.

Kellman, P. J., Yin, C., & Shipley, T. F. (in press). A common mechanism for illusory and occluded object completion. *Journal of Experimental Psychology: Human Perception & Performance.*

Kemler Nelson, D. G., Hirsh-Pasek, K., Jusczyk, P. W., & Cassidy, K. W. (1989). How the prosodic cues in motherese might assist language learning. *Journal of Child Language, 16*(1), 55–68.

Kestenbaum, R., & Nelson, C. A. (1990). The recognition and categorization of upright and inverted emotional expressions by 7-month-old infants. *Infant Behavior and Development, 13,* 597–511.

Kim, I. K., & Spelke, E. S. (1992). Infants' sensitivity to effects of gravity on visible object motion. *Journal of Experimental Psychology: Human Perception & Performance, 18*(2), 385–393.

Kisilevsky, B. S., Stach, D. M., & Muir, D. W. (1991). Fetal and infant response to tactile stimulation. In M. J. S. Weiss & P. R. Zelazo (Eds.), *Newborn attention: Biological constrains and the influence of experience* (pp. 63–98). Norwood, NJ: Ablex.

Klatzky, R. L., & Lederman, S. J. (1993). Spatial and nonspatial avenues to object recognition by the human haptic system. In N. Eilan, R. A. McCarthy, & B. Brewer (Eds.), *Spatial representation: Problems in philosophy and psychology* (pp. 191–205). Oxford: Blackwell.

Klein, A. J. (1984). Frequency and age-dependent auditory evoked potential thresholds in infants. *Hearing Research, 16*(3), 291–297.

Klein, R. P., & Jennings, K. D. (1979). Responses to social and inanimate stimuli in early infancy. *Journal of Genetic Psychology, 135,* 3–9.

Kleiner, K. A. (1987). Amplitude and phase spectra as indices of infants' pattern preferences. *Infant Behavior and Development, 10,* 49–59.

Kleiner, K. A. (1990). Models of neonates' preferences for facelike patterns: A response to Morton, Johnson, and Maurer. *Infant Behavior and Development, 13*(1), 105–108.

Kleiner, K. A., & Banks, M. S. (1987). Stimulus energy does not account for 2-month-olds' face preferences. *Journal of Experimental Psychology: Human Perception & Performance, 13,* 594–600.

Klinnert, M. D. (1984). The regulation of infant behavior by maternal facial expression. *Infant Behavior and Development, 7,* 447–465.

Klinnert, M. D., Emde, R. N., Butterfield, P., & Campos, J. J. (1986). Social referencing: The infant's use of emotional signals from a friendly adult with mother present. *Developmental Psychology, 22*(4), 427–432.

Knudsen, E. I. (1983). Early auditory experience aligns the auditory map of space in the optic tectum of the barn owl. *Science, 222*(4626), 939–942.

Knudsen, E. I. (1984). The role of auditory experience in the development and maintenance of sound localization. *Trends in Neurosciences, 7*(9), 326–330.

Knudsen, E. I., & Brainard, M. S. (1995). Creating a unified representation of visual and auditory space in the brain. *Annual Review of Neuroscience, 18*, 19–43.

Knudsen, E. I., & Knudsen, P. F. (1985). Vision guides the adjustment of auditory localization in young barn owls. *Science, 230*(4725), 545–548.

Knudsen, E. I., Knudsen, P. F., & Esterly, S. D. (1982). Early auditory experience modifies sound localization in barn owls. *Nature, 295*(5846), 238–240.

Koffka, K. (1935). *Principles of Gestalt Psychology.* New York: Harcourt, Brace & World.

Kostovic, I., & Goldman-Rakic, P. S. (1983). Transient cholinesterase staining in the mediodorsal nucleus of the thalamus and its connections in the developing human and monkey brain. *Journal of Comparative Neurology, 219*(4), 431–447.

Kremenitzer, J. P., Vaughan, H. G., Kurtzberg, D., & Dowling, K. (1979). Smooth-pursuit eye movements in the newborn infant. *Child Development, 50*(2), 442–448.

Kuhl, P. K. (1979). Speech perception in early infancy: Perceptual constancy for spectrally dissimilar vowel categories. *Journal of the Acoustical Society of America, 66*, 1668–1679.

Kuhl, P. K. (1983). Perception of auditory equivalence classes for speech in early infancy. *Infant Behavior and Development, 6*(3), 263–285.

Kuhl, P. K. (1987). Perception of speech and sound in early infancy. In P. Salapatek & L. Cohen (Eds.), *Handbook of infant perception.* Vol. 1. *From sensation of perception* (pp. 275–382). Orlando: Academic Press.

Kuhl, P. K., & Meltzoff, A. N. (1982). The bimodal perception of speech in infancy. *Science, 218*(4577), 1138–1141.

Kuhl, P. K., & Meltzoff, A. N. (1984). The intermodal representation of speech in infants. *Infant Behavior and Development, 7*(3), 361–381.

Kuhl, P. K., & Meltzoff, A. N. (1988). Speech as an intermodal object of perception. In A. Yonas (Ed.), *Perceptual development in infancy. The Minnesota symposia on child psychology* (Vol. 20, pp. 235–266). Hillsdale, NJ: Erlbaum.

Kuhl, P. K., & Miller, J. D. (1975). Speech perception by the chinchilla: Voiced-voiceless distinction in alveolar plosive consonants. *Science, 190*(4209), 69–72.

Kuhl, P. K., & Miller, J. D. (1982). Discrimination of auditory target dimensions in the presence or absence of variation in a second dimension by infants. *Perception & Psychophysics, 31*(3), 279–292.

Kuhl, P. K., & Padden, D. M. (1982). Enhanced discriminability at the phonetic boundaries for the voicing feature in macaques. *Perception & Psychophysics, 32*, 542–550.

Kuhl, P. K., Williams, K. A., Lacerda, F., Stevens, K. N., & Lindblom, B. (1992). Linguistic experience alters phonetic perception in infants by 6 months of age. *Science, 255*(5044), 606–608.

Kuypers, H. G. J. M. (1962). Corticospinal connections: Postnatal development in rhesus monkey. *Science, 138*, 678–680.

Kuypers, H. G. J. M. (1973). The anatomical organization of the descending pathways and their contributions to motor control especially in primates. In J. E. Desmedt (Ed.), *New developments in electromyography and clinical neuropsychology* (Vol. 3, pp. 38–68). Basel: Karger.

Langlois, J. H., Roggman, L. A., & Rieser-Danner, L. A. (1990). Infants' differential social responses to attractive and unattractive faces. *Developmental Psychology, 26*, 153–159.

Lasky, R. E., Klein, R. E., & Martinez, S. (1974). Age and sex discriminations in five- and six-month-old infants. *Journal of Psychology, 88*, 317–324.

Lasky, R. E., Syrdal-Lasky, A., & Klein, R. E. (1975). VOT discrimination by four- to six-and-a-half-month-old infants from Spanish environments. *Journal of Experimental Child Psychology, 20*(2), 215–225.

Lauffer, H., & Wenzel, D. (1986). Maturation of central somatosensory conduction time in infancy and childhood. *Neuropediatrics, 17*(2), 72–74.

Lawrence, D. G., & Hopkins, D. A. (1972). Developmental aspects of pyramidal motor control in the rhesus monkey. *Brain Research, 40*, 117–118.

Lederman, S. J., & Klatzky, R. L. (1987). Hand movements: A window into haptic object recognition. *Cognitive Psychology, 19*(3), 342–368.

Lederman, S. J., & Klatzky, R. L. (1990). Haptic classification of common objects: Knowledge-driven exploration. *Cognitive Psychology, 22*(4), 421–459.

Lee, D. N. (1974). Visual information during locomotion. In R. B. MacLeod & H. Pick (Eds.), *Perception: Essays in honor of J. J. Gibson* (pp. 250–267). Ithaca, NY: Cornell University Press.

Lee, D. N., & Aronson, E. (1974). Visual proprioceptive control of standing in human infants. *Perception & Psychophysics, 15*(3), 529–532.

Lee, D. N., & Lishman, J. R. (1975). Visual proprioceptive control of stance. *Journal of Human Movement Studies, 1*(2), 87–95.

Lee, D. N., Lishman, J. R., & Thomson, J. A. (1982). Regulation of gait in long jumping. *Journal of Experimental Psychology: Human Perception & Performance, 8*(3), 448–459.

Lee, D. N., & Reddish, P. E. (1981). Plummeting gannets: A paradigm of ecological optics. *Nature, 293*(5830), 293–294.

Legerstee, M. (1990). Infants use multimodal information to imitate speech sounds. *Infant Behavior and Development, 13*, 343–354.

Legerstee, M. (1991a). Changes in the quality of infant sounds as a function of social and nonsocial stimulation. *First Language, 11*, 327–343.

Legerstee, M. (1991b). The role of person and object in eliciting early imitation. *Journal of Experimental Child Psychology, 51*, 423–433.

Legerstee, M. (1994). The role of familiarity and sound in the development of person and object perception. *British Journal of Developmental Psychology, 12*, 455–468.

Legerstee, M., Corter, C., & Kienapple, K. (1990). Hand, arm and facial actions of young infants to a social and nonsocial stimulus. *Child Development, 61*, 774–784.

Legerstee, M., Pomerleau, A., Malcuit, G., & Feider, H. (1987). The development of infants' response to people and a doll: Implications for research in communication. *Infant Behavior and Development, 10*, 81–95.

Lesher, G. W., & Mingolla, E. (1993). The role of edges and line-ends in illusory contour formation. *Vision Research, 33*(16), 2253–2270.

Leslie, A. M. (1982). The perception of causality in infants. *Perception, 11*(2), 173–186.

Leslie, A. M. (1984). Spatiotemporal continuity and the perception of causality in infants. *Perception, 13*(3), 287–305.

Leslie, A. M. (1988). The necessity of illusion: Perception and thought in infancy. In L. Weiskrantz (Ed.), *Thought without language* (pp. 185–210). New York: Oxford University Press.

Leslie, A. M. (1995). A theory of agency. In D. Sperber, D. Premack, and A. J. Premack (Eds.), *Causal cognition: A multidisciplinary debate*. Symposia of the Fyssen Foundation (pp. 121–149). New York: Clarendon Press/Oxford University Press.

Leslie, A, M., & Keeble, S. (1987). Do six-month-old infants perceive causality? *Cognition, 25*, 265–288.

LeVay, S., Wiesel, T. N., & Hubel, D. H. (1980). The development of ocular dominance columns in normal and visually deprived monkeys. *Journal of Comparative Neurology, 191*, 1–51.

Lewkowicz, D. J. (1992). Infants' response to temporally based intersensory equivalence: The effect of synchronous sounds on visual preferences for moving stimuli. *Infant Behavior & Development, 15,* 297–324.

Lewkowicz, D. J. (1985). Bisensory response to temporal frequency in four-month-old infants. *Developmental Psychology, 21*(2), 306–317.

Lewkowicz, D. J. (1986). Developmental changes in infants' bisensory response to synchronous durations. *Infant Behavior and Development, 9*(3), 335–353.

Lewkowicz, D. J. (1992). Infants' response to temporally based intersensory equivalence: The effect of synchronous sounds on visual preferences for moving stimuli. *Infant Behavior and Development, 15*(3), 297–324.

Lewkowitz, D. J. (1994). Development of intersensory perception in human infants. *The development of intersensory perception: Comparative perspectives* (pp. 165–203). Hillsdale, NJ: Erlbaum.

Lewkowicz, D. J., & Turkewitz, G. (1980). Cross-modal equivalence in early infancy: Auditory-visual intensity matching. *Developmental Psychology, 16*(6), 597–607.

Liberman, A. M., Cooper, F. S., Shankweiler, D. P., & Studdert-Kennedy, M. (1967). Perception of the speech code. *Psychological Review, 74,* 431–461.

Lieberman, P. (1980). On the development of vowel production in young children. In J. Yeni-Komshian, J. Kavanagh & C. Ferguson (Eds.), *Child Phonology*. Vol. 1. *Production*. (pp. 113–142) New York: Academic Press.

Lipsitt, L., Engen, T., & Kaye, H. (1963). Developmental changes in the olfactory threshold of the neonate. *Child Development, 34,* 371–374.

Locke, J. (1690/1971). *Essay concerning the human understanding.* New York: World Publishing Co.

Lockman, J. J., & Ashmead, D. H. (1983). Asynchronies in the development of manual behavior. In L. P. Lipsitt and C. K. Rovee-Collier (Eds.), *Advances in Infancy Research, 2* (pp. 113–136). Norwood, NJ: Ablex.

Lockman, J. J., Ashmead, D. H., & Bushnell, E. W. (1984). The development of anticipatory hand orientation during infancy. *Journal of Experimental Child Psychology, 37*(1), 176–186.

Loomis, J. M., & Lederman, S. J. (1986). Tactual perception. In K. R. Boff, L. Kaufman, & J. P. Thomas (Eds.), *Handbook of perception and human performance*. Vol. 2. *Cognitive processes and performance* (pp. 1–41). New York: John Wiley & Sons.

Loomis, J. M., Da Silva, J. A., Philbeck, J. W., & Fukusima, S. S. (1996). Visual perception of location and distance. *Current Directions in Psychological Science, 5,* 72–77.

Ludemann, P., & Nelson, C. A. (1988). The categorical representation of facial expressions by 7-month-old infants. *Developmental Psychology, 24,* 492–501.

Mace, W. M. (1974). Ecologically stimulating cognitive psychology: Gibsonian perspectives. In W. B. Weimer & D. S. Palermo (Eds.), *Cognition and the symbolic process* (pp. 137–164). Hillsdale, NJ: Erlbaum.

Macfarlane, A. (1975). Olfaction in the development of social preferences in the human neonate. *Ciba Foundation Symposium, 33,* 103–113.

Mach, E. (1885/1959). *The analysis of sensations, and the relation of the physical to the psychical.* Translated from the 1st German ed. by C. M. Williams. Rev. and supplemented from the 5th German ed. by Sydney Waterlow. New York: Dover Publications.

Mandler, J. M. (1988). How to build a baby: On the development of an accessible representational system. *Cognitive Development, 3*(2), 113–136.

Mandler, J. M. (1992). How to build a baby: II. Conceptual primitives. *Psychological Review, 99*(4), 587–604.

Mandler, J. M. (1997). Representation. In D. Kuhn & R. Siegler (Eds.), *Handbook of Child Psychology* (5th ed.), *Cognition, perception, and language* (Vol. 2). New York: Wiley.

Mandler, J. M., & McDonough, L. (1993). Concept formation in infancy. *Cognitive Development*, 8(3), 291–318.

Manny, R. E., & Klein, S. A. (1985). A three alternative tracking paradigm to measure vernier acuity of older infants. *Vision Research*, 25(9), 1245–1252.

Marg, E., Freeman, D. N., Peltzman, D., & Goldstein, P. J. (1976). Visual acuity development in human infants: Evoked potential measurements. *Investigative Ophthalmology*, 15, 150–153.

Marr, D. (1982). *Vision*. San Francisco: Freeman.

Marr, D., & Hildreth, E. (1980). Theory of edge detection. *Proceedings of the Royal Society*, 201B, 187–217.

Massaro, D. W., Thompson, L. A., Barron, B., & Laren, E. (1986). Developmental changes in visual and auditory contributions to speech perception. *Journal of Experimental Child Psychology*, 41, 93–113.

Maurer, D. (1975). Infant visual perception: Methods of study. In L. B. Cohen & P. Salapatek (Eds.), *Infant perception: From sensation to cognition. Basic visual processes.* (Vol. 1, pp. 1–76). New York: Academic Press.

Maurer, D. (1985). Infants' perception of facedness. In T. M. Field & N. A. Fox (Eds.), *Social Perception in infants* (pp. 73–100). Norwood, NJ: Ablex.

Maurer, D. (1993). Neonatal synesthesia: Implications for the processing of speech and faces. In B. de Boysson-Bardies, S. de Schonen, P. W. Jusczyk, P. McNeilage, & J. Morton (Eds.), *Developmental neurocognition: Speech and face processing in the first year of life* (pp. 109–124). Dordrecht, Netherlands: Kluwer Academic Publishers.

Maurer, D., & Adams, R. J. (1987). Emergence of the ability to discriminate a blue from gray at one month of age. *Journal of Experimental Child Psychology*, 44(2), 147–156.

Maurer, D., & Salapatek, P. (1976). Developmental changes in the scanning of faces. *Child Development*, 47, 523–527.

McCall, R. B., & Kagan, J. (1967). Attention in the infant: Effects of complexity, contour, perimeter, and familiarity. *Child Development*, 38, 939–952.

McGinnis, J. M. (1930). Eye movements and optic nystagmus in early infancy. *Genetic Psychology Monographs*, 8, 321–430.

McGurk, H., & Lewis, M. (1974). Space perception in early infancy: Perception within a common auditory-visual space? *Science*, 186(4164), 649–650.

McGurk, H., & MacDonald, J. (1976). Hearing lips and seeing voices. *Nature*, 264(5588), 746–748.

McKenzie, B. E., Skouteris, H., Day, R. H., Hartman, B., & Yonas, A. (1993). Effective action by infants to contact objects by reaching and learning. *Child Development*, 64, 415–529.

Medin, D., & Barsalou, L. W. (1987). Categorization processes and categorical perception. In S. Harnad (Ed.), *Categorical perception: The groundwork of cognition* (pp. 455–490). New York: Cambridge University Press.

Meltzoff, A. N. (1988a). Imitation of televised models by infants. *Child Development*, 59, 1221–1229.

Meltzoff, A. N. (1988b). Infant imitation after a 1-week delay: Long-term memory for novel acts and multiple stimuli. *Developmental Psychology*, 24, 470–476.

Meltzoff, A. N. (1988c). Infant imitation and memory: Nine-month-olds in immediate and deferred tests. *Child Development*, 56, 62–72.

Meltzoff, A. N. (1995). Understanding the intentions of others: Reenactment of intended acts by 18-month-old children. *Developmental Psychology*, 31(5), 838–850.

Meltzoff, A. N., & Borton, R. W. (1979). Intermodal matching by human neonates. *Nature*, 282, 403–404.

Meltzoff, A. N., & Gopnik, A. (1993). The role of imitation in understanding persons and developing a theory of mind. In S. Baron-Cohen, H. Tager-Flusberg & D. J. Cohen

(Eds.), *Understanding other minds: Perspectives from autism*. Oxford: Oxford University Press.

Meltzoff, A. N., & Moore, M. K. (1983). Newborn infants imitate adult facial gestures. *Child Development, 54*, 702–709.

Meltzoff, A. N., & Moore, M. K. (1989). Imitation in newborn infants: Exploring the range of gestures imitated and the underlying mechanisms. *Developmental Psychology, 25*, 954–962.

Meltzoff, A. N., & Moore, M. K. (1992). Early imitation within a functional framework: The importance of person identity, movement, and development. *Infant Behavior and Development, 15*, 479–505.

Meltzoff, A. N., & Moore, M. K. (1994). Imitation, memory, and the representation of persons. *Infant Behavior and Development, 17*, 83–89.

Meltzoff, A. N., & Moore, M. K. (1977). Imitation of facial and manual gestures by human neonates. *Science, 198*, 75–78.

Mendelson, M. J., & Haith, M. M. (1976). The relation between audition and vision in the human newborn. *Monographs of the Society for Research in Child Development, 41*(4), 72.

Meredith. M. A., & Stein, B. E. (1986). Visual, auditory, and somatosensory convergence on cells in superior colliculus results in multisensory integration. *Journal of Neurophysiology, 56*(3), 640–662.

Michotte, A. (1963). *The perception of causality*. New York: Basic Books.

Michotte, A., Thines, G., Crabbe, G. (1964). Les complements amodaux des structures perceptives. *Studia psycologica*. Louvain: Publications Universitataires de Louvain.

Mikami, A., Newsome, W. T., & Wurtz, R. H. (1986). Motion selectivity in macaque visual cortex: II. Spatiotemporal range of directional interactions in MT and V1. *Journal of Neurophysiology, 55*, 1328–1339.

Milewski, A. E. (1976). Infants' discrimination of internal and external pattern elements. *Journal of Experimental Child Psychology, 22*(2), 229–246.

Milewski, A. E. (1978). Young infants' visual processing of internal and adjacent shapes. *Infant Behavior and Development, 1*, 359–371.

Mill, J. S. (1865/1965). Examination of Sir William Hamilton's philosophy. In R. Herrnstein & E. G. Boring (Eds.), *A source book in the history of psychology* (pp. 182–188). Cambridge, MA: Harvard University Press.

Millenson, J. R. (1967). *Principles of behavioral analysis*. New York: Macmillan.

Mills, A. (1958). On the minimum audible angle. *Journal of the Acoustical Society of America, 30*, 103–108.

Mills, M., & Melhuish, E. (1974). Recognition of mother's voice in early infancy. *Nature, 252*(5479), 123–124.

Moore, B. C. J. (1982). *An introduction to the psychology of hearing*. London: Academic Press.

Moore, D. S. G., & Gibbons, J. L. (1988, April). Early auditory and visual integration in 4-month-old infants. Paper presented at the International Conference on Infant Studies, Washington, D.C.

Morgan, J. L., & Saffran, J. R. (1995). Emerging integration of sequential and suprasegmental information in preverbal speech segmentation. *Child Development, 66*(4), 911–936.

Morrongiello, B. A. (1988). Infant's localization of sounds along the horizontal axis: Estimates of minimum audible angle. *Developmental Psychology, 24*(1), 8–13.

Morrongiello, B. A. (1994). Effects of colocation on auditory-visual interactions and cross-modal perception in infants. In D. J. Lewkowicz & R. Lickliter (Ed.), *The development of intersensory perception: Comparative perspectives* (pp. 235–263). Hillsdale, NJ: Erlbaum.

Morrongiello, B. A., Fenwick, K. D., Hillier, L., & Chance, G. (1994). Sound localization in newborn human infants. *Developmental Psychobiology, 27*(8), 519–538.

Morrongiello, B. A., & Trehub, S. E. (1987). Age-relaged changes in auditory temporal perception. *Journal of Experimental Child Psychology, 44*(3), 413–426.

Morton, J., & Johnson, M. H. (1991). CONSPEC and CONLERN: A two-process theory of infant face recognition. *Psychological Review, 98*(2), 164–181.

Morton, J., Johnson, M. H., & Maurer, D. (1990). On the reasons for newborns' responses to faces. *Infant Behavior and Development, 13*(1), 99–103.

Muir, D., & Field, J. (1979). Newborn infants orient to sounds. *Child Development, 50*(2), 431–436.

Muir, D. W., Clifton, R. K., & Clarkson, M. G. (1989). The development of a human auditory localization response: A U-shaped function. Special Issue: Infant perceptual development. *Canadian Journal of Psychology, 43*(2), 199–216.

Müller, J. (1965). Handbuch der Physiologie des Menschen, bk. V, Coblenz. Translated by William Baly as Elements of physiology, vol. II (London, 1842). In R. Herrnstein and E. G. Boring (Eds.). *A sourcebook in the history of psychology* (pp. 26–33), Cambridge, MA: Harvard University Press. (Originally published 1838)

Nakayama, K., & Shimojo, S. (1992). Experiencing and perceiving visual surfaces. *Science, 257,* 1357–1363.

Nanez, J. (1988). Perception of impending collision in 3- to 6-week-old infants. *Infant Behavior and Development, 11,* 447–463.

Nanez, J., & Yonas, A. (1994). Effects of luminance and texture motion on infant defensive reactions to optical collision. *Infant Behavior and Development, 17,* 165–174.

Needham, A., & Baillargeon, R. (1993). Intuitions about support in four-and-a-half-month-old infants. *Cognition, 47*(2), 121–148.

Neisser, U. (1964). Visual search. *Scientific American, 210,* 94–102.

Neisser, U. (1976). *Cognitive Psychology.* New York: Appleton-Century-Crofts.

Nelson, C. A. (1987). The recognition of facial expressions in the first two years of life: Mechanisms of development. *Child Development, 58,* 889–909.

Nelson, C. A., & Dolgin, K. (1985). The generalized discrimination of facial expressions by 7-month-old infants. *Child Development, 56,* 58–61.

Newtson, D., & Engquist, G. (1976). The perceptual organization of ongoing behavior. *Journal of Experimental Social Psychology, 12,* 436–450.

Newtson, E. I., Engquist, G., & Bois, J. (1977). The objective basis of behavior units. *Journal of Personality and Social Psychology, 35,* 847–862.

Noback, C. R., & Demarest, R. J. (1986). *The nervous system.* New York: McGraw-Hill.

Norcia, A. M., & Tyler, C. W. (1985). Spatial frequency sweep VEP: Visual acuity during the first year of life. *Vision Research, 25*(10), 1399–1408.

Norcia, A. M., Tyler, C. W., & Hamer, R. D. (1990). Development of contrast sensitivity in the human infant. *Vision Research, 30*(10), 1475–1486.

Nystrom, M., Hansson, M. B., & Marklund, K. (1975). Infant preference for intermittent light. *Psychological Research Bulletin, Lund U, 15*(4), 11.

Oakes, L. M. (1994). Development of infants' use of continuity cues in their perception of causality. *Developmental Psychology, 30,* 869–879.

Oakes, L. M., & Cohen, L. B. (1990). Infant perception of a causal event. *Cognitive Development, 5,* 193–207.

Oakes, L. M., Madole, K. L., & Cohen, L. B. (1991). Infants' object examining: Habituation and categorization. *Cognitive Development, 6*(4), 377–392.

Okado, N. (1981). Onset of synapse formation in the human spinal cord. *Journal of Comparative Neurology, 201*(2), 211–219.

Oldfield, S. R., & Parker, S. P. (1986). Acuity of sound localisation: A topography of auditory space: III. Monaural hearing conditions. *Perception, 15,* 67–81.

Olshausen, B. A., & Field, D. J. (1996). Emergence of simple-cell receptive field properties by learning a sparse code for natural images. *Nature, 381,* 607–609.

Olsho, L. W., Koch, E. G., Halpin, C. F., & Carter, E. A. (1987). An observer-based psycho-acoustic procedure for use with young infants. *Developmental Psychology, 23*(5), 627–640.

Olsho, L. W., Schoon, C., Sakai, R., Turpin, R., & Sperduto, V. (1982a). Auditory frequency discrimination in infancy. *Developmental Psychology, 18*(5), 721–726.

Olsho, L. W., Schoon, C., Sakai, R., Turpin, R., & Sperduto, V. (1982b). Preliminary data on frequency discrimination in infancy. *Journal of the Acoustical Society of America, 72,* 1788–1803.

Olson, G. M., & Sherman, T. (1983). Attention, learning, and memory in infants. In M. M. Haith & J. J. Campos (Eds.), *Handbook of Child Psychology* (Vol. 2, pp. 1001–1080). New York: Wiley.

Olzak, L. A., & Thomas, J. P. (1991). When orthogonal orientations are not processed independently. *Vision Research, 31*(1), 51–57.

Oross, S., Francis, E., Mauk, D., & Fox, R. (1987). The Ames window illusion: Perception of illusory motion by human infants. Special Issue: The ontogenesis of perception. *Journal of Experimental Psychology: Human Perception & Performance, 13*(4), 609–613.

Oster, H. E. (1975). Color perception in human infants. Doctoral dissertation, University of California, Berkeley.

Owsley, C. (1983). The role of motion in infants' perception of solid shape. *Perception, 12*(6), 707–717.

Packer, O. S., Hartmann, E. E., & Teller, D. Y. (1984). Infant color vision: The effect of test field size on Rayleigh discriminations. *Vision Research, 24*(10), 1247–1260.

Palmer, C. F. (1989). The discriminating nature of infants' exploratory actions. *Developmental Psychology, 25*(6), 885–893.

Pascalis, O., de Schonen, S., Morton, J., Deruelle, C., & Fabre-Grenet, M. (1995). Mother's face recognition by neonates: A replication and an extension. *Infant Behavior and Development, 18,* 79–85.

Pavlov, I. (1910/1927). *Conditioned reflexes: An investigation of the physiological activity of the cerebral cortex* (G. V. Anrep, Trans.). London: Oxford.

Peeples, D. R., & Teller, D. Y. (1975). Color vision and brightness discrimination in two-month-old human infants. *Science, 189*(4208), 1102–1103.

Pegg, J. E., Werker, J. F., & McLeod, P. J. (1992). Preference for infant-directed over adult-directed speech: Evidence from 7-week-old infants. *Infant Behavior and Development, 15*(3), 325–345.

Pentland, A. (1990). Photometric motion. *Investigative Ophthalmology and Visual Science Supplements, 31*(172).

Perris, E. E., & Clifton, R. K. (1988). Reaching in the dark toward sound as a measure of auditory localization in infants. *Infant Behavior and Development, 11*(4), 473–491.

Petrig, B., Julesz, B., Kropfl, W., Baumgartner, G., & Anliker, M. (1981). Development of stereopsis and corical binocularity in human infants: Electrophysiological evidence. *Science, 213,* 1402–1405.

Pettigrew, J. D. (1974). The effect of visual experience on the development of stimulus specificity by kitten cortical neurones. *Journal of Physiology, 237,* 49–74.

Piaget, J. (1952). *The origins of intelligence in children.* New York: International Universities Press.

Piaget, J. (1954). *The construction of reality in the child.* New York: Basic Books.

Piaget, J. (1969). *Perceptual activities and secondary illusions. The mechanisms of perception.* New York: Basic Books.

Piaget, J. (1970). *The children's conception of movement and speed.* (G. E. T. Holloway & M. J. MacKenzie, Trans.). New York: Ballantine Books.

Piaget, J. (1973). *The grasp of consciousness: Action and concept in the young child.* Cambridge, MA: Harvard University Press.

Piaget, J., (1976). *The psychology of intelligence.* [Translated from the French by Malcolm Piercy and D. E. Berlyne]. Totowa, NJ: Littlefield, Adams.

Piaget, J. (1981). *Intelligence and affectivity: Their relationship during child development.* Palo Alto, CA: Annual Reviews.

Pieraut-Le Bonniec, G. (1990). Reaching and hand adjusting to the target properties. In H. Bloch & B. Bertenthal (Eds.), *Sensory-motor organizations and development in infancy and early childhood.* (Vol. 56, pp. 301–314). Dordrecht, Netherlands: Kluwer.

Pirchio, M., Spinelli, D., Fiorentini, A., & Maffei, L. (1978). Infant contrast sensitivity evaluated by evoked potentials. *Brain Research, 141*(1), 179–184.

Pisoni, D. B., Aslin, R. N., Perey, A. J., & Hennessy, B. L. (1982). Some effects of laboratory training on identification and discrimination of voicing contrasts in stop consonants. *Journal of Experimental Psychology: Human Perception & Performance, 8,* 297–314.

Polat, U., & Sagi, D. (1993). Lateral interactions between spatial channels: Suppression and facilitation revealed by lateral masking experiments. *Vision Reasearch, 33*(7), 993–999.

Polka, L., & Werker, J. F. (1994). Developmental changes in perception of nonnative vowel contrasts. *Journal of Experimental Psychology: Human Perception & Performance, 20*(2), 421–435.

Pomerantz, J. R., Sager, L. C., & Stoever, R. J. (1977). Perception of wholes and of their component parts: Some configural superiority effects. *Journal of Experimental Psychology: Human Perception & Performance, 3*(3), 422–435.

Porter, R. H., Makin, M. W., Davis, L. B., & Christensen, K. M. (1991). An assessment of the salient olfactory environment of formula-fed infants. *Physiology and Behavior, 50,* 907–911.

Poulin-Dubois, D., & Shultz, T. R. (1990). The infant's concept of agency: The distinction between social and nonsocial objects. *Journal of Genetic Psychology, 151,* 77–90.

Predebon, J. & Woolley, J. S. (1994). The familiar-size cue to depth under reduced-cue viewing conditions. *Perception, 23,* 1301–1312.

Provine, R. R., & Westerman, J. A. (1979). Crossing the midline: Limits of early eye-hand behavior. *Child Development, 50*(2), 437–441.

Purpura, D. P. (1975). Dendritic differentiation in human cerebral cortex: Normal and aberrant developmental patterns. In G. W. Kreutzberg (Ed.), *Advances in neurology* (Vol. 12 pp. 91–116). New York: Raven Press.

Putnam, H. (1975). *Mind, language, and reality: Philosophical papers* (Vol. 2). London: Cambridge University Press.

Pylyshyn, Z. (1973). What the mind's eye tells the mind's brain: A critique of mental imagery. *Psychological Bulletin, 80,* 1–24.

Querleu, D., Renard, X., Versyp, F., Paris-Delrue, L., & Crepin, G. (1988). Fetal hearing. *European Journal of Obstetrics, Gynecology, and Reproductive Biology, 28*(3), 191–212.

Quinn, P. C. (1994). The categorization of above and below spatial relations by young infants. *Child Development, 65*(1), 58–69.

Quinn, P. C., & Eimas, P. D. (1986). On categorization in early infancy. *Merrill-Palmer Quarterly, 32*(4), 331–363.

Quinn, P. C., & Eimas, P. D. (1996). Perceptual organization and categorization in young infants. In C. Rovee-Collier & L. P. Lipsitt (Eds.), *Advances in infancy research* (Vol. 10 pp. 1–36). Norwood, NJ: Ablex.

Quinn, P. C., Siqueland, E. R., & Bomba, P. C. (1985). Delayed recognition memory for orientation by human infants. *Journal of Experimental Child Psychology, 40*(2), 293–303.

Ramachandran, V. S., Clarke, P. G., & Whitteridge, D. (1977). Cells selective to binocular disparity in the cortex of newborn lambs. *Nature, 268*(5618), 333–335.

Ratoosh, P. (1949). On interposition as a cue for the perception of distance. *Proceedings of the National Academy of Sciences. Washington, 35,* 257–259.

Regal, D. M. (1981). Development of critical flicker frequency in human infants. *Vision Research, 21*(4), 549–555.

Regan, D., & Cynader, M. (1979). Neurons in area 18 of cat visual cortex selectively sensitive to changing size: Non-linear interactions between responses to two edges. *Vision Research, 19,* 699–711.

Regolin, L., & Vallortigara, G. (1995). Perception of partly occluded objects by young chicks. *Perception & Psychophysics, 57,* 971–976.

Reid, T. (1785/1969). *Essays on the intellectual powers of man.* Cambridge, MA: MIT Press.

Reissland, N. (1988). Neonatal imitation in the first hour of life: Observations in rural Nepal. *Developmental Psychology, 24,* 646–649.

Riesen, A. H. (1947). The development of visual perception in man and chimpanzee. *Science,* 1947, v106: 107–108.

Ringach, D. L. & Shapley, R. (1996). Spatial and temporal properties of illusory contours and amodal boundary completion. *Vision Research, 36*(19), 3037–3050.

Rochat, P. (1987). Mouthing and grasping in neonates. Evidence for the early detection of what hard or soft substances afford for action. *Infant Behavior and Development, 25,* 871–884.

Rochat, P. (1989). Object manipulation and exploration in 2- to 5-month-old infants. *Developmental Psychology, 25*(6), 871–884.

Rock, I. (1983). *The logic of perception.* Cambridge, MA: MIT Press.

Rock, I., & Anson, R. (1979). Illusory contours as the solution to a problem. *Perception, 8,* 665–681.

Rock, I., & Harris, C. S. (1967). Vision and touch. *Scientific American, 216,* 96–104.

Rose, S. A., Gottfried, A. W., & Bridger, W. H. (1981a). Cross-modal transfer and information processing by the sense of touch in infancy. *Developmental Psychology, 17,* 90–98.

Rose, S. A., Gottfried, A. W., & Bridger, W. H. (1981b). Cross-modal transfer and six-month-old infants. *Developmental Psychology, 17,* 661–669.

Rosenstein, D., & Oster, H. (1988). Differential facial responses to four basic tastes in newborns. *Child Development, 59,* 1136–1143.

Roucoux, A., Culee, C., & Roucoux, M. (1983). Development of fixation and pursuit eye movements in human infants. *Behavioural Brain Research, 10,* 133–139.

Royer, F. L. (1981). Detection of symmetry. *Journal of Experimental Psychology: Human Perception & Performance, 7,* 1186–1210.

Rubin, E. (1915). *Synoplevede Figurer.* Copenhagen: Gyldendalske.

Ruff, H. A. (1978). Infant recognition of the invariant form of objects. *Child Development, 49*(2), 293–306.

Ruff, H. A. (1984). Infants' manipulative exploration of objects: Effects of age and object characteristics. *Developmental Psychology, 20*(1), 9–20.

Ruff, H. A. (1986). Components of attention during infants' manipulative exploration. *Child Development, 57,* 105–114.

Ruff, H. A., & Kohler, C. J. (1978). Tactual-visual transfer in six-month-old infants. *Infant Behavior and Development, 1,* 259–264.

Runeson, S. (1977). On the possibility of "smart" perceptual mechanisms. *Scandinavian Journal of Psychology, 18,* 172–179.

Runeson, S., & Frykholm, G. (1981). Visual perception of lifted weight. *Journal of Experimental Psychology: Human Perception & Performance, 7*(4), 733–740.

Runeson, S., & Frykholm, G. (1983). Kinematic specification of dynamics as an information basis for person-and-action perception: Expectation, gender recognition, and deception intention. *Journal of Experimental Psychology: General, 112,* 585–615.

Saffran, J. R., Aslin, R. N., & Newport, E. L. (1996). Statistical learning by 8-month-old infants. *Science, 274,* 1926–1928.

Sai, F., & Bushnell, I. W. R. (1988). The perception of faces in different poses by 1-month-olds. *British Journal of Developmental Psychology, 6,* 35–41.

Salapatek, P. (1975). Pattern perception in early infancy. In L. B. Cohen & P. Salapatek (Eds.), *Infant perception: From sensation to cognition.* Vol. 1. *Basic visual processes.* (pp 133–248) New York: Academic Press.

Salapatek, P., & Kessen, W. (1966). Visual scanning of triangles by the human newborn. *Journal of Experimental Child Psychology, 3,* 155–167.

Salapatek, P., & Kessen, W. (1973). Prolonged investigation of a plane geometric triangle by the human newborn. *Journal of Experimental Child Psychology, 15*(1), 22–29.

Scaife, M., & Bruner, J. S. (1975). The capacity for joint visual attention in the infant. *Nature, 253,* 265–266.

Schaller, M. J. (1975). Chromatic vision in human infants: Conditioned operant fixation to "hues" of varying intensity. *Bulletin of the Psychonomic Society, 6*(1), 39–42.

Schaffer, R. (1984). *The child's entry into a social world.* New York: Academic Press.

Schieffelin, B. B. (1979). Getting it together: An ethnographic approach to the study of the development of communicative competence. In E. Ochs & B. B. Schieffelin (Eds.), *Developmental pragmatics.* New York: Academic Press.

Schieffelin, B. B. (1990). *The give and take of everyday life: Language socialization of Kaluli children.* New York: Cambridge University Press.

Schiff, W. (1965). Perception of impending collision: A study of visually directed avoidant behavior. *Psychological Monographs, 79* (Whole No. 604).

Schiff, W., & Oldak, R. (1990). Accuracy of judging time to arrival: Effects of modality, trajectory, and gender. *Journal of Experimental Psychology: Human Perception & Performance, 16*(2), 303–316.

Schmidt, H., & Spelke, E. S. (1984, April). Gestalt relations and object perception in infancy. Paper presented at the International Conference on Infant Studies, New York.

Schmuckler, M. A., & Gibson, E. J. (1989). The effect of imposed optical flow on guided locomotion in young walkers. *British Journal of Developmental Psychology, 7*(3), 193–206.

Schneider, B. A., Morrongiello, B. A., & Trehub, S. E. (1990). Size of critical band in infants, children, and adults. *Journal of Experimental Psychology: Human Perception & Performance, 16*(3), 642–652.

Schneider, G. E. (1969). Two visual systems. *Science, 163,* 895–902.

Schneirla, T. C. (1959). An evolutionary and developmental theory of biphasic processes underlying approach and withdrawal. Paper presented at the Nebraska symposium on motivation, Lincoln.

Schwartz, M., & Day, R. H. (1979). Visual shape perception in early infancy, *Monographs of the Society for Research in Child Development, 44*(7), 63.

Serrano, J. M., Iglesias, J., & Loeches, A. (1992). Visual discrimination and recognition of facial expressions of anger, fear, and surprise in 4- to 6-month-old infants. *Developmental Psychobiology, 25,* 411–425.

Shapley, R., & Gordon, J. (1987). The existence of interpolated illusory contours depends on contrast and spatial separation. In S. Petry & G. E. Meyer (Eds.), Perception of illusory contours (pp. 109–116). New York: Springer-Verlag.

Shaw, L., Roder, B., & Bushnell, E. W. (1986). Infants' identification of three-dimensional form from transformations of linear perspective. *Perception & Psychophysics, 40*(5), 301–310.

Shea, S. L., & Aslin, R. N. (1990). Oculomotor responses to step-ramp targets by young human infants. *Vision Research, 30,* 1077–1092.

Shepard, R. N. (1984). Ecological constraints on internal representation: Resonant kinematics of perceiving, imagining, thinking, and dreaming. *Psychological Review, 91*(4), 417–447.

Sherman, T. (1985). Categorization skills in infants. *Child Development*, 56(6), 1561–1573.

Shimojo, S., Birch, E. E., Gwiazda, J., & Held, R. (1984). Development of vernier acuity in infants. *Vision Research*, 24(7), 721–728.

Shipley, T. F., & Kellman, P. J. (1990). The role of discontinuities in the perception of subjective figures. *Perception & Psychophysics*, 48(3), 259–270.

Shipley, T. F., & Kellman, P. J. (1992a). Perception of partly occluded objects and illusory figures: Evidence for an identity hypothesis. *Journal of Experimental Psychology: Human Perception & Performance*, 18(1), 106–120.

Shipley, T. F., & Kellman, P. J. (1992b). Strength of visual interpolation depends on the ratio of physically specified to total edge length. *Perception & Psychophysics*, 52(1), 97–106.

Shipley, T. F., & Kellman, P. J. (1994). Spatiotemporal boundary formation: Boundary, form, and motion perception from transformations of surface elements. *Journal of Experimental Psychology: General*, 123(1), 3–20.

Simons, K. (Ed.) (1993). *Early visual development: Normal and abnormal*. New York: Oxford University Press.

Sinnott, J. M., & Aslin, R. N. (1985). Frequency and intensity discrimination in human infants and adults. *Journal of the Acoustical Society of America*, 78(6), 1986–92.

Sireteanu, R., Kellerer, R., & Boergen, K. P. (1984). The development of peripheral visual acuity in human infants. A preliminary study. *Human Neurobiology*, 3(2), 81–85.

Sitskoorn, M. M., & Smitsman, A. W. (1995). Infants' perception of dynamic relations between objects: Passing through or support? *Developmental Psychology*, 31(3), 437–447.

Slater, A. M., & Findlay, J. M. (1975). Binocular fixation in the newborn baby. *Journal of Experimental Child Psychology*, 20(2), 248–273.

Slater, A., Johnson, S. P., Kellman, P. J., & Spelke, E. S. (1994). The role of three-dimensional depth cues in infants' perception of partly occluded objects. *Early Development and Parenting*, 3, 187–191.

Slater, A., Mattock, A., & Brown, E. (1990). Size constancy at birth: Newborn infants' responses to retinal and real size. *Journal of Experimental Child Psychology*, 49(2), 314–322.

Slater, A., & Morison, V. (1985). Shape constancy and slant perception at birth. *Perception*, 14(3), 337–344.

Slater, A., Morison, V., & Rose, D. (1983). Locus of habituation in the human newborn. *Perception*, 12(5), 593–598.

Slater, A., Morison, V., & Somers, M. (1988). Orientation discrimination and cortical function in the human newborn. *Perception*, 17(5), 597–602.

Slater, A., Morison, V., Somers, M., Mattock, A., Brown, E., & Taylor, D. (1990). Newborn and older infants' perception of partly occluded objects. *Infant Behavior and Development*, 13(1), 33–49.

Slater, A., & Sykes, M. (1977). Newborn infants' visual responses to square wave gratings. *Child Development*, 48(2), 545–554.

Snow, C. E. (1977). Mothers' speech research: From input to interaction. In C. E. Snow & C. A. Ferguson (Eds.), *Talking to children: Language input and acquisition* (pp. 31–49). Cambridge: Cambridge University Press.

Snow, C. E., & Ferguson, C. A. (1977). *Talking to children: Language input and acquisition*. Cambridge: Cambridge University Press.

Sokol, S. (1978). Measurement of infant visual acuity from pattern reversal evoked potentials. *Vision Research*, 18(1), 33–39.

Sokolov, E. N. (1963). *Perception and the conditioned reflex*. New York: MacMillian.

Source, J. F., Emde, R. N., Campos, J. J., & Klinnert, M. D. (1985). Maternal emotional signaling: Its effect on the visual cliff behavior of one-year-olds. *Developmental Psychology*, 21, 195–200.

Spelke, E. S. (1976). Infants' intermodal perception of events. *Cognitive Psychology, 8*(4), 553–560.

Spelke, E. S. (1979). Perceiving bimodally specified events in infancy. *Developmental Psychology, 15*(6), 626–636.

Spelke, E. S. (1985). Perception of unity, persistence and identity: Thoughts on infants' conceptions of objects. In J. Mehler & R. Fox (Eds.), *Neonate cognition: Beyond the blooming buzzing confusion* (pp. 89–113). Hillsdale, NJ: Erlbaum.

Spelke, E. S. (1987). The development of intermodal perception. In P. Salapatek & L. Cohen (Eds.), *Handbook of infant perception* (Vol. 2, pp. 233–273). Orlando: Academic.

Spelke, E. S. (1988). Where perceiving ends and thinking begins: The apprehension of objects in infancy. In A. Yonas (Ed.), *Perceptual development in infancy: The Minnesota symposia on child psychology* (Vol. 20, pp. 197–234). Hillsdale, NJ: Erlbaum.

Spelke, E. S. (1994). Preferential looking and intermodal perception in infancy: Comment on Lewkowicz (1992). *Infant Behavior and Development, 17,* 285–287.

Spelke, E. S. (1996, April). Development and knowledge: Some lessons from Piaget. Paper presented at the Tenth Biennial Meetings of the International Society on Infant Studies, Providence, RI.

Spelke, E. S., Born, W. S., & Chu, F. (1983). Perception of moving, sounding objects by four-month-old infants. *Perception, 12*(6), 719–732.

Spelke, E. S., Breinlinger, K., Jacobson, K., & Phillips, A. (1993). Gestalt relations and object perception: A developmental study. *Perception, 22*(12), 1483–1501.

Spelke, E. S., Breinlinger, K., Macomber, J., & Jacobson, K. (1992). Origins of knowledge. *Psychological Review, 99*(4), 605–632.

Spelke, E. S., Katz, G., Purcell, S. E., Ehrlich, S. M., Breinlinger, K. (1994). Early knowledge of object motion: Continuity and inertia. *Cognition, 51*(2), 131–176.

Spelke, E. S., & Owsley, C. J. (1979). Intermodal exploration and knowledge in infancy. *Infant Behavior and Development, 2*(1), 13–27.

Spence, M. J., & Freeman, M. S. (1996). Newborn infants prefer the maternal low-pass filtered voice, but not the maternal whispered voice. *Infant Behavior and Development, 19,* 199–212.

Starkey, P., & Cooper, R. G. (1980). Perception of numbers by human infants. *Science, 210,* 1033–1035.

Starkey, P., Spelke, E. S., & Gelman, R. (1983). Detection of intermodal numerical correspondences by human infants. *Science, 222,* 179–181.

Starkey, P., Spelke, E. S., & Gelman, R. (1990). Numerical abstraction by human infants. *Cognition, 36*(2), 97–127.

Stein, B. E., Meredith, M. A., & Wallace, M. T. (1994). Development and neural basis of multisensory integration. In D. J. Lewkowicz & R. Litckliter (Ed.), *The development of intesensory perception: Comparative perspectives* (pp. 81–105). Hillsdale, NJ: Erlbaum.

Stern, D. N. (1985). *The interpersonal world of the infant.* New York: Basic Books.

Stevens, B., & Johnston, C. C. (1993). Pain in the infant: Theoretical and conceptual issues. *Maternal-Child Nursing Journal, 21*(1), 3–14.

Stoffregen, T. A. (1985). Flow structure versus retinal location in the optical control of stance. *Journal of Experimental Psychology: Human Perception & Performance, 11*(5), 554–565.

Stoffregen, T. A. (1986). The role of optical velocity in the control of stance. *Perception & Psychophysics, 39*(5), 355–360.

Stoffregen, T. A., Schmuckler, M. A., & Gibson, E. J. (1987). Use of central and peripheral optical flow in stance and locomotion in young walkers. *Perception, 16*(1), 113–119.

Strauss, M. S., & Curtis, L. E. (1981). Infant perception of numerosity. *Child Development, 52*(4), 1146–1152.

Streeter, L. A. (1976). Language perception of 2-month-old infants shows effects of both innate mechanisms and experience. *Nature, 259,* 39–41.

Streri, A. (1987). Tactile discrimination of shape and intermodal transfer in two- to three-month-old infants. *British Journal of Developmental Psychology, 5,* 213–220.

Streri, A. (1993). *Seeing, reaching, touching.* Cambridge, MA: MIT Press.

Streri, A., & Molina, M. (1993). Visual-tactual and tactual-visual transfer between objects and pictures in 2-month-old-infants. *Perception, 22,* 1299–1318.

Streri, A., & Molina, M. (1994). Constraints on intermodal transfer between touch and vision in infancy. In D. J. Lewkowicz & R. Lickliter (Eds.), *The development of intersensory perception: Comparative perspectives* (pp. 285–307). Hillsdale, NJ: Erlbaum.

Streri, A., & Spelke, E. S. (1988). Haptic perception of objects in infancy. *Cognitive Psychology, 20*(1), 1–23.

Streri, A., Spelke, E., & Rameix, E. (1993). Modality-specific and amodal aspects of object perception in infancy: The case of active touch. *Cognition, 47*(3), 251–279.

Studdert-Kennedy, M., Liberman, A. M., Harris, K. S., & Cooper, F. S. (1970). Motor theory of speech perception: A reply to Lane's critical review. *Psychological Review, 77,* 234–249.

Sugarman, S. (1978). Some organizational aspects of preverbal communication. In I. Markova (Ed.), *The social context of language* (pp. 49–66). New York: Wiley.

Sumby, W. H., & Pollack, I. (1954). Visual contribution to speech intelligibility in noise. *Journal of the Acoustical Society of America, 26,* 212–215.

Sumi, S. (1984). Upside-down presentation of the Johansson moving light-spot pattern. *Perception, 13*(3), 283–286.

Sutherland, N. S. (1961). *The methods and findings of experiments on the visual discrimination of shape by animals.* Cambridge, UK: Heffer.

Tauber, E., & Koffler, S. (1966). Optomotor response in human infants to apparent motion: Evidence of innateness. *Science, 152,* 382–383.

Teller, D. Y. (1979). The forced-choice preferential looking procedure: A psychophysical technique for use with human infants. *Infant Behavior and Development, 2*(2), 135–153.

Teller, D. Y., & Bornstein, M. H. (1987). Infant color vision and color perception. In P. Salapatek & L. Cohen (Eds.), *Handbook of infant perception.* Vol. 1. *From sensation to perception* (pp. 185–236). Orlando: Academic Press.

Teller, D. Y., & Lindsey, D. T. (1993). Motion nulling techniques and infant color vision. In C. E. Granrud (Ed.), *Visual perception and cognition in infancy: Carnegie-Mellon symposia on cognition* (pp. 47–73). Hillsdale, NJ: Erlbaum.

Teller, D. Y., & Palmer, J. (1996). Infant color vision: Motion nulls for red/green versus luminance-modulated stimuli in infants and adults. *Vision Research, 36*(7), 955–974.

Teller, D. Y., Peeples, D. R., & Sekel, M. (1978). Discrimination of chromatic from white light by two-month-old human infants. *Vision Research, 18*(1), 41–48.

Timney, B. (1981). Development of binocular depth perception in kittens. *Investigative Ophthalmology and Visual Science, 21,* 493–496.

Titchener, E. B. (1902). *A textbook of psychology.* New York: Macmillan.

Todd, J. T. (1982). Visual information about rigid and nonrigid motion: A geometric analysis. *Journal of Experimental Psychology Human Perception & Performance, 8*(2), 238–252.

Trehub, S. E. (1976). The discrimination of foreign speech contrasts by infants and adults. *Child Development, 47*(2), 466–472.

Trevarthen, C. (1975). Growth of visuomotor coordination in infants. *Journal of Movement Studies, 1,* 57.

Trevarthen, C. (1979). Communication and cooperation in early infancy: A description of primary intersubjectivity. In M. Bullowa (Ed.), *Before speech: The beginning of interpersonal communication.* Cambridge: Cambridge University Press.

Turkewitz, G., Lewkowicz, D., & Gardner, J. (1966). Effect of intensity of auditory stimulation on directional eye movements in the human neonate. *Animal Behaviour, 14*(1), 93–101.

Turvey, M. T., Shaw, R. E., Reed, E. S., & Mace, W. M. (1981). Ecological laws of perceiving and acting: In reply to Fodor and Pylyshyn. *Cognition, 9,* 237–304.

Ullman, S. (1979). *The interpretation of visual motion.* Cambridge, MA: MIT Press.

Ullman, S. (1980). Against direct perception. *Behavioral and Brain Sciences, 3,* 373–415.

Van der Meer, A. L. H., Van der Weel, F. R., & Lee, D. N. (1995). The functional significance of arm movements in neonates. *Science, 267,* 693–695.

Van de Walle, G. A., & Spelke, E. S. (1996). Spatiotemporal integration and object perception in infancy: Perceiving unity versus form. *Child Development, 67,* 2621–2640.

van Loosbroek, E., & Smitsman, A. W. (1990). Visual perception of numerosity in infancy. *Developmental Psychology, 26*(6), 911–922.

Varner, D., Cook, J. E., Schneck, M. E., McDonald, M., & Teller, D. Y. (1985). Tritan discriminations by 1- and 2-month-old human infants. *Vision Research, 25*(6), 821–831.

Volkmann, F. C., & Dobson, M. V. (1976). Infant responses of ocular fixtion to moving visual stimuli. *Journal of Experimental Child Psychology, 22*(1), 86–99.

von der Heydt, R., Peterhans, E., & Baumgartner, G. (1984). Illusory contours and cortical neuron responses. *Science, 224*(4654), 1260–1262.

von der Malsburg, C. (1973). Self-organization of orientation sensitive cells in striate cortex. *Kybernetik, 14,* 85–100.

von Hofsten, C. (1974). Proximal velocity change as a determinant of space perception. *Perception & Psychophysics, 15*(3), 488–494.

von Hofsten, C. (1976). The role of convergence in visual space perception. *Vision Research, 16,* 193–198.

von Hofsten, C. (1977). Binocular convergence as a determinant of reaching behavior in infancy. *Perception, 6,* 139–144.

von Hofsten, C. (1980). Predictive reaching for moving objects by human infants. *Journal of Experimental Child Psychology, 30*(3), 369–382.

von Hofsten, C. (1982). Eye-hand coordination in the newborn. *Developmental Psychology, 18*(3), 450–461.

von Hofsten, C. (1983). Catching skills in infancy. *Journal of Experimental Psychology: Human Perception & Performance, 9*(1), 75–85.

von Hofsten, C. (1983a). Foundations for perceptual development. In L. P. Lipsitt and C. K. Rovee-Collier (Eds.), *Advances in infancy research.* Vol. 2 (pp. 241–264). Norwood, NJ: Ablex.

von Hofsten, C. (1990). Early development of grasping an object in space-time. In M. A. Goodale (Ed.), *Vision and action: The control of grasping. The Canadian Institute for Advanced Research series in artificial intelligence and robotics* (pp. 65–79). Norwood, NJ: Ablex.

von Hofsten, C. (1993). Prospective control: A basic aspect of action development. *Human Development, 36,* 253–270.

von Hofsten, C., Kellman, P., & Putaansuu, J. (1992). Young infants' sensitivity to motion parallax. *Infant Behavior and Development, 15*(2), 245–264.

von Hofsten, C., & Ronnqvist, L. (1993). The structuring of neonatal arm movements. *Child Development, 64,* 1046–1057.

von Hofsten, C., & Siddiqui, A. (1993). Using the mother's actions as a reference for object exploration in six- and twelve-month-old infants. *British Journal of Developmental Psychology, 11,* 61–74.

von Hofsten, C., & Spelke, E. S. (1985). Object perception and object-directed reaching in infancy. *Journal of Experimental Psychology: General, 114*(2), 198–212.

von Hornbostel, E. M. (1927). The unity of the senses (E. Koffka & W. Vinton, Trans.). *Psyche*, 7(28), 83–89.

Walden, T. A., & Ogan, T. A. (1988). The development of social referencing. *Child Development*, 59(5), 1230–1240.

Walk, R. D., & Gibson, E. J. (1961). A comparative and analytical study of visual depth perception. *Psychological Monographs, 75*(519).

Walker, A. S. (1982). Intermodal perception of expressive behaviors by human infants. *Journal of Experimental Child Psychology, 33*, 514–535.

Walker, A. S., Owsley, C. J., Megaw-Nyce, J., Gibson, E. J., & Bahrick, L. E. (1980). Detection of elasticity as an invariant property of objects by young infants. *Perception, 9*, 713–718.

Walker-Andrews, A. S. (1986). Intermodal perception of expressive behaviors: Relation of eye and voice? *Developmental Psychology, 22*, 373–377.

Walker-Andrews, A. (1994). Taxonomy for intermodal relations. In D. J. Lewkowicz & R. Lickliter (Eds.), *The development of intersensory perception: Comparative perspectives* (pp. 39–56). Hillsdale, NJ: Erlbaum.

Walker-Andrews, A. S., Bahrick, L. E., Raglioni, S. S., & Diaz, I. (1991). Infants' bimodal perception of gender. *Ecological Psychology, 3*, 55–75.

Walker-Andrews, A. S., & Grolnick, W. (1983). Discrimination of vocal expressions by young infants. *Infant Behavior and Development, 6*, 491–498.

Wallach, H. (1985). Learned stimulation in space and motion perception. *American Psychologist, 40*(4), 399–404.

Wallach, H., & Floor, L. (1971). The use of size matching to demonstrate the effectiveness of accommodation and convergence as cues for distance. *Perception & Psychophysics, 10*(6), 423–428.

Wallach, H., Newman, E. B., & Rosenzweig, M. R. (1949). The precedence effect in sound localization. *American Journal of Psychology, 62*, 315–336.

Wallach, H., & O'Connell, D. N. (1953). The kinetic depth effect. *Journal of Experimental Psychology, 45*, 205–217.

Wallach, H., & O'Leary, A. (1982). Slope of regard as a distance cue. *Perception & Psychophysics, 31*(2), 145–148.

Wallach, H., & Slaughter, V. (1988). The role of memory in perceiving subjective contours. *Perception & Psychophysics, 43*(2), 101–106.

Wallach, H., & Zuckerman, C. (1963). The constancy of stereoscopic depth. *American Journal of Psychology, 76*, 404–412.

Wandell, B. A. (1995). *Foundations of vision*. Sunderland, MA: Sinauer.

Warren, R., & Wertheim, A. H. (1990). *Perception and control of self-motion*. Hillsdale, NJ: Erlbaum.

Watson, J. B. (1919). *Psychology from the standpoint of a behaviorist*. Philadelphia: Lippincott.

Wattam-Bell, J. (1991). Development of motion-specific cortical responses in infancy. *Vision Research, 31*(2), 287–297.

Wattam-Bell, J. (1992). The development of maximum displacement limits for discrimination of motion direction. *Vision Research, 32*, 621–630.

Wattam-Bell, J. (1996a). Visual motion processing in one-month-old infants: Preferential looking experiments. *Vision Research, 36*(11), 1671–1677.

Wattam-Bell, J. (1996b). Visual motion processing in one-month-old infants: Habituation experiments. *Vision Research, 36*(11), 1679–1685.

Webb, J. A., & Aggarwal, J. K. (1982). Structure from motion of rigid and jointed objects. *Artificial Intelligence, 19*, 107–130.

Werker, J. F., Gilbert, J. H., Humphrey, K., & Tees, R. C. (1981). Developmental aspects of cross-language speech perception. *Child Development, 52*(1), 349–355.

Werker, J. F., & Tees, R. C. (1983). Developmental changes across childhood in the perception of non-native speech sounds. *Canadian Journal of Psychology, 37*(2), 278–286.

Werker, J. F., & Tees, R. C. (1984). Cross-language speech perception: Evidence for perceptual reorganization during the first year of life. *Infant Behavior and Development, 7*(1), 49–63.

Werner, L. A., & Bargones, J. Y. (1992). Psychoacoustic development of human infants. In C. Rovee-Collier & L. Lipsitt (Eds.), *Advances in infancy research* (Vol. 7, pp. 103–145). Norwood, NJ: Ablex.

Wertheimer, M. (1912). Experimentelle Studien uber das Sehen von Beuegung. *Zeitschrift fuer Psychologie, 61,* 161–265.

Wertheimer, M. (1923). Untersunchungen zur Lehre der Gestalt. *Psychologische Forschung, 4:* 301–50.

Wertheimer, M. (1961). Psychomotor coordination of auditory and visual space at birth. *Science, 134,* 1692.

Westheimer, G., & McKee, S. P. (1980). Stereoscopic acuity with defocused and spatially filtered retinal images. *Journal of the Optical Society of America, 70*(7), 772–778.

White, B., Castle, R., & Held, R. (1964). Observations on the development of visually directed reaching. *Child Development, 35,* 349–364.

Whitfield, I. C., Cranford, J., Ravizza, R,. & Diamond, I. T. (1972). Effects of unilateral ablation of auditory cortex in cat on complex sound localization. *Journal of Neurophysiology, 35*(5), 718–731.

Whyte, V. A., McDonald, P. V., Baillargeon, R., & Newell, K. M. (1994). Mouthing and grasping of objects by young infants. *Ecological Psychology, 6,* 205–218.

Wiesel, T. N., & Hubel, D. H. (1974). Ordered arrangement of orientation columns in monkeys lacking visual experience. *Journal of Comparative Neurology, 158,* 307–318.

Wundt, W. (1862). *Beitrage zur Theorie der Sinneswahrnehmung.* Leipzig: C. F. Winter.

Wynn, K. (1992). Addition and subtraction by human infants. *Nature, 358,* 749–750.

Yonas, A. (1981). Infants' responses to optical information for collision. In R. N. Aslin, J. Alberts & M. Petersen (Eds.), *Development of perception: Psychobiological perspectives: The visual system* (Vol. 2, pp. 313–334). New York: Academic Press.

Yonas, A., Arterberry, M. E., & Granrud, C. E. (1987a). Four-month-old infants' sensitivity to binocular and kinetic information for three-dimensional object shape. *Child Development, 58,* 910–917.

Yonas, A., Arterberry, M. E., & Granrud, C. E. (1987b). Space perception in infancy. In R. Vasta (Ed.), *Annals of child development* (pp. 1–34). Greenwich, CT: JAI Press.

Yonas, A., & Arterberry, M. E. (1994). Infants' perceive spatial structure specified by line junctions. *Perception, 23,* 1427–1435.

Yonas, A., Bechtold, A. G., Frankel, D., Gordon, F. R., McRoberts, G., Norcia, A., & Sternfels, S. (1977). Development of sensitivity to information for impending collision. *Perception & Psychophysics, 21,* 97–104.

Yonas, A., Cleaves, W. T., & Pettersen, L. (1978). Development of sensitivity to pictorial depth. *Science, 200,* 77–79.

Yonas, A., & Granrud, C. E. (1984). The development of sensitivity to kinetic, binocular and pictorial depth information in human infants. In D. Ingle, D. Lee & M. Jeannerod (Eds.), *Brain mechanisms and spatial vision* (pp. 113–145). Amsterdam: Nijhoff.

Yonas, A., & Granrud, C. E. (1985a). Development of visual space perception in young infants. In J. Mehler & R. Fox (Eds.), *Neonate cognition: Beyond the blooming buzzing confusion* (pp. 45–67). Hillsdale, NJ: Erlbaum.

Yonas, A., & Granrud, C. E. (1985b). Reaching as a measure of visual development. In G. Gottlieb & N. Krasnegor (Eds.), *The measurement of audition and vision during the first year of life: A methodological overview* (pp. 301–322). Norwood, NJ: Ablex.

Yonas, A., Granrud, C. E., Arterberry, M. E., & Hanson, B. L. (1986). Distance perception from linear perspective and texture gradients. *Infant Behavior and Development, 9*, 247–256.

Yonas, A., & Hartman, B. (1993). Perceiving the affordance of contact in four- and five-month-old infants. *Child Development, 64*(1), 298–308.

Yonas, A., & Owsley, C. (1987). Development of visual space perception. In P. Salapatek & L. Cohen (Eds.), *Handbook of infant perception* (Vol. 2, pp. 79–122). Orlando, FL: Academic Press.

Yonas, A., Pettersen, L., & Granrud, C. E. (1982). Infants' sensitivity to familiar size as information for distance. *Child Development, 53*(5), 1285–1290.

Yonas, A., Pettersen, L., & Lockman, J. J. (1979). Young infants' sensitivity to optical information for collision. *Canadian Journal of Psychology, 33*(4), 268–276.

Younger, B. (1990). Infant categorization: Memory for category-level and specific item information. *Journal of Experimental Child Psychology, 50*(1), 131–155.

Younger, B. (1992). Developmental change in infant categorization: The perception of correlations among facial features. *Child Development, 63*(6), 1526–1535.

Younger, B. A. (1993). Understanding category members as "the same sort of thing": Explicit categorization in ten-month infants. *Child Development, 64*(1), 309–320.

Younger, B. A., & Gotlieb, S. (1988). Development of categorization skills: Changes in the nature or structure of infant form categories? *Developmental Psychology, 24*(5), 611–619.

Younger, B. A. (1985). The segregation of items into categories by ten-month-old infants. *Child Development, 56*(6), 1574–1583.

Younger, B. A., & Cohen, L. B. (1983). Infant perception of correlations among attributes. *Child Development, 54*(4), 858–869.

Younger, B. A., & Cohen, L. B. (1986). Developmental change in infants' perception of correlations among attributes. *Child Development, 57*(3), 803–815.

Yuodelis, C., & Hendrickson, A. (1986). A qualitative and quantitative analysis of the human fovea during development. *Vision Research, 26*(6), 847–855.

Zelazo, P. R., Weiss, M. J. S., & Tarquinio, N. (1991). Habituation and recovery of neonatal orienting to auditory stimuli. In M. J. S. Weiss & P. R. Zelazo (Eds.), *Newborn attention: Biological constraints and the influence of experience* (pp. 120–141). Norwood, NJ: Ablex.

Author Index

Subject Index

Monocular cues (*See* Pictorial cues)
Motherese, 233–235
Motion
 apparent (*See* Motion, stroboscopic)
 biological, 171–174
 detection, 54–56, 97, 184–189
 direction selectivity, 54–56
 nonrigid, 171–174
 observer, 156–158, 191–194
 perspective (or parallax), 81–84, 87, 90–92, 106, 167, 193
 stroboscopic, 181–182, 188, 302
 structure from, 83, 145, 165, 167
 velocity sensitivity, 183–184
Motion perception, 90–93,181–188
 during observer motion, 155–158
 neural mechanisms, 181, 191, 184–186
 optical displacement, 182, 186
 optical expansion & contraction, 83, 188
 optical pursuit, 182, 187
 and reaching, 186
 and unit formation, 155–157
Motor development, 74–76
 crawling, 255
 posture (*See* Posture)
 prereaching, 251
 reaching (*See* Reaching)
 sensorimotor period, 282
 visually guided reaching
 visual-manual coordination, 218–219, 251
 walking, 76, 145, 257–260

Nativism, 127–128
Neural development, 28–33
 dendritic arborization, 29
 myelination, 31–32
 synaptic development, 29–31
 in visual cortex
Newborn, 12
 as altricial vs. precocial, 27–28
 gustation and olfaction
 hearing, 207–210
 imitation, 267
 motion perception, 182–183, 188–189
 motor abilities, 75–76
 nervous system of the, 27–32
 perception of faces, 274
 perception of objects, 105–107
 perception of speech, 231
 reflexes, 207–209
 vision, 33–37, 46
Numerical competence, 289–292

Object exploration, 254
 in blind children, 259
Object perception, 135–177 (*See also* Shape
 constancy; Size constancy; Unit
 formation; Form perception)
 edge-insensitive (EI) process in, 154, 158, 176
 edge relatability in 143–144, 151–152, 160
 edge-sensitive (ES) process in, 151, 160–161, 307, 312
 global vs. local processing in, 131–132, 144, 163, 171, 219
 solidity, 302
 substance, 145, 175
 transparency, 2, 4
 transposition, 127–130
Object permanence, 194–197
Observer-based psychoacoustic procedure (OPP) (*See* Methods)
Occlusion, 88–89, 141–143, 150–163, 195
Ocular dominance columns, 29, 31, 96
Oculomotor information, 16–17, 56–58, 87–88, 96–97
 accommodation, 57, 87–88, 96
 convergence, 57–58, 87–88, 96–97
Olfactory development, 73–74
Operant conditioning, 39–40, 69
Optic array, 33, 83
Optic flow, 83, 248–250
Optical expansion and contraction, 83, 90–91, 182, 188, 191
Optical pursuit, 182, 187–188
Optokinetic nystagmus (OKN), 39, 56, 182, 187–188
Orientation sensitivity, 48–50

Pain sensitivity, 71–73
Parallax information (*See* Space perception)
Pattern perception, 111–134
Perception
 levels of analysis in, 2–9, 11–12
 role of energy in, 10–11, 201–202
 theories of, 15–25
Perception-action loops, 11, 246, 263
Perceptual adaptation, 187
Perceptual learning, 22–25, 80, 132, 311
Perceptual systems, 20–22
Peripheral vision, 34, 44–45
Phoneme perception (*See* Speech, perception of)